Fifth Workshop on Computational Approaches to Linguistic Code-Switching 2021

Online
11 June 2021

ISBN: 978-1-7138-3018-4

Printed from e-media with permission by:

Curran Associates, Inc.
57 Morehouse Lane
Red Hook, NY 12571

Some format issues inherent in the e-media version may also appear in this print version.

Printed with permission by Curran Associates, Inc. (2021)

For permission requests, please contact the Association for Computational Linguistics at the addrcss below.

Association for Computational Linguistics
209 N. Eighth Street
Stroudsburg, Pennsylvania 18360

Phone: 1-570-476-8006
Fax: 1-570-476-0860

acl@aclweb.org

Additional copies of this publication are available from:

Curran Associates, Inc.
57 Morehouse Lane
Red Hook, NY 12571 USA
Phone: 845-758-0400
Fax: 845-758-2633
Email: curran@proceedings.com
Web: www.proceedings.com

NAACL 2021

Computational Approaches to Linguistic Code-Switching

Proceedings of the Fifth Workshop

June 11, 2021

This workshop was sponsored by Facebook

Message from the Program Chairs

Bienvenidos to the proceedings of the fifth edition of the workshop on computational approaches for linguistic code-switching (CALCS-2021)! Code-switching is this very interesting phenomenon where multilingual speakers communicate by moving back and forth between the languages they speak when communicating with other multilingual speakers. Code-switching (CSW) is predominantly used in speech but since it also tends to be more prevalent in casual settings, we can observe CSW in genres like social media platforms where interactions tend to be more casual.

However interesting, our current NLP technology is lagging behind in the development of resources and methodologies that can effectively process code-switched language. This is true for even the large multilingual pretrained models such as mBERT and BART. At the same time, the growing adoption of smart devices and automated assistants that rely on speech interfaces, makes it even more pressing that our field addresses CSW language data.

This workshop series brings together experts and practitioners that are currently working on different aspects of CSW with a special focus on motivating tighter collaborations between speech and text researchers. We received 18 regular workshop submissions, of which we accepted 13. But this year we also had a special submission type called "Rising Stars". The goal of the Rising Stars is to allow young scientists that have recently published work in the space of CSW to present this work again to a specialized audience. These submissions are non-archival and are intended to increase visibility of CSW research by young researchers. We received two submissions of this type and we hope to continue this new track in future editions.

Our workshop also aims to motivate new research and energize the community to take on the challenges posed by CSW data. With this in mind, we hosted a new shared task on machine translation in CSW settings colocated with the workshop. This shared task provided two modalities for participation, supervised and unsupervised. For the supervised mode we asked participants to translate English data into Hinglish (Hindi-English). For the unsupervised setting we provided the following language pairs: Spanish-English (Spanglish) to English, English to Spanglish, Modern Standard Arabic-Egyptian Arabic (MSA-EA) to English and English to MSA-EA. The current leaderboard for the task shows 12 individual public system submissions coming out of 5 different teams. The overview of the shared task and the individual system submissions will be presented at the workshop.

The workshop program includes short talks from regular workshop submissions, rising star talks and system description talks. We also have a stellar invited speaker program with talks by Özlem Çetinoğlu, Manish Shrivastava and Ngoc Thang Vu. In addition, the one day program will also feature an exciting panel discussing research challenges unique to Machine Translation in CSW environments. Panelists include: Kalika Bali, Pushpak Bhattacharyya, Marina Fomicheva, Philipp Koehn, and Holger Schwenk.

We would like to thank the NAACL workshop organizers, Bhavana Dalvi, Mamoru Komachi and Michel Galley for their help during the organization of the workshop. We also extend our appreciation to Priscilla Rasmussen for her continuous help in the organization of these events. Last, but not least, we thank the NAACL organizing team for handling the conference organization in such a smooth way, even in the face of the current pandemic.

It would have been great to see everyone face to face in Mexico City, but alas we have another virtual event this year. Nonetheless, we hope that you join us on Friday June 11th and that you enjoy the program we put together.

Let's talk code-switching in June!

The Workshop Organizers

Workshop Organizers:

Alan W. Black, Carnegie Mellon University (USA)
Mona Diab, Facebook (USA)
Shuguang Chen, University of Houston (USA)
Sunayana Sitaram, Microsoft Research (India)
Thamar Solorio, University of Houston (USA)
Victor Soto, Amazon Alexa AI (USA)
Anirudh Srinivasan, Microsoft Research India (India)
Emre Yilmaz, SRI International (USA)

Program Committee:

Gustavo Aguilar, University of Houston (USA)
Elena Álvarez Mellado, University of Southern California (USA)
Segun Aroyehun, Instituto Politécnico Nacional (Mexico)
Kalika Bali, Microsoft Research India (India)
Astik Biswas, Oracle (India)
Monojit Choudhury, Microsoft Research India (India)
Amitava Das, Wipro AI Lab (India)
Indranil Dutta, Jadavpur University (India)
Alexander Gelbukh, Insituto Politécnico Nacional (Mexico)
Genta Indra Winata, HKUST (Hong Kong)
Sudipta Kar, Amazon (USA)
Grandee Lee, National University of Singapore (Singapore)
Els Lefever, Ghent University (Belgium)
Constantine Lignos, University of Pennsylvania (USA)
Yang Liu, Amazon (USA)
Manuel Mager, Universität Stuttgart (Germany)
Parth Patwa, Indian Institute of Information Technology Sri City (India)
Sai Krishna Rallabandi, Carnegie Mellon University (USA)
Yihong Theis, Kansas State University (USA)
Van Tung Pham, Nanyang Technological University (Singapore)
Khyathi Raghavi Chandu, Carnegie Mellon University (USA)
Seza Doğruöz, Ghent University (Belgium)

Table of Contents

Conference Program

Friday, June 11, 2021 (Mexico City Time, CDT, GMT -5)

8:00–10:30 **Morning Session I**

8:00–8:15 *Welcome Remarks*
Thamar Solorio

8:15–9:00 *Invited Talk*
Manish Shrivastava

9:00–9:30 *Lighting Talks*
Thamar Solorio

9:30–9:40 *Political Discourse Analysis: A Case Study of Code Mixing and Code Switching in Political Speeches*
Dama Sravani, Lalitha Kameswari and Radhika Mamidi

9:40–9:50 *Challenges and Limitations with the Metrics Measuring the Complexity of Code-Mixed Text*
Vivek Srivastava and Mayank Singh

9:50–10:00 *Translate and Classify: Improving Sequence Level Classification for English-Hindi Code-Mixed Data*
Devansh Gautam, Kshitij Gupta and Manish Shrivastava

10:00–10:30 ***Break I***

Friday, June 11, 2021 (Mexico City Time, CDT, GMT -5) (continued)

10:30–13:00 Morning Session II

10:30–10:40 *Shared Task Overview*
Thamar Solorio

10:40–10:50 *Gated Convolutional Sequence to Sequence Based Learning for English-Hingilsh Code-Switched Machine Translation.*
Suman Dowlagar and Radhika Mamidi

10:50–11:00 *IITP-MT at CALCS2021: English to Hinglish Neural Machine Translation using Unsupervised Synthetic Code-Mixed Parallel Corpus*
Ramakrishna Appicharla, Kamal Kumar Gupta, Asif Ekbal and Pushpak Bhattacharyya

11:00–11:10 *Exploring Text-to-Text Transformers for English to Hinglish Machine Translation with Synthetic Code-Mixing*
Ganesh Jawahar, El Moatez Billah Nagoudi, Muhammad Abdul-Mageed and Laks Lakshmanan, V.S.

11:10–11:20 *CoMeT: Towards Code-Mixed Translation Using Parallel Monolingual Sentences*
Devansh Gautam, Prashant Kodali, Kshitij Gupta, Anmol Goel, Manish Shrivastava and Ponnurangam Kumaraguru

11:20–11:30 *Investigating Code-Mixed Modern Standard Arabic-Egyptian to English Machine Translation*
El Moatez Billah Nagoudi, AbdelRahim Elmadany and Muhammad Abdul-Mageed

11:30–12:15 *Invited Talk*
Özlem Çetinoğlu

12:15–13:00 *Lunch Break*

Friday, June 11, 2021 (Mexico City Time, CDT, GMT -5) (continued)

13:00–15:30 Afternoon Session I

13:00–13:10 *Much Gracias: Semi-supervised Code-switch Detection for Spanish-English: How far can we get?*
Dana-Maria Iliescu, Rasmus Grand, Sara Qirko and Rob van der Goot

13:10–13:20 *A Language-aware Approach to Code-switched Morphological Tagging*
Şaziye Betül Özateş and Özlem Çetinoğlu

13:20–13:30 *Can You Traducir This? Machine Translation for Code-Switched Input*
Jitao Xu and François Yvon

13:30–13:40 *On the logistical difficulties and findings of Jopara Sentiment Analysis*
Marvin Agüero-Torales, David Vilares and Antonio López-Herrera

13:40–15:00 *Panel Discussion Moderated by Mona Diab*
Panelists: Kalika Bali, Pushpak Bhattacharyya, Marina Fomicheva, Philipp Koehn, Holger Schwenk

15:00–15:30 ***Midday Short Break***

15:30–16:45 Afternoon Session II

15:30–16:15 *Invited Talk*
Ngoc Thang Vu

16:15–16:45 ***Evening Break***

16:45–18:15	**Evening Session**
16:45–16:55	*Unsupervised Self-Training for Sentiment Analysis of Code-Switched Data* Akshat Gupta, Sargam Menghani, Sai Krishna Rallabandi and Alan W Black
16:55–17:05	*CodemixedNLP: An Extensible and Open NLP Toolkit for Code-Mixing* Sai Muralidhar Jayanthi, Kavya Nerella, Khyathi Raghavi Chandu and Alan W Black
17:05–17:15	*Normalization and Back-Transliteration for Code-Switched Data* Dwija Parikh and Thamar Solorio
17:15–17:25	*Abusive content detection in transliterated Bengali-English social media corpus* Salim Sazzed
17:25–17:35	*Developing ASR for Indonesian-English Bilingual Language Teaching* Zara Maxwelll-Smith and Ben Foley
17:35–17:45	*Transliteration for Low-Resource Code-Switching Texts: Building an Automatic Cyrillic-to-Latin Converter for Tatar* Chihiro Taguchi, Yusuke Sakai and Taro Watanabe
17:45–17:55	*Code-Mixing on Sesame Street: Dawn of the Adversarial Polyglots* Samson Tan and Shafiq Joty
17:55–18:05	*Are Multilingual Models Effective in Code-Switching?* Genta Indra Winata, Samuel Cahyawijaya, Zihan Liu, Zhaojiang Lin, Andrea Madotto and Pascale Fung
18:05–18:15	***Closing Remarks***

Political Discourse Analysis: A Case Study of Code Mixing and Code Switching in Political Speeches

Dama Sravani, Lalitha Kameswari, Radhika Mamidi
Language Technologies Research Centre
International Institute of Information Technology
Hyderabad, Telangana, India
{dama.sravani, v.a.lalitha}@research.iiit.ac.in
radhika.mamidi@iiit.ac.in

Abstract

Political discourse is one of the most interesting data to study power relations in the framework of Critical Discourse Analysis. With the increase in the modes of textual and spoken forms of communication, politicians use language and linguistic mechanisms that contribute significantly in building their relationship with people, especially in a multilingual country like India with many political parties with different ideologies. This paper analyses code-mixing and code-switching in Telugu political speeches to determine the factors responsible for their usage levels in various social settings and communicative contexts. We also compile a detailed set of rules capturing dialectal variations between Standard and Telangana dialects of Telugu.

1 Introduction

Gumperz (1982) defines Code Switching (CS) as the juxtaposition within the same speech exchange of passages of speech belonging to two different grammatical systems or sub-systems. On the other hand, Code Mixing(CM) refers to the embedding of linguistic units such as phrases, words and morphemes of one language into an utterance of another language (Myers-Scotton, 1997). So broadly speaking, CS occurs across sentences/phrases and CM within a sentence/phrases (though some researchers do not distinguish the two).

Gumperz (1982) researched specific speech events to examine the relationship between speakers' linguistic choices. They also looked for CS instances, either between languages or between varieties of the same language, to find out in what situation and with what interlocutors, CS occurs and CS may signal various group memberships and identities. Gumperz (1977) found that local dialect carried great prestige, and as a person's native speech is regarded as an integral part of his family background, a sign of his local identity. However, when interacting with members of other communities and with tourists, the residents would use the standard dialect.

Foster et al. (1981) states that language is not neutral or universal in a political context. Language is used to reflect many historical, cultural and social identities associated with the politician. In a multilingual country like India, CM and CS are a norm. They not only reflect a person's association with more than one language or a dialect, but also conveys their social identity in a given context. In this paper, our aim is to look at CM and CS as two distinctive techniques used for political gain.

The matrix language we have chosen to study these phenomena is Telugu, a South-Central Dravidian language predominantly spoken in India's Southern parts, especially in Andhra Pradesh and Telangana. There are many regional dialects and sub-dialects in Telugu, but the three major dialects are the Coastal Andhra dialect, the Telangana dialect which has a significant influence of Urdu/Dakhni, and the Rayalaseema dialect. The variety spoken by the educated class from the interior districts of Andhra area was modernised and elevated to 'Standard Telugu' status in 1969 and since then has been widely used in textbooks, newspapers and other formal communication. It is also referred to as Modern Standard Telugu (MST) in Krishnamurti et al. (1968).

Even though Telugu is one of India's largest spoken languages with more than 80 million speakers, there is a severe dearth of resources in Telugu, which makes it hard for NLP research. For our purpose, we did not find any corpus for Code Mixing and Switching in Telugu. Hence, we created a corpus of political speeches in Telugu consisting of 1134 sentences and about 10000 words. Since our work is closely associated with a set of rules and statistical observations corresponding to those rules, the corpus size was sufficient to give us good results. We will further examine the factors re-

Proceedings of the Fifth Workshop on Computational Approaches to Linguistic Code-Switching, pages 1–5
June 11, 2021. ©2021 Association for Computational Linguistics
https://doi.org/10.26615/978-954-452-056-4_001

sponsible for varying levels of CM and CS in these speeches.

2 Related Work

Kameswari and Mamidi (2018) conducted a study about various interpersonal speech choices in election campaign speeches, including the usage patterns of nouns, pronouns, kinship terms, rhetorical questions, etc. There are a few more studies (Martinez Guillem (2009), Ilic and Radulovic (2015), Kampf and Katriel (2016)) which analyse the deeper intention behind the choice of words and phrases using the famous Speech Act theory by Searle et al. (1980) and the Sociocognitive model by Van Dijk (2014).

There has been some work recently on CM and CS involving Indian languages. But most of the work is done in the social media domain and involves Hindi-English pair because of the easier availability of data. Bali et al. (2014) worked on code mixed tweets in English-Hindi. They tried to differentiate between borrowing and code-mixing based on the frequency of co-occurrence of words in tweets.

In Dravidian languages, there is very little work done in this area so far. Srirangam et al. (2019) created a corpus for Named Entity recognition in English-Telugu code mixed tweets,Jitta et al. (2017) created a English-Telugu code mixed conversational data for Dialog Act recognition.

There has been very less work on analysing the Telangana dialect. Bhaskar wrote a book named *Telanagana Padakosam* with Telangana words and their corresponding words in Standard dialect. Also, he has drawn few observations that are common in Telangana dialect.Chakravarthy (2016), An Annotated Translation of Kalarekhalu A Historical Novel by Ampasayya Naveen, describes the important phases that lead to the Telangana state. Few cultural words have been retained without translating into English. Sastry (1987) provided a prosodic analysis of Telangana dialect.

To our knowledge, this work is the first of its kind, which analyses CM and CS together in political discourse along with dialectal level code-mixing analysis. We aim to understand these phenomena as a speech choice and its effect on the audience in politics.

3 Dataset and Annotation

3.1 Dataset collection

Even with the advent of social and print media, in-person modes of communication such as campaigns and political speeches remain the most preferred ways of communicating with the general public for politicians. They try to ensure that the audience feels connected to them, thereby increasing their potential votes. This is done strategically and persuasively.

We chose our speakers as Mr K Chandrasekhar Rao (KCR), the Chief Minister of Telangana and Mr Chandra Babu Naidu(CBN), former Chief Minister of Andhra Pradesh. KCR is the founder of the Telangana Rashtra Samiti (TRS) party and is widely regarded as the face of the Telangana movement for a separate state in 2014. CBN is the leader of the Telugu Desam Party. They use a variety of dialects and languages such as Telangana Telugu, Modern Standard Telugu, Urdu, English and Hindi in their speeches.

We chose a total of 6 speeches of both the speakers in three different social settings and communicative contexts to analyse the levels of code-mixing and code-switching as follows:

1. **Public Meetings in Telangana**: KCR's speech was during the Telangana movement, meant for the creation of a new state. He addressed the pathetic situation of Telangana residents and also discussed the plan and policies for the new state.CBN's speech is during the Telangana elections in 2018. The audience were residents of Telangana. We will refer to this as communicative event 1.

2. **Felicitating Dr. Venkaiah Naidu when honoured as Vice President**: KCR and CBN's speeches were with MLAs and other parliament members of their respective states,*viz.* They spoke about Dr Venkaiah Naidu's great qualities and praised him for his service to the nation and attaining one of its highest positions. We will refer to this as communicative event 2.

3. **Capital Development**: In these speeches, both the speakers were talking about developments of capitals. In the KCR speech, the audience were Government officials and local politicians of Telangana. CBN addressed the

collectors of Andhra Pradesh. We will refer to this one as communicative event 3.

Though the speeches were available on YouTube, none of the existing off-the-shelf speech to text systems could serve to capture the speech effectively along with the dialectal variations in the language. Therefore, we manually transcribed the speeches in the WX format (Diwakar et al., 2010) and verified the transcription with the help of native speakers. The duration of the speeches is 100 minutes for each speaker, and after transcription, it consists of 1134 sentences. The total word count is around 10000.

3.2 Annotation

All speeches are annotated for the usage of CM and CS at the word level. Each speech is annotated for Dialectal level code-mixing(DCM), Language level code-mixing (LCM) and Code-Switching(CS). We will further examine how CM and CS will vary in different social settings and communicative contexts for pragmatic reasons.

3.2.1 Guidelines to handle dialectal level code-mixing

The subjects of our study use Telangana dialect and MST more often compared.

To our knowledge, there has been no exhaustive set of observations differentiating these two varieties Telangana from MST. We took some observations from the book by Bhaskar and Sastry (1987). Few more observations are drawn from texts of Chakravarthy (2016). Also, we compiled a few more observations from a TV news program named *Teenmar news* which uses Telangana dialect. After removing duplicates, we categorised the observations and segregated them into three categories: Vowel rule (V), Consonant rule (C) and the other rules which apply to syllables (S). The rules in each of these three categories are further classified as *Addition, Deletion or Replacement*, based on the kind of operation performed.

We came up with over 50 tags for these observations capturing the pattern differences between the Standard and Telangana dialects. If a word follows any of these observations, then it is marked as 1 under the category DCM. Else, it is marked as 0. In this paper, we present a few observations which are prominent in our data. The writing convention followed is:
[Standard dialect word] - [Telangana dialect word]:

1. **Vowel rules**
   - **Deletion**: In Telangana dialect, vowels are dropped at the end of some words. For example:

     nenu - nen
   - **Replacement**: Long vowels are replaced with short vowels.

     vastAru - vastaru
2. **Consonant rules**
   - **Addition**: In Telangana dialect g is added at the start for few words.

     ippuDu - gippuDu
   - **Deletion**: In some words *v* is dropped at the beginning of the word. This occurs in nouns, pronouns and verbs

     vAna - Ana
   - **Replacement**: Voiced consonants are replaced with voiceless consonants in some words.

     pedda + kAleV- peddagAleV -
     cAlu - jAlu
     peTTAru - beTTAru
3. **Syllable rules**
   - **Deletion**: Dropping of the syllable which precedes the /d/ sound. In some cases, after the dropping, the preceding vowel is lengthened. This is mostly observed in terms associated with spatial deixis.

     ikkaDa - IDa
   - **Replacement**: For the verbs in past tense, The second last syllable's long vowel gets replaced with *in/i/shortening of vowel/ina*. These are further subcategorised based on gender, number and person.

     cesAru - jeSinru
     cesAvA - jeSinavA
     cesAru - jeSiru

3.2.2 Guidelines to handle language level code-mixing

In our paper, language level code-mixing is said to occur when two or more languages or language varieties are used at a morphological level. To be more precise, it occurred when English root words were suffixed with Telugu plural markers, and morphological suffixes in one word or English/Hindi words are used.

pArtIlu - party + lu
kAlejIlo - College + lo
rejiyanga - region + ga

If a word follows these observations, then it is marked as 1. Else, it is marked as 0 for language level code-mixing.

3.2.3 Guidelines to handle code-switching

All the language variations at the sentence level, i.e. if the sentence or phrase with more than one word is in a different language, then it is considered under code-switching. Here as our speeches are in Telugu, sentences or phrases in languages other than Telugu come under this category. All the words in these sentences/phrases are marked as 1.

mIru ganaka commitement won tIskunte, Yes sir come on let us move annAru

In the above sentence, all the words in the phrase *Yes sir come on let us move* are marked as 1 under the category code-switching.

4 Observations and Results

After annotating based on these guidelines, the results are tabulated as follows.

Speech	No.of Words	Dialectal level Code-mixing	Language level Code-mixing	Code-Switching
1	2153	19.9%	E-5.4% H-0.8%	E-0.1% H-17.4%
2	1137	12%	E-3.1% H-0%	E- 2.1% H-0%
3	2654	15%	E-9.2% H-0%	E-9.9% H-0%

Table 1: KCR Speech Statistics (E-English, H-Hindi/Urdu)

Speech	No.of Words	Dialectal level Code-mixing	Language level Code-mixing	Code-Switching
1	1357	8.91%	E-4.64% H-0%	E-1.76% H-0%
2	1960	3.82%	E-4.7% H-0%	E- 4.33% H-0%
3	984	2.7%	E-7.01% H-0%	E-39.63% H-0%

Table 2: CBN Speech Statistics

In communicative event 1, as they were addressing Telangana residents, relatively higher levels of Telangana dialect are observed in speeches by both the speakers to get more *connection with the audience*. However, KCR has used more Telangana dialect in his speech than CBN. KCR was fighting for a separate Telangana state. CBN speech was during the Telangana elections in 2018. His ideology doesn't align with KCR. In addition to connection with the audience, *ideologies of the speaker* also impact the levels of code-mixing and code-switching. KCR also uses high levels of code-switching in Hindi for establishing a better connection with the audience as the Telangana dialect is influenced by Hindi/Urdu.

In communicative event 2, KCN and CBN addressed MLAs and other parliament members of Telangana and Andhra Pradesh. In CBN's speech, the usage of MST can be due to the absence of Telangana residents. However, in KCR speech, most of them are Telangana residents, yet lesser levels of Telangana dialect are observed. So, *context of the speech* also determines the levels of code-mixing and code-switching. In this communicative event, as they were addressing a national topic, MST, lesser language level code-mixing and lower code-switching levels are observed.

In communicative event 3, English usage is high in both speeches than other speeches as the meeting is about capitals and all government officials may not be aware of the local language. In KCR speech, local politicians are also part of the meeting, so Telangana dialect usage is prominent. Whereas in CBN speech, very high levels of English is used as the meeting is only with collectors.

5 Conclusions and Future Work

In this paper, we looked at the phenomenon of CM/CS between dialects of Telugu, MST and languages like English and Hindi/Urdu for different communicative contexts. The audience, ideologies of the speaker and context of the speech impacted the speakers linguistic choices.

Our transcribed and annotated speeches[1] can be further be used to develop dialectal speech recognition systems.We present a very detailed set of observations and annotation guidelines to capture the dialectal variations between the MST and Telangana dialect of Telugu. These could be studied and extended to handle dialectal variations in other languages, especially Dravidian languages like Tamil and Kannada. These can also help develop Machine Translation systems equipped for several dialects within a given language pair. Further, we would like to expand our data and examine other factors responsible for code-switching and code-mixing.

[1] https://github.com/damasravani19/CodeMIxingCodeSwitchingInPoliticalSpeeches

6 Acknowledgements

We thank SriHarshitha Bondugula for aiding us in transcribing political speeches in the Telangana dialect.

References

Kalika Bali, Jatin Sharma, Monojit Choudhury, and Yogarshi Vyas. 2014. "i am borrowing ya mixing?" an analysis of english-hindi code mixing in facebook. In *Proceedings of the First Workshop on Computational Approaches to Code Switching*, pages 116–126.

Nalimela Bhaskar. *Bhaskar*,.

I Pavan Chakravarthy. 2016. *An Annotated Translation of Kalarekhalu A Historical Novel by Ampasayya Naveen*. Ph.D. thesis, The English and Foreign Languages University, Hyderabad.

Sapan Diwakar, Pulkit Goyal, and Rohit Gupta. 2010. Transliteration among indian languages using wx notation. In *Proceedings of the Conference on Natural Language Processing 2010*, CONF, pages 147–150. Saarland University Press.

Leslie D Foster, Dennis J Gallant, William D Drew, and Cecil R Lohrey. 1981. Columnar patient care service facility. US Patent App. 06/004,211.

John J. Gumperz. 1977. The sociolinguistic significance of conversational code-switching. *RELC Journal*, 8(2):1–34.

John J Gumperz. 1982. *Discourse strategies*, volume 1. Cambridge University Press.

Biljana Misic Ilic and Milica Radulovic. 2015. Commissive and expressive illocutionary acts in political discourse. *Lodz Papers in Pragmatics*, 11(1):19.

D. S. Jitta, K. R. Chandu, H. Pamidipalli, and R. Mamidi. 2017. "nee intention enti?" towards dialog act recognition in code-mixed conversations. In *2017 International Conference on Asian Language Processing (IALP)*, pages 243–246.

Lalitha Kameswari and Radhika Mamidi. 2018. Political discourse analysis: A case study of 2014 andhra pradesh state assembly election of interpersonal speech choices. In *PACLIC*.

Zohar Kampf and Tamar Katriel. 2016. Political condemnations: Public speech acts and the moralization of discourse. *The handbook of communication in cross-cultural perspective*, 312:324.

B. Krishnamurti, P.S. Sarma, and K. Civam. 1968. *A Basic Course in Modern Telugu*. sole distributors Motilal Banarsidass, Delhi.

Susana Martinez Guillem. 2009. Argumentation, metadiscourse and social cognition: organizing knowledge in political communication. *Discourse & Society*, 20(6):727–746.

Carol Myers-Scotton. 1997. *Duelling languages: Grammatical structure in codeswitching*. Oxford University Press.

J. Sastry. 1987. A study of telugu regional and social dialects : a prosodic analysis.

John R Searle, Ferenc Kiefer, Manfred Bierwisch, et al. 1980. *Speech act theory and pragmatics*, volume 10. Springer.

Vamshi Krishna Srirangam, Appidi Abhinav Reddy, Vinay Singh, and Manish Shrivastava. 2019. Corpus creation and analysis for named entity recognition in telugu-english code-mixed social media data. In *Proceedings of the 57th Annual Meeting of the Association for Computational Linguistics: Student Research Workshop*, pages 183–189.

Teun A Van Dijk. 2014. *Discourse and knowledge: A sociocognitive approach*. Cambridge University Press.

Challenges and Limitations with the Metrics Measuring the Complexity of Code-Mixed Text

Vivek Srivastava
TCS Research
Pune, Maharashtra, India
srivastava.vivek2@tcs.com

Mayank Singh
IIT Gandhinagar
Gandhinagar, Gujarat, India
singh.mayank@iitgn.ac.in

Abstract

Code-mixing is a frequent communication style among multilingual speakers where they mix words and phrases from two different languages in the same utterance of text or speech. Identifying and filtering code-mixed text is a challenging task due to its co-existence with monolingual and noisy text. Over the years, several code-mixing metrics have been extensively used to identify and validate code-mixed text quality. This paper demonstrates several inherent limitations of code-mixing metrics with examples from the already existing datasets that are popularly used across various experiments.

1 Introduction

Code-mixing is the phenomenon of mixing words and phrases from multiple languages in the same utterance of a text or speech (Bokamba, 1989). Multilingual societies observe a high frequency of code-mixed communication in the informal setting such as social media, online messaging, discussion forums, and online gaming (Tay, 1989). Various studies indicate the overwhelming growth in the number of code-mixed speakers in various parts of the world, such as India, Spain, and China (Baldauf, 2004). The phenomenal increase of the code-mixed data on various platforms such as Twitter, Facebook, WhatsApp, Reddit, and Quora, has led to several interesting research directions such as token-level language identification (Shekhar et al., 2020; Singh et al., 2018a), POS tagging (Vyas et al., 2014; Singh et al., 2018b), machine translation (Dhar et al., 2018; Srivastava and Singh, 2020), and question-answering (Chandu et al., 2019; Banerjee et al., 2016).

Despite such active participation from the computational linguistic community in developing tools and resources for the code-mixed languages, we observe many challenges in processing the code-mixed data. One of the most compelling problems with the code-mixed data is the co-existence with the noisy and monolingual data. In contrast to the monolingual languages, we do not find any platform where the code-mixed language is the only medium of communication. The co-existing nature of the code-mixed languages with the noisy and monolingual languages posits the fundamental challenge of filtering and identifying the code-mixed text relevant for a given study. Over the years, various works have employed human annotators for this task. However, employing humans for identifying and filtering the code-mixed text (in addition to the task-specific annotations) is extremely expensive on both fronts of time and cost. Also, since code-mixed languages do not follow specific linguistic rules and standards, it becomes increasingly challenging to evaluate human annotations and proficiency.

In order to address some of the above challenges, several code-mixing metrics (Das and Gambäck, 2014; Gambäck and Das, 2016; Barnett et al., 2000; Guzmán et al., 2017) have been proposed to measure the degree of code-mixing in the text. However, we observe several limitations in the metric formulations. This paper outlines several such limitations and supports our claims with examples from multiple already existing datasets for various tasks. For illustrations, we choose Hinglish (code-mixing of Hindi and English language) due to two major reasons: (i) popularity of Hinglish and (ii) active research community. Baldauf (2004) projected that number of Hinglish speakers might soon outrun the number of native English speakers in the world. This strengthens our belief that even though Hinglish (and other code-mixed languages) does not enjoy the official status, we need to build robust systems to serve the multilingual societies. With the availability of datasets and tools for the Hinglish language, we seek a boom in the active participation from the computational linguistic community to address various challenges.

Proceedings of the Fifth Workshop on Computational Approaches to Linguistic Code-Switching, pages 6–14
June 11, 2021. ©2021 Association for Computational Linguistics
https://doi.org/10.26615/978-954-452-056-4_002

Data source	Task	Dataset size	Reported CMI
Singh et al. (2018c)	Named-entity recognition	3,638	Unavailable
Swami et al. (2018)	Sarcasm detection	5,520	Unavailable
Joshi et al. (2016)	Sentiment analysis	3,879	Unavailable
Patwa et al. (2020)	Sentiment analysis	20,000	25.32
Barman et al. (2014)	Language identification	771	13
Bohra et al. (2018)	Hate-speech detection	4,575	Unavailable
Dhar et al. (2018)	Machine translation	6,096	30.5
Srivastava and Singh (2020)	Machine translation	13,738	75.76
Vijay et al. (2018)	Irony detection	3,055	Unavailable
Khanuja et al. (2020)	Natural language inference	2,240	>20

Table 1: We explore 10 Hinglish code-mixed datasets to showcase the limitations of code-mixing metrics.

Outline of the paper: We formally define Hindi-English code-mixing in Section 2. Section 3 describes several code-mixing metrics. We outline various limitations supported with multiple examples from various datasets in Section 4. We conclude and present future direction in Section 5.

2 Hinglish: Mixing Hindi with English

Hinglish is a portmanteau of Hindi and the English language. Figure 1 shows example Hinglish sentences. Also, we see two example sentences in Figure 1 that are non-code-mixed but might appear to contain words from two languages. The presence of named entities from the Hindi language does not make the sentence code-mixed.

Code-mixed sentences

SENTENCE 1: ye ek code mixed sentence ka example hai

SENTENCE 2 : kal me movie dekhne ja raha hu. How are the reviews?

Non-code-mixed sentences

SENTENCE 1: Tendulkar scored more centuries than Kohli in Delhi.

SENTENCE 2: Bhartiya Janta Party won the 2019 general elections.

Figure 1: Example code-mixed sentences with words from Hindi and English languages. The non-code-mixed sentences might get confused with the code-mixed sentence due to the presence of named entities.

In this study, we explore 10 Hinglish datasets encompassing eight different tasks, namely named entity recognition, sarcasm detection, sentiment analysis, language identification, hate-speech detection, machine translation, irony detection, and natural language inference (see Table 1 for more details). Contrasting against monolingual datasets for similar tasks, the Hinglish datasets are significantly smaller in size. We support our claims by providing illustrative examples from these datasets.

3 Code-Mixing Metrics

In this section, we describe several popular code-mixing metrics that measure the complexity of the code-mixed text. Among the following metrics, code-mixing index (CMI, Das and Gambäck (2014); Gambäck and Das (2016)) is the most popular metric.

3.1 Code-mixing Index

CMI metric (Das and Gambäck, 2014) is defined as follows:

$$CMI = \begin{cases} 100 * [1 - \frac{max(w_i)}{n-u}] & n > u \\ 0 & n = u \end{cases} \quad (1)$$

Here, w_i is the number of words of the language i, max$\{w_i\}$ represents the number of words of the most prominent language, n is the total number of tokens, u represents the number of language-independent tokens (such as named entities, abbreviations, mentions, and hashtags).

A low CMI score indicates monolingualism in the text whereas the high CMI score is an indicator of the high degree of code-mixing in the text. In the later work, (Gambäck and Das, 2016) also introduced number of code alternation points in the original CMI formulation. An *alternation point* (a.k.a. *switch point*) is defined as any token in the text that is preceded by a token with a different language tag. Let f_p denotes ratio of number of code alternation points P per token, $f_p = \frac{P}{n}$ where

$0 \leq P < n$. Let CMI$_{old}$ denotes the CMI formulation defined in Eq. 1. The updated CMI formulation (CMI$_{new}$) is defined as:

$$CMI_{new} = a.CMI_{old} + b.f_p \tag{2}$$

where a and b are weights, such that $a + b = 1$. Again, CMI_{new} = 0 for monolingual text, as CMI_{old} = 0 and $P = 0$. Hereafter, throughout the paper, we refer to CMI_{new} as CMI metric.

3.2 M-index

Barnett et al. (2000) proposed the Multilingual Index (M-index). M-index measures the inequality of the distribution of language tags in a text comprising at least two languages. If p_j is the total number of words in the language j over the total number of words in the text, and $j \in k$, where k is total number of languages in the text, M-index is defined as:

$$M - index = \frac{1 - \sum p_j^2}{(k-1)\sum p_j^2} \tag{3}$$

The index varies between 0 (monolingual utterance) and 1 (a perfect code-mixed text comprising equal contribution from each language).

3.3 I-index

The Integration-index proposed by Guzmán et al. (2017) measures the probability of switching within a text. I-index approximates the probability that any given token in the corpus is a switch point. Consider a text comprised of n tokens, I-index is defined as:

$$I - index = \frac{\sum_{1 \leq i < n-1} S(i, i+1)}{n-1} \tag{4}$$

Here, $S(i, i+1) = 1$ if language tag of ith token is different than the language tag of $(i+1)^{th}$ token, otherwise $S(i, i+1) = 0$. I-index varies between 0 (monolingual utterance) and 1 (a perfect code-mixed text comprising consecutive tokens with different language tag). Guzmán et al. (2017) also adapted two metrics that quantify burstiness and memory in complex systems (Goh and Barabási, 2008) to measure the complexity of code-mixed text. Next, we introduce these complex system-based metrics.

3.4 Burstiness

Burstiness (Goh and Barabási, 2008) measures whether switching occurs in bursts or has a more periodic character. Let σ_r denote the standard deviation of the language spans and m_r the mean of the language spans. Burstiness is calculated as:

$$Burstiness = \frac{\sigma_r - m_r}{\sigma_r + m_r} \tag{5}$$

The burstiness metric is bounded within the interval [-1, 1]. Text with periodic dispersions of switch points yields a burstiness value closer to -1. In contrast, text with high burstiness and containing less predictable switching patterns take values closer to 1.

3.5 Memory

Memory (Goh and Barabási, 2008) quantifies the extent to which the length of language spans tends to be influenced by the length of spans preceding them. Let n_r be the number of language spans in the utterance and τ_i denote a specific language span in that utterance ordered by i. Let σ_1 and μ_1 be the standard deviation and mean of all language spans but the last, where σ_2 and μ_2 are the standard deviation and mean of all language spans but the first.

$$Memory = \frac{1}{n_r - 1} \sum_{1}^{n_r - 1} \frac{(\tau_i - \mu_1)(\tau_{i+1} - \mu_2)}{\sigma_1 \sigma_2} \tag{6}$$

Memory varies in an interval [-1,1]. Memory values close to -1 describe the tendency for consecutive language spans to be negatively correlated, that is, short spans follow long spans, and vice-versa. Conversely, memory values closer to 1 describe the tendency for consecutive language spans to be positively correlated, meaning similar in length.

In addition to the above metrics, there exist several other code-mixing metrics such as Language Entropy and Span Entropy that can be derived from the above metrics (Guzmán et al., 2017). Due to the space constraints, we refrain from further discussing them in the paper.

Evaluating metric scores on code-mixed datasets: To understand the effectiveness of these metrics, we randomly sample one sentence each from the ten datasets and calculate the score on all the code-mixing metrics. In addition, we employ three human annotators proficient in both the languages (English and Hindi) to rate the sentences

Hinglish sentence	CMI	M-index	I-index	Burstiness	Memory	Human 1		Human 2		Human 3	
						DCM	RA	DCM	RA	DCM	RA
Deepak ji, channel ko kitna fund diya hai congress ne? 2006 me ameithi rape case kyu nahi discuss kiya kabhi?	3.53	7.59	7.27	-0.46	-0.12	8	10	9	10	10	8
4 din me 2 accidents, kuch to jhol hai, shayad politics ho rahi hai..	1.67	6.2	5	-0.19	-0.31	4	9	5	10	10	9
Bhai kasam se bata do ki shadi kab karr rahe ho warna mai kuwara marr jaunga	0	0	0	-1	-0.41	0	10	1	10	9	7
@Mariam_Jamali Nice one but logo filhal KK ki jaga Pakistan ka lagwa do. Pic is good	4.6	9.7	4.7	-0.28	-0.37	6	6	8	8	7	9
abe .,., joke marna hai hi to aur hi kabi maar .,.,. confession page ki bejaati maat ker bhai .. JOKE MARA???????????? HASU? \"haha..!\"	2	6.67	4.28	-0.08	-0.18	6	5	3	8	7	5
Wale log jante hai par atankwadiyo nafrat failane walo ke liye meri yehi language rahegi	0.6	1.42	1.42	0.09	0	4	6	2	8	7	6
mujhe hasi aa rahi thi , while I ws reading them . :P	5	9.32	2.5	-0.24	-0.64	10	10	9	10	6	6
laufed ... first u hav to correct ur english baad me suchna use !!!	3.33	6.67	3.07	0.2	-0.06	10	8	8	9	6	7
The ultimate twist Dulhan dandanate huye brings Baraat .... Dulha	4.44	6.9	5.55	-0.08	0.48	8	6	7	2	5	7
RAHUL jab dieting par hota hai toh green tea peeta hai.	3.63	6.61	5.45	-0.44	0	10	10	2	10	10	9

Table 2: Measuring the complexity of various Hindi-English code-mixed text. Language independent tokens are marked with black color. We select one sentence each from the 10 datasets (in the same order as given in Table 1). Here, DCM stands for degree of code-mixing and RA stands for readability. We scale the CMI, M-index, and I-index metric scores in the range 0 to 10. The range for Burstiness and Memory score is -1 to 1.

on two parameters: the degree of code-mixing and readability. We provide the following guidelines to the annotators for this task:

- **Degree of code-mixing (DCM)**: The score can vary between 0 to 10. A DCM score of 0 corresponds to the monolingual sentence with no code-mixing, whereas the DCM score of 10 suggests the high degree of code-mixing.
- **Readability (RA)**: RA score can vary between 0 to 10. A completely unreadable sentence due to large number of spelling mistakes, no sentence structuring, or meaning, yields a RA score of 0. A RA score of 10 suggests a highly readable sentence with clear semantics and easy-to-read words.

Table 2 shows the 10 example Hinglish sentences with the corresponding metric scores and the human evaluation. Some major observations are:

- We do not observe any metric to independently measure the readability of code-mixed text as quantified by humans.
- We also observe contrasting scores given by different metrics, making it difficult to choose the best-suited metric for the given code-mixed dataset.
- At times, we observe a high disagreement even among the human ratings. This behavior indicates the complexity of the task for humans as well.
- We do not observe any significant relationship between the degree of code-mixing and the readability score as provided by humans. This observation is critical in building high-quality datasets for various code-mixing tasks.

4 Limitations of code-mixing metrics

This section describes various limitations of the existing metrics that measure the complexity of the code-mixed text. As CMI is most popular among code-mixing metrics, it is reported in five (Patwa et al., 2020; Barman et al., 2014; Dhar et al., 2018; Srivastava and Singh, 2020; Khanuja et al., 2020) out of the 10 datasets listed in Table 1. We describe major limitations of code-mixing metrics from three different perspectives:

1. **Metric formulation**: Most of the code-mixing metrics are based on the word frequency from different languages in the text.

Data source	**Spelling variations**	**Noisy/monolingual**	**Readability/semantic**
Singh et al. (2018c)	Ab boliye teen talak harram h ya nai aapke khud ki lady's chate h ki aap sai dur hona. Shame on u again...#TripleTalaq	#TripleTalaq Don't post this	@BJP4UP @narendramodi @AmitShah @BJPLive @bjpsamvad @BJP4India #NoteBandi ke baad ab poori
Swami et al. (2018)	Shareef wo hai jisay moqa nae milta! #irony	Resigned: Sri Lanka Cricket aniyin thodar thoalviyinaal Therivuk kuluth Thalaivar Sanath Jayasuriya ullitta athan uruppinarhal Raajinaamaa	Kudakudhinge dhuvasthamee? #Maldives #Politics
Joshi et al. (2016)	Nhi ye log apny lie ayeen change karty he ye konsa mulk k lie sochty he har koi apny lie aur apny families k lie politics me he sary chor he	#Cricket News 6 Saal Team Ki Qeyadat Karna Mare Liye Izaz Hai Ab Kisi Our Ko Aagay Aana Chahiye Sabiq Captain AB De Villiers	Hiii kam chhe
Patwa et al. (2020)	@DivyanshMohit @GulBukhari Tum apny Indian ki fikkar Karo Pakistan ko hum khud dykh lyngy. Mukti bahini 2 nahi ban	@BTS_army_Fin Also Stade de France is preparing for the concert. Looks so beautiful! See their post on Instagram https://t.co/OwhP	Now this i too much ab sare tweet arsal ke support me Jab jiya ka man nhi and wo chai nhi bana sakti yasit ke liy
Barman et al. (2014)	@Liaqat842 tum sahi keh rhy thy yeh zayda buri timings hain 3 wali match ki subah purany office bhi jna hai kaam hai	@saadiaafzaal Pagl he ye Qaom Jo misbah ka Cmprezm imraan se kr rhe he. khuda ko maano kaha misbah kaha imran.. shoib Akhtar	@aashikapokharel Haha okay. Office time, aba bus ma bore hune wala chhu. Also, Alumni ko imp kaam chha. Viber ma aaye hune. :P
Bohra et al. (2018)	Gf khoon peene k liye hoti hai aur apne babu ko thana thilane k liye bas	Mere marnay ki ya hate deni ki?	ke karya karta aise hi baithe hai.kal ye ghatna aap or Hum
Dhar et al. (2018)	Modi ji aap jesa koi nhi dhanywad aap desh ki kitni sewa karte hai jese ak beta apni ma ko poojta hai	Girna samal nai lage	Etni lambi speech sa kuch mi hotta sirf 2 word khna or unka suna sa frk atta h........ sekho i love you sallu??
Srivastava and Singh (2020)	unhone pehle pic ni dkhi ti kya tmhari jo milne k baad hi ignore kia tmhe...?	kaun hai ye zaleel insaan?	@indiantweeter Jain ration gap ho jaega.
Vijay et al. (2018)	35 sal ma koi hospital esa nai banaya jaha khud ka ilaj hosakai. .. Irony	and then the irony,, sab ko jurisakyo lahana le kahile juraucha ?	hi Vanitha Garu hai Andi this is irony , arledy rep icharu ga
Khanuja et al. (2020)	3 kam padey they	KASTURI is speaking to his son	31 minutes time hua

Table 3: Examples from the 10 datasets highlighting the various inherent limitations that could lead to misleading code-mxing metric score. For the marked words in **spelling variations**, we observe multiple spellings across datasets. We observe that the **noisy** sentences have low **readability**.

This formulation makes the metric vulnerable to several limitations, such as the bag-of-words model and assigning higher metric scores to meaningless sentences that are difficult to read and comprehend.

2. **Resource limitation**: The existing code-mixed datasets too have several shortcomings, such as noisy and monolingual text (see Table 3). Besides, we observe the poor quality of the token-level language identification (LID) systems which are fundamental in calculating the various code-mixing metric scores.

3. **Human annotation**: In the absence of good quality code-mixed LID systems, various works employ human annotators to perform language identification. Evaluating human proficiency is a challenging task since code-mixed languages lacks standard syntax and semantics. Additionally, human annotation is a time and effort extensive process.

Next, we describe four major limitations that combine one or more than one perspective (see Table 4). Figure 2 shows a general flow diagram to obtain the code-mixed data from the large-scale noisy text. It shows the three major bottlenecks (metric formulation, resource limitation, and human annotation) in the entire data filtering process. The resultant code-mixed data is noisy and suffers from several other limitations (see Table 3).

Limitation	**Perspective**
Bag of words	MF
Code-mixed LID	MF, RL
Misleading score	MF, RL, HA
High inference time	MF, RL, HA

Table 4: Combination of perspectives for each of the limitation to code-mixing metrics. Here, MF: Metric Formulation, RL: Resource Limitation, HA: Human Annotation.

1. **Bag-of-words**: None of the code-mixing metrics consider inherent ordering between the

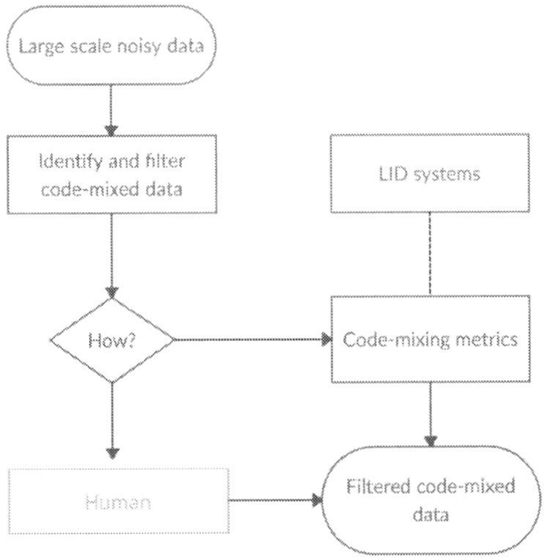

Figure 2: A general flow diagram for identifying and filtering the code-mixed data from the large scale noisy text. We observe three major limitations: metric formulation, resource limitation, and human annotation. There is a time-quality trade-off between the two paths to filter the code-mixed data. Employing humans takes more time and relatively better quality code-mixed sentences as compared to code-mixing metrics that takes less time and shows poor performance.

Pair I

HINGLISH1 (Khanuja et al., 2020): FATHER ab hospital mein hi rahenge.
HINGLISH2 (shuffled HINGLISH1) : hospital ab FATHER mein hi rahenge.
Observation: Same CMI, M-index, I-index, Burstiness and Memory scores

Pair II

HINGLISH1 (Bohra et al., 2018): TAJMAHAL p jake atka hai
HINGLISH2 (shuffled HINGLISH1) : atka p jake TAJMAHAL hai
Observation: Same CMI, M-index, and I-index scores

Figure 3: Example to demonstrate the *bag of words* assumption of code-mixing metrics. We shuffle tokens in HINGLISH1 to get HINGLISH2. Observation shows that metric scores remain unchanged after the shuffling while the semantic of the original sentence is lost.

words in the code-mixed sentence[1]. This limitation makes these metric scores vulnerable to multiple challenges, such as poor grammatical structure. Figure 3 shows examples of good quality code-mixed sentences and corresponding noisy sentences, both having the same metric scores.

2. **Code-mixed language identification**: The presence of more than one language in the code-mixed text presents several challenges for the various downstream NLP tasks such as POS tagging, summarization and named entity recognition. Identifying the token-level language of the code-mixed text is the fundamental step in calculating the code-mixing metric scores. Often various works have employed human annotators to obtain the token-level language tags. However, both human annotators and the language identification systems suffer from the poor token-level language tagging. Table 5 shows the variation in the output of five multilingual/code-mixed LID systems (Langdetect[2], Polyglot[3], CLD3[4], FastText[5], and iNLTK[6]) on the code-mixed text against human-annotated language tags. Contrasting human-annotated tag sequence, the same metric yields significantly different scores due to variation in the language tag sequence obtained from different LID tools. We identify three major reasons for the poor performance of humans and the LID systems in identifying the language of the code-mixed text:

    - **Spelling variations and non-contextual LID**: Spelling variation is one of the most significant challenges in developing code-mixed LID systems. Due to the lack of standard grammar and spellings in code-mixed language, we observe multiple variations of the same word across datasets (see Table 3). For example, Hindi tokens *'hn'* or *'hay'* can also be written as *'hun'* or *'hai'*, respectively. As outlined in Table 5, we observe incorrect language identification by popular multilingual and code-mixed LID systems. This behavior could be highly attributed to the spelling

[1]Note that, *Burstiness* and *Memory* metric only considers span length and not the word ordering within a span.

[2]https://pypi.org/project/langdetect/

[3]https://github.com/aboSamoor/polyglot

[4]https://github.com/google/cld3/

[5]https://fasttext.cc/blog/2017/10/02/blog-post.html

[6]https://inltk.readthedocs.io/en/latest/index.html

	@user	bus	office	me	hn	,	Sat	thora	thanda	hota	hay	kaam	k	point	of	view	say	you	know	:)
Langdetect	et	id	en	nl	vi	unk	tl	en	en	cs	so	so	sw	fi	en	af	tl	sw	en	unk
Polyglot	en	en	en	en	da	un	en	en	en	to	es	fy	en	en	en	en	en	en	en	un
CLD3	no	la	ja	mi	sv	ja	sd	la	ko	mi	es	et	sl	de	en	en	id	en	en	ja
FastText	en	en	en	en	en	ru	pt	war	en	en	es	az	ja	en	en	en	en	en	en	uz
iNLTK	en	en	en	en	en	en	en	en	en	en	en	en	en	en	en	en	en	en	en	en
Human	univ	en	en	hi	hi	univ	en	hi	hi	hi	hi	hi	hi	en	en	en	hi	en	en	univ

Table 5: Example to demonstrate the limitations of LID systems in calculating the code-mixing metric scores. Hinglish sentence is from the dataset used in (Barman et al., 2014). The language name corresponding to the language code can be found at the corresponding LID system's web page.

Token	@	nehantics	Haan	yaar	neha	kab	karega	woh	post	Usne	na	sach	mein
Language	O	Hin	Hin	Hin	Hin	Hin	Hin	Hin	Hin	Hin	Hin	Hin	Hin
Token	photoshoot	karna	chahiye	phir	woh	post	karega	...	https	//	tco	/	5RSISbZNtt
Language	Eng	Hin	Hin	Hin	Hin	Hin	Hin	O	Eng	O	Eng	O	Eng

(a) Example sentence from Patwa et al. (2020)

Token	are	cricket	se	sanyas	le	liya	kya	viru	aur	social	service	suru
Language	Hin	Eng	Hin	Hin	Hin	Hin	Hin	Hin	Hin	Eng	Eng	Hin
Token	kardiya	.	khel	hi	bhul	gaye	.	2	innings	0	n	0
Language	Hin	O	Hin	Hin	Hin	Hin	O	O	Hin	O	Hin	O

(b) Example sentence from Swami et al. (2018)

Table 6: Example sentences to demonstrate the limitations with the language tags in the current code-mixed datasets. We use the color coding to represent three major reasons for such behaviour: ambiguous, annotator's proficiency, and non-contextual. 'O' in the language tag represent the tag 'Other'.

variation of words. Additionally, the non-contextual language tag sequence generation by LID systems and humans leads to a similar set of challenges (see Table 6). In both the examples in Table 6, we observe the incorrect language tag to words like *'tco'* and *'n'* due to the missing context by the human annotator. Also, as observed in Table 6, incorrect LID by humans could be attributed to considering the code-mixed tokens out of context.

- **Ambiguity**: Ambiguity in identifying named-entities, abbreviations, community-specific jargons, etc., leads to incorrect language identification. Table 6 shows the example sentences having incorrect language tags due to ambiguity in the code-mixed sentences. For example, tokens like *'nehatics'*, *'neha'*, and *'viru'* are person named-entities, incorrectly tagged with *hi* tag.
- **Annotator's proficiency**: Evaluating the human proficiency for a code-mixed language is much more challenging as compared to the monolingual languages due to lack of standard, dialect variation, and ambiguity in the text. Table 6 shows an example of incorrect language annotation by the human annotators, which could be attributed to low human proficiency/varied interpretation of the code-mixed text. For example, English tokens like *'post'* and *'innings'* are tagged as *hi* tokens by human annotators.

3. **Misleading score**: We observe several inconsistencies in the interpretation of the code-mixing metric scores. We identify three major reasons for this inconsistent behavior:

   - **Coherence**: Coherency in a multi-sentence code-mixed text is one of the fundamental properties of good quality data. Future works in code-mixed NLP, such as text summarization, question-answering, and natural language inference, will require highly coherent datasets. However, the current metrics cannot measure the coherency of the code-mixed text. We witness a large number of real scenarios where the code-mixing metric scores for multi-sentence text are high, but the coherency is very poor. In such cases, the code-mixing metrics in the present form will lead to undesirable behavior. For instance, we query a Hinglish question-answering system *WebShodh*[7] (Chandu et al., 2017) with the question: *India ka PM kaun hai? Cricket dekhne jaana hai?* The list of eight probable answers (*'ipl', 'puma', 'kohli', 'sports news feb', ''amazoncom', 'sport news nov', 'hotstar vip', 'rugged flip phone unlocked water shock proof att tmobile metro cricket straight talk consumer cellular carrier cell phones'*) shows the poor performance of the system due to low coherency in the question text (in addition to other architectural limitations) even though the question text is highly code-mixed on various metrics.

- **Readability**: The co-existence of the code-mixed data with the monolingual and the noisy text results in the poor readability of the code-mixed text. The code-mixing metrics do not take into account the readability of the code-mixed text. Low readability of the code-mixed text will also lead to incorrect annotations by the annotators, which will eventually lead to incorrect metric scores for the given data. Table 3 shows example sentences from multiple datasets with low readability.
- **Semantics**: The last column in Table 3 shows example sentences from multiple datasets where it is extremely difficult to extract the meaning of the code-mixed sentence. Due to the current formulation of the code-mixing metrics where we consider the independent language tokens and the bag-of-words approach, it is not feasible to identify such low semantic sentences.

4. **High inference time**: We require an efficient automatic NLP system that identifies and filters the code-mixed text from a large-scale noisy text or monolingual text. Even though theoretically, the code-mixing metrics can help identify text with high levels of code-mixing, but practically they fail due to inefficiencies in LID systems. We showcase the inability of LID systems to detect correct language tags (see point 2 above). One possible remedy is to employ humans in language identification. However, human involvement significantly increases the time and the cost of performing the labeling task. Also, human annotations are also prone to errors (see Table 6). We might also need task-specific annotations (e.g., POS tags, NER, etc.) which will further increase the time and cost of the annotation task. Due to this reason, we see majority of the datasets (see Table 1) relatively smaller in size (<5000 data points). Human annotation significantly increases the inference time in calculating the code-mixing metric scores.

[7] `http://tts.speech.cs.cmu.edu/webshodh/cmqa.php`

5 Conclusion and Future Work

In this paper, we extensively discuss the limitations of code-mixing metrics. We explored 10 Hinglish datasets for presenting examples to support our claims. Overall, we showcase the need for extensive efforts in addressing these limitations. In the future, we plan to develop a robust code-mixing metric that measures the extent of code-mixing and quantifies the readability and grammatical correctness of the text. Also, we aim to create a large-scale Hinglish dataset with manual token-level language annotation.

References

Scott Baldauf. 2004. A hindi-english jumble, spoken by 350 million. *The Christian Science Monitor*, 1123(1):3.

Somnath Banerjee, Sudip Kumar Naskar, Paolo Rosso, and Sivaji Bandyopadhyay. 2016. The first cross-script code-mixed question answering corpus. In *MultiLingMine@ ECIR*, pages 56–65.

Utsab Barman, Amitava Das, Joachim Wagner, and Jennifer Foster. 2014. Code mixing: A challenge for language identification in the language of social media. In *Proceedings of the First Workshop on Computational Approaches to Code Switching*, pages 13–23, Doha, Qatar. Association for Computational Linguistics.

Ruthanna Barnett, Eva Codó, Eva Eppler, Montse Forcadell, Penelope Gardner-Chloros, Roeland van Hout, Melissa Moyer, Maria Carme Torras, Maria Teresa Turell, Mark Sebba, Marianne Starren, and Sietse Wensing. 2000. The lides coding manual: A document for preparing and analyzing language interaction data version 1.1—july, 1999. *International Journal of Bilingualism*, 4(2):131–132.

Aditya Bohra, Deepanshu Vijay, Vinay Singh, Syed Sarfaraz Akhtar, and Manish Shrivastava. 2018. A dataset of hindi-english code-mixed social media text for hate speech detection. In *Proceedings of the second workshop on computational modeling of people's opinions, personality, and emotions in social media*, pages 36–41.

Eyamba G Bokamba. 1989. Are there syntactic constraints on code-mixing? *World Englishes*, 8(3):277–292.

Khyathi Chandu, Ekaterina Loginova, Vishal Gupta, Josef van Genabith, Günter Neumann, Manoj Chinnakotla, Eric Nyberg, and Alan W Black. 2019. Code-mixed question answering challenge: Crowdsourcing data and techniques. In *Third Workshop on Computational Approaches to Linguistic Code-Switching*, pages 29–38. Association for Computational Linguistics (ACL).

Khyathi Raghavi Chandu, Manoj Chinnakotla, Alan W Black, and Manish Shrivastava. 2017. Webshodh: A code mixed factoid question answering system for web. In *International Conference of the Cross-Language Evaluation Forum for European Languages*, pages 104–111. Springer.

Amitava Das and Björn Gambäck. 2014. Identifying languages at the word level in code-mixed indian social media text. In *Proceedings of the 11th International Conference on Natural Language Processing*, pages 378–387.

Mrinal Dhar, Vaibhav Kumar, and Manish Shrivastava. 2018. Enabling code-mixed translation: Parallel corpus creation and mt augmentation approach. In *Proceedings of the First Workshop on Linguistic Resources for Natural Language Processing*, pages 131–140.

Björn Gambäck and Amitava Das. 2016. Comparing the level of code-switching in corpora. In *Proceedings of the Tenth International Conference on Language Resources and Evaluation (LREC'16)*, pages 1850–1855.

K-I Goh and A-L Barabási. 2008. Burstiness and memory in complex systems. *EPL (Europhysics Letters)*, 81(4):48002.

Gualberto A Guzmán, Joseph Ricard, Jacqueline Serigos, Barbara E Bullock, and Almeida Jacqueline Toribio. 2017. Metrics for modeling code-switching across corpora. In *INTERSPEECH*, pages 67–71.

Aditya Joshi, Ameya Prabhu, Manish Shrivastava, and Vasudeva Varma. 2016. Towards sub-word level compositions for sentiment analysis of hindi-english code mixed text. In *Proceedings of COLING 2016, the 26th International Conference on Computational Linguistics: Technical Papers*, pages 2482–2491.

Simran Khanuja, Sandipan Dandapat, Sunayana Sitaram, and Monojit Choudhury. 2020. A new dataset for natural language inference from code-mixed conversations. In *Proceedings of the The 4th Workshop on Computational Approaches to Code Switching*, pages 9–16.

Parth Patwa, Gustavo Aguilar, Sudipta Kar, Suraj Pandey, PYKL Srinivas, Björn Gambäck, Tanmoy Chakraborty, Thamar Solorio, and Amitava Das. 2020. Semeval-2020 task 9: Overview of sentiment analysis of code-mixed tweets. In *Proceedings of the Fourteenth Workshop on Semantic Evaluation*, pages 774–790.

Shashi Shekhar, Dilip Kumar Sharma, and MM Sufyan Beg. 2020. Language identification framework in code-mixed social media text based on quantum lstm—the word belongs to which language? *Modern Physics Letters B*, 34(06):2050086.

Kushagra Singh, Indira Sen, and Ponnurangam Kumaraguru. 2018a. Language identification and named entity recognition in hinglish code mixed tweets. In *Proceedings of ACL 2018, Student Research Workshop*, pages 52–58.

Kushagra Singh, Indira Sen, and Ponnurangam Kumaraguru. 2018b. A twitter corpus for hindi-english code mixed pos tagging. In *Proceedings of the Sixth International Workshop on Natural Language Processing for Social Media*, pages 12–17.

Vinay Singh, Deepanshu Vijay, Syed Sarfaraz Akhtar, and Manish Shrivastava. 2018c. Named entity recognition for hindi-english code-mixed social media text. In *Proceedings of the seventh named entities workshop*, pages 27–35.

Vivek Srivastava and Mayank Singh. 2020. Phinc: A parallel hinglish social media code-mixed corpus for machine translation. In *Proceedings of the Sixth Workshop on Noisy User-generated Text (W-NUT 2020)*, pages 41–49.

Sahil Swami, Ankush Khandelwal, Vinay Singh, Syed Sarfaraz Akhtar, and Manish Shrivastava. 2018. A corpus of english-hindi code-mixed tweets for sarcasm detection. *arXiv preprint arXiv:1805.11869*.

Mary WJ Tay. 1989. Code switching and code mixing as a communicative strategy in multilingual discourse. *World Englishes*, 8(3):407–417.

Deepanshu Vijay, Aditya Bohra, Vinay Singh, Syed Sarfaraz Akhtar, and Manish Shrivastava. 2018. A dataset for detecting irony in hindi-english code-mixed social media text. *EMSASW@ ESWC*, 2111:38–46.

Yogarshi Vyas, Spandana Gella, Jatin Sharma, Kalika Bali, and Monojit Choudhury. 2014. Pos tagging of english-hindi code-mixed social media content. In *Proceedings of the 2014 Conference on Empirical Methods in Natural Language Processing (EMNLP)*, pages 974–979.

Translate and Classify: Improving Sequence Level Classification for English-Hindi Code-Mixed Data

Devansh Gautam **Kshitij Gupta** **Manish Shrivastava**
International Institute of Information Technology Hyderabad
{devansh.gautam,kshitij.gupta}@research.iiit.ac.in,
m.shrivastava@iiit.ac.in

Abstract

Code-mixing is a common phenomenon in multilingual societies around the world and is especially common in social media texts. Traditional NLP systems, usually trained on monolingual corpora, do not perform well on code-mixed texts. Training specialized models for code-switched texts is difficult due to the lack of large-scale datasets. Translating code-mixed data into standard languages like English could improve performance on various code-mixed tasks since we can use transfer learning from state-of-the-art English models for processing the translated data. This paper focuses on two sequence-level classification tasks for English-Hindi code mixed texts, which are part of the GLUECoS benchmark - Natural Language Inference and Sentiment Analysis. We propose using various pre-trained models that have been fine-tuned for similar English-only tasks and have shown state-of-the-art performance. We further fine-tune these models on the translated code-mixed datasets and achieve state-of-the-art performance in both tasks. To translate English-Hindi code-mixed data to English, we use mBART, a pre-trained multilingual sequence-to-sequence model that has shown competitive performance on various low-resource machine translation pairs and has also shown performance gains in languages that were not in its pre-training corpus.

1 Introduction

In the last decade, social media has become a significant part of the lives of a large population in the world. Unlike previously popular communication platforms, online messaging is very informal, and in recent years, it has led to an increase in the usage of emojis, slang, and even a hybrid form of language, code-mixed language.

Code-mixed language is a mixture of multiple languages where words belonging to different languages are interleaved with each other in the same conversation. It is commonly used by multilingual speakers. It does not follow a formally defined structure and often varies from person to person, although some studies (Poplack, 1980; Belazi et al., 1994) have proposed linguistic constraints on code-switching. Code-mixing and code-switching are similar terms that slightly differ technically, but they are often used interchangeably by the research community. We will also be using them interchangeably in our paper.

In this paper, we work with English-Hindi code-mixed data. English-Hindi code-mixed language often called *Hinglish* is very common in India because of a large number of bilingual speakers who often use English in their professional lives while using Hindi in their personal lives. An example of an English-Hindi code-mixed sentence from a dataset released by Dhar et al. (2018) is shown below:

- **Original Sentence:** My brother always told me ki in retrospect, badi dikkatein chhoti lagti hain.
- **Gloss:** [My brother always told me] that [in retrospect], big problems small seem are.
- **Translation:** My brother always told me that, in retrospect, big problems seem to be small.

Although there is a large population globally that communicates using code-mixed languages, annotated datasets remain scarce even when the monolingual constituent languages have large-scale datasets. Recent work suggests that multilingual models trained on several monolingual datasets perform well with zero-shot cross-lingual transfer in code-switched settings (Patwa et al., 2020; Khanuja et al., 2020b). However, Khanuja et al. (2020b) conclude that their model had varying performance across tasks and especially struggled with NLI and sentiment analysis tasks. Another challenge with code-mixed language research is that,

Proceedings of the Fifth Workshop on Computational Approaches to Linguistic Code-Switching, pages 15–25
June 11, 2021. ©2021 Association for Computational Linguistics
https://doi.org/10.26615/978-954-452-056-4_003

unlike monolingual data, there are no formal data sources like news articles or books written in code-mixed languages. Instead, most research uses informal sources such as social media texts or messages, which are usually challenging to obtain. Also, most of the data is written in the Roman script, and Hindi words are transliterated informally without any standard rules. Instead, individuals generally provide a rough phonetic transcription of the intended word, which can vary from individual to individual due to any number of factors, including regional or dialectal differences in pronunciations, differing conventions of transcription, or simple idiosyncrasy (Roark et al., 2020). This makes it challenging to prepare reliable datasets to train robust deep learning models. Most of the existing datasets focus on a few language pairs and have been prepared by several shared task organizers.

To address these issues, we propose translating the code-mixed data to English (a high-resource language) and applying powerful models trained on English data to perform sequence-level classification tasks on the translated data. To translate the code-mixed data to English, we propose using mBART (Liu et al., 2020), a pre-trained multilingual sequence-to-sequence model. We experiment with our pipeline on two English-Hindi code-mixed sequence classification tasks of the GLUECoS (Khanuja et al., 2020b) benchmark - Natural Language Inference and Sentiment Analysis. We achieve state-of-the-art performance in both tasks. The code for our proposed system is available at `https://github.com/devanshg27/cm_translatify`.

The main contributions of our work are as follows:

- We explore the effectiveness of using mBART for low resource code-mixed Hinglish-English translation with transfer learning from Hindi-English translation.
- We propose performing sequence-level classifications on the code-mixed data by first translating it to English and then using powerful models trained on English data to classify the translated data.
- We achieve state-of-the-art performance on two classification tasks of the GLUECoS benchmark - Natural Language Inference and Sentiment Analysis with an absolute increase of 12.4% and 5.3%, respectively.

The rest of the paper is organized as follows. We discuss prior work related to code-mixed language processing and also discuss work related to machine translation, Natural language Inference, and Sentiment Analysis. We describe the translation system we use and show the effect of different training choices. We describe our pipeline for code-mixed sequence level classification tasks on the chosen tasks - Natural Language Inference and Sentiment Analysis and show its performance against past work. We conclude with a direction for future work and highlight our main findings.

2 Related Work

Code-mixing occurs when a speaker uses words belonging to different languages interleaved with each other in the same conversation. With the rise of social media and messaging platforms, there has been a significant increase in code-mixed language usage.

Several shared tasks have been conducted as a part of code-switching workshops (Diab et al., 2014, 2016; Aguilar et al., 2018b) which were held in notable conferences. These tasks include language identification (Solorio et al., 2014; Molina et al., 2016), named entity recognition (Aguilar et al., 2018a; Rao and Devi, 2016), information retrieval (Roy et al., 2013; Choudhury et al., 2014; Sequiera et al., 2015; Banerjee et al., 2018), Part-of-speech tagging (Jamatia et al., 2016), sentiment analysis (Patra et al., 2018; Patwa et al., 2020), and question answering (Chandu et al., 2018).

Although these tasks have helped progress code-switching language research, most tasks require building specialized systems for the specific task and language pair due to the limited dataset sizes. Recently, large pre-trained multilingual models have been used for various code-mixed tasks (Patwa et al., 2020; Khanuja et al., 2020b).

Machine Translation refers to translating a text from a source language to its counterpart in a target language using machines. It has widespread applications in the real world and has been an active area of research.

Earlier works in machine translation mostly focused on statistical or rule-based approaches. In contrast, neural machine translation gained popularity in the last decade after Kalchbrenner and Blunsom (2013) successfully proposed the first DNN model for translation. Recent works use transformer-based approaches (Vaswani et al.,

2017). Some approaches utilize multilingual pre-training (Song et al., 2019; Conneau and Lample, 2019; Edunov et al., 2019; Liu et al., 2020); however, these works focus only on monolingual language pairs.

Despite the significant usage of English-Hindi code-mixing, there has been little work regarding English-Hindi code-mixed translation (Srivastava and Singh, 2020; Singh and Solorio, 2018; Dhar et al., 2018), which leads to a massive gap in communication as these texts can only be understood by people who are proficient in both these languages.

Natural Language Inference is the task of determining if the given "premise" supports a given "hypothesis" and classifying the hypothesis as true (entailment), false (contradiction), or undetermined (neutral). It is arguably one of the most fundamental tasks in natural language understanding. Wang et al. (2018) and Yin et al. (2019) suggest that various NLP tasks can be reduced to Natural Language Inference, which makes it an even more valuable task to solve.

Natural Language Inference for English texts has been an active area of research. It has been extensively studied under different tasks such as RTE (Recognizing Textual Entailment) (Dagan et al., 2006), NLI (Natural Language Inference) (Bowman et al., 2015), FEVER (Fact Extraction and VERification) (Thorne et al., 2018). In recent years, large-scale pre-trained models (Devlin et al., 2019; Yang et al., 2019; Liu et al., 2019) have dominated these tasks and have achieved close-to-human performance.

Although NLI on English data has seen many advances, there has been little work on NLI for code-mixed data. Khanuja et al. (2020a) release the first NLI dataset for code-mixed languages. It consists of conversations from Hindi movies (Bollywood) as premises. Chakravarthy et al. (2020) compare the effectiveness of various approaches on the dataset.

Sentiment Analysis is the task of understanding the sentiment expressed in the text and classifying the text into positive, negative, or neutral classes. It has several applications such as customer feedback, marketing, and social media monitoring. There has been extensive research on sentiment analysis of English texts with various shared tasks and datasets. Sentiment analysis for code-mixed texts is an essential task due to the widespread usage of code-mixed texts on social media in multilingual societies. There has been some work related to code-mixed sentiment analysis with a few shared tasks (Patra et al., 2018; Patwa et al., 2020). The participants of the task organized by Patwa et al. (2020) explored various approaches such as pre-trained language models, RNN, CNN, and word embeddings.

	Dhar et al. (2018)	Srivastava and Singh (2020)
# of sentences	6,096	13,738
# of tokens	63,913	200,326
# of Hindi tokens	37,673	103,887
# of English tokens	16,182	38,511
# of 'Other' tokens	10,094	57,928

Table 1: The statistics of the English-Hindi code-mixed sentences in the two datasets we use. We use the language tokens predicted by the CSNLI library for both the datasets.

3 Translating Code-Mixed Text

In this section, we describe our proposed model, which uses mBART (Liu et al., 2020) to translate code-mixed texts to English.

3.1 mBART

We fine-tune mBART, which is a multilingual sequence-to-sequence denoising auto-encoder. It has been pre-trained using the BART (Lewis et al., 2020) objective on large-scale monolingual corpora of 25 languages extracted from Common Crawl[1] (Wenzek et al., 2020; Conneau et al., 2020). Both English and Hindi are part of the pre-training corpus with 55,608 million tokens (300.8 GB) and 1,715 million tokens (20.2 GB), respectively. It uses a standard sequence-to-sequence Transformer architecture (Vaswani et al., 2017), with 12 encoder and decoder layers each and a model dimension of 1024 on 16 heads resulting in ~680 million parameters.

3.2 Data Preparation

We use the datasets released by Dhar et al. (2018) and Srivastava and Singh (2020), the statistics of the datasets are provided in the Table 1. Since both the datasets contain Hindi words in Roman script, we use the CSNLI library[2] (Bhat et al., 2017, 2018) as a preprocessing step. It transliterates the Hindi words to Devanagari and also performs text normalization. We split the datasets into an 8:1:1

[1] https://commoncrawl.org/

[2] https://github.com/irshadbhat/csnli

train:validation:test split. We merge the training and validation sets of the two datasets and use the merged datasets for all our experiments.

We also use the dataset released by Kunchukuttan et al. (2018) which contains parallel sentences for English and Hindi. We use the training set, which contains 1,609,682 sentences, for training our systems.

3.3 Optimization

We use the implementation of mBART available in the fairseq library[3] (Ott et al., 2019). We fine-tune on 4 Nvidia GeForce RTX 2080 Ti GPUs with an effective batch size of 1024 tokens per GPU. We use the Adam optimizer ($\epsilon = 10^{-6}, \beta_1 = 0.9, \beta_2 = 0.98$) (Kingma and Ba, 2015) with 0.2 label smoothing, 0.3 dropout, 0.1 attention dropout and polynomial decay learning rate scheduling. We validate the models every 8000 steps and select the best checkpoint based on the lowest validation loss. To train our systems efficiently, we prune mBART's vocabulary by removing the tokens which are not present in any of the datasets mentioned in the previous section.

We compare the following 3 strategies for fine-tuning mBART:

- **mBART-cm:** We fine-tune mBART on the merged dataset with parallel English-Hindi code-mixed sentences. We fine-tune for 20,000 steps with 2,500 warm-up steps and a learning rate of $3 * 10^{-5}$.
- **mBART-hien:** We fine-tune mBART on the dataset with parallel English-Hindi sentences. We fine-tune for 80,000 steps with 2,500 warm-up steps and a learning rate of $3 * 10^{-5}$.
- **mBART-hien-cm:** We fine-tune mBART on the dataset with parallel English-Hindi sentences for 80,000 steps with 2,500 warm-up steps and a learning rate of $3 * 10^{-5}$, followed by further fine-tuning on on the merged dataset with parallel English-Hindi code-mixed sentences for 10,000 steps with 2,500 warm-up steps and a learning rate of 10^{-5}.

3.4 Results

We use BLEU scores as the metric for comparing our systems, the scores are computed using the

Model	Datasets	
	Dhar et al. (2018)	Srivastava and Singh (2020)
mBART-hien	17.2	16.7
mBART-cm	30.5	31.6
mBART-hien-cm	**31.7**	**33.0**

Table 2: BLEU scores of our systems on the test sets of the two datasets.

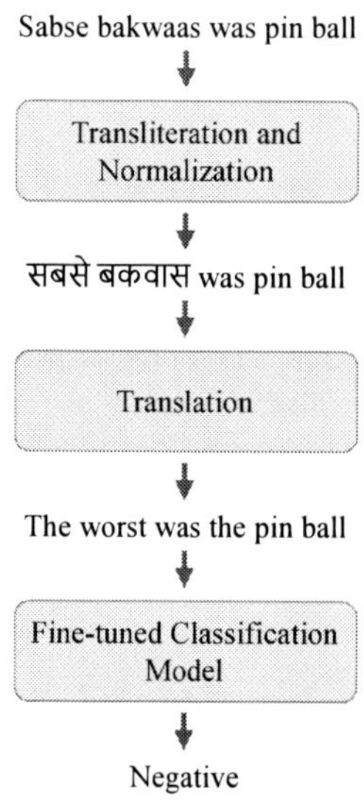

Figure 1: The working of our pipeline for the task of code-mixed Natural Language Inference is demonstrated on an example (with minor edits) from the dataset (the details of the dataset are discussed later).

SacreBLEU library[4] (Post, 2018) after tokenization using the `TweetTokenizer` available with the NLTK library[5] (Bird et al., 2009). The scores of our systems are shown in Table 2. We find that **mBART-hien** which was only fine-tuned for Hindi-English translation, performs considerably worse than the other models, showing that fine-tuning on English-Hindi code-mixed data improves the performance substantially. We also find that **mBART-hien-cm** has the best performance among the systems we consider. It uses transfer learning from Hindi to English translation to improve Hinglish-English translation.

4 Code-Mixed Sequence-level Classification

In this section, we describe our approach for code-mixed sequence-level classification tasks using our

[3] https://github.com/pytorch/fairseq

[4] https://github.com/mjpost/sacrebleu

[5] https://www.nltk.org/

Model	Architecture	Dataset(Number of samples)				#Parameters
		SNLI (570k)	MultiNLI (433k)	FEVER-NLI (250k)	ANLI(R1,R2,R3) (170k)	
(1) (Liu et al., 2019)	RoBERTa $_{large}$		✓			~355M
(2) (Nie et al., 2020)	RoBERTa $_{large}$	✓	✓	✓	✓	~355M
(3) (Nie et al., 2020)	XLNet $_{large}$	✓	✓	✓	✓	~340M
(4) (Nie et al., 2020)	ALBERT $_{xxlarge}$	✓	✓	✓	✓	~223M
(5) (He et al., 2021)	DeBERTa $_{large}$		✓			~390M

Table 3: The pre-trained checkpoints we use along with their architecture, number of parameters and finetuning datasets.

	Train Set	Dev Set	Test Set
# of sentences	1,392	400	447
# of entailed sentences	696	200	224
# of contradictory sentences	696	200	223
# of tokens	123,366	33,932	40,072
# of Hindi tokens	75,865	20,837	24,413
# of English tokens	19,952	5,457	6,624
# of 'Other' tokens	27,549	7,638	9,035

Table 4: The statistics of the Natural Language Inference dataset. We use the language tokens predicted by the CSNLI library.

translation system. Our pipeline is shown in Figure 1. We evaluate the performance of our pipeline on two tasks - Natural Language Inference and Sentiment Analysis.

4.1 Natural Language Inference

4.1.1 Data Preparation

We use the dataset released by Khanuja et al. (2020a), which is a part of the GLUECoS benchmark. The dataset consists of code-mixed conversations from Hindi Movies (*Bollywood*) as premises that have been annotated with hypotheses that are either entailed or contradicted by the conversational premise. The statistics for the dataset are shown in Table 4. Since the dataset consists of Hindi words in Roman script, we use the CSNLI library to transliterate the Hindi words to Devanagari and perform text normalization. The data is then translated to English using our best-performing translation system - **mBART-hien-cm**. The dataset has a split between a train set and a test set with 1792 and 447 premise-hypothesis pairs in each, respectively. We split the train set into a validation set to create a 3.5:1:1.25 train:validation:test split finally.

4.1.2 System Overview

Our systems use different models which have shown competitive performance on Natural Language Inference for English texts. We use publicly available checkpoints for each model, which have been fine-tuned for Natural Language Inference on various English datasets such as SNLI (Bowman et al., 2015), MultiNLI (Williams et al., 2018), FEVER-NLI (Nie et al., 2019), ANLI (R1, R2, R3) (Nie et al., 2020). We fine-tune the checkpoints further on the code-mixed data translated to English. The details about the checkpoints we use are shown in Table 3.

4.1.3 Optimization

For the implementation of our systems, we use the HuggingFace Transformers library[6] (Wolf et al., 2020) and the AdamW optimizer ($\epsilon = 10^{-8}, \beta_1 = 0.9, \beta_2 = 0.999, \text{wd} = 0.01$) available in PyTorch[7] (Paszke et al., 2019) with a learning rate of 10^{-6}. All models were fine-tuned using 4 Nvidia GeForce RTX 2080 Ti GPU with a batch size of 8. The maximum sequence length was 512 for **(1)** and **(2)** and 256 for the other models. We fine-tune the models for 5 epochs with validation every 100 steps and choose the model with the best performance on the validation set. We use cross-entropy as the loss function.

4.1.4 Results

We compare the performance of our systems against the system with the highest test set performance discussed in Chakravarthy et al. (2020) and the baselines provided by Khanuja et al. (2020b).

The performance of our systems is shown in Table 5. All our systems perform better than the current state-of-the-art. We find that **(2)** performs better than **(1)**, which shows that transfer learning from a larger English dataset improves the performance on code-mixed texts. The confusion matrix for the predictions from our best model is shown

[6] https://huggingface.co/transformers/
[7] https://pytorch.org/

Model	Accuracy
mBERT (Khanuja et al., 2020b)	61.09
Mod. mBERT (Khanuja et al., 2020b)	63.1
mod-mBERT (Chakravarthy et al., 2020)	62.41
(1) - RoBERTa $_{large}$	73.65 $_{\pm 0.82}$
(2) - RoBERTa $_{large}$	**75.53** $_{\pm 1.08}$
(3) - XLNet $_{large}$	68.97 $_{\pm 1.16}$
(4) - ALBERT $_{xxlarge}$	70.74 $_{\pm 1.66}$
(5) - DeBERTa $_{large}$	73.92 $_{\pm 0.61}$

Table 5: NLI Performance with different checkpoints: Mean and standard deviation of the metrics from 5 independent runs.

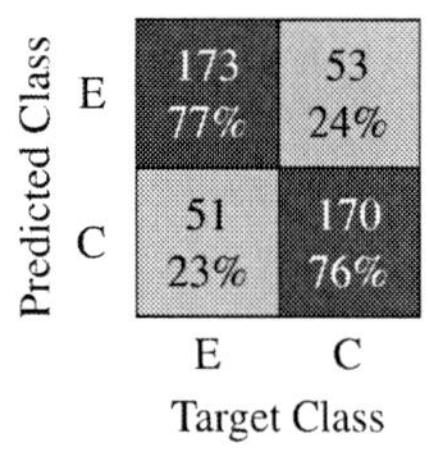

Figure 2: Confusion matrix of the test set predictions by our best model. The percentages show the ratio of the target class, which was predicted as that class. C: Contradictory, E: Entailed.

in Figure 2. We find that the performance of our system on entailed and contradictory statements is similar.

4.2 Sentiment Analysis

4.2.1 Data Preparation

We use the dataset released by Patra et al. (2018), which is part of the GLUECoS benchmark. The dataset was created by collecting code-mixed tweets using common Hindi words as search keywords. The tweets were annotated with word-level language tags and sentiment tags (positive, negative, or neutral). A transliterated version of the dataset is also provided where the Hindi words are in the Devanagari script. We use the transliterated version and translate it to English using **mBART-hien-cm** after normalizing the text with the `DevanagariNormalizer` function available in the IndicNLP Library[8] (Kunchukuttan, 2020). The statistics for the dataset are shown in Table 6. We use the provided train:validation:test split, which is in the ratio 8:1:1.

[8] http://anoopkunchukuttan.github.io/indic_nlp_library/

	Train Set	Dev Set	Test Set
# of sentences	10,079	1,260	1,262
# of negative sentences	2,319	283	290
# of neutral sentences	4,559	578	586
# of positive sentences	3,202	399	385
# of tokens	159,528	20,652	18,985
# of Hindi tokens	65,245	8,486	7,841
# of English tokens	62,678	8,028	7,453
# of 'Other' tokens	31,605	4,138	3,691

Table 6: The statistics of the Sentiment Analysis dataset. We use the word-level language tags provided along with the dataset.

4.2.2 System Overview

We use the following models which have shown competitive performance on sentiment analysis of English tweets:

(1) BERTweet (Nguyen et al., 2020): A large-scale pre-trained language model for English tweets which has been pre-trained on a large corpus of 850M English tweets. It has the same architecture as BERT$_{base}$ with ~110M parameters.

(2) RoB-RT (Barbieri et al., 2020): The pre-trained RoBERTa$_{base}$ model which has been re-trained on a corpus of 58M English tweets. It has ~125M parameters.

We use publicly available checkpoints of the above models, which have been fine-tuned on the sentiment analysis dataset released for SemEval-2017 Task 4 (Rosenthal et al., 2017) which is part of the TweetEval (Barbieri et al., 2020) benchmark. The dataset consists of ~60,000 tweets. We fine-tune the checkpoints further for sentiment analysis of code-mixed tweets that have been translated to English.

4.2.3 Optimization

For the implementation of our systems, we again use the HuggingFace Transformers library and the AdamW ($\epsilon = 10^{-8}, \beta_1 = 0.9, \beta_2 = 0.999, \text{wd} = 0.01$) optimizer available in PyTorch with a learning rate of 10^{-6}. All models were fine-tuned using 4 Nvidia GeForce RTX 2080 Ti GPU with a batch size of 16. The maximum sequence length was 128 for **(1) BERTweet** and 512 for **(2) RoB-RT**. We fine-tune the models for 5 epochs with validation every 100 steps and choose the model with

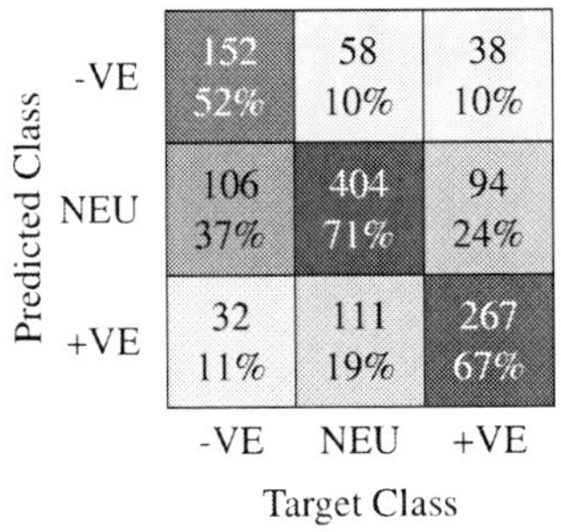

Figure 3: Confusion matrix of the test set predictions by our best model. The percentages show the ratio of the target class, which was predicted as that class. -VE: Negative, NEU: Neutral, +VE: Positive.

Model	F1-weighted
IIIT-NBP (Patra et al., 2018)	56.9
mBERT (Khanuja et al., 2020b)	58.24
Mod. mBERT (Khanuja et al., 2020b)	59.35
(1) BERTweet	**64.6** ± 0.3
(2) RoB-RT $_{\text{base}}$	**64.6** ± 0.4

Table 7: Sentiment Analysis Performance with different checkpoints: Mean and standard deviation of the metrics from 5 independent runs.

the best performance on the validation set. We use cross-entropy as the loss function.

4.2.4 Results

We compare the performance of our systems against the system achieving the highest score in the task organized by Patra et al. (2018) and the two best-performing baselines provided by Khanuja et al. (2020b).

The performance of our systems is shown in Table 7. Both the systems we consider have similar performance and perform better than the current state-of-the-art. The confusion matrix for the predictions from our best model is shown in Figure 3. We find that our model struggles with negative sentiment tweets and misclassifies them as neutral sentiment in 37% of cases.

5 Conclusion

In this paper, we demonstrate that mBART can be used to translate English-Hindi code-mixed sentences to English and show that transfer learning from Hindi-English translation improves its performance on code-mixed translation. We evaluate how our translation system can be used to improve performance in code-mixed sequence classification tasks. We develop a pipeline that uses our translation system to translate code-mixed data to English and then uses large-scale pre-trained English models for the downstream tasks. Our experiments show that our pipeline achieves state-of-the-art performance on two tasks of the GLUECoS benchmark - Natural Language Inference and Sentiment Analysis.

The performance of our pipeline shows that improving code-mixed translation can improve the performance of several code-mixed tasks. In future work, we would like to improve our translation system by creating a larger parallel corpus or synthetically generating parallel sentences for data augmentation. We would also like to extend our system to other code-mixing language pairs.

Acknowledgments

We would like to thank the anonymous reviewers for their time and insightful comments.

References

Gustavo Aguilar, Fahad AlGhamdi, Victor Soto, Mona Diab, Julia Hirschberg, and Thamar Solorio. 2018a. Named entity recognition on code-switched data: Overview of the CALCS 2018 shared task. In *Proceedings of the Third Workshop on Computational Approaches to Linguistic Code-Switching*, pages 138–147, Melbourne, Australia. Association for Computational Linguistics.

Gustavo Aguilar, Fahad AlGhamdi, Victor Soto, Thamar Solorio, Mona Diab, and Julia Hirschberg, editors. 2018b. *Proceedings of the Third Workshop on Computational Approaches to Linguistic Code-Switching*. Association for Computational Linguistics, Melbourne, Australia.

Somnath Banerjee, Kunal Chakma, Sudip Kumar Naskar, Amitava Das, Paolo Rosso, Sivaji Bandyopadhyay, and Monojit Choudhury. 2018. Overview of the mixed script information retrieval (msir) at fire-2016. In *Text Processing*, pages 39–49, Cham. Springer International Publishing.

Francesco Barbieri, Jose Camacho-Collados, Luis Espinosa Anke, and Leonardo Neves. 2020. TweetEval: Unified benchmark and comparative evaluation for tweet classification. In *Findings of the Association for Computational Linguistics: EMNLP 2020*, pages 1644–1650, Online. Association for Computational Linguistics.

Hedi M. Belazi, Edward J. Rubin, and Almeida Jacqueline Toribio. 1994. Code switching and x-bar theory: The functional head constraint. *Linguistic Inquiry*, 25(2):221–237.

Irshad Bhat, Riyaz A. Bhat, Manish Shrivastava, and Dipti Sharma. 2017. Joining hands: Exploiting monolingual treebanks for parsing of code-mixing data. In *Proceedings of the 15th Conference of the European Chapter of the Association for Computational Linguistics: Volume 2, Short Papers*, pages 324–330, Valencia, Spain. Association for Computational Linguistics.

Irshad Bhat, Riyaz A. Bhat, Manish Shrivastava, and Dipti Sharma. 2018. Universal Dependency parsing for Hindi-English code-switching. In *Proceedings of the 2018 Conference of the North American Chapter of the Association for Computational Linguistics: Human Language Technologies, Volume 1 (Long Papers)*, pages 987–998, New Orleans, Louisiana. Association for Computational Linguistics.

Steven Bird, Ewan Klein, and Edward Loper. 2009. *Natural Language Processing with Python*. O'Reilly Media.

Samuel R. Bowman, Gabor Angeli, Christopher Potts, and Christopher D. Manning. 2015. A large annotated corpus for learning natural language inference. In *Proceedings of the 2015 Conference on Empirical Methods in Natural Language Processing*, pages 632–642, Lisbon, Portugal. Association for Computational Linguistics.

Sharanya Chakravarthy, Anjana Umapathy, and Alan W Black. 2020. Detecting entailment in code-mixed Hindi-English conversations. In *Proceedings of the Sixth Workshop on Noisy User-generated Text (W-NUT 2020)*, pages 165–170, Online. Association for Computational Linguistics.

Khyathi Chandu, Ekaterina Loginova, Vishal Gupta, Josef van Genabith, Günter Neumann, Manoj Chinnakotla, Eric Nyberg, and Alan W. Black. 2018. Code-mixed question answering challenge: Crowd-sourcing data and techniques. In *Proceedings of the Third Workshop on Computational Approaches to Linguistic Code-Switching*, pages 29–38, Melbourne, Australia. Association for Computational Linguistics.

Monojit Choudhury, Gokul Chittaranjan, Parth Gupta, and Amitava Das. 2014. Overview of fire 2014 track on transliterated search. *Proceedings of FIRE*, pages 68–89.

Alexis Conneau, Kartikay Khandelwal, Naman Goyal, Vishrav Chaudhary, Guillaume Wenzek, Francisco Guzmán, Edouard Grave, Myle Ott, Luke Zettlemoyer, and Veselin Stoyanov. 2020. Unsupervised cross-lingual representation learning at scale. In *Proceedings of the 58th Annual Meeting of the Association for Computational Linguistics*, pages 8440–8451, Online. Association for Computational Linguistics.

Alexis Conneau and Guillaume Lample. 2019. Cross-lingual language model pretraining. In *Advances in Neural Information Processing Systems*, volume 32. Curran Associates, Inc.

Ido Dagan, Oren Glickman, and Bernardo Magnini. 2006. The pascal recognising textual entailment challenge. In *Machine Learning Challenges. Evaluating Predictive Uncertainty, Visual Object Classification, and Recognising Tectual Entailment*, pages 177–190, Berlin, Heidelberg. Springer Berlin Heidelberg.

Jacob Devlin, Ming-Wei Chang, Kenton Lee, and Kristina Toutanova. 2019. BERT: Pre-training of deep bidirectional transformers for language understanding. In *Proceedings of the 2019 Conference of the North American Chapter of the Association for Computational Linguistics: Human Language Technologies, Volume 1 (Long and Short Papers)*, pages 4171–4186, Minneapolis, Minnesota. Association for Computational Linguistics.

Mrinal Dhar, Vaibhav Kumar, and Manish Shrivastava. 2018. Enabling code-mixed translation: Parallel corpus creation and MT augmentation approach. In *Proceedings of the First Workshop on Linguistic Resources for Natural Language Processing*, pages 131–140, Santa Fe, New Mexico, USA. Association for Computational Linguistics.

Mona Diab, Pascale Fung, Mahmoud Ghoneim, Julia Hirschberg, and Thamar Solorio, editors. 2016. *Proceedings of the Second Workshop on Computational Approaches to Code Switching*. Association for Computational Linguistics, Austin, Texas.

Mona Diab, Julia Hirschberg, Pascale Fung, and Thamar Solorio, editors. 2014. *Proceedings of the First Workshop on Computational Approaches to Code Switching*. Association for Computational Linguistics, Doha, Qatar.

Sergey Edunov, Alexei Baevski, and Michael Auli. 2019. Pre-trained language model representations for language generation. In *Proceedings of the 2019 Conference of the North American Chapter of the Association for Computational Linguistics: Human Language Technologies, Volume 1 (Long and Short Papers)*, pages 4052–4059, Minneapolis, Minnesota. Association for Computational Linguistics.

Pengcheng He, Xiaodong Liu, Jianfeng Gao, and Weizhu Chen. 2021. Deberta: Decoding-enhanced bert with disentangled attention. In *International Conference on Learning Representations*.

Anupam Jamatia, Björn Gambäck, and Amitava Das. 2016. Collecting and annotating indian social media code-mixed corpora. In *International Conference on Intelligent Text Processing and Computational Linguistics*, pages 406–417. Springer.

Nal Kalchbrenner and Phil Blunsom. 2013. Recurrent continuous translation models. In *Proceedings of the 2013 Conference on Empirical Methods in Natural Language Processing*, pages 1700–1709, Seattle, Washington, USA. Association for Computational Linguistics.

Simran Khanuja, Sandipan Dandapat, Sunayana Sitaram, and Monojit Choudhury. 2020a. A new dataset for natural language inference from code-mixed conversations. In *Proceedings of the The 4th Workshop on Computational Approaches to Code Switching*, pages 9–16, Marseille, France. European Language Resources Association.

Simran Khanuja, Sandipan Dandapat, Anirudh Srinivasan, Sunayana Sitaram, and Monojit Choudhury. 2020b. GLUECoS: An evaluation benchmark for code-switched NLP. In *Proceedings of the 58th Annual Meeting of the Association for Computational Linguistics*, pages 3575–3585, Online. Association for Computational Linguistics.

Diederik P. Kingma and Jimmy Ba. 2015. Adam: A method for stochastic optimization. In *3rd International Conference on Learning Representations, ICLR 2015, San Diego, CA, USA, May 7-9, 2015, Conference Track Proceedings*.

Anoop Kunchukuttan. 2020. The IndicNLP Library. `https://github.com/anoopkunchukuttan/indic_nlp_library/blob/master/docs/indicnlp.pdf`.

Anoop Kunchukuttan, Pratik Mehta, and Pushpak Bhattacharyya. 2018. The IIT Bombay English-Hindi parallel corpus. In *Proceedings of the Eleventh International Conference on Language Resources and Evaluation (LREC 2018)*, Miyazaki, Japan. European Language Resources Association (ELRA).

Mike Lewis, Yinhan Liu, Naman Goyal, Marjan Ghazvininejad, Abdelrahman Mohamed, Omer Levy, Veselin Stoyanov, and Luke Zettlemoyer. 2020. BART: Denoising sequence-to-sequence pre-training for natural language generation, translation, and comprehension. In *Proceedings of the 58th Annual Meeting of the Association for Computational Linguistics*, pages 7871–7880, Online. Association for Computational Linguistics.

Yinhan Liu, Jiatao Gu, Naman Goyal, Xian Li, Sergey Edunov, Marjan Ghazvininejad, Mike Lewis, and Luke Zettlemoyer. 2020. Multilingual denoising pre-training for neural machine translation.

Yinhan Liu, Myle Ott, Naman Goyal, Jingfei Du, Mandar Joshi, Danqi Chen, Omer Levy, Mike Lewis, Luke Zettlemoyer, and Veselin Stoyanov. 2019. Roberta: A robustly optimized bert pretraining approach.

Giovanni Molina, Fahad AlGhamdi, Mahmoud Ghoneim, Abdelati Hawwari, Nicolas Rey-Villamizar, Mona Diab, and Thamar Solorio. 2016. Overview for the second shared task on language identification in code-switched data. In *Proceedings of the Second Workshop on Computational Approaches to Code Switching*, pages 40–49, Austin, Texas. Association for Computational Linguistics.

Dat Quoc Nguyen, Thanh Vu, and Anh Tuan Nguyen. 2020. BERTweet: A pre-trained language model for English tweets. In *Proceedings of the 2020 Conference on Empirical Methods in Natural Language Processing: System Demonstrations*, pages 9–14, Online. Association for Computational Linguistics.

Yixin Nie, Haonan Chen, and Mohit Bansal. 2019. Combining fact extraction and verification with neural semantic matching networks. In *The Thirty-Third AAAI Conference on Artificial Intelligence, AAAI 2019, The Thirty-First Innovative Applications of Artificial Intelligence Conference, IAAI 2019, The Ninth AAAI Symposium on Educational Advances in Artificial Intelligence, EAAI 2019, Honolulu, Hawaii, USA, January 27 - February 1, 2019*, pages 6859–6866. AAAI Press.

Yixin Nie, Adina Williams, Emily Dinan, Mohit Bansal, Jason Weston, and Douwe Kiela. 2020. Adversarial NLI: A new benchmark for natural language understanding. In *Proceedings of the 58th Annual Meeting of the Association for Computational Linguistics*, pages 4885–4901, Online. Association for Computational Linguistics.

Myle Ott, Sergey Edunov, Alexei Baevski, Angela Fan, Sam Gross, Nathan Ng, David Grangier, and Michael Auli. 2019. fairseq: A fast, extensible toolkit for sequence modeling. In *Proceedings of the 2019 Conference of the North American Chapter of the Association for Computational Linguistics (Demonstrations)*, pages 48–53, Minneapolis, Minnesota. Association for Computational Linguistics.

Adam Paszke, Sam Gross, Francisco Massa, Adam Lerer, James Bradbury, Gregory Chanan, Trevor Killeen, Zeming Lin, Natalia Gimelshein, Luca Antiga, Alban Desmaison, Andreas Kopf, Edward Yang, Zachary DeVito, Martin Raison, Alykhan Tejani, Sasank Chilamkurthy, Benoit Steiner, Lu Fang, Junjie Bai, and Soumith Chintala. 2019. Pytorch: An imperative style, high-performance deep learning library. In H. Wallach, H. Larochelle, A. Beygelzimer, F. d'Alché-Buc, E. Fox, and R. Garnett, editors, *Advances in Neural Information Processing Systems 32*, pages 8024–8035. Curran Associates, Inc.

Braja Gopal Patra, Dipankar Das, and Amitava Das. 2018. Sentiment analysis of code-mixed indian languages: An overview of sail_code-mixed shared task @icon-2017.

Parth Patwa, Gustavo Aguilar, Sudipta Kar, Suraj Pandey, Srinivas PYKL, Björn Gambäck, Tanmoy Chakraborty, Thamar Solorio, and Amitava Das. 2020. SemEval-2020 task 9: Overview of sentiment analysis of code-mixed tweets. In *Proceedings of the Fourteenth Workshop on Semantic Evaluation*, pages 774–790, Barcelona (online). International Committee for Computational Linguistics.

Shana Poplack. 1980. Sometimes i'll start a sentence in spanish y termino en espaÑol: toward a typology of code-switching 1. *Linguistics*, 18:581–618.

Matt Post. 2018. A call for clarity in reporting BLEU scores. In *Proceedings of the Third Conference on Machine Translation: Research Papers*, pages 186–191, Brussels, Belgium. Association for Computational Linguistics.

Pattabhi R. K. Rao and S. Devi. 2016. Cmee-il: Code mix entity extraction in indian languages from social media text @ fire 2016 - an overview. In *FIRE*.

Brian Roark, Lawrence Wolf-Sonkin, Christo Kirov, Sabrina J. Mielke, Cibu Johny, Isin Demirsahin, and Keith Hall. 2020. Processing South Asian languages written in the Latin script: the dakshina dataset. In *Proceedings of the 12th Language Resources and Evaluation Conference*, pages 2413–2423, Marseille, France. European Language Resources Association.

Sara Rosenthal, Noura Farra, and Preslav Nakov. 2017. SemEval-2017 task 4: Sentiment analysis in Twitter. In *Proceedings of the 11th International Workshop on Semantic Evaluation (SemEval-2017)*, pages 502–518, Vancouver, Canada. Association for Computational Linguistics.

Rishiraj Saha Roy, Monojit Choudhury, Prasenjit Majumder, and Komal Agarwal. 2013. Overview of the fire 2013 track on transliterated search. In *Post-Proceedings of the 4th and 5th Workshops of the Forum for Information Retrieval Evaluation*, FIRE '12 & '13, New York, NY, USA. Association for Computing Machinery.

Royal Sequiera, Monojit Choudhury, Parth Gupta, Paolo Rosso, Shubham Kumar, Somnath Banerjee, Sudip Kumar Naskar, Sivaji Bandyopadhyay, Gokul Chittaranjan, Amitava Das, et al. 2015. Overview of fire-2015 shared task on mixed script information retrieval. In *FIRE Workshops*, volume 1587, pages 19–25.

Thoudam Doren Singh and Thamar Solorio. 2018. Towards translating mixed-code comments from social media. In *Computational Linguistics and Intelligent Text Processing*, pages 457–468, Cham. Springer International Publishing.

Thamar Solorio, Elizabeth Blair, Suraj Maharjan, Steven Bethard, Mona Diab, Mahmoud Ghoneim, Abdelati Hawwari, Fahad AlGhamdi, Julia Hirschberg, Alison Chang, and Pascale Fung. 2014. Overview for the first shared task on language identification in code-switched data. In *Proceedings of the First Workshop on Computational Approaches to Code Switching*, pages 62–72, Doha, Qatar. Association for Computational Linguistics.

Kaitao Song, Xu Tan, Tao Qin, Jianfeng Lu, and Tie-Yan Liu. 2019. MASS: Masked sequence to sequence pre-training for language generation. In *Proceedings of the 36th International Conference on Machine Learning*, volume 97 of *Proceedings of Machine Learning Research*, pages 5926–5936. PMLR.

Vivek Srivastava and Mayank Singh. 2020. PHINC: A parallel Hinglish social media code-mixed corpus for machine translation. In *Proceedings of the Sixth Workshop on Noisy User-generated Text (W-NUT 2020)*, pages 41–49, Online. Association for Computational Linguistics.

James Thorne, Andreas Vlachos, Christos Christodoulopoulos, and Arpit Mittal. 2018. FEVER: a large-scale dataset for fact extraction and VERification. In *Proceedings of the 2018 Conference of the North American Chapter of the Association for Computational Linguistics: Human Language Technologies, Volume 1 (Long Papers)*, pages 809–819, New Orleans, Louisiana. Association for Computational Linguistics.

Ashish Vaswani, Noam Shazeer, Niki Parmar, Jakob Uszkoreit, Llion Jones, Aidan N Gomez, Ł ukasz Kaiser, and Illia Polosukhin. 2017. Attention is all you need. In *Advances in Neural Information Processing Systems*, volume 30. Curran Associates, Inc.

Alex Wang, Amanpreet Singh, Julian Michael, Felix Hill, Omer Levy, and Samuel Bowman. 2018. GLUE: A multi-task benchmark and analysis platform for natural language understanding. In *Proceedings of the 2018 EMNLP Workshop BlackboxNLP: Analyzing and Interpreting Neural Networks for NLP*, pages 353–355, Brussels, Belgium. Association for Computational Linguistics.

Guillaume Wenzek, Marie-Anne Lachaux, Alexis Conneau, Vishrav Chaudhary, Francisco Guzmán, Armand Joulin, and Edouard Grave. 2020. CCNet: Extracting high quality monolingual datasets from web crawl data. In *Proceedings of the 12th Language Resources and Evaluation Conference*, pages 4003–4012, Marseille, France. European Language Resources Association.

Adina Williams, Nikita Nangia, and Samuel Bowman. 2018. A broad-coverage challenge corpus for sentence understanding through inference. In *Proceedings of the 2018 Conference of the North American Chapter of the Association for Computational Linguistics: Human Language Technologies, Volume 1 (Long Papers)*, pages 1112–1122, New Orleans, Louisiana. Association for Computational Linguistics.

Thomas Wolf, Lysandre Debut, Victor Sanh, Julien Chaumond, Clement Delangue, Anthony Moi, Pierric Cistac, Tim Rault, Remi Louf, Morgan Funtowicz, Joe Davison, Sam Shleifer, Patrick von Platen, Clara Ma, Yacine Jernite, Julien Plu, Canwen Xu, Teven Le Scao, Sylvain Gugger, Mariama Drame, Quentin Lhoest, and Alexander Rush. 2020. Transformers: State-of-the-art natural language processing. In *Proceedings of the 2020 Conference on Empirical Methods in Natural Language Processing: System Demonstrations*, pages 38–45, Online. Association for Computational Linguistics.

Zhilin Yang, Zihang Dai, Yiming Yang, Jaime Carbonell, Russ R Salakhutdinov, and Quoc V Le. 2019. Xlnet: Generalized autoregressive pretraining for language understanding. In *Advances in Neural Information Processing Systems*, volume 32. Curran Associates, Inc.

Wenpeng Yin, Jamaal Hay, and Dan Roth. 2019. Benchmarking zero-shot text classification: Datasets, evaluation and entailment approach. In *Proceedings of the 2019 Conference on Empirical Methods in Natural Language Processing and the 9th International Joint Conference on Natural Language Processing (EMNLP-IJCNLP)*, pages 3914–3923, Hong Kong, China. Association for Computational Linguistics.

Gated Convolutional Sequence to Sequence Based Learning for English-Hingilsh Code-Switched Machine Translation.

Suman Dowlagar
LTRC
IIIT-Hyderabad
suman.dowlagar
@research.iiit.ac.in

Radhika Mamidi
LTRC
IIIT-Hyderabad
radhika.mamidi
@iiit.ac.in

Abstract

Code-Switching is the embedding of linguistic units or phrases from two or more languages in a single sentence. This phenomenon is practiced in all multilingual communities and is prominent in social media. Consequently, there is a growing need to understand code-switched translations by translating the code-switched text into one of the standard languages or vice versa. Neural Machine translation is a well-studied research problem in the monolingual text. In this paper, we have used the gated convolutional sequences to sequence networks for English-Hinglish translation. The convolutions in the model help to identify the compositional structure in the sequences more easily. The model relies on gating and performs multiple attention steps at encoder and decoder layers.

1 Introduction

Language is a social phenomenon. The day-to-day interactions are made possible via language. The adaptive nature of languages and the flexibility to use multiple languages in one text message might help the speakers to communicate efficiently. This form of language interaction/contact is considered to be an essential phenomenon, especially in multilingual societies. In bilingual or multilingual communities, speakers use their native tongue and their second language during interactions. This form of alternation of two or more languages is called Code-Switching (CS) (Muysken et al., 2000).

Through the advent of social media, people from around the world can connect and exchange information instantly. Users from a Multilingual community often express their thoughts or opinions on social media by mixing different languages in the same utterance (Dowlagar and Mamidi, 2021). This mixing or alteration of two or more languages is known as code-mixing or code-switching (Wardhaugh, 2011).

There are no standard grammar rules that are meant to be practiced in the code-switched text. The code-switched data often contain variations of spellings and grammar. The computational processing of code-mixed or code-switched data is challenging due to the nature of the mixing and the presence of non-standard variations in spellings and grammar, and transliteration (Bali et al., 2014). Because of such linguistic complexities, code-switching poses several unseen difficulties in fundamental fields of natural language processing (NLP) tasks such as language identification, part-of-speech tagging, shallow parsing, Named entity recognition, sentiment analysis, offensive language identification etc.

To encourage research on code-mixing text, the Computational Approaches to Linguistic Code-Switching (CALCS) community has organized several workshops on language identification, Named Entity Recognition (Aguilar et al., 2018). This task focus on machine translation in the code-switched environment in multiple language combinations and directions [1].

This paper presents a gated convolutional sequence to sequence encoder and decoder models (Gehring et al., 2017) for machine translation on the code-mixed text. We have used the convolutional model because of its sliding window concept to deal with contextual words and the convolutions to extract rich representations.

The paper is organized as follows. Section 2 provides related work on the code-switched text for machine translation. Section 3 provides information on the task and dataset. Section 4 describes the proposed work. Section 5 presents the experimental setup and the performance of the model. Section 6 concludes our work.

[1] https\protect\leavevmode@ifvmode\kern+.2222em\relax//code-switching.github.io/2021#shared-task

Proceedings of the Fifth Workshop on Computational Approaches to Linguistic Code-Switching, pages 26–30
June 11, 2021. ©2021 Association for Computational Linguistics
https://doi.org/10.26615/978-954-452-056-4_004

#	English (source translation)	Hinglish (target translation)
1	Hello! do you like comedy, adventure, and animation movies?	namaskaar! kya aapako komedee, edavenchar aur eneemeshan philmen pasand hain?
2	It was a strange choice	bahut strange choice thi ye
3	are you still there?	TUM ABHEE BHI VAHAAN HO
4	Hello.	Hello.

Table 1: Example translations

2 Related Work

There is relatively less research in the field of the machine translation of the code-switched text, partially due to the relative lack of structured corpora and also potentially because it also poses significant linguistic challenges such as ambiguity in language identification, spelling variations, informal style of writing, Misplaced/skipped punctuation, etc. Nonetheless, some researchers have provided datasets to enable research in code-mixed machine translation, specifically in Hindi-English code-switched scenario (Srivastava and Singh, 2020; Dhar et al., 2018). Dhar et al. (2018) presented a parallel corpus of the 13,738 code-mixed Hindi-English sentences and their corresponding human translation in English. In addition, they also provided a translation pipeline built on top of Google Translate. The pipeline fragments the input sentence into multiple chunks and identifies the language of each word in the chunk before feeding it to google-translate. The pipeline gives a BLEU-1 metric of 0.153 on the given English dataset. Dhar et al. (2018) translated the 6,096 code-mixed English-Hindi sentences into English and presented a translation augmentation pipeline. The pipeline is presented as a pre-processing step and can be plugged into any existing MT system. The pre-processed data is then given to translation systems like Moses, Google Neural Machine Translation System (NMTS), and Bing Translator, where the pre-processed data with NMTS has outperformed all the baselines with a BLEU score of 28.4.

3 Task Description

The goal of this task is the machine translation for code-switching settings in multiple language combinations and directions, such as involving English, Hinglish, Spanish, Spanglish, Modern Standard Arabic, and Egyptian Arabic languages. The code-mixed dataset is obtained from comments/posts from social media. In this paper, we have focussed on the English-Hinglish dataset. The English-Hinglish code-mixed dataset has 8060 train, 952 dev, and 960 test with source, and target translations. The task is to translate the given English sentence into a code-mixed Hindi-English sentence. The examples of the given English-Hinglish translation are given in the table 1.

In the first translation, one can see that the Hinglish sentence has a mixture of non-standard variations of words such as komedee(comedy), edavenchar(adventure), eneemeshan(animation), and the second translation exhibits the switching of English and Hindi phrases. In the third translation, the sentence is completely translated to Hindi (with roman script). The fourth translation shows that no translation is followed. The above sentences depict the diversity of the code-mixed translations, thus making the research and translation of the code-mixed text a complex task.

4 The proposed work

This section presents the proposed gated convolutional neural networks with encoder and decoder models for machine translation from English to code-mixed Hinglish text. The encoder model encode the source sentence into a vector and the decoder model takes the encoder information and decodes the given target sentences. The encoded vector is also known context vector. The context vector can be visualized as an abstract representation of the entire input sentence. The vector is decoded by a decoder model that learns to output the target sentence. The context needs to contain all of the information about the source sentence. It can be done by using attention.

Our encoder and decoder attention-based models use convolutions to encode the source sentence and to decode it into the target sentence. The convolutional layer uses filters. These filters have a window size. For example, if a filter has a window size of 3, then it can process three consecutive tokens. This window helps in determining the context. The convolutional layer has many of these filters, where each filter will slide across the entire sequence by looking at all three consecutive tokens at a time. These filters will help extract different features in the given text and aid the machine translation model.

The description of the encoder and decoder convolutional models is given in the subsequent subsections.

4.1 Encoder

In the encoder model, each token in the source sentence is passed through an embedding layer. As the convolutional model has no recurrent connections, the model has no idea about the order of the tokens within a sequence. So it is necessary to add the positional embedding layer. In the positional embedding, the position of the tokens, including the start of the sequence and the end of the sequence, are encoded. Next, the token and positional embeddings are combined by elementwise sum. The obtained embedding vector contains the token and also its position within the sequence.

The given embedding vector is passed through a series of convolutional blocks. We follow the (Gehring et al., 2017) paper to implement the gated convolutional block architecture. It is formulated as,

$$h_i^l = v\left(\mathbf{W}^l\left[h_{i-k/2}^{l-1}, \ldots, h_{i+k/2}^{l-1}\right] + \mathbf{b}_w^l\right) + h_i^{l-1} \quad (1)$$

Where h_i^l is the output of the ith sequence in l^{th} block. v is the gated gated linear units (GLU) (Dauphin et al., 2016) activation function. $\left[h_{i-k/2}^{l-1}, \ldots, h_{i+k/2}^{l-1}\right]$ are convolutional transformations of previous layer, $\mathbf{W}^l$ and $\mathbf{b}_w^l$ are learnable parameters and h_i^{l-1} is the residual output from the previous layer.

Passing the embedding vector through the convolutional blocks gives the convolved vector for each token in the given source sentence. The embedding vector is added as a residual connection is added to the convolved vector to get a combined vector.

4.2 Decoder

The decoder is similar to the encoder, with a few additional paddings to both the main model and the convolutional blocks inside the model.

In the decoder, the encoder convolved and combined outputs are used with attention. Finally, the output of the decoder is passed through a feed-forward layer to match the output target dimension in order to get the translated sentence.

5 Experiments

Here, we demonstrate the performance of the machine translation systems on the code-mixed text. We experiment with the popular RNN based encoder-decoder machine translation and vanilla transformer models and evaluate their performance on the given English-Hinglish machine translation task. We use BLEU metrics to evaluate system performance (Papineni et al., 2002).

5.1 Baseline MT models

RNN based encoder-decoder model (Bahdanau et al., 2014) The model uses RNN blocks to encode and decode the given sequence. The model allows the decoder to look at the entire source sentence at each decoding step by using attention.

Transformer We have implemented the Transformer model from the paper Vaswani et al. (2017). The transformer model uses multi-headed attention, layer normalizations, and feed-forward networks to implement the transformer models. The positional embeddings are used to remember the sequence of the sentence.

5.2 Hyperparameters and libraries

The parameters used to train our neural machine translation model are: the number of epochs used to train the model is 10. The Adam optimizer is used with cross-entropy loss with the gradient clipping of 0.1. The embedding and hidden dimensionalities are set as 256 and 512. The number of encoder and decoder convolutional layers used is 10. The default kernel window of size three is maintained. The dropout is kept at 0.25, and the maximum length used for the positional embeddings is 400. The Pytorch library is used to implement the model and is made publicly accessible [2].

5.3 Results and Error analysis

The results are guven in the table 2. From the table, it is clear that the convolutional model has obtained a better accuracy when compared to the vanilla transformer and encoder-decoder models. The use of convolutions and using the window size helped the convolutional model understand its context. We have even observed that the small length sequences and code-switching points are detected better by a convolutional model. As there is no

[2] `https://github.com/suman101112/CMMT.git`

Model	BLEU score (based on validation data)
Encoder-Decoder RNN model	1.52
Transformer model	2.51
proposed model (Conv seq2seq)	**2.58**

Table 2: BLEU metrics of the proposed model when compared to baselines.

	Incorrect Translation
Source Sentence (English)	Plus how many times are you going to leave your kid behind. I see they added another scene. How the robbers got caught and Kevin reuniting with his mom and family
Target Translation (Hinglish)	aur kitne baar apne bete ko chod doge. maine dekha hai ki woh log aur ek scene add kar diya. Robbers kaise pakde gaye aur kevin apni mom aur family se mila.
Translation by our model	mujhe us kahani pasand hein, jho tho yeh sach ko bahut pasand hein jab mein kabhi kabhi ko dekhna nahi hein lekin mein kabhi kabhi ko apney kabhi ko nahi nahi hein jab mujhe yakeen hai ki yah kuchh daraatee hai ki mujhe kabhi ko apney kabhi ko nahi
	Proper Translation
Source Sentence (English)	yes, it is good
Target Translation (Hinglish)	han, ye accha hai
Translation by our model	han, ye good hai

Table 3: Output of our convolutional sequence to sequence model on English-Hinglish text

recurrence in the convolutions, the computations are performed faster than the RNN's. Compared to recurrent networks, our convolutional approach allows discovering compositional structure in the sequences more easily since representations. Our model relies on gating and performs multiple attention steps. The vanilla transformer model did not perform well on this task because of the limited dataset used by the model. The vanilla transformer model is designed to be trained on larger datasets. It might be possible that the pre-trained transformer models can achieve better results when the dataset is finetuned on such models. The encoder-decoder RNN model performed worst and were very slow when compared to the other models.

During the error analysis we have found that there were repetitions in translations for the long sentences that are incorrectly translated by our model. This often lead to decrease in BLEU metric. The example is given table 3. Where as the short sentences are correctly translated by the given model. This is due to the low dependencies exhibited because of low window size and also due to presence of more Out of vocabulary (OOV) words because of the limited dataset. The improvement in the size of datasets will improve the translation accuracy of the proposed model.

6 Conclusion

This paper presents the performance of a neural machine translation model for the shared task on code-switched English-Hinglish translation. The model uses the convolutional sequence to sequence-based neural network architecture to translate the given sequence. The contextual window and the state-of-the-art convolution model helped the model learn better representations from the text and improved the model's performance compared to RNN encoder-decoder and vanilla transformer models. In the future, we wish to use the pre-trained BERT models and their ensembles and also consider other code-mixing factors such as pre-processing of the code-switched text to improve the quality of the code-switched machine translation.

References

Gustavo Aguilar, Fahad AlGhamdi, Victor Soto, Mona Diab, Julia Hirschberg, and Thamar Solorio. 2018. Named entity recognition on code-switched data: Overview of the CALCS 2018 shared task. In *Proceedings of the Third Workshop on Computational Approaches to Linguistic Code-Switching*, pages 138–147, Melbourne, Australia. Association for Computational Linguistics.

Dzmitry Bahdanau, Kyunghyun Cho, and Yoshua Bengio. 2014. Neural machine translation by jointly learning to align and translate. *arXiv preprint arXiv:1409.0473*.

Kalika Bali, Jatin Sharma, Monojit Choudhury, and Yogarshi Vyas. 2014. "i am borrowing ya mixing?" an analysis of english-hindi code mixing in facebook. In *Proceedings of the First Workshop on Computational Approaches to Code Switching*, pages 116–126.

Yann N Dauphin, Angela Fan, Michael Auli, and David Grangier. 2016. Language modeling with gated convolutional networks. arxiv.

Mrinal Dhar, Vaibhav Kumar, and Manish Shrivastava. 2018. Enabling code-mixed translation: Parallel corpus creation and mt augmentation approach. In *Proceedings of the First Workshop on Linguistic Resources for Natural Language Processing*, pages 131–140.

Suman Dowlagar and Radhika Mamidi. 2021. Graph convolutional networks with multi-headed attention for code-mixed sentiment analysis. In *Proceedings of the First Workshop on Speech and Language Technologies for Dravidian Languages*, pages 65–72.

Jonas Gehring, Michael Auli, David Grangier, Denis Yarats, and Yann N Dauphin. 2017. Convolutional sequence to sequence learning. In *International Conference on Machine Learning*, pages 1243–1252. PMLR.

Pieter Muysken, Pieter Cornelis Muysken, et al. 2000. *Bilingual speech: A typology of code-mixing*. Cambridge University Press.

Kishore Papineni, Salim Roukos, Todd Ward, and Wei-Jing Zhu. 2002. Bleu: a method for automatic evaluation of machine translation. In *Proceedings of the 40th annual meeting of the Association for Computational Linguistics*, pages 311–318.

Vivek Srivastava and Mayank Singh. 2020. Phinc: a parallel hinglish social media code-mixed corpus for machine translation. *arXiv preprint arXiv:2004.09447*.

Ashish Vaswani, Noam Shazeer, Niki Parmar, Jakob Uszkoreit, Llion Jones, Aidan N Gomez, Lukasz Kaiser, and Illia Polosukhin. 2017. Attention is all you need. *arXiv preprint arXiv:1706.03762*.

Ronald Wardhaugh. 2011. *An introduction to sociolinguistics*, volume 28. John Wiley & Sons.

IITP-MT at CALCS2021: English to Hinglish Neural Machine Translation using Unsupervised Synthetic Code-Mixed Parallel Corpus

Ramakrishna Appicharla,[*] Kamal Kumar Gupta,[*] Asif Ekbal, Pushpak Bhattacharyya
Department of Computer Science and Engineering
Indian Institute of Technology Patna
Patna, Bihar, India
{appicharla_2021cs01,kamal.pcs17,asif,pb}@iitp.ac.in

Abstract

This paper describes the system submitted by IITP-MT team to Computational Approaches to Linguistic Code-Switching (CALCS 2021) shared task on MT for English → Hinglish. We submit a neural machine translation (NMT) system which is trained on the synthetic code-mixed (cm) English-Hinglish parallel corpus. We propose an approach to create code-mixed parallel corpus from a clean parallel corpus in an *unsupervised manner*. It is an alignment based approach and we do not use any linguistic resources for explicitly marking any token for code-switching. We also train NMT model on the gold corpus provided by the workshop organizers augmented with the generated synthetic code-mixed parallel corpus. The model trained over the generated synthetic cm data achieves 10.09 BLEU points over the given test set.

1 Introduction

In this paper, we describe our submission to shared task on Machine Translation (MT) for English → Hinglish at CALCS 2021. The objective of this shared task to generate Hinglish (Hindi-English Code-Mixed[1]) data from English. In this task, we submit an NMT system which is trained on the parallel code-mixed English-Hinglish synthetic corpus. We generate synthetic corpus in unsupervised fashion and the methodology followed to generate data is independent of languages involved. Since the target Hindi tokens are written in roman script, during the synthetic corpus creation, we transliterate the Hindi tokens from Devanagari script to Roman script.

Code-Mixing (CM) is a very common phenomenon in various social media contents, product description and reviews, educational domain etc. For better understanding and ease in writing, users write posts, comments on social media in code-mixed fashion. It is not consistent or convenient always to translate all the words, especially the named entities, quality related terms etc.

But translating in code-mixed fashion required code-mixed parallel training data. It is possible to generate code-mixed parallel corpus from a clean parallel corpus. From the term 'clean parallel corpus', we refer to a parallel corpus which consists of the non code-mixed parallel sentences. Generally noun tokens, noun phrases and adjectives are the major candidates to be preserved as it is (without translation) in the code-mixed output. This requires a kind of explicit token marking using parser, tagger (part of speech, named entity etc.) to find the eligible candidate tokens for code-mixed replacement. Since this method is dependent on linguistic resources, it is limited to the high resource languages only.

We introduce an alignment based unsupervised approach for generating code-mixed data from parallel corpus which can be used to train the NMT model for code-mixed text translation.

The paper is organized as follows. In section 2, we briefly mention some notable works on translation and generation of synthetic code-mixed corpus. In section 3, we describe our approach to generate synthetic code-mixed corpus along with the system description. Results are described in section 4. Finally, the work is concluded in section 5.

2 Related Works

Translation of code-mixed data has gained popularity in recent times. Menacer et al. (2019) conducted experiments on translating Arabic-English CM data to pure Arabic and/or to pure English with Statistical Machine Translation (SMT) and Neural Machine Translation (NMT) approaches. Dhar et al. (2018) proposed an MT augmentation pipeline which takes CM sentence and determines the most dominating language and translates the

[*]Equal contribution

[1]Hindi words are romanized

Proceedings of the Fifth Workshop on Computational Approaches to Linguistic Code-Switching, pages 31–35
June 11, 2021. ©2021 Association for Computational Linguistics
https://doi.org/10.26615/978-954-452-056-4_005

remaining words into that language. The resulting sentence will be in one single language and can be translated to other language with the existing MT systems. Yang et al. (2020) have used code-mixing phenomenon and proposed a pre-training strategy for NMT. Song et al. (2019) augmented the code-mixed data with clean data while training the NMT system and reported that this type of data augmentation improves the translation quality of constrained words such as named entities. Singh and Solorio (2017); Masoud et al. (2019); Mahata et al. (2019) also explored various approaches which utilize linguistic resources (such as language identification etc.) to translate the code-mixed data.

There have been some efforts for creating code-mixed data. Gupta et al. (2020) proposed an Encoder-Decoder based model which takes English sentence along with linguistic features as input and generates synthetic code-mixed sentence. Pratapa et al. (2018) explored 'Equivalence Constraint' theory to generate the synthetic code-mixed data which is used to improve the performance of Recurrent Neural Network (RNN) based language model. While Winata et al. (2019) proposed a method to generate code-mixed data using a pointer-generator network, Garg et al. (2018) explored SeqGAN for code-mixed data generation.

3 System Description

In this section, we describe the synthetic parallel corpus creation, dataset and experimental setup of our system.

3.1 Unsupervised Synthetic Code-Mixed Corpus Creation

We utilize the existing parallel corpus to create synthetic code-mixed data. First we learn word-level alignments between source and target sentences of a given parallel corpus of a specific language pair. We use the implementation[2] of *fast_align* algorithm (Dyer et al., 2013) to obtain the alignment matrix. Let $X = \{x_1, x_2, ..., x_m\}$ be the source sentence and $Y = \{y_1, y_2, ..., y_n\}$ be the target sentence. We consider only those alignment pairs $\{x_j, y_k\}$ [for $j = (1, ..., m)$ and $k = (1, ..., n)$] which are having one-to-one mapping, as candidate tokens. By 'One-to-one mapping', we mean that neither $\{x_j\}$ nor $\{y_k\}$ should be aligned to more than one token from their respective counter sides except $\{y_k\}$ and $\{x_j\}$ respectively. The obtained candidate token set is further pruned by removing the pairs where x_j is a stopword. Based on the resulting candidate set, the source token x_j is replaced with aligned target token y_k. The generated code-mixed sentence is in the form: $CM = \{x_1, x_2, ..., y_k, y_l, ..., x_m\}$. Figure 1 shows an example of English-Hindi code-mixed sentence generated through this method.

[2]https://github.com/clab/fast_align/

3.2 Romanization of the Hindi text

The task is to generate Hinglish data in which Hindi words are written in Roman script. But in the generated synthetic code-mixed corpus, Hindi words are written in Devanagari script. In order to convert the Devanagari script to Roman script, we utilize Python based transliteration tool.[3] This convert the Devanagari script to Roman script.

We also create another version of the synthetic code-mixed corpus by replacing the two consecutive vowels with single vowel (Belinkov and Bisk, 2018). We call this version of code-mixed corpus as synthetic code-mixed corpus with user patterns. The main reason to create noisy version of the corpus is to simulate the user writing patterns when writing romanized code-mixed sentences in real-life. An example of such scenario would be, user may write 'Paani' (water) as 'Pani' (water). We tried to capture these scenarios by replacing the consecutive vowels with single vowel. These vowel replacement is done at target side (Hinglish) of the synthetic code-mixed corpus only and source (English) is kept as it is. The gold corpus provided by organizers is not modified in any way and also kept as it is.

3.3 Dataset

We consider English-Hindi IIT Bombay (Kunchukuttan et al., 2018) parallel corpus. We tokenize and true-case English using Moses tokenizer (Koehn et al., 2007) and truecaser [4] scripts and Indic-nlp-library [5] to tokenize Hindi. We remove the sentences having length greater that 150 tokens and created synthetic code-mixed corpus on the resulting corpus as described earlier. The statistics of data used in the experiments are shown in Table 1.

[3]https://github.com/libindic/Transliteration

[4]3https://github.com/mosessmt/mosesdecoder/blob/RELEASE-3.0/scripts/tokenizer/tokenizer.perl

[5]https://github.com/anoopkunchukuttan/indic_nlp_library

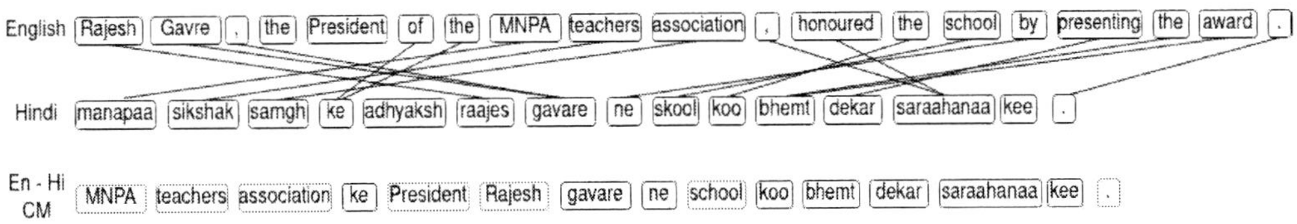

Figure 1: An example of alignment between parallel sentence pair and generated CM sentence. In the CM sentence, the source words that are replaced are shown with red border.

Corpus	Train	Dev
Synthetic CM	1,549,115	-
Synthetic CM + User Patterns	1,549,115	-
Gold	8,060	942
Total	3,106,290	942

Table 1: Data statistics used in the experiment. Synthetic CM: Size of synthetic code-mixed data. Synthetic CM + User Patterns: Size of synthetic code-mixed data with addition of user writing patterns. Gold: Size of gold standard parallel corpus provided by organizers. Train, Dev denotes Training and Development set statistics respectively. In the experiments we use only gold standard corpus as development set.

3.4 Experimental Setup

We conduct the experiments on Transformer based Encoder-Decoder NMT architecture (Vaswani et al., 2017). We use 6 layered Encoder-Decoder stacks with 8 attention heads. Embedding size and hidden sizes are set to 512, dropout rate is set to 0.1. Feed-forward layer consists of 2048 cells. Adam optimizer (Kingma and Ba, 2015) is used for training with 8,000 warmup steps with initial learning rate of 2. We use Sentencepiece (Kudo and Richardson, 2018) with joint vocabulary size of 50K. Models are trained with OpenNMT toolkit [6] (Klein et al., 2017) with batch size of 2048 tokens till convergence and checkpoints are created after every 10,000 steps. All the checkpoints that are created during the training are averaged and considered as the best parameters for each model. During inference, beam size is set to 5.

4 Results

We train two models. Baseline model which is trained on the Gold standard corpus. Second model on the synthetic code-mixed data. We upload our model predictions on the test set provided by organizers to shared task leaderboard[7]. The test set contains 960 sentences. Our model achieved BLEU (Papineni et al., 2002) score of 10.09. Table 2 shows the BLEU scores obtained from the trained models on Development and Test sets. Table 3 shows some sample translations.

Model	Dev	Test
Baseline	2.55	2.45
Synthetic CM	11.52	10.09

Table 2: BLEU scores of the Baseline model and Synthetic Code-Mixed model on Development and Test sets.

Source	Who is your favorite member from the first avengers?
Reference	Tumhara favorite member kaun hai first avengers mein se?
Output	first avengers se aapka favorite member kon hai?
Source	I think it was a robotic shark, but am not sure.
Reference	me sochta hoon voh robotic shark thi, but me sure nahi hoon.
Output	mujhe lagata hai ki yah ek robotik shark hai ,lekin sure nahi hai.
Source	Do you like action movies?
Reference	aap ko action movies pasand hein kya?
Output	Kya tumhe action movies pasand hai?

Table 3: Sample translations generated by trained model

5 Conclusion

In this paper, we described our submission to shared task on MT for English → Hinglish at CALCS 2021. We submitted a system which is trained on synthetic code-mixed corpus generated in unsupervised way. We trained an NMT model

[6]https://opennmt.net/

[7]https://ritual.uh.edu/lince/leaderboard

on the synthetic code-mixed corpus and gold standard data provided by organizers. On the test set, the model trained over the gold data provided by the workshop achieves 2.45 BLEU points while the model trained over our generated synthetic cm data yields BLEU score of 10.09. We believe that the proposed method to generate synthetic code-mixed data can be very useful for training MT systems in code-mixed settings as the proposed method does not require any linguistic resources to generate code-mixed data.

References

Yonatan Belinkov and Yonatan Bisk. 2018. Synthetic and natural noise both break neural machine translation. In *International Conference on Learning Representations*.

Mrinal Dhar, Vaibhav Kumar, and Manish Shrivastava. 2018. Enabling code-mixed translation: Parallel corpus creation and MT augmentation approach. In *Proceedings of the First Workshop on Linguistic Resources for Natural Language Processing*, pages 131–140, Santa Fe, New Mexico, USA. Association for Computational Linguistics.

Chris Dyer, Victor Chahuneau, and Noah A. Smith. 2013. A simple, fast, and effective reparameterization of IBM model 2. In *Proceedings of the 2013 Conference of the North American Chapter of the Association for Computational Linguistics: Human Language Technologies*, pages 644–648, Atlanta, Georgia. Association for Computational Linguistics.

Saurabh Garg, Tanmay Parekh, and Preethi Jyothi. 2018. Code-switched language models using dual RNNs and same-source pretraining. In *Proceedings of the 2018 Conference on Empirical Methods in Natural Language Processing*, pages 3078–3083, Brussels, Belgium. Association for Computational Linguistics.

Deepak Gupta, Asif Ekbal, and Pushpak Bhattacharyya. 2020. A semi-supervised approach to generate the code-mixed text using pre-trained encoder and transfer learning. In *Findings of the Association for Computational Linguistics: EMNLP 2020*, pages 2267–2280, Online. Association for Computational Linguistics.

Diederik P. Kingma and Jimmy Ba. 2015. Adam: A method for stochastic optimization. In *3rd International Conference on Learning Representations, ICLR 2015, San Diego, CA, USA, May 7-9, 2015, Conference Track Proceedings*.

Guillaume Klein, Yoon Kim, Yuntian Deng, Jean Senellart, and Alexander Rush. 2017. OpenNMT: Open-source toolkit for neural machine translation. In *Proceedings of ACL 2017, System Demonstrations*, pages 67–72, Vancouver, Canada. Association for Computational Linguistics.

Philipp Koehn, Hieu Hoang, Alexandra Birch, Chris Callison-Burch, Marcello Federico, Nicola Bertoldi, Brooke Cowan, Wade Shen, Christine Moran, Richard Zens, Chris Dyer, Ondřej Bojar, Alexandra Constantin, and Evan Herbst. 2007. Moses: Open source toolkit for statistical machine translation. In *Proceedings of the 45th Annual Meeting of the Association for Computational Linguistics Companion Volume Proceedings of the Demo and Poster Sessions*, pages 177–180, Prague, Czech Republic. Association for Computational Linguistics.

Taku Kudo and John Richardson. 2018. SentencePiece: A simple and language independent subword tokenizer and detokenizer for neural text processing. In *Proceedings of the 2018 Conference on Empirical Methods in Natural Language Processing: System Demonstrations*, pages 66–71, Brussels, Belgium. Association for Computational Linguistics.

Anoop Kunchukuttan, Pratik Mehta, and Pushpak Bhattacharyya. 2018. The IIT Bombay English-Hindi parallel corpus. In *Proceedings of the Eleventh International Conference on Language Resources and Evaluation (LREC 2018)*, Miyazaki, Japan. European Language Resources Association (ELRA).

Sainik Kumar Mahata, Soumil Mandal, Dipankar Das, and Sivaji Bandyopadhyay. 2019. Code-mixed to monolingual translation framework. In *Proceedings of the 11th Forum for Information Retrieval Evaluation*, pages 30–35.

Maraim Masoud, Daniel Torregrosa, Paul Buitelaar, and Mihael Arčan. 2019. Back-translation approach for code-switching machine translation: A case study. In *27th AIAI Irish Conference on Artificial Intelligence and Cognitive Science*. AICS2019.

Mohamed Amine Menacer, David Langlois, Denis Jouvet, Dominique Fohr, Odile Mella, and Kamel Smaïli. 2019. Machine translation on a parallel code-switched corpus. In *Canadian Conference on Artificial Intelligence*, pages 426–432. Springer.

Kishore Papineni, Salim Roukos, Todd Ward, and Wei-Jing Zhu. 2002. Bleu: a method for automatic evaluation of machine translation. In *Proceedings of the 40th Annual Meeting of the Association for Computational Linguistics*, pages 311–318, Philadelphia, Pennsylvania, USA. Association for Computational Linguistics.

Adithya Pratapa, Gayatri Bhat, Monojit Choudhury, Sunayana Sitaram, Sandipan Dandapat, and Kalika Bali. 2018. Language modeling for code-mixing: The role of linguistic theory based synthetic data. In *Proceedings of the 56th Annual Meeting of the Association for Computational Linguistics (Volume 1: Long Papers)*, pages 1543–1553, Melbourne, Australia. Association for Computational Linguistics.

Thoudam Doren Singh and Thamar Solorio. 2017. Towards translating mixed-code comments from social media. In *International Conference on Computational Linguistics and Intelligent Text Processing*, pages 457–468. Springer.

Kai Song, Yue Zhang, Heng Yu, Weihua Luo, Kun Wang, and Min Zhang. 2019. Code-switching for enhancing NMT with pre-specified translation. In *Proceedings of the 2019 Conference of the North American Chapter of the Association for Computational Linguistics: Human Language Technologies, Volume 1 (Long and Short Papers)*, pages 449–459, Minneapolis, Minnesota. Association for Computational Linguistics.

Ashish Vaswani, Noam Shazeer, Niki Parmar, Jakob Uszkoreit, Llion Jones, Aidan N Gomez, Łukasz Kaiser, and Illia Polosukhin. 2017. Attention is all you need. In *Advances in neural information processing systems*, pages 5998–6008.

Genta Indra Winata, Andrea Madotto, Chien-Sheng Wu, and Pascale Fung. 2019. Code-switched language models using neural based synthetic data from parallel sentences. In *Proceedings of the 23rd Conference on Computational Natural Language Learning (CoNLL)*, pages 271–280, Hong Kong, China. Association for Computational Linguistics.

Zhen Yang, Bojie Hu, Ambyera Han, Shen Huang, and Qi Ju. 2020. CSP:code-switching pre-training for neural machine translation. In *Proceedings of the 2020 Conference on Empirical Methods in Natural Language Processing (EMNLP)*, pages 2624–2636, Online. Association for Computational Linguistics.

Exploring Text-to-Text Transformers for English to Hinglish Machine Translation with Synthetic Code-Mixing

Ganesh Jawahar[1,2] **El Moatez Billah Nagoudi**[1]
Muhammad Abdul-Mageed[1,2] **Laks V.S. Lakshmanan**[2]
Natural Language Processing Lab[1]
Department of Computer Science[2]
The University of British Columbia
ganeshjwhr@gmail.com, {moatez.nagoudi, muhammad.mageed}@ubc.ca, laks@cs.ubc.ca

Abstract

We describe models focused at the understudied problem of translating between monolingual and code-mixed language pairs. More specifically, we offer a wide range of models that convert monolingual English text into Hinglish (code-mixed Hindi and English). Given the recent success of pretrained language models, we also test the utility of two recent Transformer-based encoder-decoder models (i.e., mT5 and mBART) on the task finding both to work well. Given the paucity of training data for code-mixing, we also propose a dependency-free method for generating code-mixed texts from bilingual distributed representations that we exploit for improving language model performance. In particular, armed with this additional data, we adopt a curriculum learning approach where we first finetune the language models on synthetic data then on gold code-mixed data. We find that, although simple, our synthetic code-mixing method is competitive with (and in some cases is even superior to) several standard methods (backtranslation, method based on equivalence constraint theory) under a diverse set of conditions. Our work shows that the mT5 model, finetuned following the curriculum learning procedure, achieves best translation performance (12.67 BLEU). Our models place first in the overall ranking of the English-Hinglish official shared task.

1 Introduction

Code-mixing is a phenomenon of mixing two or more languages in speech and text (Gumperz, 1982). Code-mixing is prevalent in multilingual societies, where the speakers typically have similar fluency in two or more languages (Sitaram et al., 2019). For example, Hindi, Tamil and Telugu speakers from India frequently code-mix with English. Code-mixing can happen between dialects, for example, Modern Standard Arabic is frequently code-mixed with Arabic dialects (Abdul-Mageed et al., 2020). Building NLP systems that can handle code-mixing is challenging as the space of valid grammatical and lexical configurations can be large due to presence of syntactic structures from more than one linguistic system (Pratapa et al., 2018).

In this work, we focus on building a machine translation (MT) system that converts a monolingual sequence of words into a code-mixed sequence. More specifically, we focus on translating from English to Hindi code-mixed with English (i.e., Hinglish). In the literature, work has been done on translating from Hinglish into English (Dhar et al., 2018; Srivastava and Singh, 2020). To illustrate both directions, we provide Figure 1. The Figure presents sample translation pairs for Hinglish to English as well as English to Hinglish. The challenges for solving this task include: (i) lack of Hindi data in roman script (words highlighted in cyan color), (ii) non-standard spellings (e.g., 'isme' vs 'is me'), (iii) token-level ambiguity across the two languages (e.g., Hindi 'main' vs. English 'main'), (iv) non-standard casing (e.g., ROTTEN TOMATOES), (v) informal writing style, and (vi) paucity of English-Hinglish parallel data. Compared with Hinglish to English translation, the English to Hinglish translation direction is a less studied research problem.

English-Hinglish translation can have several practical applications. For example, it can be used to create engaging conversational agents that mimic the code-mixing norm of a human user who uses code-mixing. Another use of resulting Hinglish data would be to create training data for some downstream applications such as token-level language identification.

Our proposed machine translation system exploits a multilingual text-to-text Transformer model along with synthetically generated code-mixed data. More specifically, our system utilizes the state-of-the-art pre-trained multilingual generative model, mT5 (a multilingual variant of "Text-to-Text Trans-

Proceedings of the Fifth Workshop on Computational Approaches to Linguistic Code-Switching, pages 36–46
June 11, 2021. ©2021 Association for Computational Linguistics
https://doi.org/10.26615/978-954-452-056-4_006

Hinglish to English translation (Dhar et al. (2018), Srivastava and Singh (2020))		
Hinglish: Hi there! Chat ke liye ready ho?	→	English: Hi there! Ready to chat?
Hinglish: isme kids keliye ache message hein, jo respectful hein sabhi keliye	→	English: It does show a really good message for kids, to be respectful of everybody
English to Hinglish translation (our task)		
English: Maybe it's to teach kids to challenge themselves	→	Hinglish: maybe kida ko teach karna unka challenge ho saktha hein
English: It's seem to do OK on rotten tomatoes I got a 79%	→	Hinglish: ROTTEN TOMATOES KA SCORE 79% DIYA HEIN JO OK HEIN KYA

Table 1: Sample translation pairs for Hinglish to English and English to Hinglish machine translation task. Words highlighted in cyan color are in Hindi language in roman script, while non-highlighted words are in English language.

fer Transformer" model (Raffel et al., 2020)) as a backbone. The mT5 model is pretrained on large amounts of monolingual text from 107 languages, making it a good starting point for multilingual applications such as question answering and MT. It is not clear, however, how mT5's representation fares in a code-mixed context such as ours. *This is the question we explore, empirically, in this paper, on our data.* We also introduce a simple approach for generating code-mixed data and show that by explicitly finetuning the model on this code-mixed data we are able to acquire sizeable improvements. For this finetuning, we adopt a *curriculum learning* method, wherein the model is finetuned on the synthetically generated code-mixed data and then finetuned on the gold code-mixed data.

To synthetically generate code-mixed data, we propose a novel lexical substitution method that exploits bilingual word embeddings trained on shuffled context obtained from English-Hindi bitext. The method works by replacing select n-grams in English sentences with their Hindi counterparts obtained from the bilingual word embedding space. For meaningful comparisons, we also experiment with five different methods to create code-mixed training data: (i) *romanization of monolingual Hindi* from English-Hindi parallel data, (ii) *paraphrasing of monolingual English* from English-Hinglish parallel data, (iii) *backtranslation* of output from the mT5 model trained on English-Hinglish parallel data, (iv) *adapting social media data* containing parallel English-Hinglish sentences by removing emoticons, hashtags, mentions, URLs (Srivastava and Singh, 2020), and (v) code-mixed data generated based on *equivalence constraint theory* (Pratapa et al., 2018). We study the impact of different settings (e.g., size of training data, number of paraphrases per input) applicable for most methods on the translation performance. We observe that the mT5 model finetuned on the code-mixed data generated by our proposed method based on bilingual word embeddings followed by finetuning on gold data achieves a BLEU score of 12.67 and places us first in the overall ranking for the shared task. Overall, our major contributions are as follows:

1. We propose a simple, yet effective and dependency-free, method to generate English-Hinglish parallel data by leveraging bilingual word embeddings trained on shuffled context obtained via English-Hindi bitext.

2. We study the effect of several data augmentation methods (based on romanization, paraphrasing, backtranslation, etc.) on the translation performance.

3. Exploiting our code-mixing generation method in the context of curriculum learning, we obtain state-of-the-art performance on the English-Hinglish shared task data with a BLEU score of 12.67.

2 Related Work

Our work involves code-mixed data generation, machine translation involving code-mixed language, and multilingual pretrained generative models.

2.1 Code-Mixed Data Generation

Due to the paucity of code-mixed data, researchers have developed various methods to automatically generate code-mixed data. An ideal method for code-mixed data generation should aim to generate *syntactically valid* (i.e., fluent), semantically correct words (i.e., adequate), *diverse* code-mixed data of *varying lengths*. To create grammatically valid code-mixed sentences, Pratapa et al. (2018) leverages a linguistically motivated technique based on equivalence constraint theory (Poplack, 1980). They observe that the default distribution of synthetic code-mixed sentences created by their method can be quite different from the distribution of real code-mixed sentences in terms of code-mixing measures. This distribution gap can be largely bridged by post-processing the generated code-mixed sentences by binning them into switch point fraction bins and appropriately sampling from these bins. However, the method depends on availability of a word alignment model, which can be erroneous for distant languages (e.g., Hindi and Chinese) (Gupta et al., 2020). Winata et al. (2019) show that a Seq2Seq model with a copy mechanism can be trained to consume parallel monolingual data (concatenated) as input and produce code-mixed data as output, that is distributionally similar to real code-mixed data. Their method needs an external NMT system to obtain monolingual fragment from code-switched text and is expensive to scale to more language pairs. Garg et al. (2018) introduces a novel RNN unit for an RNN based language model that includes separate components to focus on each language in code-switched text. They utilize training data generated from SeqGAN along with syntactic features (e.g., Part-of-Speech tags, Brown word clusters, language ID feature) to train their RNN based language model. Their method involves added cost to train SeqGAN model and expensive to scale to more language pairs.

Samanta et al. (2019) propose a two-level hierarchical variational autoencoder that models syntactic signals in the lower layer and language switching signals in the upper layer. Their model can leverage modest real code-switched text and large monolingual text to generate large amounts of code-switched text along with its language at token level. The code-mixed data generated by their model seems syntactically valid, yet distributionally different from real code-mixed data and their model is harder to scale for large training data. Gupta et al. (2020) proposes a two-phase approach: (i) creation of synthetic code-mixed sentences from monolingual bitexts (English being one of the languages) by replacing aligned named entities and noun phrases from English; and (ii) training a Seq2Seq model to take English sentence as input and produce the code-mixed sentences created in the first phase. Their approach depends on the availability of a word alignment tool, a part-of-speech tagger, and knowledge of what constituents to replace in order to create a code-mixed sentence. By contrast, our proposed method based on bilingual word embeddings to generate code-mixed data does not require external software such as a word alignment tool, part-of-speech tagger, or constituency parser. Rizvi et al. (2021) develops the toolkit for code-mixed data generation for a given language pair using two linguistic theories: equivalence constraint (code-mixing following the grammatical structure of both the languages) and matrix language theory (McClure, 1995) (code-mixing by fixing a language that lends grammatical structure while other language lends its vocabulary). For comparison, we use this tool to implement the code-mixed data generation method based on equivalence constraint theory.

2.2 Code-Mixed MT

Building MT systems involving code-mixed language is a less researched area. Existing MT systems trained on monolingual data fail to translate code-mixed language such as from Hinglish to English (Dhar et al., 2018; Srivastava and Singh, 2020). Given that neural MT systems require large training data, Dhar et al. (2018) collects a parallel corpus of $6,096$ Hinglish-English bitexts. They propose a machine translation pipeline where they first identify the languages involved in the code-mixed sentence, determine the matrix language, translate the longest word sequence belonging to the embedded language to the matrix language, and then translate the resulting sentence into the target language. The last two steps are performed by monolingual translation systems trained to translate embedded language to matrix language and matrix language to target language respectively. Their proposed pipeline improves the performance of Google and Bing translation systems. Srivastava and Singh (2020) collect a large parallel corpus (called PHINC) of $13,738$ Hinglish-English bitexts that they claim is topically diverse and has better annotation quality than the corpus collected by Dhar et al. (2018). They propose a translation pipeline where they perform token level language identification and translate select phrases involving mostly Hindi to English using a monolingual translation system, while keeping the rest of phrases intact. This proposed pipeline outperforms Google and Bing systems on the PHINC dataset. For our work, we make use of the PHINC dataset by adapting the text by removing mentions, hashtags, emojis, emoticons as well as non-meaning bearing constituents such as URLs.

2.3 Multilingual Pretrained Models

Neural models pretrained on monolingual data using a self-supervised objective such as BERT (Devlin et al., 2019), BART (Lewis et al., 2020), and T5 (Raffel et al., 2020) have become integral to NLP systems as they serve as a good starting point for building SOTA models for diverse monolingual tasks. Recently, there is increasing attention to pretraining neural models on multilingual data, resulting in models such as mBERT (Devlin et al., 2019), XLM (Conneau et al., 2019), mBART (Liu et al., 2020) and mT5 (Xue et al., 2021). Especially, generative multilingual models such as mBART (Liu et al., 2020) and mT5 (Xue et al., 2021) can be utilized directly without additional neural network components to solve summarization, MT, and other natural language generation tasks. These generative models are trained using a self-supervised pretraining objective based on span-corruption objective (mBART and mT5) and sentence shuffling objective (mBART). Training data for these models are prepared by concatenating monolingual texts from multiple languages (e.g., 25 for mBART, 107 for mT5). It is not clear how much code-mixed data these models have seen during pretraining, making it an important question to investigate how they fare in processing text in varieties such as Hinglish. In this work, we target this question by exploring the challenges of applying one of these models (mT5) for the English to Hinglish translation task.

3 Shared Task

The goal of the shared task is to encourage MT involving code-mixing. We focus on translating English to Hinglish. A sentence in Hinglish may contain English tokens and roman Hindi tokens, as shown in Figure 1. The organizers provide $8,060$, 942 and 960 examples for training, validation, and test respectively.

4 Our Approach

Our approach to the English-Hinglish MT task is simple. We first identify the best text-to-text Transformer model on the validation set and follow a curriculum learning procedure to finetune the model for the downstream task. The curriculum learning procedure works such that we first finetune the model using synthetic code-mixed data from our generation method, then further finetune on the gold code-mixed data. This training recipe has been explored previously by Choudhury et al. (2017) and Pratapa et al. (2018) to build code-mixed language models. Curriculum learning itself has been explored previously for different NLP tasks such as parsing (Spitkovsky et al., 2010) and language modeling (Graves et al., 2017). We now present our proposed method to *generate* synthetic code-mixed text for a given language pair.

For our method, we assume having access to large amounts of bitext from a given pair of languages (LG_1 and LG_2) for which we need to generate code-mixed data. Let $B_i = \{x_i, y_i\}$ denote the bitext data, where x_i and y_i correspond to sentences in LG_1 and LG_2, respectively. Let $\texttt{ngrams}(n, x_i, y_i)$ denote the set of unique n-grams in x_i and y_i. Let $\texttt{cumulative-ngrams}(n, x_i, y_i) = \cup_{j=1}^{j=n} \texttt{ngrams}(j, x_i, y_i)$ denote the cumulative set of unique n-grams in the set of pairs x_i and y_i. We shuffle the n-grams in the cumulative set and create a "shuffled" code-mixed sentence by concatenating the shuffled set with n-grams separated by a space. For example, let LG_1 denote English and LG_2 denote Hindi (assuming Roman script for illustration). A sample bitext instance B_i can be "I've never seen it" (x_i) and "maine ye kabhi nah dekhi" (y_i). Set of unique 1-grams will be {"I've", "never", "seen", "it", "maine", "ye", "kabhi", "nah", "dekhi"} ($\texttt{ngrams}(1, x_i, y_i)$, assuming a whitespace tokenizer for simplicity). Then, $\texttt{cumulative-ngrams}(2, x_i, y_i)$ correspond to {"I've", "never", "seen", "it", "maine", "ye", "kabhi", "nah", "dekhi", "I've never", "never seen", "seen it", "maine ye", "ye kabhi", "kabhi nah", "nah dekhi"}. A shuffled code-mixed sentence can be, "I've ye_kabhi never seen_it seen never_seen it kabhi_nah I've_never maine_ye ye kabhi nah dekhi maine nah_dekhi". We create one shuffled code-mixed sentence per bitext instance, thereby creating a shuffled code-mixed corpus. We train a word2vec model on this shuffled code-mixed corpus to learn embeddings for n-grams in both languages. The resulting word embeddings seem cross-lingually aligned (based on manual inspection), thereby allowing us to do n-gram translation from one language to another language. For example, nearest English neighbor of a Hindi 1-gram "nah" can be "never".

Once the word embeddings are learned, we can create a code-mixed sentence for the given languages: LG_1 and LG_2. We first find the n-grams in $x_i \in LG_1$ and then sort all the n-grams by cosine similarity of the n-gram with its most similar n-gram in LG_2. Let `num-substitutions` denote the number of substitutions performed to convert x_i to a code-mixed sentence. We pick one n-gram at a time from the sorted list and replace all occurrences of that n-gram with its top n-gram belonging to language LG_2 based on word embeddings. We continue this substitution process until we exhaust the `num-substitutions`.

For our machine translation task, we assume LG_1 and LG_2 to be English and Hindi (native) respectively. [1] We feed the OPUS corpus [2] containing 17.2M English-Hindi bitexts (Hindi in native script) as input to the algorithm that outputs English-Hinglish code-mixed parallel data.

5 Experiments

In this section, we first discuss how we choose a text-to-text Transformer model from available models and then introduce our five baseline methods.

5.1 Choosing a Text-to-Text Transformer

Multilingual encoder-decoder models such as mT5 (Xue et al., 2021)[3] and mBART (Liu et al., 2020)[4] are suited to the MT task, and already cover both English and Hindi. It is not clear, however, how these models will perform on a task involving code-mixing at the target side such as ours (where we need to output Hinglish). For this reason, we first explore the potential of these two models on the code-mixed translation task to select the best model among these two. Once we identify the best model, we use it as the basis for further experiments as we will explain in Section 5.3. For both mT5 and mBART, we use the implementation provided by the HuggingFace library (Wolf et al., 2020) with the default settings for all hyperparameters except the maximum number of training epochs, which we choose based on the validation set.

[1] We can assume LG_1 and LG_2 to be Hindi and English respectively, but we leave this exploration for future.

[2] https://opus.nlpl.eu/

[3] https://github.com/google-research/multilingual-t5

[4] https://github.com/pytorch/fairseq/tree/master/examples/mbart

cs method (hyper.)	Valid	Test
Romanization		
IIT-B (100K)	14.27	12.95
IIT-B (250K)	**14.74**	**12.75**
IIT-B (500K)	14.12	12.46
OPUS (100K)	14.67	12.62
OPUS (250K)	14.57	12.71
Paraphrasing		
Para (1)	14.39	12.72
Para (2)	14.4	12.62
Para (3)	**15.07**	**12.63**
Backtranslation		
Forward model	**14.07**	**12.16**
Backward model	**14.51**	**13.03**
Social media		
PHINC	**14.71**	**12.68**
CMDR (ours)		
CMDR-unigram	**14.6**	**12.69**
CMDR-bigram	14.58	12.4

Table 2: Performance in BLEU of mT5 model finetuned using curriculum learning — finetuning on one of the different code-mixed data generation method followed by finetuning on gold data. **CMDR:** Code-Mixing from Distributed Representations refers to our proposed method. Note that we did not study the method based on equivalence constraint theory in this experiment. For CMDR, we perform n-gram translation of Hindi from native to roman script.

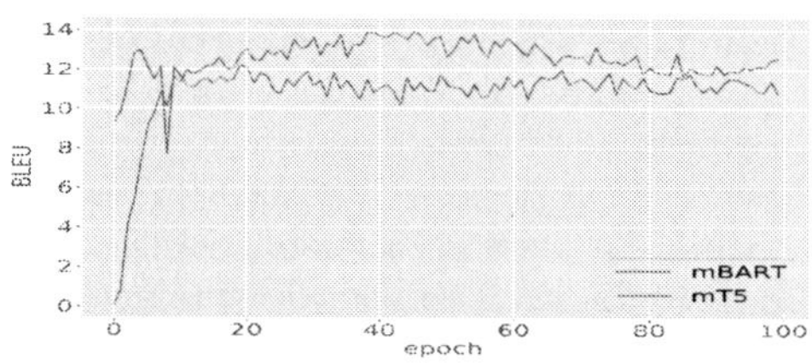

Figure 1: Validation BLEU of mBART and mT5 model on 541 randomly picked examples from the official training set after deduplication, while the rest of the 7000 examples are used for training.

Data Splits. For this set of experiments, we use "custom" splits using the official shared task training data after deduplication[5] and shuffling, as follows: $7,000$ examples for training set and 541 examples for validation set. For testing test, we use the official validation data (n=942 examples). We finetune both mT5 and mBART on the custom

[5] Deduplication is done based on exact overlap of source and target text.

split, and show results in Figure 1. We observe that mBART converges quickly within 5 epochs, while mT5 model takes ~ 46 epochs for convergence. Importantly, the best validation performance of 13.95 BLEU is obtained by the mT5 model, which helped us choose mT5 as the backbone model to build our final MT system. For subsequent experiments, we choose 50 as the maximum number of epochs to finetune the mT5 model. We now introduce our baseline code-mixing data generation methods.

5.2 Baseline Code-Mixing Generation Methods

We experiment with five different baseline methods to generate English-Hinglish bitexts that can be used in the first stage of finetuning. We now describe each of these methods.

5.2.1 Monolingual Target Romanization

In this method, we focus on creating monolingual bitexts by taking the Hindi sentence from parallel English-Hindi data and changing the script of Hindi from native script (Devanagari) to Roman script while keeping the English sentence intact. Although the resulting Hindi sentence is monolingual, the generated bitexts can help mT5 model to learn the semantics of Romanized Hindi language (mT5 model might be pretrained on native Hindi), along with the relationships between English and romanized Hindi language. To this end, we exploit two large parallel data sources for English-Hindi pairs (Hindi in native script) — IIT Bombay Parallel corpus (Kunchukuttan et al., 2018) (1.49M bitexts) and OPUS corpus (17.2M bitexts). We utilize the Aksharamukha tool to convert native Hindi to romanized Hindi.[6]

5.2.2 Monolingual Source Paraphrasing

Here, we paraphrase each English source sentence in the gold data to create a new training example, while keeping the target Hinglish sentence intact. Since good paraphrases can typically retain the meaning of the original sentence although the form can be different, we hypothesize the resulting bitext can improve the robustness of our translation system. To generate paraphrases, we use the $T5_{BASE}$ (Raffel et al., 2020) model finetuned on paraphrases from diverse English sources. For our experiments, we use n paraphrases of each source sentence, with n chosen from the set $\{1,2,3\}$. Details about our paraphrasing model are in Appendix A.1.

[6]https://aksharamukha.appspot.com

5.2.3 Backtranslation

We also use the traditional backtranslation pipeline to generate more data for our task. Specifically, we create two models: *forward model* that is obtained by finetuning the mT5 model on English as source and Hinglish as target, *backward model* that is obtained by finetuning mT5 on Hinglish as source and English as target, on the gold training data in both cases. For each gold bitext, the process involves two steps: *forward model inference*, where the gold English sentence is fed to the forward model that generates the intermediate Hinglish sentence; *backward model inference*, where the intermediate Hinglish sentence is fed to the backward model that generates the final English sentence. The new bitext is obtained by pairing up the final English sentence with the gold Hinglish sentence (which is parallel to the English fed to the forward model as source). This method can be treated as an alternative method to creating paraphrases of an English sentence.

5.2.4 Social Media Adaptation

We adapt a publicly available English-Hinglish social media dataset, PHINC (Srivastava and Singh, 2020), to our task. PHINC consists of 13, 738 manually annotated English-Hinglish code-mixed sentences, mainly sourced from social media platforms such as Twitter and Facebook. It covers a wide range of topics (such as sports and politics) and has high quality text (e.g., it handles spelling variations and filters abusive and ambiguous sentences). We perform post-processing on PHINC by removing tokens particular to the social media context such as hashtags, mentions, emojis, emoticons and URLs. We use the resulting, adapted, dataset to finetune mT5 for the first stage (as explained in Section 4).

5.2.5 Equivalence Constraint Theory

This method generates code-mixed data based on *equivalence constraint theory* (EC), as originally proposed by Pratapa et al. (2018). The method works by producing parse trees for English-Hindi sentence pair and replaces common nodes between the two trees based on the EC theory. We use the implementation provided by the GCM tool (Rizvi et al., 2021). We feed the English-Hindi bitexts (Hindi in native script) from the OPUS corpus to generate English-Hinglish (Hindi in native script) parallel data. We now describe our results with mT5 on our custom splits.

5.3 Performance With mT5

As briefly introduced earlier, we finetune the mT5 model using curriculum learning where we have two stages. In stage one, we finetune one of the code-mixed data generation methods. We follow that by stage two where we finetune on the gold code-mixed data (official shared task training data). Also, for stage one, to cap GPU hours with the large synthetic code-mixed data, we experiment with a maximum of 5 epochs. For the stage two, where we have smaller amount of gold data, we experiment with 50 as the maximum number of epochs choosing the best epoch on the validation set.

Table 2 displays the validation and the test performance of mT5 finetuned using curriculum learning. [7] For romanization of monolingual target method, as the Table shows, more data does not strictly improve validation (nor test) performance. That is, there seems to be a 'sweet spot' after which quality deteriorates with noise. The behavior is similar for the models exploiting paraphrases of the source monolingual English data: Adding more paraphrases for a single gold instance can lead to overfitting of the model, as noticed by consistent degradation in test performance. For backtranslation, we experiment with two variants: *forward model* where predictions (Hinglish) from the forward model is paired up with English sentence from the gold, *backward model* which corresponds to the traditional backtranslation bitext. Performance of the backward model is consistently better on both the validation and the test set. For the social media adaptation method, mT5 achieves validation performance that is better than any of the methods based on romanization or backtranslation. For our proposed method based on code-mixing from bilingual distributed representations (CMDR), we experiment with different values of `num-substitutions` and change the script of replaced Hindi words from native to roman script using the Aksharamukha tool. Manual inspection of the data reveals that script conversion at word level is noisy due to lack of sentential context. This might lead to decline in the performance as our method makes more substitutions. Nevertheless, our proposed method, simple as it is, leads to results competitive with any of the other methods.

[7] The best epoch for each stage in the pipeline is displayed in Appendix B.

English (Gold): And they grow apart. She is the protector of the Moors forest. **Hinglish (Prediction)**: Aur wo apart grow karte hai. Wo Moors forest ka (ki) protector hai.
English (Gold): I watched it at least twice.. it was that good. I love female superheros **Hinglish (Prediction)**: Maine ise kam se kam ek (do) baar dekha hai. Ye itni achi thi. Mujhe female superheros pasand hai.
English (Gold): I loved the story & how true they made it in how teen girls act but I honestly don't know why I didn't rate it highly as all the right ingredients were there. I cannot believe it was 2004 it was released though, 14 years ago! **Hinglish (Prediction)**: mujhe story bahut pasand aaya aur teen girls ka act kaise hota lekin main honestly nahi janta kyon ki main ise highly rate nahi kar raha tha kyunki sahi ingredients wahan they. mujhe yakin nahi hota ki 2004 mein release huyi thi, 14 saal pehle!

Table 3: Translations of our proposed system that uses native script and 3 as `num-substitutions`. Errors in translations are highligthed in red color, with their the right translation in paranthesis and highlighted in green color.

5.4 Qualitative Analysis

We manually inspect translations from our proposed system that uses native script and 3 as `num-substitutions` on 25 randomly picked examples from the official test set. 64% of the translations are correct, while 24% and 12% of the translations have grammatical error (e.g., incorrect gender) and semantic errors (e.g., factual inconsistency) respectively. 12% of the translations exactly match with the source. Few of these translations are shown in Table 3. The first translation has grammatical gender error, as it contains male posessive noun, 'ka' (instead of female possessive noun, 'ki'). The second translation has semantic error, where the number of times that the movie has been watched is incorrectly translated as one time ('ek') when the source mentions it as two ('do') times. The third example is long (43 words), which our system translates without errors.

6 Official Results

In this section, we describe the official test performance obtained by our models. First, we experiment with mT5 model finetuned using promising code-mixing methods identified in our previous experiments (see Section 5.3). The best performing baseline method is based on equivalence constraint theory for $100K$ examples and yields a

cs method	BLEU
baseline (mBART model)	11.00
LinCE leaderboard (only best results)	
LTRC Team	12.22
IITP-MT Team	10.09
CMMTOne Team	2.58
Romanization	
OPUS	12.38
Paraphrasing	
Para	12.1
Backtranslation	
Backward model	11.47
Social media	
PHINC	11.9
Equivalence constraint theory	
ECT (100K)	12.45
CMDR (ours)	
CMDR-unigram (roman)	12.25
CMDR-bigram (native)	12.63
CMDR-bigram (roman)	12.08
CMDR-trigram (native)	**12.67**
CMDR-trigram (roman)	12.05
Method Combinations	
CMDR-unigram (roman) + PHINC	11.58
ECT (100K) + CMDR-trigram (native)	12.27

Table 4: Official test performance of mT5 model finetuned using curriculum learning — finetuning on one of the different code-mixed data generation method (max. epochs is 5) followed by finetuning on concatenation of gold training data and gold validation data (leaving out 200 examples for validation) (max. epochs is 50)

BLEU score of 12.45. For the proposed CMDR method, we experiment not only with the value for `num-substitutions`, but also the script type. Surprisingly, the best combination for our proposed method is based on maximum substitutions of 3, sticking to the original native script, and yields the highest BLEU score of 12.67. The variants of our proposed method that romanizes the replacement n-gram consistently perform poorly, which confirms our observation that n-gram level romanization is deprived of sentential context and is prone to errors.

7 Discussion

The lessons learned in this shared task can be summarized as follows.

Similar Text-to-Text Models. *Off-the-shelf mT5 and mBART models perform similarly, with mT5 being slightly better in our experiments (for English-Hinglish MT).* A down side of mT5 is that it takes many more epochs than mBART to converge. In the future, it will be interesting to explore recent extensions of mBART[8], which are already finetuned for multilingual translation. These extensions involve training on English-Hindi (native) bitexts, and so can act as an interesting zero-shot translation baseline without further finetuning. They may also serve as a better baseline when finetuned using the curriculum learning approach adopted in our work.

Code-Mixing from Distributed Representations is Useful. *Our proposed code-mixed data generation method based on bilingual word embeddings can be exploited by mT5 model to achieve the state-of-the-art translation performance,* especially when the number of substitutions is high and the script remains in native form. It will be interesting to see the sweet spot for the number of substitutions, as too low value can result in very less code-mixing while too high value can result in more code-mixing along with more noise (possibly grammatically incorrect and unnatural to bilingual speaker).

Combinations of Code-Mixed Data not Ideal. *Combining code-mixed generations from two methods likely introduces more noise and does not improve the performance of the mT5 model compared to performance obtained using generations from individual method,* as seen in the 'Misc.' section of Table 4. It might be interesting to explore more than two stages of curriculum learning, where the mT5 model is successively finetuned on code-mixed data generated using different methods.

8 Conclusion

We proposed an MT pipeline for translating between English and Hinglish. We test the utility of existing pretrained language models on the task and propose a simple, dependency-free, method for generating synthetic code-mixed text from bilingual distributed representations of words and phrases. Comparing our proposed method to five baseline methods, we show that our method achieves competitively. The method results in best translation performance on the shared task blind test data, placing us first in the official competition. In the future, we plan to (i) scale up the size of code-mixed data, (ii) experiment with different domains of English-Hindi bitexts such as Twitter, (iii) experiment with recent extensions of mBART, and (iv) assess the generalizability of our proposed code-mixing method to other NLP tasks such as question answering and dialogue modeling.

[8]These are `mbart-large-50-many-to-many-mmt`, `mbart-large-50-one-to-many-mmt`, and `mbart-large-50-many-to-one-mmt`.

Acknowledgements

We gratefully acknowledges support from the Natural Sciences and Engineering Research Council of Canada, the Social Sciences and Humanities Research Council of Canada, Canadian Foundation for Innovation, Compute Canada (www.computecanada.ca), and UBC ARC-Sockeye (https://doi.org/10.14288/SOCKEYE).

References

Muhammad Abdul-Mageed, Chiyu Zhang, AbdelRahim Elmadany, and Lyle Ungar. 2020. Micro-dialect identification in diaglossic and code-switched environments. In *Proceedings of the 2020 Conference on Empirical Methods in Natural Language Processing (EMNLP)*, pages 5855–5876.

Monojit Choudhury, Kalika Bali, Sunayana Sitaram, and Ashutosh Baheti. 2017. Curriculum design for code-switching: Experiments with language identification and language modeling with deep neural networks. In *Proceedings of the 14th International Conference on Natural Language Processing (ICON-2017)*, pages 65–74, Kolkata, India. NLP Association of India.

Alexis Conneau, Kartikay Khandelwal, Naman Goyal, Vishrav Chaudhary, Guillaume Wenzek, Francisco Guzmán, Edouard Grave, Myle Ott, Luke Zettlemoyer, and Veselin Stoyanov. 2019. Unsupervised cross-lingual representation learning at scale. *arXiv preprint arXiv:1911.02116*.

Mathias Creutz. 2018. Open subtitles paraphrase corpus for six languages. *arXiv preprint arXiv:1809.06142*.

Jacob Devlin, Ming-Wei Chang, Kenton Lee, and Kristina Toutanova. 2019. BERT: Pre-training of Deep Bidirectional Transformers for Language Understanding. In *Proceedings of the 2019 Conference of the North American Chapter of the Association for Computational Linguistics: Human Language Technologies, Volume 1 (Long and Short Papers)*, pages 4171–4186.

Mrinal Dhar, Vaibhav Kumar, and Manish Shrivastava. 2018. Enabling code-mixed translation: Parallel corpus creation and MT augmentation approach. In *Proceedings of the First Workshop on Linguistic Resources for Natural Language Processing*, pages 131–140, Santa Fe, New Mexico, USA. Association for Computational Linguistics.

Saurabh Garg, Tanmay Parekh, and Preethi Jyothi. 2018. Code-switched language models using dual RNNs and same-source pretraining. In *Proceedings of the 2018 Conference on Empirical Methods in Natural Language Processing*, pages 3078–3083, Brussels, Belgium. Association for Computational Linguistics.

Alex Graves, Marc G. Bellemare, Jacob Menick, Remi Munos, and Koray Kavukcuoglu. 2017. Automated curriculum learning for neural networks.

John J. Gumperz. 1982. *Discourse Strategies*. Studies in Interactional Sociolinguistics. Cambridge University Press.

Deepak Gupta, Asif Ekbal, and Pushpak Bhattacharyya. 2020. A semi-supervised approach to generate the code-mixed text using pre-trained encoder and transfer learning. In *Findings of the Association for Computational Linguistics: EMNLP 2020*, pages 2267–2280, Online. Association for Computational Linguistics.

Ari Holtzman, Jan Buys, Li Du, Maxwell Forbes, and Yejin Choi. 2020. The Curious Case of Neural Text Degeneration. In *International Conference on Learning Representations*.

Anoop Kunchukuttan, Pratik Mehta, and Pushpak Bhattacharyya. 2018. The IIT Bombay English-Hindi parallel corpus. In *Proceedings of the Eleventh International Conference on Language Resources and Evaluation (LREC 2018)*, Miyazaki, Japan. European Language Resources Association (ELRA).

Wuwei Lan, Siyu Qiu, Hua He, and Wei Xu. 2017. A continuously growing dataset of sentential paraphrases. In *Proceedings of the 2017 Conference on Empirical Methods in Natural Language Processing*, pages 1224–1234, Copenhagen, Denmark. Association for Computational Linguistics.

Mike Lewis, Yinhan Liu, Naman Goyal, Marjan Ghazvininejad, Abdelrahman Mohamed, Omer Levy, Veselin Stoyanov, and Luke Zettlemoyer. 2020. BART: Denoising sequence-to-sequence pre-training for natural language generation, translation, and comprehension. In *Proceedings of the 58th Annual Meeting of the Association for Computational Linguistics*, pages 7871–7880, Online. Association for Computational Linguistics.

Yinhan Liu, Jiatao Gu, Naman Goyal, Xian Li, Sergey Edunov, Marjan Ghazvininejad, Mike Lewis, and Luke Zettlemoyer. 2020. Multilingual Denoising Pre-training for Neural Machine Translation.

Erica McClure. 1995. Duelling languages: Grammatical structure in codeswitching. *Studies in Second Language Acquisition*, 17(1):117–118.

Shana Poplack. 1980. Sometimes i'll start a sentence in spanish y termino en espaÑol: toward a typology of code-switching. 18(7-8):581–618.

Adithya Pratapa, Gayatri Bhat, Monojit Choudhury, Sunayana Sitaram, Sandipan Dandapat, and Kalika Bali. 2018. Language modeling for code-mixing: The role of linguistic theory based synthetic data. In

Proceedings of the 56th Annual Meeting of the Association for Computational Linguistics (Volume 1: Long Papers), pages 1543–1553, Melbourne, Australia. Association for Computational Linguistics.

Colin Raffel, Noam Shazeer, Adam Roberts, Katherine Lee, Sharan Narang, Michael Matena, Yanqi Zhou, Wei Li, and Peter J. Liu. 2020. Exploring the limits of transfer learning with a unified text-to-text transformer. *Journal of Machine Learning Research*, 21(140):1–67.

Mohd Sanad Zaki Rizvi, Anirudh Srinivasan, Tanuja Ganu, Monojit Choudhury, and Sunayana Sitaram. 2021. GCM: A toolkit for generating synthetic code-mixed text. In *Proceedings of the 16th Conference of the European Chapter of the Association for Computational Linguistics: System Demonstrations*, pages 205–211, Online. Association for Computational Linguistics.

Bidisha Samanta, Sharmila Reddy, Hussain Jagirdar, Niloy Ganguly, and Soumen Chakrabarti. 2019. A deep generative model for code-switched text. *CoRR*, abs/1906.08972.

Sunayana Sitaram, Khyathi Raghavi Chandu, Sai Krishna Rallabandi, and Alan W. Black. 2019. A survey of code-switched speech and language processing. *CoRR*, abs/1904.00784.

Valentin I. Spitkovsky, Hiyan Alshawi, and Daniel Jurafsky. 2010. From baby steps to leapfrog: How "less is more" in unsupervised dependency parsing. In *Human Language Technologies: The 2010 Annual Conference of the North American Chapter of the Association for Computational Linguistics*, pages 751–759, Los Angeles, California. Association for Computational Linguistics.

Vivek Srivastava and Mayank Singh. 2020. PHINC: A parallel Hinglish social media code-mixed corpus for machine translation. In *Proceedings of the Sixth Workshop on Noisy User-generated Text (W-NUT 2020)*, pages 41–49, Online. Association for Computational Linguistics.

Genta Indra Winata, Andrea Madotto, Chien-Sheng Wu, and Pascale Fung. 2019. Code-switched language models using neural based synthetic data from parallel sentences. In *Proceedings of the 23rd Conference on Computational Natural Language Learning (CoNLL)*, pages 271–280, Hong Kong, China. Association for Computational Linguistics.

Thomas Wolf, Lysandre Debut, Victor Sanh, Julien Chaumond, Clement Delangue, Anthony Moi, Pierric Cistac, Tim Rault, Remi Louf, Morgan Funtowicz, Joe Davison, Sam Shleifer, Patrick von Platen, Clara Ma, Yacine Jernite, Julien Plu, Canwen Xu, Teven Le Scao, Sylvain Gugger, Mariama Drame, Quentin Lhoest, and Alexander Rush. 2020. Transformers: State-of-the-art natural language processing. In *Proceedings of the 2020 Conference on Empirical Methods in Natural Language Processing: System Demonstrations*, pages 38–45, Online. Association for Computational Linguistics.

Wei Xu, Chris Callison-Burch, and Bill Dolan. 2015. SemEval-2015 task 1: Paraphrase and semantic similarity in Twitter (PIT). In *Proceedings of the 9th International Workshop on Semantic Evaluation (SemEval 2015)*, pages 1–11, Denver, Colorado. Association for Computational Linguistics.

Linting Xue, Noah Constant, Adam Roberts, Mihir Kale, Rami Al-Rfou, Aditya Siddhant, Aditya Barua, and Colin Raffel. 2021. mt5: A massively multilingual pre-trained text-to-text transformer.

Appendix

A Baseline Code-Mixing Generation Methods

A.1 Monolingual Source Paraphrasing

To generate paraphrases, we use the $T5_{BASE}$ (Raffel et al., 2020) model finetuned on paraphrases from diverse English sources: paraphrase and semantic similarity in Twitter shared task (PIT-2015) (Xu et al., 2015), LanguageNet (tweet) (Lan et al., 2017), Opusparcus (Creutz, 2018) (video subtitle), and Quora question pairs (Q&A website). [9] For all datasets excluding Quora question pairs, we keep sentence pairs with a semantic similarity score $\geq 70\%$. We merge all the datasets, split the resulting data into training, validation, and testing (80%, 10%, and 10%). The T5 model is finetuned on the training split for 20 epochs with constant learning rate of $3e^{-4}$. Given an English sentence to paraphrase, the finetuned model uses top-p sampling (Holtzman et al., 2020) during inference to generate 10 diverse paraphrases. We pick relevant paraphrases for a given sentence by ranking all the generated paraphrases based on the semantic similarity score with the original English sentence and discarding those paraphrases whose semantic similarity score $\geq 95\%$.

B Performance With mT5 On Custom Splits

Table 5 presents the performance of our proposed system on custom splits, along with best epoch for each stage in the pipeline.

[9] `https://www.quora.com/q/quoradata/First-Quora-Dataset-Release-Question-Pairs`

cs method (hyper.)	S1 epoch	S2 epoch	Valid	Test
Romanization				
IIT-B (100K)	3	50	14.27	12.95
IIT-B (250K)	5	47	**14.74**	**12.75**
IIT-B (500K)	3	46	14.12	12.46
OPUS (100K)	3	43	14.67	12.62
OPUS (250K)	3	50	14.57	12.71
Paraphrasing				
Para (1)	5	43	14.39	12.72
Para (2)	5	43	14.4	12.62
Para (3)	5	44	**15.07**	**12.63**
Backtranslation				
Forward model	3	37	**14.07**	**12.16**
Backward model	3	36	**14.51**	**13.03**
Social media				
PHINC	5	29	**14.71**	**12.68**
CMDR (ours)				
CMDR-unigram	3	48	**14.6**	**12.69**
CMDR-bigram	5	42	14.58	12.4

Table 5: Performance in BLEU of mT5 model finetuned using curriculum learning — finetuning on one of the different code-mixed data generation method (max. epochs is 5) followed by finetuning on gold data (max. epochs is 50). **CMDR:** Code-Mixing from Distributed Representations refers to our proposed method. Validation performance is calculated on 541 randomly picked examples from the official training set after deduplication, while the rest of the $7,000$ examples are used for training. Test performance is calculated on the official validation set. Note that we did not study the method based on equivalence constraint theory in this experiment. For CMDR, we perform n-gram translation of Hindi from native to Roman script.

CoMeT: Towards Code-Mixed Translation Using Parallel Monolingual Sentences

Devansh Gautam[†] **Prashant Kodali**[†] **Kshitij Gupta**[†] **Anmol Goel**[††]
Manish Shrivastava[†] **Ponnurangam Kumaraguru**[‡]
[†]International Institute of Information Technology Hyderabad
[‡]Indraprastha Institute of Information Technology Delhi
[††]Guru Gobind Singh Indraprastha University, Delhi
{devansh.gautam,prashant.kodali,kshitij.gupta}@research.iiit.ac.in,
agoel00@gmail.com, m.shrivastava@iiit.ac.in, pk@iiitd.ac.in

Abstract

Code-mixed languages are very popular in multilingual societies around the world, yet the resources lag behind to enable robust systems on such languages. A major contributing factor is the informal nature of these languages which makes it difficult to collect code-mixed data. In this paper, we propose our system for Task 1 of CACLS 2021[1] to generate a machine translation system for English to Hinglish in a supervised setting. Translating in the given direction can help expand the set of resources for several tasks by translating valuable datasets from high resource languages. We propose to use mBART, a pre-trained multilingual sequence-to-sequence model, and fully utilize the pre-training of the model by transliterating the roman Hindi words in the code-mixed sentences to Devanagri script. We evaluate how expanding the input by concatenating Hindi translations of the English sentences improves mBART's performance. Our system gives a BLEU score of 12.22 on test set. Further, we perform a detailed error analysis of our proposed systems and explore the limitations of the provided dataset and metrics.

1 Introduction

Code-mixing[2] is the mixing of two or more languages where words from different languages are interleaved with each other in the same conversation. It is a common phenomenon in multilingual societies across the globe. In the last decade, due to the increase in the popularity of social media and various online messaging platforms, there has been an increase in various forms of informal writing, such as emojis, slang, and the usage of code-mixed languages.

Due to the informal nature of code-mixing, code-mixed languages do not follow a prescriptively defined structure, and the structure often varies with the speaker. Nevertheless, some linguistic constraints (Poplack, 1980; Belazi et al., 1994) have been proposed that attempt to determine how languages mix with each other.

Given the increasing use of code-mixed languages by people around the globe, there is a growing need for research related to code-mixed languages. A significant challenge to research is that there are no formal sources like books or news articles in code-mixed languages, and studies have to rely on sources like Twitter or messaging platforms. Another challenge with Hinglish, in particular, is that there is no standard system of transliteration for Hindi words, and individuals provide a rough phonetic transcription of the intended word, which often varies with individuals.

In this paper, we describe our systems for Task 1 of CALCS 2021, which focuses on translating English sentences to English-Hindi code-mixed sentences. The code-mixed language is often called *Hinglish*. It is commonly used in India because many bilingual speakers use both Hindi and English frequently in their personal and professional lives. The translation systems could be used to augment datasets for various Hinglish tasks by translating datasets from English to Hinglish. An example of a Hinglish sentence from the provided dataset (with small modifications) is shown below:

- **Hinglish Sentence:** Bahut strange choice thi ye.
- **Gloss of Hinglish Sentence:** Very [strange choice] was this.
- **English Sentence:** This was a very strange choice.

We propose to fine-tune mBART for the given task by first transliterating the Hindi words in the

[1]https://code-switching.github.io/2021

[2]Code-switching is another term that slightly differs in its meaning but is often used interchangeably with code-mixing in the research community. We will also be following the same convention and use both the terms interchangeably in our paper.

Proceedings of the Fifth Workshop on Computational Approaches to Linguistic Code-Switching, pages 47–55
June 11, 2021. ©2021 Association for Computational Linguistics
https://doi.org/10.26615/978-954-452-056-4_007

target sentences from Roman script to Devanagri script to utilize its pre-training. We further translate the English input to Hindi using pre-existing models and show improvements in the translation using parallel sentences as input to the mBART model. The code for our systems, along with error analysis, is public[3].

The main contributions of our work are as follows:

- We explore the effectiveness of fine-tuning mBART to translate to code-mixed sentences by utilizing the Hindi pre-training of the model in Devanagri script. We further explore the effectiveness of using parallel sentences as input.

- We propose a normalized BLEU score metric to better account for the spelling variations in the code-mixed sentences.

- Along with BLEU scores, we analyze the code-mixing quality of the reference translations along with the generated outputs and propose that for assessing code-mixed translations, measures of code-mixing should be part of evaluation and analysis.

The rest of the paper is organized as follows. We discuss prior work related to code-mixed language processing, machine translation, and synthetic generation of code-mixed data. We describe our translation systems and compare the performances of our approaches. We discuss the amount of code-mixing in the translations predicted by our systems and discuss some issues present in the provided dataset. We conclude with a direction for future work and highlight our main findings.

2 Background

Code-mixing occurs when a speaker switches between two or more languages in the context of the same conversation. It has become popular in multilingual societies with the rise of social media applications and messaging platforms.

In attempts to progress the field of code-mixed data, several code-switching workshops (Diab et al., 2014, 2016; Aguilar et al., 2018b) have been organized in notable conferences. Most of the workshops include shared tasks on various of the language understanding tasks like language identification (Solorio et al., 2014; Molina et al., 2016), NER (Aguilar et al., 2018a; Rao and Devi, 2016), IR (Roy et al., 2013; Banerjee et al., 2018), PoS tagging (Jamatia et al., 2016), sentiment analysis (Patra et al., 2018; Patwa et al., 2020), and question answering (Chandu et al., 2018).

Although these workshops have gained traction, the field lacks standard datasets to build robust systems. The small size of the datasets is a major factor that limits the scope of code-mixed systems.

Machine Translation refers to the use of software to translate text from one language to another. In the current state of globalization, translation systems have widespread applications and are consequently an active area of research.

Neural machine translation has gained popularity only in the last decade, while earlier works focused on statistical or rule-based approaches. Kalchbrenner and Blunsom (2013) first proposed a DNN model for translation, following which transformer-based approaches (Vaswani et al., 2017) have taken the stage. Some approaches utilize multilingual pre-training (Song et al., 2019; Conneau and Lample, 2019; Edunov et al., 2019; Liu et al., 2020); however, these works focus only on monolingual language pairs.

Although a large number of multilingual speakers in a highly populous country like India use English-Hindi code-mixed language, only a few studies (Srivastava and Singh, 2020; Singh and Solorio, 2018; Dhar et al., 2018) have attempted the problem. Enabling translation systems in the following pair can bridge the communication gap between several people and further improve the state of globalization in the world.

Synthetic code-mixed data generation is a plausible option to build resources for code-mixed language research and is a very similar task to translation. While translation focuses on retaining the meaning of the source sentence, generation is a simpler task requiring focus only on the quality of the synthetic data generated.

Pratapa et al. (2018) started by exploring linguistic theories to generate code-mixed data. Later works attempt the problem using several approaches including Generative Adversarial Networks (Chang et al., 2019), an encoder-decoder framework (Gupta et al., 2020), pointer-generator networks (Winata et al., 2019), and a two-level

[3] `https://github.com/devanshg27/cm_translation`

	Train	Valid	Test
# of sentences	8,060	942	960
# of tokens in source sentences	98,080	12,275	12,557
# of tokens in target sentences	101,752	12,611	-
# of Hindi tokens in target sentences	68,054	8,310	-
# of English tokens in target sentences	21,502	2,767	-
# of 'Other' tokens in target sentences	12,196	1,534	-

Table 1: The statistics of the dataset. We use the language tags predicted by the CSNLI library[4]. Since the target sentences of the test set are not public, we do not provide its statistics.

variational autoencoder (Samanta et al., 2019). Recently, Rizvi et al. (2021) released a tool to generate code-mixed data using parallel sentences as input.

3 System Overview

In this section, we describe our proposed systems for the task, which use mBART (Liu et al., 2020) to translate English to Hinglish.

3.1 Data Preparation

We use the dataset provided by the task organizers for our systems, the statistics of the datasets are provided in Table 1. Since the target sentences in the dataset contain Hindi words in Roman script, we use the CSNLI library[4] (Bhat et al., 2017, 2018) as a preprocessing step. It transliterates the Hindi words to Devanagari and also performs text normalization. We use the provided train:validation:test split, which is in the ratio 8:1:1.

3.2 Model

We fine-tune mBART, which is a multilingual sequence-to-sequence denoising auto-encoder pretrained using the BART (Lewis et al., 2020) objective on large-scale monolingual corpora of 25 languages including English and Hindi. It uses a standard sequence-to-sequence Transformer architecture (Vaswani et al., 2017), with 12 encoder and decoder layers each and a model dimension of 1024 on 16 heads resulting in ~680 million parameters. To train our systems efficiently, we prune mBART's vocabulary by removing the tokens which are not present in the provided dataset or the dataset released by Kunchukuttan et al. (2018) which contains 1,612,709 parallel sentences for English and Hindi.

We compare the following two strategies for fine-tuning mBART:

- **mBART-en:** We fine-tune mBART on the train set, feeding the English sentences to the encoder and decoding Hinglish sentences. We use beam search with a beam size of 5 for decoding.
- **mBART-hien:** We fine-tune mBART on the train set, feeding the English sentences along with their parallel Hindi translations to the encoder and decoding Hinglish sentences. For feeding the data to the encoder, we concatenate the Hindi translations, followed by a separator token '##', followed by the English sentence. We use the Google NMT system[5] (Wu et al., 2016) to translate the English source sentences to Hindi. We again use beam search with a beam size of 5 for decoding.

3.3 Post-Processing

We transliterate the Hindi words in our predicted translations from Devanagari to Roman. We use the following methods to transliterate a given Devanagari token (we use the first method which provides us with the transliteration):

1. When we transliterate the Hindi words in the target sentences from Roman to Devanagari (as discussed in Section 3.1), we store the most frequent Roman transliteration for each Hindi word in the train set. If the current Devanagari token's transliteration is available, we use it directly.
2. We use the publicly available Dakshina Dataset (Roark et al., 2020) which has 25,000 Hindi words in Devanagari script along with their attested romanizations. If the current Devanagari token is available in the dataset, we use the transliteration with the maximum number of attestations from the dataset.
3. We use the `indic-trans` library[6] (Bhat et al., 2015) to transliterate the token from Devanagari to Roman.

4 Experimental Setup

4.1 Implementation

We use the implementation of mBART available in the fairseq library[7] (Ott et al., 2019). We fine-tune on 4 Nvidia GeForce RTX 2080 Ti GPUs

[4] `https://github.com/irshadbhat/csnli`

[5] `https://cloud.google.com/translate`

[6] `https://github.com/libindic/indic-trans`

[7] `https://github.com/pytorch/fairseq`

Model	Validation Set		Test Set	
	BLEU	$BLEU_{normalized}$	BLEU	$BLEU_{normalized}$
mBART-en	**15.3**	18.9	**12.22**	–
mBART-hien	14.6	**20.2**	11.86	–

Table 2: Performance of our systems on the validation set and test set of the dataset. Since the target sentences of the test set are not public, we do not calculate the scores ourselves. We report the BLEU scores of our systems on the test set from the official leader board.

with an effective batch size of 1024 tokens per GPU. We use the Adam optimizer ($\epsilon = 10^{-6}, \beta_1 = 0.9, \beta_2 = 0.98$) (Kingma and Ba, 2015) with 0.3 dropout, 0.1 attention dropout, 0.2 label smoothing and polynomial decay learning rate scheduling. We fine-tune the model for 10,000 steps with 2,500 warm-up steps and a learning rate of $3 * 10^{-5}$. We validate the models for every epoch and select the best checkpoint based on the best BLEU score on the validation set. To train our systems efficiently, we prune mBART's vocabulary by removing the tokens which are not present in any of the datasets mentioned in the previous section.

4.2 Evaluation Metrics

We use the following two evaluation metrics for comparing our systems:

1. **BLEU:** The BLEU score (Papineni et al., 2002) is the official metric used in the leader board. We calculate the score using the SacreBLEU library[8] (Post, 2018) after lowercasing and tokenization using the `TweetTokenizer` available with the NLTK library[9] (Bird et al., 2009).

2. **$BLEU_{normalized}$:** Instead of calculating the BLEU scores on the texts where the Hindi words are transliterated to Roman, we calculate the score on texts where Hindi words are in Devanagari and English words in Roman. We transliterate the target sentences using the CSNLI library and we use the outputs of our system before performing the post-processing (Section 3.3). We again use the SacreBLEU library after lowercasing and tokenization using the `TweetTokenizer` available with the NLTK library.

[8]`https://github.com/mjpost/sacrebleu`
[9]`https://www.nltk.org/`

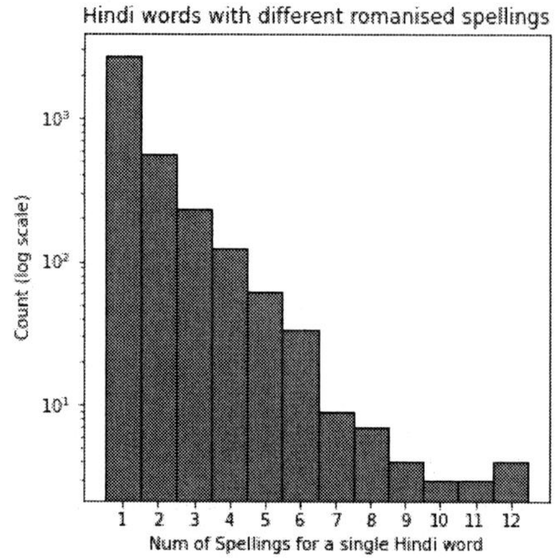

Figure 1: Multiple roman spellings for the same Hindi Word. These spelling variations can cause the BLEU score to be low, even if the correct Hindi word is predicted.

5 Results

Table 2 shows the BLEU scores of the outputs generated by our models described in Section 3.2. In Hinglish sentences, Hindi tokens are often transliterated to roman script, and that results in spelling variation. Since BLEU score compares token/n-gram overlap between source and target, lack of canonical spelling for transliterated words, reduces BLEU score and can mischaracterize the quality of translation. To estimate the variety in roman spellings for a Hindi word, we perform normalization by back transliterating the Hindi words in a code-mixed sentence to Devanagari and aggregated the number of different spellings for a single Devanagari token. Figure 1 shows the extent of this phenomena in the dataset released as part of this shared task, and it is evident that there are Hindi words that have multiple roman spellings. Thus, even if the model is generating the correct Devanagari token, the BLEU scores will be understated due to the spelling variation in the transliterated reference sentence. By back-transliterating Hindi tokens to Devanagari, **$BLEU_{normalized}$** score thus provides a better representation of translation quality.

5.1 Error Analysis of Translations of Test set

Since BLEU score primarily look at n-gram overlaps, it does not provide any insight into the quality of generated output or the errors therein. To

	mBART-en	mBART-hien
Mistranslated/Partially Translated	28	23
MWE/NER mistranslation	7	4
Morphology/Case Marking/Agreement/Syntax Issues	13	2
No Error	52	71

Table 3: Error Analysis of 100 randomly sampled translations from test set for both mBART-en and mBART-hien model

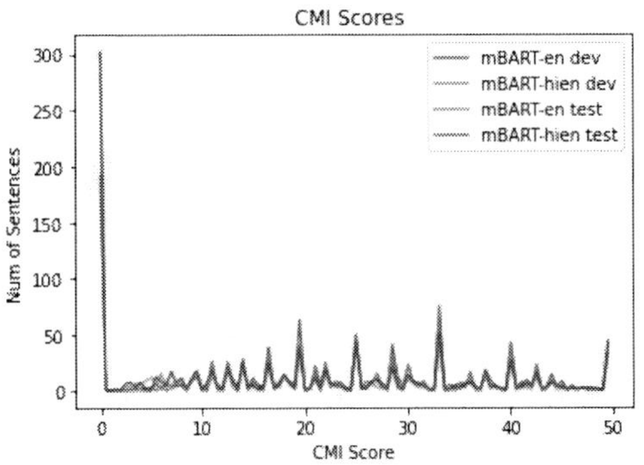

Figure 2: Code Mixing Index(CMI) for the generated translation of dev and test set .

	Avg CMI Score	% of Sents.with CMI = 0
Train Gold	19.4	26.1%
Dev Gold	21.6	19.3%
mBART-en Dev	21.8	19.4%
mBART-hien Dev	16.9	30.0%
mBART-en Test	21.8	20.0%
mBART-hien Test	16.7	31.4%

Table 4: Avg. CMI scores, Percentage of sentences with CMI = 0. Train Gold and Dev Gold are calculated on the target sentences given in the dataset. Rest are calculated on the outputs generated by our models.

	Validation Set	Test Set
mBART-en		
# of English tokens	3,282 (25.5%)	3,571 (27.6%)
# of Hindi tokens	8,155 (63.4%)	8,062 (62.3%)
# of 'Other' tokens	1,435 (11.1%)	1,302 (10.1%)
mBART-hien		
# of English tokens	2,462 (18.5%)	2,519 (18.8%)
# of Hindi tokens	9,471 (71.3%)	9,616 (72.0%)
# of 'Other' tokens	1,356 (10.2%)	1,233 (9.2%)

Table 5: The number of tokens of each language in our predicted translations. The language tags are based on the script of the token.

analyse the quality of translations on the test set, we randomly sampled 100 sentences (> 10% of test set) from the outputs generated by the two models: **mBART-en** and **mBART-hien**, and bucketed them into various categories. Table 3 shows the categories of errors and their corresponding frequency. Mistranslated/partially translated category indicates that the generated translation has no or very less semantic resemblance with the source sentence. Sentences, where Multi-Word Expressions/Named Entities are wrongly translated, is the second category. Morphology/Case Marking/Agreement/Syntax Issues category indicates sentences where most of the semantic content is faithfully captured in the generated output. However, the errors on a grammatical level render the output less fluent. **mBART-hien** makes fewer errors when compared to **mBART-en**, but that can possibly be attributed to the fact that this model generates a higher number of Hindi tokens while being low in code-mixing quality, and makes lesser grammatical errors. A more extensive and fine-grained analysis of these errors will undoubtedly help improve the models' characterization, and we leave it for future improvements.

5.2 Code Mixing Quality of generated translations

In the code-mixed machine translation setting, it is essential to observe the quality of the code-mixing in the generated translations. While BLEU scores indicate how close we are to the target translation in terms of n-gram overlap, a measure like Code-Mixing Index (CMI) (Gambäck and Das, 2016) provides us means to assess if the generated output is a mix of two languages or not. Relying on just the BLEU score for assessing translations can misrepresent the quality of translations, as models could generate monolingual outputs and still have a basic BLEU score due to n-gram overlap. If a measure of code mixing intensity, like CMI, is also part of the evaluation regime, we would be able to assess the code mixing quality of generated outputs as well. Figure 2 shows us that the distribution of CMI for outputs generated by our various models (mBART-en and mBART-hien) for both validation and test set.

Figure 2 and Table 4 show that the code mixing quality of the two models is is more or less similar across the validation and test set. The high

	Num of Pairs
Meaning of target similar to source	759
Meaning of target distored compared to source	141
Total	900

Table 6: Statistics of the errors in randomly sampled subset of train + dev.

percentages of sentences having a 0 CMI score shows that in a lot of sentences, the model does not actually perform code-mixing. We also find that even though the outputs generated by the **mBART-hien** model have a higher $BLEU_{normalized}$ score, the average CMI is lower and the percentage of sentences with a 0 CMI score is higher. This suggests that **mBART-hien** produces sentences with a lower amount of code-mixing. This observation, we believe, can be attributed to the **mBART-hien** model's propensity to generate a higher percentage of Hindi words, as shown in Table 5. We also find that in the train set, more than 20% of the sentences have a CMI score of 0. Replacing such samples with sentence pairs with have a higher degree of code mixing will help train the model to generate better code mixed outputs. Further analysis using different measures of code-mixing can provide deeper insights. We leave this for future work.

5.3 Erroneous Reference Translations in the dataset

We randomly sampled ∼10% (900 sentence pairs) of the parallel sentences from the train and validation set and annotated them for translation errors. For annotation, we classified the sentence pairs into one of two classes : 1) Error - semantic content in the target is distorted as compared to source; 2) No Error - semantic content of source and target are similar and the target might have minor errors. Minor errors in translations that are attributable to agreement issues, case markers issues, pronoun errors etc were classified into the No Error bucket. Out of the 900 samples that were manually annoatated, 141 samples, i.e 15% of annotated pairs, had targets whose meaning was distorted as compared to source sentence. One such example is shown below:

- **English Sentence:** I think I know the football player it was based on.
- **Hinglish Sentence:** Muje lagtha ki yeh football player ke baare mein hein.
- **Translation of Hinglish Sentence:** I thought that this is about football player.

Table 6 shows the analysis of these annotated subset. The annotated file with all 900 examples can be found in our code repository. Filtering such erroneous examples from training and validation datasets, and augmenting the dataset with better quality translations will certainly help in improving the translation quality.

6 Discussion

In this paper, we presented our approaches for English to Hinglish translation using mBART. We analyse our model's outputs and show that the translation quality can be improved by including parallel Hindi translations, along with the English sentences, while translating English sentences to Hinglish. We also discuss the limitations of using BLEU scores for evaluating code-mixed outputs and propose using $BLEU_{normalized}$ - a slightly modified version of BLEU. To understand the code-mixing quality of the generated translations, we propose that a code-mixing measure, like CMI, should also be part of the evaluation process. Along with the working models, we have analysed the model's shortcomings by doing error analysis on the outputs generated by the models. Further, we have also presented an analysis on the shared dataset : percentage of sentences in the dataset which are not code-mixed, the erroneous reference translations. Removing such pairs and replacing them with better samples will help improve the translation quality of the models.

As part of future work, we would like to improve our translation quality by augmenting the current dataset with parallel sentences with a higher degree of code-mixing and good reference translations. We would also like to further analyse the nature of code-mixing in the generated outputs, and study the possibility of constraining the models to generated translations with a certain degree of code-mixing.

References

Gustavo Aguilar, Fahad AlGhamdi, Victor Soto, Mona Diab, Julia Hirschberg, and Thamar Solorio. 2018a. Named entity recognition on code-switched data: Overview of the CALCS 2018 shared task. In *Proceedings of the Third Workshop on Computational Approaches to Linguistic Code-Switching*, pages 138–147, Melbourne, Australia. Association for Computational Linguistics.

Gustavo Aguilar, Fahad AlGhamdi, Victor Soto, Thamar Solorio, Mona Diab, and Julia Hirschberg, editors. 2018b. *Proceedings of the Third Workshop on Computational Approaches to Linguistic Code-Switching*. Association for Computational Linguistics, Melbourne, Australia.

Somnath Banerjee, Kunal Chakma, Sudip Kumar Naskar, Amitava Das, Paolo Rosso, Sivaji Bandyopadhyay, and Monojit Choudhury. 2018. Overview of the mixed script information retrieval (msir) at fire-2016. In *Text Processing*, pages 39–49, Cham. Springer International Publishing.

Hedi M. Belazi, Edward J. Rubin, and Almeida Jacqueline Toribio. 1994. Code switching and x-bar theory: The functional head constraint. *Linguistic Inquiry*, 25(2):221–237.

Irshad Bhat, Riyaz A. Bhat, Manish Shrivastava, and Dipti Sharma. 2017. Joining hands: Exploiting monolingual treebanks for parsing of code-mixing data. In *Proceedings of the 15th Conference of the European Chapter of the Association for Computational Linguistics: Volume 2, Short Papers*, pages 324–330, Valencia, Spain. Association for Computational Linguistics.

Irshad Bhat, Riyaz A. Bhat, Manish Shrivastava, and Dipti Sharma. 2018. Universal Dependency parsing for Hindi-English code-switching. In *Proceedings of the 2018 Conference of the North American Chapter of the Association for Computational Linguistics: Human Language Technologies, Volume 1 (Long Papers)*, pages 987–998, New Orleans, Louisiana. Association for Computational Linguistics.

Irshad Ahmad Bhat, Vandan Mujadia, Aniruddha Tammewar, Riyaz Ahmad Bhat, and Manish Shrivastava. 2015. Iiit-h system submission for fire2014 shared task on transliterated search. In *Proceedings of the Forum for Information Retrieval Evaluation*, FIRE '14, pages 48–53, New York, NY, USA. ACM.

Steven Bird, Ewan Klein, and Edward Loper. 2009. *Natural Language Processing with Python*. O'Reilly Media.

Khyathi Chandu, Ekaterina Loginova, Vishal Gupta, Josef van Genabith, Günter Neumann, Manoj Chinnakotla, Eric Nyberg, and Alan W. Black. 2018. Code-mixed question answering challenge: Crowdsourcing data and techniques. In *Proceedings of the Third Workshop on Computational Approaches to Linguistic Code-Switching*, pages 29–38, Melbourne, Australia. Association for Computational Linguistics.

Ching-Ting Chang, Shun-Po Chuang, and Hung-Yi Lee. 2019. Code-Switching Sentence Generation by Generative Adversarial Networks and its Application to Data Augmentation. In *Proc. Interspeech 2019*, pages 554–558.

Alexis Conneau and Guillaume Lample. 2019. Cross-lingual language model pretraining. In *Advances in Neural Information Processing Systems*, volume 32. Curran Associates, Inc.

Mrinal Dhar, Vaibhav Kumar, and Manish Shrivastava. 2018. Enabling code-mixed translation: Parallel corpus creation and MT augmentation approach. In *Proceedings of the First Workshop on Linguistic Resources for Natural Language Processing*, pages 131–140, Santa Fe, New Mexico, USA. Association for Computational Linguistics.

Mona Diab, Pascale Fung, Mahmoud Ghoneim, Julia Hirschberg, and Thamar Solorio, editors. 2016. *Proceedings of the Second Workshop on Computational Approaches to Code Switching*. Association for Computational Linguistics, Austin, Texas.

Mona Diab, Julia Hirschberg, Pascale Fung, and Thamar Solorio, editors. 2014. *Proceedings of the First Workshop on Computational Approaches to Code Switching*. Association for Computational Linguistics, Doha, Qatar.

Sergey Edunov, Alexei Baevski, and Michael Auli. 2019. Pre-trained language model representations for language generation. In *Proceedings of the 2019 Conference of the North American Chapter of the Association for Computational Linguistics: Human Language Technologies, Volume 1 (Long and Short Papers)*, pages 4052–4059, Minneapolis, Minnesota. Association for Computational Linguistics.

Björn Gambäck and Amitava Das. 2016. Comparing the level of code-switching in corpora. In *Proceedings of the Tenth International Conference on Language Resources and Evaluation (LREC'16)*, pages 1850–1855, Portorož, Slovenia. European Language Resources Association (ELRA).

Deepak Gupta, Asif Ekbal, and Pushpak Bhattacharyya. 2020. A semi-supervised approach to generate the code-mixed text using pre-trained encoder and transfer learning. In *Findings of the Association for Computational Linguistics: EMNLP 2020*, pages 2267–2280, Online. Association for Computational Linguistics.

Anupam Jamatia, Björn Gambäck, and Amitava Das. 2016. Collecting and annotating indian social media code-mixed corpora. In *International Conference on Intelligent Text Processing and Computational Linguistics*, pages 406–417. Springer.

Nal Kalchbrenner and Phil Blunsom. 2013. Recurrent continuous translation models. In *Proceedings of the 2013 Conference on Empirical Methods in Natural Language Processing*, pages 1700–1709, Seattle, Washington, USA. Association for Computational Linguistics.

Diederik P. Kingma and Jimmy Ba. 2015. Adam: A method for stochastic optimization. In *3rd International Conference on Learning Representations,*

ICLR 2015, San Diego, CA, USA, May 7-9, 2015, Conference Track Proceedings.

Anoop Kunchukuttan, Pratik Mehta, and Pushpak Bhattacharyya. 2018. The IIT Bombay English-Hindi parallel corpus. In *Proceedings of the Eleventh International Conference on Language Resources and Evaluation (LREC 2018)*, Miyazaki, Japan. European Language Resources Association (ELRA).

Mike Lewis, Yinhan Liu, Naman Goyal, Marjan Ghazvininejad, Abdelrahman Mohamed, Omer Levy, Veselin Stoyanov, and Luke Zettlemoyer. 2020. BART: Denoising sequence-to-sequence pretraining for natural language generation, translation, and comprehension. In *Proceedings of the 58th Annual Meeting of the Association for Computational Linguistics*, pages 7871–7880, Online. Association for Computational Linguistics.

Yinhan Liu, Jiatao Gu, Naman Goyal, Xian Li, Sergey Edunov, Marjan Ghazvininejad, Mike Lewis, and Luke Zettlemoyer. 2020. Multilingual denoising pre-training for neural machine translation.

Giovanni Molina, Fahad AlGhamdi, Mahmoud Ghoneim, Abdelati Hawwari, Nicolas Rey-Villamizar, Mona Diab, and Thamar Solorio. 2016. Overview for the second shared task on language identification in code-switched data. In *Proceedings of the Second Workshop on Computational Approaches to Code Switching*, pages 40–49, Austin, Texas. Association for Computational Linguistics.

Myle Ott, Sergey Edunov, Alexei Baevski, Angela Fan, Sam Gross, Nathan Ng, David Grangier, and Michael Auli. 2019. fairseq: A fast, extensible toolkit for sequence modeling. In *Proceedings of the 2019 Conference of the North American Chapter of the Association for Computational Linguistics (Demonstrations)*, pages 48–53, Minneapolis, Minnesota. Association for Computational Linguistics.

Kishore Papineni, Salim Roukos, Todd Ward, and Wei-Jing Zhu. 2002. Bleu: a method for automatic evaluation of machine translation. In *Proceedings of the 40th Annual Meeting of the Association for Computational Linguistics*, pages 311–318, Philadelphia, Pennsylvania, USA. Association for Computational Linguistics.

Braja Gopal Patra, Dipankar Das, and Amitava Das. 2018. Sentiment analysis of code-mixed indian languages: An overview of sail_code-mixed shared task @icon-2017.

Parth Patwa, Gustavo Aguilar, Sudipta Kar, Suraj Pandey, Srinivas PYKL, Björn Gambäck, Tanmoy Chakraborty, Thamar Solorio, and Amitava Das. 2020. SemEval-2020 task 9: Overview of sentiment analysis of code-mixed tweets. In *Proceedings of the Fourteenth Workshop on Semantic Evaluation*, pages 774–790, Barcelona (online). International Committee for Computational Linguistics.

Shana Poplack. 1980. Sometimes i'll start a sentence in spanish y termino en espaÑol: toward a typology of code-switching 1. *Linguistics*, 18:581–618.

Matt Post. 2018. A call for clarity in reporting BLEU scores. In *Proceedings of the Third Conference on Machine Translation: Research Papers*, pages 186–191, Brussels, Belgium. Association for Computational Linguistics.

Adithya Pratapa, Gayatri Bhat, Monojit Choudhury, Sunayana Sitaram, Sandipan Dandapat, and Kalika Bali. 2018. Language modeling for code-mixing: The role of linguistic theory based synthetic data. In *Proceedings of the 56th Annual Meeting of the Association for Computational Linguistics (Volume 1: Long Papers)*, pages 1543–1553, Melbourne, Australia. Association for Computational Linguistics.

Pattabhi R. K. Rao and S. Devi. 2016. Cmee-il: Code mix entity extraction in indian languages from social media text @ fire 2016 - an overview. In *FIRE*.

Mohd Sanad Zaki Rizvi, Anirudh Srinivasan, Tanuja Ganu, Monojit Choudhury, and Sunayana Sitaram. 2021. GCM: A toolkit for generating synthetic code-mixed text. In *Proceedings of the 16th Conference of the European Chapter of the Association for Computational Linguistics: System Demonstrations*, pages 205–211, Online. Association for Computational Linguistics.

Brian Roark, Lawrence Wolf-Sonkin, Christo Kirov, Sabrina J. Mielke, Cibu Johny, Isin Demirsahin, and Keith Hall. 2020. Processing South Asian languages written in the Latin script: the dakshina dataset. In *Proceedings of the 12th Language Resources and Evaluation Conference*, pages 2413–2423, Marseille, France. European Language Resources Association.

Rishiraj Saha Roy, Monojit Choudhury, Prasenjit Majumder, and Komal Agarwal. 2013. Overview of the fire 2013 track on transliterated search. In *Post-Proceedings of the 4th and 5th Workshops of the Forum for Information Retrieval Evaluation*, FIRE '12 & '13, New York, NY, USA. Association for Computing Machinery.

Bidisha Samanta, Sharmila Reddy, Hussain Jagirdar, Niloy Ganguly, and Soumen Chakrabarti. 2019. A deep generative model for code switched text. In *Proceedings of the Twenty-Eighth International Joint Conference on Artificial Intelligence, IJCAI-19*, pages 5175–5181. International Joint Conferences on Artificial Intelligence Organization.

Thoudam Doren Singh and Thamar Solorio. 2018. Towards translating mixed-code comments from social media. In *Computational Linguistics and Intelligent Text Processing*, pages 457–468, Cham. Springer International Publishing.

Thamar Solorio, Elizabeth Blair, Suraj Maharjan, Steven Bethard, Mona Diab, Mahmoud

Ghoneim, Abdelati Hawwari, Fahad AlGhamdi, Julia Hirschberg, Alison Chang, and Pascale Fung. 2014. Overview for the first shared task on language identification in code-switched data. In *Proceedings of the First Workshop on Computational Approaches to Code Switching*, pages 62–72, Doha, Qatar. Association for Computational Linguistics.

Kaitao Song, Xu Tan, Tao Qin, Jianfeng Lu, and Tie-Yan Liu. 2019. MASS: Masked sequence to sequence pre-training for language generation. In *Proceedings of the 36th International Conference on Machine Learning*, volume 97 of *Proceedings of Machine Learning Research*, pages 5926–5936. PMLR.

Vivek Srivastava and Mayank Singh. 2020. PHINC: A parallel Hinglish social media code-mixed corpus for machine translation. In *Proceedings of the Sixth Workshop on Noisy User-generated Text (W-NUT 2020)*, pages 41–49, Online. Association for Computational Linguistics.

Ashish Vaswani, Noam Shazeer, Niki Parmar, Jakob Uszkoreit, Llion Jones, Aidan N Gomez, Ł ukasz Kaiser, and Illia Polosukhin. 2017. Attention is all you need. In *Advances in Neural Information Processing Systems*, volume 30. Curran Associates, Inc.

Genta Indra Winata, Andrea Madotto, Chien-Sheng Wu, and Pascale Fung. 2019. Code-switched language models using neural based synthetic data from parallel sentences. In *Proceedings of the 23rd Conference on Computational Natural Language Learning (CoNLL)*, pages 271–280, Hong Kong, China. Association for Computational Linguistics.

Yonghui Wu, Mike Schuster, Zhifeng Chen, Quoc V. Le, Mohammad Norouzi, Wolfgang Macherey, Maxim Krikun, Yuan Cao, Qin Gao, Klaus Macherey, Jeff Klingner, Apurva Shah, Melvin Johnson, Xiaobing Liu, Łukasz Kaiser, Stephan Gouws, Yoshikiyo Kato, Taku Kudo, Hideto Kazawa, Keith Stevens, George Kurian, Nishant Patil, Wei Wang, Cliff Young, Jason Smith, Jason Riesa, Alex Rudnick, Oriol Vinyals, Greg Corrado, Macduff Hughes, and Jeffrey Dean. 2016. Google's neural machine translation system: Bridging the gap between human and machine translation. *CoRR*, abs/1609.08144.

Investigating Code-Mixed Modern Standard Arabic-Egyptian to English Machine Translation

El Moatez Billah Nagoudi   AbdelRahim Elmadany   Muhammad Abdul-Mageed
Natural Language Processing Lab
The University of British Columbia
{moatez.nagoudi,a.elmadany,muhammad.mageed}@ubc.ca

Abstract

Recent progress in neural machine translation (NMT) has made it possible to translate successfully between monolingual language pairs where large parallel data exist, with pre-trained models improving performance even further. Although there exists work on translating in code-mixed settings (where one of the pairs includes text from two or more languages), it is still unclear what recent success in NMT and language modeling exactly means for translating code-mixed text. We investigate one such context, namely MT from code-mixed Modern Standard Arabic and Egyptian Arabic (MSAEA) into English. We develop models under different conditions, employing both (i) standard end-to-end sequence-to-sequence (S2S) Transformers trained from scratch and (ii) pre-trained S2S language models (LMs). We are able to acquire reasonable performance using only MSA-EN parallel data with S2S models trained from scratch. We also find LMs fine-tuned on data from various Arabic dialects to help the MSAEA-EN task. Our work is in the context of the Shared Task on Machine Translation in Code-Switching. Our best model achieves **25.72** BLEU, placing us first on the official shared task evaluation for MSAEA-EN.

	(1) MSAEA	أنا عايز شغل جامد يا جدعان.
English	**Human**	I want hard work, guys.
	GMT	I want a rigid job, Jadaan.
	S2ST	I want a solid job, jadan.
	(2) MSAEA	الدكاترة قالو انى مش همشي طبيعى تانى.
English	**Human**	The doctors said I can't walk normally again.
	GMT	The doctors said that I was not a normal marginal again.
	S2ST	Doctors said I wasn't a natural marginality again.

Table 1: Code-mixed Modern Standard Arabic-Egyptian Arabic (MSAEA) sentences with their English human translation, Google machine translation (GMT)[1], and translation by a sequence-to-sequence Transformer model (S2ST) trained from scratch on 55M MSA-English parallel sentences. **Green** refers to good translations. **Red** refers to erroneous translation.

1 Introduction

Recent year have witnessed fast progress in various areas of natural language processing (NLP), including machine translation (MT) where neural approaches have helped boost performance when translating between pairs with especially large amounts of parallel data. However, tasks involving a need to process data from different languages mixed together remain challenging for all NLP tasks. This phenomenon of using two or more languages simultaneously in speech or text is referred to as *code-mixing* (Gumperz, 1982) and is prevalent in multilingual societies (Sitaram et al., 2019). Code-mixing is challenging since the space of possibilities when processing mixed data is vast, but also because there is not usually sufficient code-mixed resources to train models on. Nor is it clear how much code-mixing existing language models may have seen during pre-training, and so ability of these language models to transfer knowledge to downstream code-mixing tasks remain largely unexplored.

In this work, we investigate translation under a code-mixing scenario where sequences at source side are a combination of two varieties of the collection of languages referred to as Arabic. More

[1] We use Google Translate API `https://cloud.google.com/translate`.

Proceedings of the Fifth Workshop on Computational Approaches to Linguistic Code-Switching, pages 56–64
June 11, 2021. ©2021 Association for Computational Linguistics
https://doi.org/10.26615/978-954-452-056-4_008

specifically, we take as our objective translating between Modern Standard Arabic (MSA) mixed with Egyptian Arabic (EA) (source; collectively abbreviated here as MSAEA) into English (target). Table1 shows two examples of MSAEA sentences and their human and machine translations. We highlight problematic translations caused by nixing of Egyptian Arabic with MSA. Through work related to the shared task, we target the following three main research questions:

1. *How do models trained from scratch on purely MSA data fare on the code-mixed MSAEA data (i.e., the zero-shot EA setting)?*
2. *How do existing language models perform under the code-mixed condition (i.e., MSAEA)?*
3. *What impact, if any, does exploiting dialectal Arabic (DA) data (i.e., from a range of dialects) have on the MSAEA code-mixed MT context?*

Our main contributions in this work lie primarily in answering these three questions. We also develop powerful models for translating from MSAEA to English.

The rest of the paper is organized as follows: Section 2 discusses related work. The shared task is described in Section 3. Section 4 describes external parallel data we exploit to build our models. Section 5 presents the proposed MT models. Section 6 presents our experiments, and our different settings. We provide evaluation on Dev data in Section 7 and official results in Section 8. We conclude in Section 9.

2 Related Work

A thread of research on code-mixed MT focuses on automatically generating synthetic code-mixed data to improve the downstream task. This includes attempts to generate linguistically-motivated sequences (Pratapa et al., 2018). Some work leverages sequence-to-sequence (S2S) models (Winata et al., 2019) to generate code-mixing exploiting an external neural MT system, while others (Garg et al., 2018) use a recurrent neural network along with data generated by a sequence generative adversarial network (SeqGAN) and grammatical information such as from a part of speech tagger to generate code-mixed sequences. These methods have dependencies and can be costly to scale beyond one language pair.

Arabic MT. For Arabic, some work has focused on translating between MSA and Arabic dialects. For instance, Zbib et al. (2012) studied the impact of combined dialectal and MSA data on dialect/MSA to English MT performance. Sajjad et al. (2013) uses MSA as a pivot language for translating Arabic dialects into English. Salloum et al. (2014) investigate the effect of sentence-level dialect identification and several linguistic features for MSA/dialect-English translation. Guellil et al. (2017) propose an neural machine translation (NMT) system for Arabic dialects using a vanilla recurrent neural networks (RNN) encoder-decoder model for translating Algerian Arabic written in a mixture of Arabizi and Arabic characters into MSA. Baniata et al. (2018) present an NMT system to translate Levantine (Jordanian, Syrian, and Palestinian) and Maghrebi (Algerian, Moroccan, Tunisia) to MSA, and MSA to English. Farhan et al. (2020), propose unsupervised dialectal NMT, where the source dialect is not represented in training data. This last problem is referred to as zero-shot MT (Lample et al., 2018).

DA Arabic MT Resources. There are also efforts to develop dialectal Arabic MT resources. For example, Meftouh et al. (2015) present the Parallel Arabic Dialect Corpus (PADIC),[2] which is a multi-dialect corpus including MSA, Algerian, Tunisian, Palestinian, and Syrian. Recently, Sajjad et al. (2020a) also introduced AraBench, an evaluation suite for dialectal Arabic to English MT. AraBench consists of five publicly available datasets: Arabic-Dialect/English Parallel Text (APT) (Zbib et al., 2012), Multi-dialectal Parallel Corpus of Arabic (MDC) (Bouamor et al., 2014), MADAR Corpus (Bouamor et al., 2018), Qatari-English speech corpus (Elmahdy et al., 2014), and the English Bible translated into MSA.[3]

3 Code-Switching Shared Task

The goal of the shared tasks on machine translation in code-switching settings[4] is to encourage building MT systems that translate a source sentence into a target sentence while one of the directions contains

[2] https://sites.google.com/site/torjmanepnr/6-corpus

[3] The United Bible Societies https://www.bible.com

[4] https://code-switching.github.io/2021.

an alternation between two languages (i.e., code-switching). We note that, in the current paper, we employ the wider term *code-mixing*. The shared task involves two subtasks:

1. **Supervised MT.** For supervised MT, gold data are provided to participants for training and evaluating models that take English as input and generate Hinglish sequences.

2. **Unsupervised MT.** In this subtask, the goal is to develop systems that can generate high quality translations for multiple language combinations. These combinations include Spanish-English to English or Spanish, English to Spanish-English, Modern Standard Arabic-Egyptian Arabic (MSAEA) to English and vice versa. For each pair, only test data are provided to participants, with no reference translations.

In the current work, we focus on the unsupervised MT subtask only. More specifically, we build models exclusively for MSAEA to English. Our approach exploits external data to train a variety of models. We now describe these external datasets.

Data	#Sentences
Bible	62.2K
EUbookshop	1.7K
GlobalVoices	52.6K
Gnome	150
Infopankki	50.8K
KDE4	116.2K
MultiUN	9.8M
News Commentary	90.1K
OpenSubtitles	29.8M
QED	500.9K
Tanzil	187K
Tatoeba	27.3K
TED2013	152.8K
Ubuntu	6K
UN	74.1K
UNPC	20M
Wikipedia	151.1K
Total	61M
Similarity $\in$ [0.3 - 0.99]	5.7M
***N*-gram deduplication** (>0.75)	55.2M

Table 2: Parallel datasets extracted from OPUS (Tiedemann, 2012). We remove duplicate and identical pairs, keeping only high quality translations.

4 Parallel Datasets

4.1 MSA-English Data

In order to develop Arabic MT models that can translate efficiently across different text domains, we make use of a large collection of parallel sentences extracted from the Open Parallel Corpus (OPUS) (Tiedemann, 2012). OPUS contains more than 2.7 billion parallel sentences in 90 languages. To train our models, we extract more than $\sim$ 61M sentences MSA-English parallel sentences from the whole collection. Since OPUS can have noise and duplicate data, we clean this collection and remove duplicates before we use it. We now describe our quality assurance method for cleaning and deduplication of the data.

Data Quality Assurance. To keep only high quality parallel sentences, we follow two steps:

1. We run a cross-lingual semantic similarity model (Yang et al., 2019) on each pair of sentences, keeping only sentences with a bilingual similarity score between 0.30 and 0.99. This allows us to filter out sentence pairs whose source and target are identical (i.e., similarity score = 1) and those that are not good translations of one another (i.e., those with a cross-lingual semantic similarity score < 0.3).

2. Observing some English sentences in the source data, we perform an analysis based on sub-string matching between source and target, using the word trigram sliding window method proposed by Barrón-Cedeño and Rosso (2009) and used in Abdul-Mageed et al. (2021) to de-duplicate the data splits. In other words, we compare each sentence in the source side (i.e., MSA) to the target sentence (i.e., English). We then inspect all pairs of sentences that match higher than a given threshold, considering thresholds between 90% and 30%. We find that a threshold of $> 75\%$ safely guarantees completely distinct source and target pairs.

More details about the MSA-English OPUS dataset before and after our quality assurance, including deduplication, are provided in Table 2.

Dataset	Egyptian	Levantine	Gulf
Bouamor et al. (2018)	18K	22K	26K
Elmahdy et al. (2014)	–	–	14.7K
Zbib et al. (2012)	38K	138K	–
Total	56K	160K	40.7K

Table 3: Our parallel DA-English datasets. Gulf comprises data from Bouamor et al. (2018), Elmahdy et al. (2014) , and Zbib et al. (2012).

4.2 Dialectal Arabic-English Data

Several recent works show that MT models trained on one dialect can be used to improve models targeting other dialects (Farhan et al., 2020; Sajjad et al., 2020b). For this reason, we exploit several parallel dialectal Arabic (DA)-English datasets in order to enhance the MSAEA to English translation.

DA-English Parallel Corpus. Zbib et al. (2012) provide 38k Egyptian Arabic (EA)-English and 138k Levantine-English sentences ($\sim$ 3.5 million tokens of Arabic dialects), collected from online user groups and dialectal Arabic weblogs. The authors use crowdsourcing to translate this dataset into English.

MADAR Corpus. MADAR Bouamor et al. (2018) is a commissioned dataset where 26 Arabic native speakers were tasked to translate 2k English sentences each into their own native dialect. In addition, Bouamor et al. (2018) translate 10k more sentences for five selected cities: Beirut, Cairo, Doha, Cairo, Tunis, and Rabat. The MADAR dataset also has region-level categorization (i.e., Gulf, Levantine, Nile, and Maghrebi). In our work, we use only the Gulf, Levantine, and Nile (Egyptian) dialects, and exclude Maghrebi.[5]

Qatari-English Speech Corpus. This parallel corpus comprises 14.7k Qatari-English sentences collected by Elmahdy et al. (2014) from talk-show programs and Qatari TV series.

More details about all our parallel dialectal-English datasets are in Table 3.

4.3 Data Splits and Pre-Processing

Data Splits. For our experiments, we split the MSA and DA data as follows:

MSA. We randomly pick 10k sentences for validation (MSA-Dev) from MSA parallel data (see Section 4.1) after cleaning, and we use the rest of this data ($\sim$ 55.14M) for training (MSA-Train).

DA. For validation (DA-Dev), we randomly pick 6k sentences from the 38k Egyptian-English data provided by Zbib et al. (2012). We then use the rest of the data (i.e., $\sim$ 250.7k) for training (DA-Train).

Pre-Processing. Pre-processing is an important step for building any MT model as it can significantly affect end results (Oudah et al., 2019). For all our models, we only perform light pre-processing in order to retain a faithful representation of the original (naturally occurring) text. We remove diacritics and replace URLs, user mentions, and hashtags with the generic string tokens `URL`, `USER`, and `HASHTAG` respectively. Our second step for pre-processing is specific to each type of models we train as we will explain in the respective sections.

5 MT Models

5.1 From-Scratch Seq2Seq Models

We train our models on the MSA-English parallel data described in section 4.1 on MSA-Train with a Transformer (Vaswani et al., 2017) model as implemented in Fairseq (Ott et al., 2019). For that, we follow Ott et al. (2018) in using 6 blocks for each of the encoder and decoder parts. We use a learning rate of 0.25, a dropout of 0.3, and a batch size 4,000 tokens. For the optimizer, we use Adam (Kingma and Ba, 2014) with beta coefficients of 0.9 and 0.99 which control an exponential decay rate of running averages, with a weight decay of 10^{-4}. We also apply an inverse square-root learning rate scheduler with a value of $5e^{-4}$ and 4,000 warm-up updates. For the loss function, we use label smoothed cross entropy with a smoothing strength of 0.1. We run the Moses tokenizer (Koehn et al., 2007) on our input before passing data to the model. For vocabulary, we use a joint Byte-Pair Encoding (BPE) (Sennrich et al., 2015) vocabulary with 64K split operations for subword segmentation.

5.2 Pre-Trained Seq2Seq Language Models

We also fine-tune two state-of-the-art pre-trained multilingual generative models, mT5 (Xue et al., 2020) and mBART (Liu et al., 2020) on DA-Train for 100 epochs. We use early stopping during fine-tuning and identify the best model on DA-Dev. We use the HuggingFace (Wolf et al., 2020) implemen-

[5]We do not make use of the Maghrebi data due to the considerable linguistic differences between Maghrebi and the the Egyptian dialect we target in this work.

Source:	مش عارفين نتأكد و مش عارفين البنات فين.
S2ST	we don't know for sure and the girls don't know finn .
mT5	we can't make sure and we don't know where the girls are
mBART	we don't know where to make sure and we don't know where the girls are
Source:	انا عايز اعرف موقف الاخوان الرسمي من التحرش بالحريري و نجاد البرعي ولو البلطجية دول مش تبعهم الرئيس يستعمل سلطته.
S2ST	i want to know the brothers' official position on harassment of liberals and nejad al-barai, even the thugs, countries that are not followed by the president are using his authority and ordering their immediate arrest.
mT5	i want to know the situation of the official brothers from harassment of the silky and najad albarea and if these pants are not their president the president uses his power and order to arrest them immediately
mBART	i want to know the position of the official brothers from harassment in the army and najad al-bara'y, even if these are not theirs , the president should use his authority and order to arrest them immediately
Source:	"user : عاوزين محامي يروح معانا القسم يا جدعان صبحي ووليد تليفوناتهم مقفولة."
S2ST	user: there is a need for a lawyer to help the section, jadan sobhi and walid televonas closed .
mT5	user: we want a lawyer to go with us to the section , guys , sobhe and waleed their telephones are closed
mBART	« user : we want a lawyer to go with us to the section, oh good morning, and their telephones are closed. »
Source	بيعقدوا الجلسات في أماكن مش محاكم ، و ما ينفعش خلق الله يدخلوا من غير تصريح ، عشان المتهمين لما ييجوا يمنعوهم و يحكموا غيابي !!
S2ST	they hold hearings in places where there are no courts, and what thrives on god's creation will enter without permission, because the accused will not prevent them and judge my absence!
mT5	they have sessions in places that are not courts, and god doesn't allow people to enter without a permit, so that when they come and prevent them and rule me absence
mBART	they hold meetings in places where there is no courts, and god doesn't allow people to enter without a permit, so that when the accused come they stop them and rule them

Table 4: MSA-EA sentences with their English translations using our Models. **S2ST:** Sequence-to-sequence Transformer model trained from scratch. Data samples are extracted from the shared task Test data. **Green** refers to good translation. **Red** refers to problematic translation.

tation of each of these models, with the default settings for all hyper-parameters.

6 Experiments and Settings

In this section, we describe the different ways we fine-tune and evaluate our models.

6.1 Zero-Shot Setting

First, we use S2ST model trained on MSA-English data exclusively to evaluate MSAEA code-mixed data . While we can refer to this setting as *zero-shot*, we note that it is not truly zero-shot in the strict sense of the word due to the code-mixed nature of the data (i.e., the data has a mixture of MSA and EA). Hence, we will refer to this setting as *zero-shot EA*.

6.2 Fine-Tuning Setting

Second, we further fine-tune the three models (i.e., S2ST, mT5, and mBART) on the DA data described in Section 4.2. While the downstream shared task data only involves EA mixed with MSA, we follow Farhan et al. (2020) and Sajjad et al. (2020b) in fine-tuning on different dialects when targeting a single downstream dialect (EA in our case). We will simply refer to this second setting as *Fine-Tuned DA*.

Model	Setting	Blue
S2ST	Zero Shot EA	8.54
	Fine-tuned DA	9.33
	Zero Shot EA (true-cased)	11.59
	Fine-tuned DA (true-cased)	12.57
mT5	Fine-tuned DA	24.70
	Fine-tuned DA (true-cased)	26.35
mBART	Fine-tuned DA	23.80
	Fine-tuned DA (true-cased)	**26.07**

Table 5: Results of models on DA-Dev data. **S2ST:** Sequence-to-sequence Transformer model trained from scratch. We note that in the zero-shot EA setting the S2ST model is trained on 55M bitext sentences.

7 Evaluation on Dev Data

We report results of all our models under different settings in BLEU scores (Papineni et al., 2002). In addition to evaluation on uncased data, we run a language modeling based truecaser (Lita et al., 2003) on the outputs of our different models.[6] Results presented in Table 5 show that S2ST achieves relatively low scores (between 8.54 and 12.57) on all settings. In comparison, both mBART and mT5 fine-tuned on DA-Train are able to translate MSAEA to English with BLEU scores of 23.80 and 24.70 respectively. We note that truecasing the output results in improving the results with an average of +2.55 BLEU points.

8 Official Shared Task (Test) Results

Table 7 shows results of all our MT models with different settings on the official shared task Test set. We observe that the Transformer model in the *zero shot EA* setting (a model that does not see Egyptian Arabic data) was able to translate MSAEA to English with 21.34 BLEU. As expected, fine-tuning all the models on DA-Train improves results across all models and leads to the best BLEU score of 25.72% with the S2ST model.

Comparing performance of the S2ST model on Dev and Test data, we observe that Test data results are better. This suggests that Test data comprises more MSA than EA sequences. To test this hypothesis, we run a binary MSA-DA classifier Abdul-Mageed et al. (2020) on both the Dev and Test data to acquire MSA and DA distributions on each

[6]We were not been able to report results based on truecasing in this paper, but we note that we will provide these results in the camera ready version of this paper.

Dataset	#Size	MSA	DA
DA-Dev	6,164	18.36%	81.64%
Official Test	6,500	72.31%	27.69%

Table 6: The data distribution (MSA Vs DA) in the DA-Dev and the official Test set.

dataset. Results of this analysis, shown in Table 6, confirm our hypothesis about Test data involving significantly more MSA (i.e., 72.31%) compared to Dev data.

Model	Setting	Blue
S2ST	Zero Shot EA	21.34
	Fine-tuned DA	22.51
	Zero Shot EA (true-cased)	23.68
	Fine-tuned DA (true-cased)	**25.72**
mT5	Fine-tuned DA	16.41
	Fine-tuned DA (true-cased)	18.80
mBART	Fine-tuned DA	17.17
	Fine-tuned DA (true-cased)	19.79

Table 7: Results of our models on official Test data. Again, in the zero-shot EA setting the S2ST model is trained on 55M bitext sentences,

Discussion. We inspect output translations from our models on Test data. We observe that even though S2ST performs better than the two language models on Test data, both of these models are especially able to translate Egyptian Arabic tokens such as فين in example (1) in Table 4 well. Again, Test data contain more MSA than DA as we explained earlier and hence the S2ST model (which is trained on 55M sentence pairs) outperforms each of the two language models. This analysis suggests that fine-tuning the language models on more MSA-ENG should result in better performance.

Returning to our three main research questions, we can reach a number of conclusions. For **RQ1**, we observe that models trained from scratch on purely MSA data fare reasonably well on the code-mixed MSAEA data (i.e., *zero-shot EA* setting). This is due to lexical overlap between MSA and EA. For **RQ2**, we also note that language models such as mT5 and mBART do well under the code-mixed condition, more so than models trained from scratch when inference data involve more EA. This is the case even though these language models in our experiments are fine-tuned with significantly less data (i.e., $\sim$ 250K pairs) than the from-scratch S2ST models (which are trained on 55M MSA + 250K DA pairs). For **RQ3**, our results show that training on data from various Arabic dialects helps translation in the MSAEA code-mixed condition. This is in line with previous research (Farhan et al., 2020) showing that exploiting data from various dialects can help downstream translation on a single dialect dialect in the zero-shot setting.

9 Conclusion

We described our contribution to the shared tasks on MT in code-switching.[7] Our models target the MSAEA to English task under the unsupervised condition. Our experiments show that training models on MSA data is useful for the MSAEA-to-English task in the zero-shot EA setting. We also show the utility of pre-trained language models such as mT5 and mBART on the code-mixing task. Our models place first in the official shared task evaluation. In the future, we intend to apply our methods on other dialects of Arabic and investigate other methods such as backtranslation for improving overall performance.

Acknowledgements

We gratefully acknowledges support from the Natural Sciences and Engineering Research Council of Canada, the Social Sciences and Humanities Research Council of Canada, Canadian Foundation for Innovation, Compute Canada (`www.computecanada.ca`) and UBC ARC-Sockeye (`https://doi.org/10.14288/SOCKEYE`) and Penguin Computing POD™ (`pod.penguincomputing.com`).

References

Muhammad Abdul-Mageed, AbdelRahim Elmadany, and El Moatez Billah Nagoudi. 2020. ARBERT & MARBERT: Deep Bidirectional Transformers for Arabic. *arXiv preprint arXiv:2101.01785*.

Muhammad Abdul-Mageed, AbdelRahim Elmadany, Dinesh Pabbi, Kunal Verma, Rannie Lin, et al. 2021. Mega-cov: A billion-scale dataset of 100+ languages for covid-19. In *Proceedings of the 16th Conference of the European Chapter of the Association for Computational Linguistics: Main Volume*, pages 3402–3420.

Laith H Baniata, Seyoung Park, and Seong-Bae Park. 2018. A neural machine translation model for arabic dialects that utilizes multitask learning (mtl). *Computational intelligence and neuroscience*, 2018.

Alberto Barrón-Cedeño and Paolo Rosso. 2009. On automatic plagiarism detection based on n-grams comparison. In *European conference on information retrieval*, pages 696–700. Springer.

Houda Bouamor, Nizar Habash, and Kemal Oflazer. 2014. A multidialectal parallel corpus of arabic. In *LREC*, pages 1240–1245.

Houda Bouamor, Nizar Habash, Mohammad Salameh, Wajdi Zaghouani, Owen Rambow, Dana Abdulrahim, Ossama Obeid, Salam Khalifa, Fadhl Eryani, Alexander Erdmann, and Kemal Oflazer. 2018. The MADAR Arabic dialect corpus and lexicon. In *Proceedings of the Eleventh International Conference on Language Resources and Evaluation (LREC 2018)*, Miyazaki, Japan. European Language Resources Association (ELRA).

Mohamed Elmahdy, Mark Hasegawa-Johnson, and Eiman Mustafawi. 2014. Development of a tv broadcasts speech recognition system for qatari arabic. In *LREC*, pages 3057–3061.

Wael Farhan, Bashar Talafha, Analle Abuammar, Ruba Jaikat, Mahmoud Al-Ayyoub, Ahmad Bisher Tarakji, and Anas Toma. 2020. Unsupervised dialectal neural machine translation. *Information Processing & Management*, 57(3):102181.

Saurabh Garg, Tanmay Parekh, and Preethi Jyothi. 2018. Code-switched language models using dual RNNs and same-source pretraining. In *Proceedings of the 2018 Conference on Empirical Methods in Natural Language Processing*, pages 3078–3083, Brussels, Belgium. Association for Computational Linguistics.

Imane Guellil, Faical Azouaou, and Mourad Abbas. 2017. Neural vs statistical translation of algerian arabic dialect written with arabizi and arabic letter. In *The 31st Pacific Asia Conference on Language, Information and Computation PACLIC*, volume 31, page 2017.

John J. Gumperz. 1982. *Discourse Strategies*. Studies in Interactional Sociolinguistics. Cambridge University Press.

Diederik P Kingma and Jimmy Ba. 2014. Adam: A method for stochastic optimization. *arXiv preprint arXiv:1412.6980*.

Philipp Koehn, Marcello Federico, Wade Shen, Nicola Bertoldi, Ondrej Bojar, Chris Callison-Burch, Brooke Cowan, Chris Dyer, Hieu Hoang, Richard Zens, et al. 2007. Open source toolkit for statistical machine translation: Factored translation models and confusion network decoding. In *Final Report of the Johns Hopkins 2006 Summer Workshop*.

[7]https://code-switching.github.io/2021

Guillaume Lample, Myle Ott, Alexis Conneau, Ludovic Denoyer, and Marc'Aurelio Ranzato. 2018. Phrase-based & neural unsupervised machine translation. *arXiv preprint arXiv:1804.07755*.

Lucian Vlad Lita, Abe Ittycheriah, Salim Roukos, and Nanda Kambhatla. 2003. Truecasing. In *Proceedings of the 41st Annual Meeting of the Association for Computational Linguistics*, pages 152–159.

Yinhan Liu, Jiatao Gu, Naman Goyal, Xian Li, Sergey Edunov, Marjan Ghazvininejad, Mike Lewis, and Luke Zettlemoyer. 2020. Multilingual denoising pre-training for neural machine translation. *Transactions of the Association for Computational Linguistics*, 8:726–742.

Karima Meftouh, Salima Harrat, Salma Jamoussi, Mourad Abbas, and Kamel Smaili. 2015. Machine translation experiments on PADIC: A parallel Arabic DIalect corpus. In *Proceedings of the 29th Pacific Asia Conference on Language, Information and Computation*, pages 26–34, Shanghai, China.

Myle Ott, Sergey Edunov, Alexei Baevski, Angela Fan, Sam Gross, Nathan Ng, David Grangier, and Michael Auli. 2019. fairseq: A fast, extensible toolkit for sequence modeling. *arXiv preprint arXiv:1904.01038*.

Myle Ott, Sergey Edunov, David Grangier, and Michael Auli. 2018. Scaling neural machine translation. *arXiv preprint arXiv:1806.00187*.

Mai Oudah, Amjad Almahairi, and Nizar Habash. 2019. The impact of preprocessing on arabic-english statistical and neural machine translation. *arXiv preprint arXiv:1906.11751*.

Kishore Papineni, Salim Roukos, Todd Ward, and Wei-Jing Zhu. 2002. Bleu: a method for automatic evaluation of machine translation. In *Proceedings of the 40th annual meeting of the Association for Computational Linguistics*, pages 311–318.

Adithya Pratapa, Gayatri Bhat, Monojit Choudhury, Sunayana Sitaram, Sandipan Dandapat, and Kalika Bali. 2018. Language modeling for code-mixing: The role of linguistic theory based synthetic data. In *Proceedings of the 56th Annual Meeting of the Association for Computational Linguistics (Volume 1: Long Papers)*, pages 1543–1553, Melbourne, Australia. Association for Computational Linguistics.

Hassan Sajjad, Ahmed Abdelali, Nadir Durrani, and Fahim Dalvi. 2020a. Arabench: Benchmarking dialectal arabic-english machine translation. In *Proceedings of the 28th International Conference on Computational Linguistics*, pages 5094–5107.

Hassan Sajjad, Ahmed Abdelali, Nadir Durrani, and Fahim Dalvi. 2020b. AraBench: Benchmarking dialectal Arabic-English machine translation. In *Proceedings of the 28th International Conference on Computational Linguistics*, pages 5094–5107, Barcelona, Spain (Online). International Committee on Computational Linguistics.

Hassan Sajjad, Kareem Darwish, and Yonatan Belinkov. 2013. Translating dialectal arabic to english. In *Proceedings of the 51st Annual Meeting of the Association for Computational Linguistics (Volume 2: Short Papers)*, pages 1–6.

Wael Salloum, Heba Elfardy, Linda Alamir-Salloum, Nizar Habash, and Mona Diab. 2014. Sentence level dialect identification for machine translation system selection. In *Proceedings of the 52nd Annual Meeting of the Association for Computational Linguistics (Volume 2: Short Papers)*, pages 772–778.

Rico Sennrich, Barry Haddow, and Alexandra Birch. 2015. Neural machine translation of rare words with subword units. *arXiv preprint arXiv:1508.07909*.

Sunayana Sitaram, Khyathi Raghavi Chandu, Sai Krishna Rallabandi, and Alan W. Black. 2019. A survey of code-switched speech and language processing. *CoRR*, abs/1904.00784.

Jörg Tiedemann. 2012. Parallel data, tools and interfaces in opus. 2012:2214–2218.

Ashish Vaswani, Noam Shazeer, Niki Parmar, Jakob Uszkoreit, Llion Jones, Aidan N Gomez, ukasz Kaiser, and Illia Polosukhin. 2017. Attention is all you need. In *Advances in neural information processing systems*, pages 5998–6008.

Genta Indra Winata, Andrea Madotto, Chien-Sheng Wu, and Pascale Fung. 2019. Code-switched language models using neural based synthetic data from parallel sentences. In *Proceedings of the 23rd Conference on Computational Natural Language Learning (CoNLL)*, pages 271–280, Hong Kong, China. Association for Computational Linguistics.

Thomas Wolf, Julien Chaumond, Lysandre Debut, Victor Sanh, Clement Delangue, Anthony Moi, Pierric Cistac, Morgan Funtowicz, Joe Davison, Sam Shleifer, et al. 2020. Transformers: State-of-the-art natural language processing. In *Proceedings of the 2020 Conference on Empirical Methods in Natural Language Processing: System Demonstrations*, pages 38–45.

Linting Xue, Noah Constant, Adam Roberts, Mihir Kale, Rami Al-Rfou, Aditya Siddhant, Aditya Barua, and Colin Raffel. 2020. mT5: A massively multilingual pre-trained text-to-text transformer.

Yinfei Yang, Daniel Cer, Amin Ahmad, Mandy Guo, Jax Law, Noah Constant, Gustavo Hernandez Abrego, Steve Yuan, Chris Tar, Yun-Hsuan Sung, et al. 2019. Multilingual universal sentence encoder for semantic retrieval. *arXiv preprint arXiv:1907.04307*.

Rabih Zbib, Erika Malchiodi, Jacob Devlin, David Stallard, Spyros Matsoukas, Richard Schwartz, John Makhoul, Omar Zaidan, and Chris Callison-Burch.

2012. Machine translation of arabic dialects. In *Proceedings of the 2012 conference of the north american chapter of the association for computational linguistics: Human language technologies*, pages 49–59.

Much Gracias: Semi-supervised Code-switch Detection for Spanish-English: How far can we get?

Dana-Maria Iliescu*, **Rasmus Grand***, **Sara Qirko***, **Rob van der Goot**
IT-University of Copenhagen
dail@itu.dk, gran@itu.dk, saqi@itu.dk, robv@itu.dk

Abstract

Because of globalization, it is becoming more and more common to use multiple languages in a single utterance, also called code-switching. This results in special linguistic structures and, therefore, poses many challenges for Natural Language Processing. Existing models for language identification in code-switched data are all supervised, requiring annotated training data which is only available for a limited number of language pairs. In this paper, we explore semi-supervised approaches, that exploit out-of-domain monolingual training data. We experiment with word uni-grams, word n-grams, character n-grams, Viterbi Decoding, Latent Dirichlet Allocation, Support Vector Machine and Logistic Regression. The Viterbi model was the best semi-supervised model, scoring a weighted F1 score of 92.23%, whereas a fully supervised state-of-the-art BERT-based model scored 98.43%.[1]

1 Introduction

Social platforms have been the cradle of the internet, driving vast amounts of communication among people from all over the world. As a consequence, the way people communicate in written text has changed, as now it is common to use, for example, abbreviations of words, emoticons, references to other users and use multiple languages within the same utterance. An annotated example sentence of this is the following tweet:

Word	El	online	exercise	de	hoy	:
Label	es	en	en	es	es	other

This phenomenon has caught particular interest in both sociolinguistics and Natural Language Processing (NLP) (Aguilar et al., 2020; Khanuja et al., 2020).

Classifying the language labels on the word level (i.e. code-switch detection) has shown to be beneficial to improve performance on downstream NLP tasks, like dependency parsing (Bhat et al., 2018) or lexical normalization (Barik et al., 2019). Previous work has shown that high performances can be achieved for this task for many language pairs (Molina et al., 2016; Banerjee et al., 2016). However, to the best of our knowledge, most previous work focused on supervised settings, restraining their usefulness to language pairs for which annotated datasets exist. Recent efforts to unify existing datasets have collected annotation for 4 (Aguilar et al., 2020) and 2 (Khanuja et al., 2020) language pairs, which confirms that annotated data is not available for most language pairs.

In supervised settings, recent transformer models (Vaswani et al., 2017; Devlin et al., 2019) have reached a new state-of-the-art (Aguilar et al., 2020; Khanuja et al., 2020), outperforming Bi-LSTMS and traditional machine learning methods used earlier (Molina et al., 2016; Banerjee et al., 2016). Yirmibeşoğlu and Eryiğit (2018) tackled this task in a semi-supervised setup as well, where they used character n-gram language models trained on monolingual data to predict perplexity on the target word for classification. They show that this obtains a micro-average F1 score of 92.9%, compared to 95.6% with a supervised CRF-model.

To overcome this limitation, **we focus on exploiting only mono-lingual datasets for performing word-level language identification in code-switched data. We refer to this setup as semi-supervised, since we have no data annotated for the task at hand (code-switch detection).** This enables the possibility to easily train models for new language pairs, and leads to the research question: *How do semi-supervised models compare and perform in the task of language identification in English-Spanish code-switched data?* **(RQ1)**.

* Equal contributions

[1] https://github.com/RalleGr/msc-code-switching

Proceedings of the Fifth Workshop on Computational Approaches to Linguistic Code-Switching, pages 65–71
June 11, 2021. ©2021 Association for Computational Linguistics
https://doi.org/10.26615/978-954-452-056-4_009

Since supervised methods have the advantage of learning from annotated data, the second research question is: *How much can we reduce the gap in performance between the aforementioned semi-supervised models and a supervised state-of-the-art model?* (**RQ2**).

Previous work in similar setups have automatically generated code-switched data from monolingual datasets (Santy et al., 2021). We consider this approach to be orthogonal to ours, and Santy et al. (2021) exploit mono-lingual in-domain data, syntactic parsers and parallel sentences.

2 Datasets

In this section, we will first describe the manually annotated code-switched data that we use for evaluating our models, then we describe the monolingual data that we will use as "training" data. It should be noted that this is not real training data, as it is not annotated for the task at hand (thus the setting is semi-supervised).

2.1 Test data

To evaluate and compare our models, we use the Spanish-English (SPA-EN) part of the LinCE benchmark (a total of 32,651 posts equivalent to 390,953 tokens) (Aguilar et al., 2020). We chose this language pair because it has the challenge of increased similarity between the languages (Tristram, 1999). In the original data, 8 labels are used, from which we only focus on the 3 labels necessary for the language identification task: `lang1`, `lang2` and `other`, for English, Spanish and punctuation, numbers, symbols and emoticons, respectively. We use the default development and test splits for our experiments.

2.2 Monolingual data

In order to perform semi-supervised code-switching detection, we use Wikipedia data, because it is available in many languages and easy to obtain. We extracted dumps from September 1st 2020 with Wikiextractor[2]. Without punctuation and numbers, the English dataset contains 420K distinct words and the Spanish dataset contains 610K distinct words.

It should be noted that there is a domain difference between the training and the dev/test data. However, collecting monolingual data from Twitter is non-trivial.[3] Furthermore, it should be noted that the Wikipedia datasets are not 100% monolingual, so there will be some Spanish data in the English dump and vice-versa. Both of these artefacts might have a negative effect on performance.

2.3 Automated annotation for monolingual tokens

Tokenization of the raw datasets is done using the English and Spanish SpaCy tokenization models[4], as it matches the tokenization of the development and test sets. Punctuation and non-word tokens (the `other` class) are identified with manually designed rules using regular expressions, and the python `emoji` package. Tokens that are not identified as `other`, are labeled with the corresponding label based on the language of the wikipedia.

3 Methods

3.1 Word uni-grams

We first clean the mono-lingual Wikipedia data by removing XML/HTML tags from the articles and special tokens that belong to the `other` class. We calculate the word probability based on the resulting data (word frequency/total number of words) using Laplace smoothing with a smoothing factor of 1.

3.2 Word n-grams

We also experiment with taking a larger context into account through bi-grams and tri-grams. Here, we divide the frequency of the n-gram containing the word with the frequency of the leading $(n-1)$-gram. The probability is computed this way for a given word in each language, and then the label with the highest probability is assigned to the word. Laplace smoothing with a factor of 1 is used. In our initial experiments, tri-grams showed very low performance, so we use bi-grams in the remainder of this paper.

3.3 Character n-grams

For this model, we calculate the joint log probability of words based on the monolingual training data, and assign the most probable label. We vary the n-gram size from 1 to 6 and use Laplace smoothing with a factor of 1.

[2] `https://github.com/attardi/wikiextractor`

[3] Twitter blog: Evaluating language identification performance

[4] `https://spacy.io/`

3.4 Viterbi decoding

The problem of code-switching can be represented as a Hidden Markov Model (HMM) problem, since a sentence can be seen as a Markov chain with hidden states that are the two different languages.

We use the Viterbi decoding algorithm (Forney, 1973) to find the most probable sequence of states given the observations - namely, to assign a language label (state) to each word (observation). We used eginhard's implementation[5] of the Viterbi algorithm and modified the starting and transition probabilities to the values specified below, which were found to be optimal using grid search on the development set using the range of initial probabilities for English from 0.1 to 0.9 with step size 0.1, transition probabilities for English from 0.05 to 0.95 with step size 0.05. The final hyperparameters are as follows:

- states: `lang1` and `lang2`, `other` tokens are identified based on heuristics (see Section 2.3);
- initial probabilities: 0.6 for English and 0.4 for Spanish;
- transition probabilities: 0.15 for transitioning to a different language and 0.85 for transitioning to the same language;
- emission probabilities: these are estimated through a relative probability model, the probability of the word being emitted from English, for example, is:

$$P(w) = \frac{P(w|EN)}{P(w|EN) + P(w|SPA)}, \quad (1)$$

where $P(w|EN)$ and $P(w|SPA)$ are probabilities given by the dictionaries described in section 3.1. In case this is 0 (i.e. the word does not occur in our monolingual data), the emission probability is calculated by a relative character bi-gram probability.

3.5 Latent Dirichlet Allocation

Generally, Latent Dirichlet Allocation (LDA) aims to find the topics a document belongs to using the words in the document as features. In our case, the documents are the words, the features are character n-grams (with n 1 to 5) and the topics are English and Spanish. The LDA algorithm does not output labels for the resulting clusters, so we select the top 10 words based on weight that represent best each cluster, and assign them a language using the word uni-gram method (Section 3.1). We use the Scikit Learn[6] implementation of LDA with the `TfidfVectorizer` and use only the first 100,000 words from each monolingual dataset, in order to reduce training time.

3.6 Support Vector Machine

For our Support Vector Machine (SVM) model, we consider the monolingual data (Section 2.2) to be the gold training data, without tokens from the `other` class. Using `TfidfVectorizer`, we extract character n-gram features from each word, with n 1 to 5. We use the Scikit Learn implementation with all default parameters and select the first 100,000 words from each dataset.

3.7 Logistic regression

We use Logistic Regression in a weakly-supervised manner, the same as with SVM, where we consider the first 100,000 words from each Wikipedia dataset to be the gold training data. Again, we use `TfidfVectorizer` to extract character n-gram features, with n 1 to 5, and rely on the default Scikit Learn implementation.

3.8 Ensemble model

We also experiment with ensembling the previous methods, where we use a simple majority voting. We compare using all models, to using the best 3 and the best 5 models, as well as an oracle.

4 Results

To evaluate the performance of our models, we use weighted F1 score[7]. As found in Table 1, Viterbi has the overall best performance scoring 95.76% on validation data and 92.23% on the test data. Word uni-grams, character n-grams, SVM and Logistic Regression models achieve results with a range of weighted F1 score from 90.34% to 92.19% on validation data and a range from 87.80% to 88.95% on test data.

We compare our performance to a supervised BERT-based classifier as implemented by the MaChAmp toolkit 0.2 (van der Goot et al., 2021).

[5] `https://github.com/eginhard/word-level-language-id/`

[6] `https://scikit-learn.org/`

[7] over only the classes of interests; as mentioned in Section 2.1, we only focus on 3/8 labels of the LinCE data

Model	Dev	Test
Word uni-grams	91.32%	88.25%
Word n-grams	50.50%	49.04%
Character n-grams	92.19%	88.95%
Viterbi	95.99%	92.23%
LDA	64.40%	62.84%
Support Vector Machine	91.39%	88.74%
Logistic regression	90.34%	87.80%
Ensemble Model		
All models	92.15%	88.99%
Models 3, 4 and 6	93.72%	90.27%
Models 1, 3, 4, 5 and 6	92.96%	89.64%
Oracle*	98.47%	-
Supervised		
MaChAmp	99.24%	98.43%

Table 1: Models evaluated using weighted F1 score on validation and test data. * Made use of gold labels

We use multilingual BERT and all default settings. Results in Table 1 show that there is still a performance gap between the semi-supervised approaches and this state-of-the-art supervised model. When comparing common confusions of our best semi-supervised model (Viterbi) to the output of MaChAmp, we found that there was more confusion in the Viterbi model about `other`, where 213 words were classified as `lang1` and 60 as `lang2` instead, compared to just 3 and 1 in MaChAmp. Full confusion matrices can be found in the appendix.

The majority voting ensembling models do not lead to improved performance. However, the oracle ensemble, which always picks the correct label if it is available from one of the models, shows that there is potential in improving the selection method for ensembling.

5 Discussion

When inspecting the performances of the models per class (see also Table 2 in the appendix), we found that, for the development dataset, all models have a better F1 score for English than for Spanish and, for the test dataset, the other way around. This might be due to a discrepancy between the label distribution of the two datasets and is a significant aspect to be investigated in future work.

Regarding the LDA model, its low performance can be explained by the results of (Zhang et al., 2014), which show that for the task of language filtering, the performance of LDA decreases when the dominating language decreases under 70% of the whole text. This is also the case in our experiments, where the test data had a 54% English and 46% Spanish ratio. Furthermore, the amount of evidence per sample is rather low compared to the normal use of LDA (it is commonly used on the document level).

For character n-grams, we observed that the more we increased the value of n, the better results we got, up until $n = 6$. The higher order n-grams performed better with around 12% difference in validation weighted F1 score, as we can capture groups of letters that are representative for a language, e.g. 'tion' in English and 'cion' in Spanish. This model achieves good results also because it addresses the problem of misspelled words. For word n-grams, using tri-grams resulted in worse predictions than using bi-grams with around 11% difference in validation weighted F1 score.

For LDA, SVM and Logistic Regression models we tried to vectorize data with `CountVectorizer` from Scikit Learn, which gives the term-frequency for each n-gram in a word. However, `TfidfVectorizer` performed approximately 1% better in LDA and Logistic Regression and 4% for SVM in validation data. This was then the preferred vectorizer in all models, as it helps decreasing the impact of very frequent character n-grams that are not expressing much value and gives more importance to less frequent character n-grams.

The fact that the oracle model has a 3% higher weighted F1 score than the best model (in validation data), suggests that there is room for improvement for the ensemble model with other methods than majority voting. Improvements on the single models could be achieved by using bigger monolingual datasets of the same size or selecting a corpus that is more similar to the test set (social media-like posts), which is not as easy to query as Wikipedia articles. The overall performance of the models can also be slightly improved by a more complex method for the `other` class (the existing rule-based method scored an F1 of 96.76, see Table 2 in the appendix).

The training efficiency of the Viterbi model and the supervised model were measured in a Windows Sub-system for Linux environment on an i7-7700K processor with 16GB ram. We ran the MaChAmp model in this environment and it completed in 53,990 seconds. In comparison, the Viterbi training completed in 1,805 seconds, which is an improvement of almost 30 times faster than the MaChAmp model.

6 Conclusion

In this study we evaluated different types of models, namely word uni-grams, word n-grams, character n-grams, Viterbi Decoding, Latent Dirichlet Allocation, Support Vector Machine and Logistic Regression, for the task of semi-supervised language identification in English-Spanish code-switched data. We found that most of the models achieved promising results, however, the Viterbi model performed the best with a weighted F1 score of 95.76% on validation data and 92.23% on test data (**RQ1**). Using this model, one can potentially train CS-detection for many more language pairs as previously possible. Furthermore, since the majority voting did not lead to improvements, we experimented with an Oracle model, which showed that by combining results form our models, the best score we could achieve is 98.47% on validation data. Even though the results were good, our models still underperformed compared to the supervised MaChAmp model, that scored 99.24% weighted F1 score on validation data and 98.43% on test data (**RQ2**). There is also a clear take away that, by using simpler, faster approaches like ours and when top performance is not crucial, one can avoid the extensive process of human-annotation and long training time that are needed by finetuning these large transformer models on supervised data.

References

Gustavo Aguilar, Sudipta Kar, and Thamar Solorio. 2020. LinCE: A centralized benchmark for linguistic code-switching evaluation. In *Proceedings of the 12th Language Resources and Evaluation Conference*, pages 1803–1813, Marseille, France. European Language Resources Association.

Somnath Banerjee, Kunal Chakma, Sudip Kumar Naskar, Amitava Das, Paolo Rosso, Sivaji Bandyopadhyay, and Monojit Choudhury. 2016. Overview of the mixed script information retrieval (MSIR) at FIRE-2016. In *Forum for Information Retrieval Evaluation*, pages 39–49. Springer.

Anab Maulana Barik, Rahmad Mahendra, and Mirna Adriani. 2019. Normalization of Indonesian-English code-mixed Twitter data. In *Proceedings of the 5th Workshop on Noisy User-generated Text (W-NUT 2019)*, pages 417–424, Hong Kong, China. Association for Computational Linguistics.

Irshad Bhat, Riyaz A. Bhat, Manish Shrivastava, and Dipti Sharma. 2018. Universal Dependency parsing for Hindi-English code-switching. In *Proceedings of the 2018 Conference of the North American Chapter of the Association for Computational Linguistics: Human Language Technologies, Volume 1 (Long Papers)*, pages 987–998, New Orleans, Louisiana. Association for Computational Linguistics.

Jacob Devlin, Ming-Wei Chang, Kenton Lee, and Kristina Toutanova. 2019. BERT: Pre-training of deep bidirectional transformers for language understanding. In *Proceedings of the 2019 Conference of the North American Chapter of the Association for Computational Linguistics: Human Language Technologies, Volume 1 (Long and Short Papers)*, pages 4171–4186, Minneapolis, Minnesota. Association for Computational Linguistics.

G. D. Forney. 1973. The Viterbi algorithm. In *The viterbi algorithm*, 3, pages 268–278.

Simran Khanuja, Sandipan Dandapat, Anirudh Srinivasan, Sunayana Sitaram, and Monojit Choudhury. 2020. GLUECoS : An evaluation benchmark for code-switched nlp. In *Proceedings of the 58th Annual Meeting of the Association for Computational Linguistics*, page 3575–3585.

Giovanni Molina, Fahad AlGhamdi, Mahmoud Ghoneim, Abdelati Hawwari, Nicolas Rey-Villamizar, Mona Diab, and Thamar Solorio. 2016. Overview for the second shared task on language identification in code-switched data. In *Proceedings of the Second Workshop on Computational Approaches to Code Switching*, pages 40–49, Austin, Texas. Association for Computational Linguistics.

Sebastin Santy, Anirudh Srinivasan, and Monojit Choudhury. 2021. BERTologiCoMix: How does code-mixing interact with multilingual BERT? In *Proceedings of the Second Workshop on Domain Adaptation for NLP*, pages 111–121, Kyiv, Ukraine. Association for Computational Linguistics.

Hildegard L. C. Tristram. 1999. *How Celtic is Standard English?* Nauka.

Rob van der Goot, Ahmet Üstün, Alan Ramponi, Ibrahim Sharaf, and Barbara Plank. 2021. Massive choice, ample tasks (MaChAmp): A toolkit for multi-task learning in NLP. In *Proceedings of the 16th Conference of the European Chapter of the Association for Computational Linguistics: System Demonstrations*, pages 176–197, Online. Association for Computational Linguistics.

Ashish Vaswani, Noam Shazeer, Niki Parmar, Jakob Uszkoreit, Llion Jones, Aidan N Gomez, Ł ukasz Kaiser, and Illia Polosukhin. 2017. Attention is all you need. In *Advances in Neural Information Processing Systems*, volume 30. Curran Associates, Inc.

Zeynep Yirmibeşoğlu and Gülşen Eryiğit. 2018. Detecting code-switching between Turkish-English language pair. In *Proceedings of the 2018 EMNLP Workshop W-NUT: The 4th Workshop on Noisy User-generated Text*, pages 110–115, Brussels, Belgium. Association for Computational Linguistics.

Wei Zhang, Robert AJ Clark, and Yongyuan Wang. 2014. Unsupervised language filtering using the latent dirichlet allocation. In *Fifteenth Annual Conference of the International Speech Communication Association*.

A Appendix

	Validation F1 score			Test F1 score		
Model	**English**	**Spanish**	**Other**	**English**	**Spanish**	**Other**
1. Word uni-grams	91.05%	88.77%	96.76%	87.42%	89.94%	95.84%
2. Word n-grams	45.41%	31.98%	96.76%	40.61%	35.73%	95.84%
3. Character n-grams	91.84%	90.19%	96.76%	88.56%	90.68%	95.84%
4. Viterbi	96.09%	95.48%	96.76%	93.13%	94.71%	95.84%
5. Latent Dirichlet Allocation	59.37%	53.09%	96.76%	53.15%	57.74%	95.84%
6. Support Vector Machine	90.84%	89.21%	96.76%	88.07%	90.55%	95.84%
7. Logistic regression	89.65%	87.74%	96.76%	86.74%	89.41%	95.84%
Ensemble Model	**English**	**Spanish**	**Other**	**English**	**Spanish**	**Other**
All models	91.92%	90.00%	96.76%	88.36%	90.91%	95.84%
Models 3, 4 and 6	93.55%	92.31%	96.76%	90.35%	92.34%	95.84%
Models 1, 3, 4, 5 and 6	92.79%	91.17%	96.76%	89.31%	91.69%	95.84%
Oracle*	98.96%	98.81%	96.76%	-	-	-
Supervised						
MaChAmp	99.14%	99.08%	99.78%	98.42%	99.00%	99.84%

Table 2: Models evaluated using F1 score per class for validation and test data

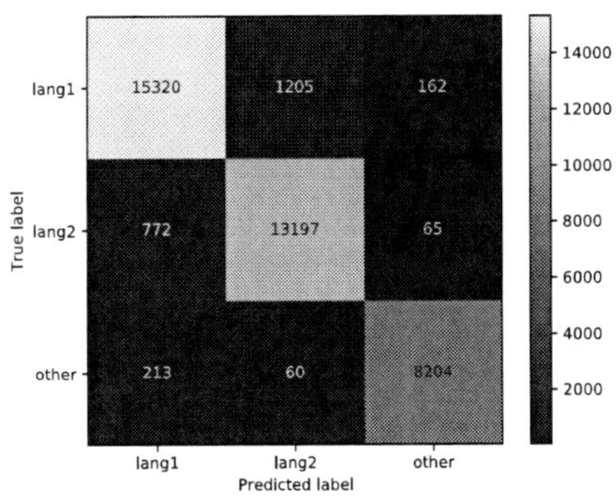

Figure 1: Confusion matrix of Viterbi predictions on test data

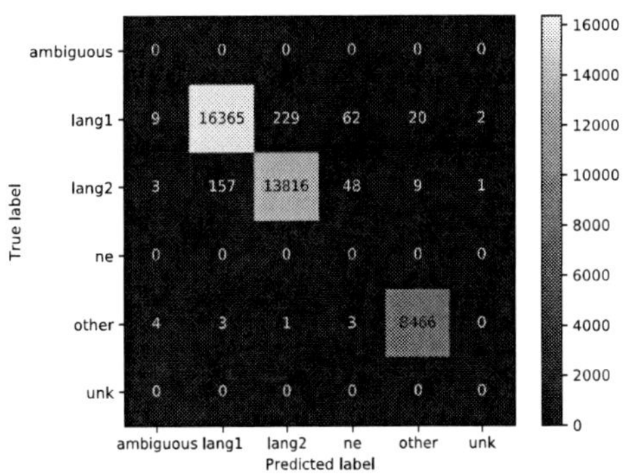

Figure 2: Confusion matrix of MaChAmp predictions on test data

Figure 1 and 2 show the confusion matrices of the Viterbi and MaChAmp model. It can be noted that the confusion matrix for MaChAmp model has more than the three labels we used, because it was trained on part of the original training set presented in Section 2.1. This set contained 8 classes, and, thus, occasionally, the model mistakenly predicted some of these classes. It can be seen that there was more confusion in Viterbi model about `other`, where 213 words were classified as `lang1` and 60 as `lang2` instead, compared to just 3 and 1 in MaChAmp, which also had 7 other misclassifications.

A Language-aware Approach to Code-switched Morphological Tagging

Şaziye Betül Özateş and **Özlem Çetinoğlu**
Institute for Natural Language Processing, University of Stuttgart, Stuttgart, Germany
{saziye.oezates,ozlem.cetinoglu}@ims.uni-stuttgart.de

Abstract

Morphological tagging of code-switching (CS) data becomes more challenging especially when language pairs composing the CS data have different morphological representations. In this paper, we explore a number of ways of implementing a language-aware morphological tagging method and present our approach for integrating language IDs into a transformer-based framework for CS morphological tagging. We perform our set of experiments on the Turkish-German SAGT Treebank. Experimental results show that including language IDs to the learning model significantly improves accuracy over other approaches.

1 Introduction

Morphological tagging is a well known sequence labelling task in Natural Language Processing (NLP). It is the task of finding the correct morphological analysis for a given word form. The analysis is usually represented with a set of morphological features. Tagging these features is beneficial in solving most NLP tasks since having knowledge about the morphological analysis of natural language words gives clues about their syntactic nature and their roles in context (Müller and Schütze, 2015). Morphological tagging becomes more important when the language in question is a morphologically rich one and the part-of-speech (POS) information about word forms is not sufficient to syntactically classify them (Tsarfaty et al., 2013).

Morphological tagging is challenging in itself[1] and it becomes more challenging when the processed language is code-switched, a phenomenon that occurs when bilingual speakers frequently switch between languages and produce utterances that include word forms and phrases from both languages. The challenge amplifies as the linguistic difference between the composing languages increases. This is because unlike POS annotation that can be made common across languages (e.g. Universal Dependencies (Nivre et al., 2016)), morphological annotation is more language-specific. The example in Figure 1 shows this difference explicitly. Even though both *Autos* in German and *arabalarda* in Turkish share the same POS tag as NOUN, they have different morphological analyses. This difference stems from inherent properties of these languages. German employs grammatical gender while Turkish does not. Additionally in the example, the Turkish *locative* case corresponds to German *dative*. Such structural differences, combined with the rich morphology of individual languages taking part in CS data, make CS morphological tagging even more challenging with respect to CS POS tagging, a task that is a more common and more studied NLP task (cf. Section 2). In fact, there has not been any research focused on CS morphological tagging before.

Form	POS	Morphological features
(a) In German:		
in	ADP	_
Autos	NOUN	Case=Dat | Gender=Neut | Number=Plur
(b) In Turkish:		
arabalarda	NOUN	Case=Loc | Number=Plur

Figure 1: The morphological analyses of German (a) and Turkish (b) translations of the phrase *in cars*.

We hypothesise that the language-dependent nature of morphological tagging can be solved more successfully for the case of CS data when the learning model has the knowledge of which language a word form belongs to. Starting from this hypothesis, we search ways of including the language ID (LID) information to tagging and present a language-aware approach. The proposed approach

[1] For instance, in the CoNLL 2018 Shared Task of Multilingual Parsing from Raw Text to Universal Dependencies, morphological tagging has the lowest range of scores among sentence segmentation, word segmentation, tokenisation, lemmatisation, and POS tagging. universaldependencies.org/conll18/results.html

Proceedings of the Fifth Workshop on Computational Approaches to Linguistic Code-Switching, pages 72–83
June 11, 2021. ©2021 Association for Computational Linguistics
https://doi.org/10.26615/978-954-452-056-4_010

integrates LIDs to the dense representation of input tokens in a transformer-based learning model. We conducted experiments on the only CS dataset with complete morphological annotation (Turkish-German SAGT Treebank (Çetinoğlu and Çöltekin, 2019)).[2] Results show that the proposed approach outperforms all of the baselines significantly and the use of LIDs is beneficial in tagging morphology for CS data. Our contributions are twofold: We present the first study on CS morphological tagging, and our data-driven method of integrating LIDs is applicable to any CS dataset and task that can exploit language IDs.

2 Related Work

Although there does not exist any prior study on CS morphological tagging, utilising language IDs in other CS tasks has been quite common. We divide how LID is utilised into three methods: as part of a pipeline, as part of joint processing, and as Machine Learning (ML) features. While one or more of these techniques have been applied to many CS tasks, e.g. parsing (Bhat et al., 2017), sentiment analysis (Vilares et al., 2016), and normalisation (van der Goot and Çetinoğlu, 2021), we focus here mainly on POS tagging, as it is a sequence labelling task and the closest one to morphological tagging.

One of the most commonly used pipeline approach is processing the data as monolingual fragments (Vyas et al., 2014; Jamatia et al., 2015; Barman et al., 2016; Bhat et al., 2017; AlGhamdi et al., 2016). For each language in the mixed data, a monolingual model is trained. During prediction, the input is split into fragments according to their language IDs and each fragment is processed by the respective monolingual model. The output is then merged into its original form. The advantage of this approach is to eliminate the need of CS data for training. However, context information is lost.

The other common pipeline approach is using LIDs in decision-making after getting predictions from monolingual models. In this setup the mixed input is given to both monolingual models. The predicted LID is then used to select the model output of the corresponding language. Solorio and Liu (2008) is the first to use this approach on English-Spanish POS tagging. Later Barman et al. (2016) and AlGhamdi et al. (2016) used this setup for English-Bengali-Hindi, and for English-Spanish and Modern Standard Arabic-Egyptian Arabic, as well as the first pipeline technique. While in Barman et al.'s (2016) case using the second pipeline method slightly outperforms the first one, AlGhamdi et al. (2016) show the first pipeline outperforms by a large margin. Thus we opted for the first architecture as one of our baselines.

Another model of Barman et al.'s (2016) was jointly trained LID and POS taggers that achieve a quite large improvement over their pipeline models. Soto and Hirschberg (2018) also trained LID and POS taggers together in their BiLSTM architecture. AlGhamdi and Diab (2019) choose joint LID and POS tagging as one of their architectures and show that distant language pairs Spanish-English and Hindi-English benefit from multi-task learning.

In many work from pre-neural era, LIDs are given as one of the features to ML models. While Solorio and Liu (2008) did not observe any significant improvement in doing so, Jamatia et al. (2015) shows that adding the LID of a token improves its POS tagging for English-Hindi. Sequiera et al. (2015) and Bhat et al. (2017) also inserted LID as a feature into their ML models. As a neural approach, Soto and Hirschberg (2018) represented the six LID labels existing in their data as boolean features and concatenated them with word vectors in a BiLSTM along with other features they used.

Different from the previous approaches, Aguilar and Solorio (2020) use language identification to create a code-switching ELMo from English ELMo (Peters et al., 2018). Later they show the effectiveness of their CS-ELMo by achieving state-of-the-art POS tagging results on a Hindi-English dataset (Singh et al., 2018). They also employ multi-task learning where their auxiliary task is language identification with a simplified LID tag set for LID, POS, and NER tagging.

3 Methodology

For morphological tagging of CS data, we chose to use STEPS[3] (Grünewald et al., 2020) as our framework. STEPS is an NLP tool for tagging and syntactic parsing in Universal Dependencies (UD) style (Nivre et al., 2016). Our motivation behind deciding on STEPS as our framework is based on two reasons. First, for token representation it utilises transformer-based language models, which

[2]There is also the NArabizi Treebank (Seddah et al., 2020) which includes partial morphological annotation where the total number of unique annotations is 46 in contrast to the SAGT Treebank which has 795 unique morphological annotations. Hence, we did not use this treebank in our study.

[3]`github.com/boschresearch/steps-parser`

have recently become famous for their outstanding success in various NLP tasks (Kondratyuk and Straka, 2019; Hoang et al., 2019). Second, STEPS is an open-source system with a minimum use of black-box modules that make the modification of the source codes very challenging, if not impossible. Moreover, STEPS is a current state-of-the-art NLP tool that outperformed other state-of-the-art tools Udify (Kondratyuk and Straka, 2019) and UDPipe 2.0 (Straka et al., 2019) in tagging and parsing of several languages (Grünewald et al., 2020).

Section 3.1 gives a brief description about STEPS. Sections 3.2 and 3.3 describe the baseline methods and our proposed approach for integrating LIDs to CS morphological tagging, respectively.

3.1 Framework

STEPS is mainly developed as a multilingual system for parsing. It also performs sequence labelling tasks such as POS and morphological tagging in a multi-task learning (MTL) setup. For our purposes, we adapted STEPS to solely perform sequence labelling. When this adapted version is used standalone, it becomes a baseline for our task. We mention this version as the `Standalone` approach throughout the paper.

The STEPS architecture follows Kondratyuk and Straka (2019) for computing token embeddings from the transformer-based language model and performing tagging and parsing. Token embeddings are calculated as a weighted sum of all intermediate outputs of the transformer layers. Coefficients of this weighted sum are learned during training. For sequence labelling, STEPS utilises a single-layer feed-forward neural network on top of token representations to extract the logit vectors for respective label vocabularies. More detailed information about the STEPS architecture can be found in (Grünewald et al., 2020).

3.2 Baselines for Language ID Integration

In a given dataset, the language-dependent morphological annotation of words that share the same POS tag gives us the intuition that feeding a model with token-wise LID information can help improve its accuracy for CS morphological tagging. Starting from this hypothesis, we designed and experimented with three ways of using token-level LID information in the model.

3.2.1 Data Split (`DSplit`)

One of the first methods that come to mind when dealing with CS data is splitting the data from CS points and treating the split parts as monolingual data as in the first pipeline method mentioned in Section 2. For our case, this method consists of three steps. First, input data is split to sub-parts containing monolingual data only. Second, monolingual models for each sub-part are trained. Each trained model processes its corresponding sub-part separately. In the last step, the output of models are joined to reach the processed version of the data.

To achieve the split of CS data into monolingual parts, we created a simple algorithm. Starting from the first token in a sentence, the algorithm creates sentence fragments whenever it encounters a switch between tokens with LIDs denoting one of the main languages in the CS data. Tokens with other LIDs (e.g., punctuation or mixed tokens where intra-word CS occurs) stay in the fragment created at that moment. Figure 2 depicts this process on a Turkish-German sentence.

3.2.2 Multi-Task Learning (`MTL`)

Another frequently applied method is the multi-task learning approach when two or more related tasks have the potential of benefitting each other through the domain information they contain. The main idea of this approach is improving the learning of a model for a task with the help of the knowledge contained by another task (Zhang and Yang, 2017). MTL has been shown effective in various areas in NLP (Collobert and Weston, 2008; Fang et al., 2019), especially in low-resource scenarios, usually as a way of transferring knowledge from a high-resource auxiliary task to a low-resource target task as in Lin et al. (2018). Our case is also a low-resource scenario where we have two related tasks, morphological tagging as the target and LID tagging as a simpler auxiliary task. In our setup, these two tasks are trained together with the same model and the loss is computed by summing losses of each task. The loss for LID tagging is scaled down 5% in training, as it was done for simpler tasks in (Grünewald et al., 2020). This loss scaling is for preventing the validation accuracy for LID tagging to go up too quickly and cause an underfitting for morphological tagging.

3.3 Proposal: LID Vectors (`LIDVec`)

Our proposal to integrate LIDs to the model is via creating LID embeddings and concatenating them

CS sentence

1	**Abendgymnasium**dan	MIXED
2	sonra	TR
3	da	TR
4	**Evangelische**	DE
5	**Hochschule**'de	MIXED
6	zaten	TR
7	**Soziale**	DE
8	**Arbeit**	DE
9	okudum	TR
10	.	OTHER

TR fragments

1	**Abendgymnasium**dan	MIXED
2	sonra	TR
3	da	TR
6	zaten	TR
9	okudum	TR
10	.	OTHER

DE fragments

4	**Evangelische**	DE
5	**Hochschule**'de	MIXED
7	**Soziale**	DE
8	**Arbeit**	DE

Figure 2: Splitting an example code-switching sentence to Turkish (TR) and German (DE) fragments. German tokens and token parts are shown in bold. (*Sentence translation: After the night school, I studied Social Work in the Protestant University.*)

to the embeddings of input tokens. The motivation behind this approach is to directly encode the LID information to each token inside the learning model and by this way to lessen the model's confusion caused by the tokens with different LIDs having different morphological annotations. Moreover, this way we can represent each LID label in contrast to `DSplit` that uses only main LID labels.

There are more than one method to represent LIDs as vectors inside the model. One-hot encoding of each LID is one of them.[4] Another method would be starting from a random embedding for each LID and training these embeddings with the rest of the model. Instead of random initialisation, LID embeddings can also be initialised with the average vectors of token embeddings in the training set, calculated for each LID label. Our motivation behind this clustering method is to see whether starting the training of the LID vectors from a more reasonable point will improve accuracy. We experimented with all of these models and chose to continue with the randomly initialised LID embeddings method based on our observation that this method works best among others. The comparison of these methods is discussed in Section 5.

In `LIDVec`, each LID label is assigned a 100-dimensional embedding vector at the beginning of training. The embedding of each input token is then concatenated with its corresponding LID embedding. These concatenated vectors are then given to the model for training. The loss at each epoch is backpropagated to both the token embeddings and the LID embeddings. We apply batch normalisation to token embeddings right after the concatenation.

[4]Soto and Hirschberg (2018) use a similar way. They represent LIDs as boolean features concatenated to word vectors in a BiLSTM architecture.

4 Experiments

4.1 Data

We evaluate our approaches on the Turkish-German SAGT Treebank (Çetinoğlu and Çöltekin, 2019) UD version 2.7.1.[5] It is based on a Turkish-German code-switching corpus created from conversation recordings of bilinguals. Although the treebank consists of spoken sentences, the transcriptions are normalised and hence the orthography does not pose a challenge in terms of morphological tagging. The SAGT Treebank includes five LID labels: `TR` for Turkish, `DE` for German, `LANG3` for tokens that belong to a third language other than Turkish and German, `OTHER` for punctuation, and `MIXED` for tokens with intra-word code-switching. Example (1) shows the structure of a mixed word from Figure 2.

(1) ***Abendgymnasium****dan*
night school.from
'from the night school'

Here the first part (*Abendgymnasium*) is a German noun and the second part (*-dan*) is a Turkish suffix. Although they are from different languages, the token ***Abendgymnasium****dan* has a single language ID since the two parts of the token are written orthographically together.

We use the original training, development, and test splits in experiments, only further splitting a small part from the development set as the fine-tuning set.[6] Sentence counts and LID distribution is given in Table 1. The average sentence length is 15.35 and the average code switches per sentence is

[5]`github.com/UniversalDependencies/UD_Turkish_German-SAGT/tree/dev`

[6]The fine-tuning set is created by randomly extracting equal amount of sentences from each document in the development set.

	Sent Count	Token Count					
		TR	DE	MIXED	LANG3	OTHER	Total
Tra	578	3,727	5,149	105	69	1,034	10,084
		37%	51%	1%	0.7%	10.3%	
FT	101	721	864	21	16	158	1,780
		41%	49%	1.2%	0.9%	8.9%	
Dev	700	4,389	5,589	122	48	1,128	11,276
		39%	49.6%	1%	0.4%	10%	
Test	805	5,341	7,139	183	46	1,384	14,093
		38%	50,6%	1.3%	0.3%	9.8%	
Total	2,184	14,178	18,741	431	179	3,704	37,233
		38%	50.3%	1.2%	0.5%	10%	

Table 1: Sentence and token counts of the Turkish-German SAGT Treebank used in the experiments (Tra: training, FT: fine-tuning, Dev: development).

	TR	DE	MIXED	LANG3	OTHER
Tags	526	293	53	5	1
Features	61	37	22	5	1

Table 2: The number of unique morphological tags and the number of unique morphological features for each language category in the SAGT Treebank.

2.19 on the whole treebank. The counts of unique morphological tags and morphological features that constitute the tags are depicted in Table 2.

Note that previous studies that follow a similar approach to DSplit use monolingual data that are usually available in large amounts in training (Vyas et al., 2014; Jamatia et al., 2015; Barman et al., 2016; Bhat et al., 2017; AlGhamdi et al., 2016). However we do not utilise monolingual Turkish and German data in the current setting of DSplit experiments. We experimented with using morphological features of two Turkish treebanks – IMST (Sulubacak et al., 2016) and BOUN (Türk et al., 2020) and two German treebanks – GSD (McDonald et al., 2013) and HDT (Borges Völker et al., 2019) as additional monolingual data but this resulted in a decrease in DSplit's accuracy possibly due to conflicting morphological annotations of these treebanks. So, we only use the corresponding parts of the SAGT Treebank in training and evaluation of DSplit. We also experimented with the second pipeline approach mentioned in Section 2. In line with our expectations, it gives worse performance. So, we stick to our current DSplit method (cf. Table 8 in Appendix A for a comparison of two approaches).

4.2 Model Configuration

STEPS can be used with both BERT (Devlin et al., 2019) and XLM-R (Conneau et al., 2020). We chose to use multilingual XLM-R observing it outperforms multilingual BERT in our preliminary experiments, which is in line with previous findings (Liang et al., 2020; Conneau et al., 2020). We use XLM-R_{Base} with 12 layers and 768 hidden states in all the experiments. We stick to the default configuration of STEPS (Grünewald et al., 2020) for all the models except LIDVec. For LIDVec, token embedding size was changed from 768 to 868 since embeddings are expanded with the concatenation of 100-dimensional LID embeddings.

4.3 Predicted Language IDs

DSplit and LIDVec need LIDs; the former during splitting the dataset into languages, the latter during the concatenation of a token embedding with its corresponding LID vector. We evaluate these models with both gold and predicted LIDs. Predicted labels are obtained by training the STEPS Standalone model for LID tagging.

4.4 Metrics

We use accuracy as the evaluation metric. We count a morphological tag prediction of a token correct only when it is an exact match with the gold one. In addition to reporting the overall accuracy, we also provide accuracy on each LID label separately. This enables us to easily observe the parts each model has the most difficulty with. The significance between the performance of the models is measured using the randomisation test (van der Voet, 1994). When we mention a performance difference being *significant*, it means the difference is found statistically significant with $p < 0.05$.

4.5 Results

Table 3 shows experimental results for each model on the development and test sets.[7] It also demonstrates the evaluation of another baseline – Udify, a well-known, state-of-the-art transformer-based multi-task tool, which uses multilingual BERT as its language model (Kondratyuk and Straka, 2019).

We see that all three models that utilise LIDs outperform Standalone as well as Udify on both development and test sets. Although Standalone and Udify have similar architectures, the performance of the former surpasses that of the latter in terms of accuracy. Besides some design decisions, the main difference between these two models is the choice of the pretrained lan-

[7] The scores on the development set are the average of three separate runs while the scores on the test set are obtained by using the run that gives the best result in the development set.

Model	Accuracy on the Development Set					
	TR	DE	MIXED	LANG3	OTHER	**ALL**
Udify (mBERT)	74.64	82.18	44.26	52.08	**99.91**	80.48
STEPS - Standalone	79.37	81.18	66.39	43.75	**99.91**	82.03
STEPS - MTL	79.94	82.05	71.04	43.75	**99.91**	82.74
STEPS - DSplit (w. gold LIDs)	81.17	83.03	69.67	**52.78**	**99.91**	83.72
STEPS - LIDVec (w. gold LIDs)	**81.87**	**83.54**	**73.22**	50.00	99.17	**84.20**
	Accuracy on the Test Set					
	TR	DE	MIXED	LANG3	OTHER	**ALL**
Udify (mBERT)	71.95	79.21	39.34	34.78	99.86	77.83
STEPS - Standalone	76.15	77.15	61.75	47.83	**99.93**	78.71
STEPS - MTL	76.47	79.04	68.31	45.65	**99.93**	79.87
STEPS - DSplit (w. gold LIDs)	78.04	80.12	65.03	**50.00**	**99.93**	80.98
STEPS - LIDVec (w. gold LIDs)	**79.20**	**80.77**	**78.69**	34.78	98.77	**81.76**

Table 3: Morphological tagging accuracy of the models on the Turkish-German SAGT Treebank.

Model	Accuracy on the Development Set					
	TR	DE	MIXED	LANG3	OTHER	**ALL**
STEPS - DSplit (w. pred. LIDs)	80.66	82.95	70.43	41.50	**100.0**	83.43
STEPS - LIDVec (w. pred. LIDs)	**81.85**	**83.53**	**73.22**	**49.31**	99.17	**84.18**
	Accuracy on the Test Set					
	TR	DE	MIXED	LANG3	OTHER	**ALL**
STEPS - DSplit (w. pred. LIDs)	77.65	80.01	65.59	**48.78**	**100.0**	80.78
STEPS - LIDVec (w. pred. LIDs)	**79.22**	**80.73**	**78.69**	34.78	98.77	**81.75**

Table 4: Morphological tagging accuracy of DSplit and LIDVec when predicted LID labels were used.

	Accuracy	
	Development set	**Test set**
TR	99.09	99.42
DE	98.43	98.80
MIXED	90.16	92.90
LANG3	52.08	67.39
OTHER	99.91	99.86
ALL	98.55	98.96

Table 5: LID prediction accuracy of STEPS on the development and test sets of the SAGT Treebank.

guage model. While Udify uses multilingual BERT, Standalone utilises XLM-R.

The best performing model is LIDVec as we expected. It outperforms Standalone more than 2 and 3 points on the development and test sets, respectively. The two baselines for LID integration, DSplit and MTL, perform better than Standalone although they are less successful than LIDVec. We observe that integrating LIDs to the system improves the accuracy in morphological tagging in all three scenarios, although the amount of the improvement differs across the models.

To see how LID prediction affects DSplit and LIDVec, we repeated the same experiments with predicted LIDs. The results are given in Table 4. As introduced in Section 4.3, Standalone is used for LID tagging. Its performance on the development and test sets is shown in Table 5.

In Table 4, we see that LID accuracy has a stronger influence on DSplit while LIDVec stays almost unaffected. This might stem from LIDs playing a key role in DSplit by splitting the data into monolingual parts that are then used to train two separate models. So, the errors in LIDs are more explicitly propagated to the two models that learn to predict the morphological features of monolingual data only. However, LIDs have a more implicit effect in LIDVec. The errors in LIDs cause the wrong LID vector to be concatenated to the embeddings of some tokens but this error can later be compensated through the training of the whole model where both token and LID embeddings being updated at each step. Considering the high overall accuracy in LID prediction in Table 5, LIDVec seems to compensate the small error rate in predicted LIDs. Although LANG3 prediction accuracy is low, this does not cause a substantial effect in the overall accuracy of LID prediction since this label is rare in the treebank.

5 Analysis on LID Integration

LID representation and initialisation In Section 3.3, we mention two more ways in addition to our preferred approach for the representation of LIDs as vectors. The first way is representing LIDs as one-hot vectors. We define each LID label as a one-hot vector and concatenate these vectors with token embeddings provided by the language model as in LIDVec. We experimented with this approach on the development set. However, this method showed poorer performance than Standalone which does not utilise LIDs in any way. We believe that one-hot vector representation might be too rigid to be used together with token embeddings due to the fact that the range of the values in these two representations greatly vary.

The second method for the LID vector representation includes the initialisation of LID embeddings by averaging the embeddings of same-LID tokens in the training set. In the initial experiments we see that when we use the average initialisation instead of a random initialisation, the training phase progresses faster and the learning stops early when the training accuracy is around 85%, in contrast to the random initialisation in which the training phase ends after a higher number of epochs and with a higher training accuracy. So, we extended the training time by changing the early stop criteria from 15 epochs to 50 epochs to give the average initialisation an opportunity to show its true capacity. Figure 3 compares the performance of these two initialisation methods for two different early stop criteria on the development set. We see that the underfitting in the average initialisation method is eliminated as the number of epochs increases. Overall, the performance of both initialisation methods is the same when they are trained sufficiently. We conclude that random initialisation can be preferred if there are time restrictions.

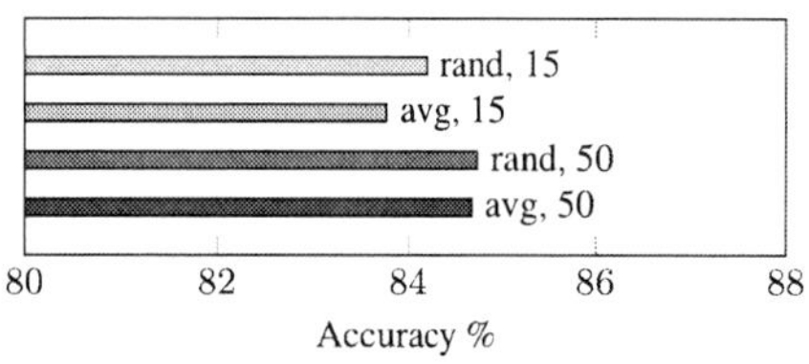

Figure 3: Comparison of random vs. average initialisation in the LIDVec model when the early stop criteria is 15 epochs vs. 50 epochs.

The impact of LID prediction We proposed three different approaches for LID integration. In terms of resources needed, MTL does not need an external LID prediction by definition, since it predicts LIDs and morphology jointly. However, it is also the worst performing one among the three approaches. DSplit and LIDVec both outperform MTL, but require predicted LIDs to function.

To test how sensitive these models to the LID prediction accuracy, we evaluated DSplit and LIDVec with MarMoT, a CRF-based sequence tagger (Müller et al., 2013) which has ~96% accuracy in LID prediction instead of the STEPS LID model with ~99% accuracy (cf. Table 9 in Appendix B for complete results). Although LIDVec's performance stays almost unaffected by the accuracy drop in LID prediction, DSplit accuracy drops approximately 1 point and more than 2 points in development and test sets, respectively. We conclude that DSplit is more vulnerable to LID accuracy whereas LIDVec can be paired with a faster and computationally less costly LID model if needed be. Another disadvantage of DSplit is the need to train multiple monolingual models to deal with different languages in CS data, in contrast to the single model architecture of LIDVec. DSplit also requires pre- and post-processing of the input and output, respectively. Considering its superior performance, and the robustness and compactness of its architecture, we suggest LIDVec as the best approach to CS morphological tagging among the models discussed in this paper.

The impact of LIDs on POS tagging We also performed experiments for POS tagging, the other possible sequence labelling task we can employ LID integration. Table 6 shows the overall accuracies for each model on the development and test sets of the SAGT Treebank. We do not observe any significant difference between the accuracies of the models, which is in line with our expectations. This is because universal POS tags used in the SAGT treebank are common to all languages in contrast to morphological tags that include many language-specific features. Hence, identifying the language a token belongs to does not add extra benefits in POS prediction.

Model	**Accuracy**	
	Dev	**Test**
STEPS - Standalone	93.72	**92.27**
STEPS - MTL	93.74	92.10
STEPS - DSplit (w. gold LIDs)	93.53	92.07
STEPS - LIDVec (w. gold LIDs)	**93.94**	92.24

Table 6: The POS tagging accuracy scores of the models on the development and test sets of the Turkish-German SAGT Treebank.

6 Qualitative Analysis

Most Common Improvements We observe that integrating language IDs contributes to a 10% increase in predicting the presence of possessive markers in Turkish nouns, which are not a feature of German nouns. This is something expected since providing LIDs enables the model to differentiate between the different sets of morphological features of two languages better. Similarly, the LID knowledge makes a 4% enhancement in predicting the existence of the *Gender* feature that is present in German nouns but absent in Turkish ones (cf. Figure 1). To understand this better, we compared `LIDVec` and `Standalone` in terms of their feature-based success. In this feature-based performance measurement, partial matches are also given scores in contrast to the evaluation metric we adopted, which counts a predicted morphological tag as correct only if it is an exact match – i.e., all the features that constitute the morphological tag are predicted correctly. We measure the feature-based performance of the models by dividing each morphological tag into features and counting each feature match as a point. Table 7 compares feature-based results of `LIDVec` and `Standalone`. We observe that `LIDVec` improves both *Precision* and *Recall* by more than 2%. These results suggest that `LIDVec` facilitates predicting the full set of features.

Model	Precision	Recall	F1	Acc
`Standalone`	87.72	87.19	87.24	82.03
`LIDVec`	**89.96**	**89.41**	**89.50**	**84.20**

Table 7: Feature-based partial scores of `Standalone` and `LIDVec` models on the development set of the Turkish-German SAGT Treebank.

When we look at what categories benefit most from including LIDs, we see that for Turkish they are verbs and nouns with an improvement of 11% and 10%, respectively. For German they are pronouns and nouns with 9% improvement. The success of morphology prediction for German verbs is already high for all models. Hence, there is not much improvement in German verbs. We observe that all the nouns and pronouns in both languages and also the verbal nouns in Turkish which are derived from verbs have the *Case* feature in their morphological analyses.

Confusion in `Case` feature values Although all models easily predicted the existence of the *Case* feature, they had the most trouble in deciding the value of it. Hence, we created confusion matrices of `Standalone` and `LIDVec` for different values of the *Case* feature on the development set as given in Figure 4. There are only four case markers in German: *nominative*, *accusative*, *dative*, and *genitive*. In Turkish, there are three additional case markers, namely *ablative*, *instrumental*, and *locative*. Albeit having a German lemma, `MIXED` tokens in the SAGT Treebank are annotated according to Turkish morphological annotation style due to the presence of Turkish suffixes in them. We observe that the most confusion occurs between *nominative* and *accusative* cases for all three token types. This confusion in `TR` and `MIXED` tokens results from the fact that the accusative suffix which makes the case of a word *accusative* and the possessive suffix in *nominative* nouns sometimes correspond to the same form in Turkish. In `DE` tokens, the situation is similar in the sense that *nominative* and *accusative* forms of German articles are different only for masculine, whereas they have the same form when their gender is feminine or neutral, or when they are in plural. `LIDVec` consistently reduces this confusion and predicts correct cases that plays an important role in its overall performance.

Improvement on `MIXED` tokens When observing the results in Tables 3 and 4, the notable success of `LIDVec` on predicting morphological analyses of `MIXED` tokens caught our attention. Even when predicted LIDs are used, `LIDVec` outperforms `Standalone` by a large margin in the development and test sets. We observe that `MIXED` tokens in the SAGT Treebank are mostly *nouns*. Therefore `MIXED` tokens get their share from overall *Case* improvements. When proportioned to the total number of cases in each category, the success of `LIDVec` is most visible in `MIXED` tokens.

Performance of `LIDVec` on `LANG3` and `OTHER` tokens We observe a pattern in the results that seems like a trade-off between the success on `TR`, `DE`, and `MIXED` and the success on `LANG3` and `OTHER`. This is most visible in `LIDVec`. We do not see the consistent improvement trend over `Standalone` in `LANG3` and `OTHER` accuracies as in `TR`, `DE`, and `MIXED` accuracies. To inspect this case, we compare confusion matrices of `Standalone` and `LIDVec` in Figure 5 for `LANG3` and `OTHER` types. Both models confused `LANG3` mostly with `DE`. We believe this situation stems from the fact that `LANG3` tokens in the treebank are mostly English proper nouns and some of them are also common in German. Nonetheless, the low success rates in this token type by all

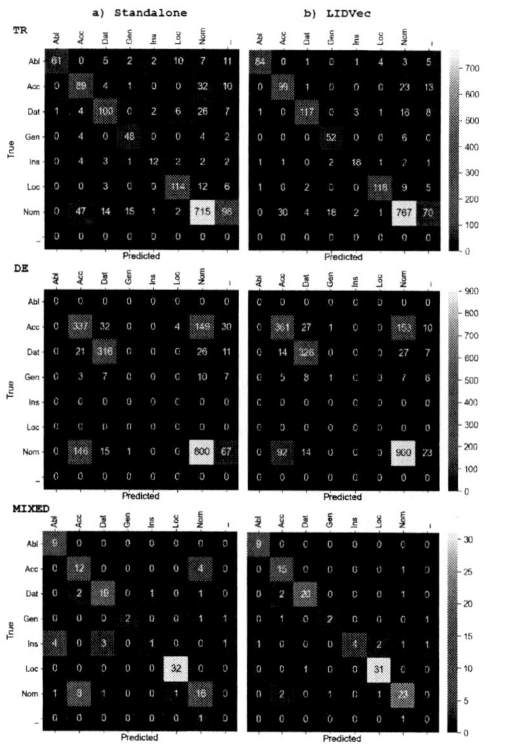

Figure 4: Confusion matrices of `Standalone` and `LIDVec` for different *Case* values.

models demonstrate once again how important the amount of training data is for data-driven models.

On the contrary, all models perform very well in predicting the absence of morphology in `OTHER` tokens. However, `LIDVec` makes a few more false predictions than `Standalone`. We believe this might stem from a slight overfitting of `LIDVec` towards `TR` tokens. Yet, accuracy of all models are above 98% for this type and we need more data to justify that there is a difference between the models for morphology prediction of `OTHER` tokens.

7 Conclusion

In this paper, we tackle the morphological tagging problem for CS data. We present some challenging aspects of the task and suggest the use of token-wise LID information. We experience with different ways of using LIDs on a transformer-based model and propose the LID Vectors approach. Our proposed model outperforms all the baselines significantly and proves to be a robust and compact way of LID integration. Being first on focusing morphological tagging on CS data,

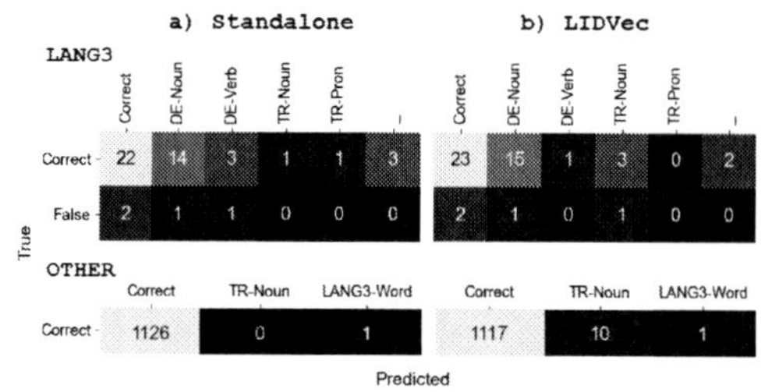

Figure 5: Confusion matrices for the tokens with `LANG3` and `OTHER` LID labels on the development set.

our study shows that utilising LIDs is an effective method in this task. We also give the first results on LID, POS, and morphological tagging on the Turkish-German SAGT dataset. An implementation of our model is available at `https://github.com/sb-b/steps-parser`.

Acknowledgements

We thank Stefan Grünewald for his valuable help in using the STEPS tool. This work is funded by DFG via project CE 326/1-1 "Computational Structural Analysis of German-Turkish Code-Switching" (SAGT).

References

Gustavo Aguilar and Thamar Solorio. 2020. From English to code-switching: Transfer learning with strong morphological clues. In *Proceedings of the 58th Annual Meeting of the Association for Computational Linguistics*, pages 8033–8044, Online. Association for Computational Linguistics.

Fahad AlGhamdi and Mona Diab. 2019. Leveraging pretrained word embeddings for part-of-speech tagging of code switching data. In *Proceedings of the Sixth Workshop on NLP for Similar Languages, Varieties and Dialects*, pages 99–109, Ann Arbor, Michigan. Association for Computational Linguistics.

Fahad AlGhamdi, Giovanni Molina, Mona Diab, Thamar Solorio, Abdelati Hawwari, Victor Soto, and Julia Hirschberg. 2016. Part of speech tagging for code switched data. In *Proceedings of the Second Workshop on Computational Approaches to Code Switching*, pages 98–107, Austin, Texas. Association for Computational Linguistics.

Utsab Barman, Joachim Wagner, and Jennifer Foster. 2016. Part-of-speech tagging of code-mixed social media content: Pipeline, stacking and joint modelling. In *Proceedings of the Second Workshop on Computational Approaches to Code Switching*, pages 30–39, Austin, Texas. Association for Computational Linguistics.

Irshad Bhat, Riyaz A. Bhat, Manish Shrivastava, and Dipti Sharma. 2017. Joining hands: Exploiting monolingual treebanks for parsing of code-mixing data. In *Proceedings of the 15th Conference of the European Chapter of the Association for Computational Linguistics: Volume 2, Short Papers*, pages 324–330, Valencia, Spain. Association for Computational Linguistics.

Emanuel Borges Völker, Maximilian Wendt, Felix Hennig, and Arne Köhn. 2019. HDT-UD: A very large Universal Dependencies treebank for German. In *Proceedings of the Third Workshop on Universal Dependencies (UDW, SyntaxFest 2019)*, pages 46–57, Paris, France. Association for Computational Linguistics.

Özlem Çetinoğlu and Çağrı Çöltekin. 2019. Challenges of annotating a code-switching treebank. In *Proceedings of the 18th International Workshop on Treebanks and Linguistic Theories (TLT, SyntaxFest 2019)*, pages 82–90, Paris, France. Association for Computational Linguistics.

Ronan Collobert and Jason Weston. 2008. A unified architecture for natural language processing: Deep neural networks with multitask learning. In *Proceedings of the 25th International Conference on Machine Learning*, ICML '08, page 160–167, New York, NY, USA. Association for Computing Machinery.

Alexis Conneau, Kartikay Khandelwal, Naman Goyal, Vishrav Chaudhary, Guillaume Wenzek, Francisco Guzmán, Edouard Grave, Myle Ott, Luke Zettlemoyer, and Veselin Stoyanov. 2020. Unsupervised cross-lingual representation learning at scale. In *Proceedings of the 58th Annual Meeting of the Association for Computational Linguistics*, pages 8440–8451, Online. Association for Computational Linguistics.

Jacob Devlin, Ming-Wei Chang, Kenton Lee, and Kristina Toutanova. 2019. BERT: Pre-training of deep bidirectional transformers for language understanding. In *Proceedings of the 2019 Conference of the North American Chapter of the Association for Computational Linguistics: Human Language Technologies, Volume 1 (Long and Short Papers)*, pages 4171–4186, Minneapolis, Minnesota. Association for Computational Linguistics.

Wei Fang, Moin Nadeem, Mitra Mohtarami, and James Glass. 2019. Neural multi-task learning for stance prediction. In *Proceedings of the Second Workshop on Fact Extraction and VERification (FEVER)*, pages 13–19, Hong Kong, China. Association for Computational Linguistics.

Stefan Grünewald, Annemarie Friedrich, and Jonas Kuhn. 2020. Graph-based universal dependency parsing in the age of the transformer: What works, and what doesn't. *arXiv preprint arXiv:2010.12699*.

Mickel Hoang, Oskar Alija Bihorac, and Jacobo Rouces. 2019. Aspect-based sentiment analysis using BERT. In *Proceedings of the 22nd Nordic Conference on Computational Linguistics*, pages 187–196, Turku, Finland. Linköping University Electronic Press.

Anupam Jamatia, Björn Gambäck, and Amitava Das. 2015. Part-of-speech tagging for code-mixed English-Hindi Twitter and Facebook chat messages. In *Proceedings of the International Conference Recent Advances in Natural Language Processing*, pages 239–248, Hissar, Bulgaria. INCOMA Ltd. Shoumen, BULGARIA.

Dan Kondratyuk and Milan Straka. 2019. 75 languages, 1 model: Parsing Universal Dependencies universally. In *Proceedings of the 2019 Conference on Empirical Methods in Natural Language Processing and the 9th International Joint Conference on Natural Language Processing (EMNLP-IJCNLP)*, pages 2779–2795, Hong Kong, China. Association for Computational Linguistics.

Yaobo Liang, Nan Duan, Yeyun Gong, Ning Wu, Fenfei Guo, Weizhen Qi, Ming Gong, Linjun Shou, Daxin Jiang, Guihong Cao, Xiaodong Fan, Ruofei Zhang, Rahul Agrawal, Edward Cui, Sining Wei, Taroon Bharti, Ying Qiao, Jiun-Hung Chen, Winnie Wu, Shuguang Liu, Fan Yang, Daniel Campos, Rangan Majumder, and Ming Zhou. 2020. XGLUE: A new benchmark dataset for cross-lingual pretraining, understanding and generation. In *Proceedings of the 2020 Conference on Empirical Methods in Natural Language Processing (EMNLP)*, pages 6008–6018, Online. Association for Computational Linguistics.

Ying Lin, Shengqi Yang, Veselin Stoyanov, and Heng Ji. 2018. A multi-lingual multi-task architecture for low-resource sequence labeling. In *Proceedings of the 56th Annual Meeting of the Association for Computational Linguistics (Volume 1: Long Papers)*, pages 799–809, Melbourne, Australia. Association for Computational Linguistics.

Ryan McDonald, Joakim Nivre, Yvonne Quirmbach-Brundage, Yoav Goldberg, Dipanjan Das, Kuzman Ganchev, Keith Hall, Slav Petrov, Hao Zhang, Oscar Täckström, Claudia Bedini, Núria Bertomeu Castelló, and Jungmee Lee. 2013. Universal Dependency annotation for multilingual parsing. In *Proceedings of the 51st Annual Meeting of the Association for Computational Linguistics (Volume 2: Short Papers)*, pages 92–97, Sofia, Bulgaria. Association for Computational Linguistics.

Thomas Müller, Helmut Schmid, and Hinrich Schütze. 2013. Efficient higher-order CRFs for morphological tagging. In *Proceedings of the 2013 Conference on Empirical Methods in Natural Language Processing*, pages 322–332, Seattle, Washington, USA. Association for Computational Linguistics.

Thomas Müller and Hinrich Schütze. 2015. Robust morphological tagging with word representations. In *Proceedings of the 2015 Conference of the North American Chapter of the Association for Computational Linguistics: Human Language Technologies*, pages 526–536, Denver, Colorado. Association for Computational Linguistics.

Joakim Nivre, Marie-Catherine de Marneffe, Filip Ginter, Yoav Goldberg, Jan Hajič, Christopher D. Manning, Ryan McDonald, Slav Petrov, Sampo Pyysalo, Natalia Silveira, Reut Tsarfaty, and Daniel Zeman. 2016. Universal Dependencies v1: A multilingual treebank collection. In Proceedings of the Tenth International Conference on Language Resources and Evaluation (LREC'16), pages 1659–1666, Portorož, Slovenia. European Language Resources Association (ELRA).

Matthew Peters, Mark Neumann, Mohit Iyyer, Matt Gardner, Christopher Clark, Kenton Lee, and Luke Zettlemoyer. 2018. Deep contextualized word representations. In *Proceedings of the 2018 Conference of the North American Chapter of the Association for Computational Linguistics: Human Language Technologies, Volume 1 (Long Papers)*, pages 2227–2237, New Orleans, Louisiana. Association for Computational Linguistics.

Djamé Seddah, Farah Essaidi, Amal Fethi, Matthieu Futeral, Benjamin Muller, Pedro Javier Ortiz Suárez, Benoît Sagot, and Abhishek Srivastava. 2020. Building a user-generated content North-African Arabizi treebank: Tackling hell. In *Proceedings of the 58th Annual Meeting of the Association for Computational Linguistics*, pages 1139–1150, Online. Association for Computational Linguistics.

Royal Sequiera, Monojit Choudhury, and Kalika Bali. 2015. POS tagging of Hindi-English code mixed text from social media: Some machine learning experiments. In *Proceedings of the 12th International Conference on Natural Language Processing*, pages 237–246, Trivandrum, India. NLP Association of India.

Kushagra Singh, Indira Sen, and Ponnurangam Kumaraguru. 2018. A Twitter corpus for Hindi-English code mixed POS tagging. In *Proceedings of the Sixth International Workshop on Natural Language Processing for Social Media*, pages 12–17, Melbourne, Australia. Association for Computational Linguistics.

Thamar Solorio and Yang Liu. 2008. Part-of-speech tagging for English-Spanish code-switched text. In *Proceedings of the 2008 Conference on Empirical Methods in Natural Language Processing*, pages 1051–1060, Honolulu, Hawaii. Association for Computational Linguistics.

Victor Soto and Julia Hirschberg. 2018. Joint part-of-speech and language ID tagging for code-switched data. In *Proceedings of the Third Workshop on Computational Approaches to Linguistic Code-Switching*, pages 1–10, Melbourne, Australia. Association for Computational Linguistics.

Milan Straka, Jana Straková, and Jan Hajič. 2019. Evaluating contextualized embeddings on 54 languages in POS tagging, lemmatization and dependency parsing. *arXiv preprint arXiv:1908.07448*.

Umut Sulubacak, Memduh Gökırmak, Francis Tyers, Çağrı Çöltekin, Joakim Nivre, and Gülşen Eryiğit. 2016. Universal Dependencies for Turkish. In *Proceedings of COLING 2016, the 26th International Conference on Computational Linguistics: Technical Papers*, pages 3444–3454, Osaka, Japan. The COLING 2016 Organizing Committee.

Reut Tsarfaty, Djamé Seddah, Sandra Kübler, and Joakim Nivre. 2013. Parsing morphologically rich languages: Introduction to the special issue. *Computational Linguistics*, 39(1):15–22.

Utku Türk, Furkan Atmaca, Şaziye Betül Özateş, Gözde Berk, Seyyit Talha Bedir, Abdullatif Köksal, Balkız Öztürk Başaran, Tunga Güngör, and Arzucan Özgür. 2020. Resources for Turkish dependency parsing: Introducing the BOUN treebank and the BoAT annotation tool. *arXiv preprint arXiv:2002.10416*.

Rob van der Goot and Özlem Çetinoğlu. 2021. Lexical normalization for code-switched data and its effect on POS tagging. In *Proceedings of the 16th Conference of the European Chapter of the Association for Computational Linguistics: Volume 1, Long Papers*. Association for Computational Linguistics.

Hilko van der Voet. 1994. Comparing the predictive accuracy of models using a simple randomization test. *Chemometrics and Intelligent Laboratory Systems*, 25(2):313–323.

David Vilares, Miguel A. Alonso, and Carlos Gómez-Rodríguez. 2016. EN-ES-CS: An English-Spanish code-switching twitter corpus for multilingual sentiment analysis. In *Proceedings of the Tenth International Conference on Language Resources and Evaluation (LREC'16)*, pages 4149–4153, Portorož, Slovenia. European Language Resources Association (ELRA).

Yogarshi Vyas, Spandana Gella, Jatin Sharma, Kalika Bali, and Monojit Choudhury. 2014. POS tagging of English-Hindi code-mixed social media content. In *Proceedings of the 2014 Conference on Empirical Methods in Natural Language Processing (EMNLP)*, pages 974–979, Doha, Qatar. Association for Computational Linguistics.

Yu Zhang and Qiang Yang. 2017. A survey on multi-task learning. *arXiv preprint arXiv:1707.08114*.

A Comparison of Two Approaches for the Data Split Method

Model	Accuracy on the Development Set					
	TR	DE	MIXED	LANG3	OTHER	**ALL**
first	**81.17**	**83.03**	**69.67**	52.78	**99.91**	**83.72**
second	81.05	82.78	60.93	**57.64**	99.88	83.48
	Accuracy on the Test Set					
	TR	DE	MIXED	LANG3	OTHER	**ALL**
first	**78.04**	**80.12**	**65.03**	50.00	**99.93**	**80.98**
second	77.44	79.59	60.11	50.00	99.86	80.42

Model	Accuracy on the Development Set					
	TR	DE	MIXED	LANG3	OTHER	**ALL**
first	**80.66**	**82.95**	**70.43**	41.50	**100.0**	**83.43**
second	80.50	82.81	63.44	41.50	99.97	83.23
	Accuracy on the Test Set					
	TR	DE	MIXED	LANG3	OTHER	**ALL**
first	**77.65**	**80.01**	**65.59**	48.78	100.0	**80.78**
second	77.05	79.54	60.75	48.78	100.0	80.26

Table 8: Morphological tagging accuracy of the two pipeline approaches for the DSplit method. The first part shows the scores in the existence of gold LIDs and the second part demonstrates the results when predicted LIDs are used instead of gold ones.

B Comparison of MarMoT and STEPS for LID Prediction

	Accuracy			
	Development set		Test set	
	MarMoT	STEPS	MarMoT	STEPS
TR	96.40	**99.09**	97.38	**99.42**
DE	97.84	**98.43**	97.88	**98.80**
MIXED	23.77	**90.16**	27.32	**92.90**
LANG3	41.67	**52.08**	0.0	**67.39**
OTHER	98.23	**99.91**	99.06	**99.86**
ALL	96.12	**98.55**	96.57	**98.96**

Table 9: Comparsion of MarMoT and STEPS tools for LID prediction on the development and test sets of the SAGT Treebank.

Can You Traducir This? Machine Translation for Code-Switched Input

Jitao Xu
Univ. Paris-Saclay,
& CNRS, LISN
Orsay, France
jitao.xu@limsi.fr

François Yvon
Univ. Paris-Saclay,
& CNRS, LISN
Orsay, France
francois.yvon@limsi.fr

Abstract

Code-Switching (CSW) is a common phenomenon that occurs in multilingual geographic or social contexts, which raises challenging problems for natural language processing tools. We focus here on Machine Translation (MT) of CSW texts, where we aim to simultaneously disentangle and translate the two mixed languages. Due to the lack of actual translated CSW data, we generate artificial training data from regular parallel texts. Experiments show this training strategy yields MT systems that surpass multilingual systems for code-switched texts. These results are confirmed in an alternative task aimed at providing contextual translations for a L2 writing assistant.

1 Introduction

Code-Switching (CSW) denotes the alternation of two languages within a single utterance (Poplack, 1980; Sitaram et al., 2019). It is a common communicative phenomenon that occurs in multilingual communities during spoken and written interactions. CSW is a well studied phenomenon in linguistic circles and has given rise to a number of theories regarding the structure of mixed language fragments (Poplack, 1978; Pfaff, 1979; Poplack, 1980; Belazi et al., 1994; Myers-Scotton, 1997). The Matrix Language Frame (MLF) theory (Myers-Scotton, 1997) defines the concept of *matrix* and *embedded* languages where the *matrix language* is the main language that the sentence structure should conform to and notably provides the syntactic morphemes, while the influence of the *embedded language* is lesser and is mostly manifested in the insertion of content morphemes.

The rise of social media and user-generated content has made written instances of code-switched language more visible. It is estimated that as much as 17% of Indian Facebook posts (Bali et al., 2014) and 3.5% of all tweets (Rijhwani et al., 2017) are code-switched. This phenomenon is also becoming more pervasive in short text messages, chats, blogs, and the like (Samih et al., 2016). Code-switching however remains understudied in natural language processing (NLP) (Aguilar and Solorio, 2020), and most work to date has focused on token-level language identification (LID) (Samih et al., 2016) and on language models for Automatic Speech Recognition (Winata et al., 2019). More tasks are being considered lately, such as Named Entity Recognition (Aguilar et al., 2018), Part-of-Speech tagging (Ball and Garrette, 2018) or Sentiment Analysis (Patwa et al., 2020).

We focus here on another task for CSW texts: Machine Translation (MT). The advent of Neural Machine Translation (NMT) technologies (Bahdanau et al., 2015; Vaswani et al., 2017) has made it possible to design multilingual models capable of translating from multiple source languages into multiple target languages (Firat et al., 2016; Johnson et al., 2017), where however both the input and output are monolingual. We study here the ability of such architectures to translate fragments freely mixing a "matrix" and an "embedded" language into monolingual utterances.

Our main contribution is to show that for the two pairs of languages considered (French-English and Spanish-English): (a) translation of CSW texts is almost as good as the translation of monolingual texts – a performance that bilingual systems are unable to match; (b) such results can be obtained by training solely with artificial data; (c) CSW translation systems achieve a near deterministic ability to recopy in the output target words found in the input, suggesting that they are endowed with some language identification abilities. Using these models, we are also able to obtain competitive results on the SemEval 2014 Task 5: L2 Writing Assistant, which we see as one potential application area of CSW translation.

Proceedings of the Fifth Workshop on Computational Approaches to Linguistic Code-Switching, pages 84–94
June 11, 2021. ©2021 Association for Computational Linguistics
https://doi.org/10.26615/978-954-452-056-4_011

2 Building translation systems for code-switched data

2.1 Code-switched data generation

Parallel corpora with natural CSW data are very scarce (Menacer et al., 2019) and, similar to Song et al. (2019a), we generate artificial CSW parallel sentences from regular translation data.

We first compute word alignments between parallel sentences using `fast_align`[1] (Dyer et al., 2013). We then extract so-called *minimal alignment units* following the approach of Crego et al. (2005): these correspond to small bilingual phrase pairs (e, f) extracted from (symmetrized) word alignments such that all alignment links outgoing from words in e reach a word in f, and vice-versa.

For each pair of parallel sentence, we first randomly select the matrix language;[2] then the number of replacements r to appear in a derived CSW sentence with an exponential distribution as:

$$P(r = k) = \frac{1}{2^{k+1}} \quad \forall k = 1, \ldots, \text{rep} \qquad (1)$$

where rep is a predefined maximum number of replacements. We also make sure that the number of replacements does not exceed half of either the original source or target sentences length, adjusting the actual number of replacements as:

$$n = \min(\frac{S}{2}, \frac{T}{2}, r) \qquad (2)$$

where S and T are respectively the length of the source and target sentences. We finally choose uniformly at random r alignment units and replace these fragments in the matrix language by their counterpart in the embedded language. Figure 1 displays examples of generated CSW sentences.

2.2 Machine translation for CSW data

2.2.1 Data preparation

We use WMT data for CSW data generation and for training MT systems. We discard sentences which do not possess the correct language by using the `fasttext` LID model[3] (Bojanowski et al., 2017). We use Moses tools (Koehn et al., 2007) to normalize punctuations, remove non-printing characters and discard sentence pairs with a source / target ratio higher than 1.5, with a maximum sentence length of 250. We tokenize all WMT data using Moses tokenizer.[4] Our procedure for artificial CSW data generation uses WMT13 En-Es parallel data with 14.5M sentences. For En-Fr, we use all WMT14 parallel data, for a grand total of 33.9M sentences. Our development sets are respectively `newstest2011` and `newstest2012` for En-Es, and `newstest2012` and `newstest2013` as development sets for En-Fr; the corresponding test sets are `newstest2013` (En-Es) and `newstest2014` (En-Fr).

2.2.2 Machine Translation systems

We use the `fairseq`[5] (Ott et al., 2019) implementation of Transformer base (Vaswani et al., 2017) for our models with a hidden size of 512 and a feedforward size of 2048. We optimize with Adam, set up with an initial learning rate of 0.0007 and an inverse square root weight decay schedule, as well as 4000 warmup steps. All models were trained with mixed precision and a batch size of 8192 tokens for 300k iterations on 4 V100 GPUs. For each language pair, we use a shared source-target inventory built with Byte Pair Encoding (BPE) of 32K merge operations, using the implementation published by Sennrich et al. (2016).[6] Note that we do not share the embedding matrices. Our experiments with sharing the decoder's input and output embeddings or sharing all encoder+decoder embeddings did not yield further gains.

We compare three settings for `Code-Switch` models:

- the `base-csw` setting, where we train two separate systems, one translating CSW into English, and the other translating CSW into Spanish or French.
- the `multi-csw` setting, where we train one model able to generate either pure matrix or embedded language in the output. To this

[1] https://github.com/clab/fast_align

[2] Note that we abuse here the terms "matrix" and "embedded" language, as we do not attempt to generate linguistically realistic CSW data matching the constraints of the MLF theory. We use these terms in a much looser sense where the sentence in the "matrix" language is the one that receives arbitrary insertions from the "embedded" language. This means that our artificial CSW sentences will contain insertions of unconstrained fragments containing both content and function words, which the theory would generally consider ungrammatical.

[3] https://dl.fbaipublicfiles.com/fasttext/supervised-models/lid.176.bin

[4] https://github.com/moses-smt/mosesdecoder

[5] https://github.com/pytorch/fairseq

[6] https://github.com/rsennrich/subword-nmt.

Matrix	In Oregon , planners are experimenting with giving drivers different choices .
$r = 1$	**Dans** Oregon , planners are experimenting with giving drivers different choices .
$r = 2$	**Dans** Oregon , **les planificateurs** are experimenting with giving drivers different choices .
$r = 3$	**Dans** Oregon , **les planificateurs** are experimenting **en offrant aux** drivers different choices .
Embedded	Dans l'Orégon, les planificateurs tentent l'expérience en offrant aux automobilistes différents choix.

Figure 1: Examples of generated CSW sentences when taking English as the matrix language and varying the number r of replacements of embedded French segments (in boldface).

end, similar to a multilingual NMT model (Johnson et al., 2017), we add a tag at the beginning of each CSW sentence to specify the desired target language. Taking En-Fr as an example, we add a `<EN>` tag for CSW-En and a `<FR>` tag for CSW-Fr. We use the combination of CSW-En and CSW-Fr data for training, which implies that each source side (CSW sentence) is duplicated in the training data, once for each possible output.

- the `joint-csw` setting, which extends `multi-csw` by using one encoder and two separate decoders and training the two output languages simultaneously *with a combined loss function*: for each training (CSW) instance, the loss function sums the two prediction terms for the embedded and the matrix language. The training data remains the same.

Note that all our `Code-Switch` systems also have the ability to translate monolingual source data, in either direction.

For comparison purposes, we also use our parallel data to train two baselines: (a) regular NMT systems for the considered language pairs (`base`), similar to `base-csw`; (b) *bilingual NMT systems*, capable of translating from and into both two languages (`bilingual`). The selection of the desired target language relies on the same tagging mechanism as `multi-csw`, which means that both types of models see exactly the same examples. All resulting baseline Transformer models have the exact same hyperparameters and use the same training scheme as `Code-Switch`. Performance is computed with SacreBLEU (Post, 2018) and METEOR (Denkowski and Lavie, 2014).

3 Machine translation experiments

3.1 Results

We run tests using artificial CSW datasets, as mentioned in Section 2.2, as well as on the original test sets, in order to evaluate our models' ability to translate both CSW and monolingual sentences. Results are in Table 1 where we also separately report scores for the 'Matrix' and 'Embedded' part of the test sets. As is obvious on the `copy` line, the 'Embedded' part contains mostly source language, and corresponds to an actual translation task whereas the 'Matrix' part mostly contains target words on the source side, and is much easier to translate.

On the left part of this table, we see that the baseline systems, either with two (`base`) or one single (`bilingual`) model(s), do better on monolingual test sets than their counterparts trained on CSW data (respectively `base-csw` and `multi-csw`). For both language pairs, the observed differences are in the range of 1-1.5 BLEU points. Conversely, when translating CSW sentences, `*-csw` models perform significantly better than the corresponding baselines models, which have never seen CSW in the source.

Moreover, we note the marked differences between BLEU scores obtained by these models when the matrix language for the CSW source is the target and when the embedded language is the target. In the former case, translation is near perfect; in the latter case they nonetheless use the little information available to improve over the monolingual scores (about 1-1.5 BLEU points), nearly matching the performance of the baseline systems. This is illustrated for Fr-En, for which `joint-csw` improved from 33.7 to 35.0; in the same condition, the `bilingual` system only improves by 0.1 point.

Among the three `Code-Switch` models, `multi-csw` is the weakest, while the other two achieve comparable performance. Interestingly, with joint training (`joint-csw`), we can recover with one single system the performance of the two separate systems used in the `base-csw` condition. On the monolingual tests, this system also matches the performance of the multilingual baseline (`bilingual`), which makes it overall our best contender of the lot.

Testset	newstest2013				csw-newstest2013			
Direction	En-Es		Es-En		CSW-Es		CSW-En	
Metrics	B	M	B	M	B	M	B	M
`copy`	-	-	-	-	50.3	57.8	46.8	31.7
					2.9	93.5	3.0	93.3
`base`	**33.2**	**58.3**	**33.8**	**36.4**	38.9	59.1	57.3	44.4
	33.1	-	34.0	-	32.5	43.4	34.6	78.7
`bilingual`	31.9	57.3	32.6	35.9	23.3	42.0	44.2	37.5
	31.9	-	32.9	-	32.3	14.5	33.3	54.5
`base-csw`	32.0	57.4	32.7	36.0	66.8	**79.8**	**66.5**	**49.4**
	31.8	-	33.0	-	33.1	97.1	34.5	97.5
`multi-csw`	31.1	56.7	31.5	35.4	66.5	79.5	64.7	48.6
	30.9	-	31.9	-	32.2	97.2	33.1	95.1
`joint-csw`	31.9	57.3	32.6	36.0	**66.9**	79.7	66.4	**49.4**
	32.0	-	32.8	-	33.2	97.2	34.2	97.5

Testset	newstest2014				csw-newstest2014			
Direction	En-Fr		Fr-En		CSW-Fr		CSW-En	
Metrics	B	M	B	M	B	M	B	M
`copy`	-	-	-	-	50.0	55.7	46.5	33.1
					2.9	93.8	2.9	93.4
`base`	**37.9**	**60.9**	**35.4**	**37.9**	45.1	64.4	61.3	47.3
	37.7	-	35.3	-	37.8	52.0	36.0	84.6
`bilingual`	36.3	59.6	34.5	37.6	54.8	71.3	56.5	45.8
	36.4	-	34.6	-	36.8	71.7	34.7	76.6
`base-csw`	36.7	59.9	34.3	37.5	**67.5**	**79.9**	**67.9**	**50.5**
	36.7	-	34.2	-	37.8	95.2	35.6	97.4
`multi-csw`	35.2	58.7	32.9	36.8	66.7	79.5	65.8	49.4
	35.3	-	32.6	-	36.3	95.1	33.7	94.6
`joint-csw`	36.2	59.5	34.0	37.3	67.4	79.8	67.7	50.3
	36.2	-	33.7	-	37.3	95.4	35.0	97.4

Table 1: Translating monolingual newstest data and artificial `csw-newstest` data for two language pairs where performance is measured via the BLEU (B) and METEOR (M) scores. We also report a trivial baseline that just recopies the source text. Small numbers contain BLEU scores computed separately when the target language is the embedded language (left) and the matrix language (right). For the monolingual tests (left part), these correspond to scores computed on the same sentences that are also included in the CSW tests.

3.2 Analysis

3.2.1 Code-Switching effect

In order to better study the effect of mixing languages, we modify the synthetic data generation method to keep one language as the matrix language, in which segments are incrementally replaced by translations of the embedded language. We relax the constraint on the maximum number of replacements and generate new test sets with an increasing number of replacements, ranging from 1 to 20, resulting in 20[7] versions of the CSW test sets (in each direction). In Figure 2, we plot the BLEU scores of both source CSW sentences and their translations for En-Fr language pair, using each language as the matrix language, to visualize the impact of progressively introducing more target fragments into the source.

The same behavior is observed for both language pairs and directions: on average, inserting random target fragments boosts the translation performance, with a larger payoff for the first few target segments. There exists an important gap for the output BLEU scores when CSW source sentences with different matrix languages reach the same (input) BLEU scores. Even though we generate a large number of replacements, the basic grammar structure of the matrix language is still maintained. Therefore, taking the target language as matrix gives the model a pre-translated sentence structure that is much easier to reproduce.

3.2.2 Implicit LID in translation

A second question concerns the ability of the translation system to identify target fragments in the source and to copy them in the target, even though these fragments are indistinguishable from genuine source segments. We use labels computed

[7]For sentences that could not accommodate 20 replacements, we performed as many replacements as possible.

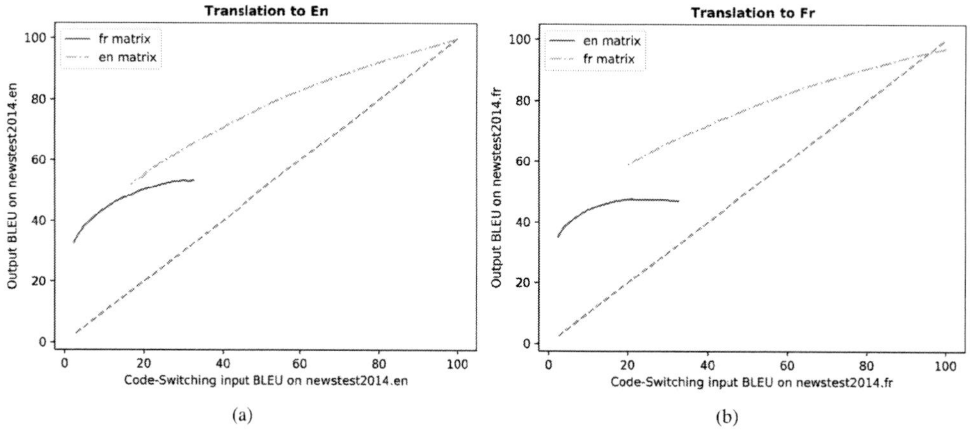

Figure 2: Evolution of the BLEU score of source CSW data and their target translation for En-Fr. (a) Direction CSW-En. The solid curve takes Fr as the matrix language, where we progressively inject more En segments; for the dash dot curve, En is the matrix language, with a growing number of Fr segments. (b) Direction CSW-Fr. Note that the target BLEU is always much higher than the source BLEU, with about a 20 points difference. The gap between the dash dot and solid curves is due to the basic sentence structure of the matrix language (see Section 3.2.1). As dash dot curves represent insertion in the *reference target* sentence, the corresponding BLEU score is always higher than the solid curve and actually reaches 100 (in the absence of any embedded language).

during the CSW generation procedure to sort out pre-translated (target) segments from actual source segments to be translated. For instance, when translating into French, only tokens with a label `eng`, denoting English, are expected to be translated. All other tokens correspond to French words are expected to be copied. As reported in Table 2, our translation models are able to copy almost all pre-translated tokens for both language pairs and directions.

Testset	csw-newstest2014		csw-newstest2013	
Direction	CSW-En	CSW-Fr	CSW-En	CSW-Es
to copy	42148	47337	37653	41053
copied	41567	46229	37421	40638
copy rate (%)	98.6	97.7	99.4	99.0
CSW rate (%)	0.13	0.30	0.16	0.23

Table 2: Analyzing the recopy of tokens on `csw-newstest2014` for En-Fr and `csw-newstest2013` for En-Es. We report the number of (pre-translated) tokens that should be copied, and the corresponding ratios.

Refining the analysis, we also study whether the relative order of target words changes, or is preserved, during the translation. Table 3 reports the percentage of exact and switched-order copies. We observe again large differences with respect to the position of the matrix language. When the matrix language is the target language, the model always preserves the observed token order since it indicates a correct sentence structure for the hypothesis. When translating into the embedded language, we observe a larger number of word order changes: in this case, inserted target segments may not appear in their correct order in the CSW sentence, an issue that the model tries to fix. An example of this is in Figure 3, where we observe a swap between the input ("différent choix") and output ("choix différent") word orders.

	En-Fr		En-Es	
Direction	Copy	Copy+Swap	Copy	Copy+Swap
CSW-En	87.1	4.5	90.7	5.2
Mat En	97.6	0.1	98.2	0.2
Mat For	61.4	15.2	72.6	17.3
CSW-For	77.4	5.5	88.5	3.7
Mat For	84.9	0.1	97.1	0.2
Mat En	59.4	18.5	65. 6	13.2

Table 3: Percentage of sentences for which all target words have been exactly copied without and with order changes, for `csw-newstest2014` (En-Fr) and `csw-newstest2013` (En-Es). We separately report numbers for the case where the foreign language (French or Spanish) is the embedded (Mat En) or matrix (Mat For) language.

Conversely, it is also interesting to look at the proportion of mixed language generated on the target side. Recall that in our training, the source is mixed-language, while the target is always monolingual. We use an in-house token-level language identification (`LID`) model to identify the language of output tokens and to detect the CSW rate on the target side. As indicated in Table 2, our models generate almost pure monolingual translations, with a very low rate of CSW text. CSW-translation models thus seem to perform some language identification, as they almost perfectly sort out target language tokens (which are almost always copied) from the source language tokens (which are always translated).

A last issue concerns morphological errors: when inserting foreign words into a matrix source, one cannot expect to always also introduce the right inflection marks, some of which can only be determined once the target context is known. Another interesting phenomenon, that we do not simulate here, is when the embedded (target) lemma is adapted bears a morphological mark that only exist in the matrix language, which means that two linguistic systems are mixed within the same word, thereby posing more extreme difficulties for MT (Manandise and Gdaniec, 2011).

To illustrate the ability to correct grammar errors in input fragments, we manually noise a CSW sentence and display its translation in Figure 3. Where the input just contains the lemma of the French word "tenter" (*to try*), the model inserts a modal "doivent" to fix the context. Another illustration is for the adjective "différent" which is moved into post-nominal position, and for which an article ("un") is inserted. This indicates that the model not only copies what already exists but also tends to adjust translations whenever necessary.

4 Computing translations in context

In this section, we evaluate CSW translation for the SemEval 2014 Task 5: L2 Writing Assistant (van Gompel et al., 2014), which can be handled as an MT task from mixed data.

4.1 Method

This task consists in translating L1 fragments in an L2 context, where the test set design is such that there is exactly one L1 insert in each utterance. We evaluated on two L1-L2 pairs: English-Spanish and French-English, and list below example test segments provided by the organizers for these pairs of languages (the insert and reference segments are in boldface):

- Input (L1=English,L2=Spanish): *"Todo ello, **in accordance** con los principios que siempre hemos apoyado."*
  Output: *"Todo ello, **de conformidad** con los principios que siempre hemos apoy-ado."*

- Input (L1=French,L2=English): *"**I rentre à la maison** because I am tired."*
  Output: *"**I return home** because I am tired."*

The official metric for the SemEval evaluation is a word-based accuracy of the translations of the L1 fragment, which means that the L2 context of each sentence is not taken into account in scoring. Since our systems are full-fledged NMT systems, their output may not contain the reference L2 prefix and suffix. Therefore, two options are explored to compute these scores. The first is to post-process the output `HYP` and align it with the L2 reference context in `REF`. This alignment allows us to only score the relevant fragment in `HYP`. We refer to this option as `free-dec`.

The second option is to ensure that the L2 context will be present in the output translation. To this end, we use the *force decoding mode* of `fairseq`, implementing the methods of Post and Vilar (2018); Hu et al. (2019). We explored two different ways to express the L2 context as decoding constraints. The first turns every token in the L2 context as a separate constraint (`token-cst`). Continuing the previous example, *"I, because, I, am, tired."* yield 5 constraints. The second uses the prefix and suffix of the L2 context as two multi-word constraints (`presuf-cst`). In this case, *"I"* and *"because I am tired."* yield just 2 constraints. In both cases, constraints are required to be present in the prescribed order in the output.

4.2 Results

Scores are computed with the SemEval evaluation tool,[8] which enables a comparison with other submissions for this task. Results are in Table 4 and 5. For En-Es, our CSW translator outperforms the best system in the official evaluation (van Gompel et al., 2014). Note that this model is not specifically designed nor tuned in any way for the SemEval task. For Fr-En, our system achieves better performance than the forth best participating system, with a clear gap with respect to the top results. In both cases, constraint decoding hurts performance: given that the automatic copy of target segments is already nearly perfect, introducing more constraints during

[8] `https://github.com/proycon/semeval2014task5`

En	In Oregon , planners are experimenting with giving drivers different choices.
Fr	Dans l'Orégon, les planificateurs tentent l'expérience en offrant aux automobilistes différents choix.
CSW	In l'Oregon , planners **tentent l' expérience** with giving **automobilistes différents choix**.
Hyp	*Dans l'Orégon , les planificateurs tentent l'expérience de donner aux automobilistes différents choix.*
Noisy CSW	In l' Oregon , planners **tenter** l'expérience with giving **automobilist différent** choix.
Hyp	*Dans l'Orégon , les planificateurs **doivent tenter** l'expérience de donner **à l' automobiliste un choix différent**.*

Figure 3: A noisy Code-Switched sentence with French as both the matrix and target language.

the search has here a clear detrimental effect for this task.

	Accuracy	Word Accuracy	Recall
UEdin-run2	0.755	0.827	1.0
UEdin-run1	0.753	0.827	1.0
UEdin-run3	0.745	0.820	1.0
`multi-csw`			
`free-dec`	0.755	0.827	1.0
`token-cst`	0.749	0.824	1.0
`presuf-cst`	0.751	0.827	1.0
`joint-csw`			
`free-dec`	0.773	0.842	1.0

Table 4: Results of SemEval 2014 Task 5 for En-Es.

	Accuracy	Word Accuracy	Recall
UEdin-run1	0.733	0.824	1.0
UEdin-run2	0.731	0.821	1.0
UEdin-run3	0.723	0.816	1.0
CNRC-run1	0.556	0.694	1.0
`multi-csw`			
`free-dec`	0.554	0.685	0.996
`token-cst`	0.531	0.665	0.990
`presuf-cst`	0.519	0.658	0.982
`joint-csw`			
`free-dec`	0.626	0.744	0.994

Table 5: Results of SemEval 2014 Task 5 for Fr-En.

To better study the performance gap between these language pairs, we additionally score the development and test data with BLEU and METEOR. Results in Table 6 show that for these metrics, we achieve performance that are in that same ballpark for the two language pairs, suggesting that the observed difference in the SemEval metric is likely due to a mismatch between references and system outputs. The official metric is a word accuracy which may exclude acceptable translations by exact token match.

5 Related work

Research in the area of NLP for CSW has mostly focused on CSW Language Modeling, especially for Automatic Speech Recognition (Pratapa et al., 2018; Garg et al., 2018; Gonen and Goldberg, 2019;

	`multi-csw`		`joint-csw`	
Dataset	B	M	B	M
Fr-En dev	97.3	75.6	97.6	76.4
Fr-En test	90.1	64.1	91.0	66.1
En-Es dev	97.4	98.8	97.6	99.0
En-Es test	89.9	95.3	90.4	95.5

Table 6: Results of other metrics on SemEval data. METEOR scores for the Fr-En SemEval test are much worse than for En-Es. This is mostly due to the high "fragmentation penalty" computed by METEOR for English; the corresponding average F_{mean} is about 0.99, showing that translations are mostly correct.

Winata et al., 2019; Lee and Li, 2020). Evaluation tasks, benchmarks have also been prepared for LID in user generated CSW content (Zubiaga et al., 2016; Molina et al., 2016), Named Entity Recognition (Aguilar et al., 2018), Part-of-Speech tagging (Ball and Garrette, 2018; Aguilar et al., 2020; Khanuja et al., 2020) and Sentiment Analysis (Patwa et al., 2020). CSW was also found useful in foreign language teaching: Renduchintala et al. (2019a,b) showed that replacing words by their counterparts in foreign language helps to learn foreign language vocabulary.

Regarding MT, most past work has focused on using artificial CSW data to help conventional translation systems. Huang and Yates (2014) used CSW corpus to improve word alignment and statistical MT. Dinu et al. (2019) experienced replacing and concatenating source terminology constraints by the corresponding translation(s) to boost the accuracy of term translations. Song et al. (2019a) shared the same idea by replacing phrases with prespecified translation to perform "soft" constraint decoding. A different line of research is in (Bulte and Tezcan, 2019; Xu et al., 2020; Pham et al., 2020), who explore ways to combine a source sentence with similar translations extracted from translation memories. Yang et al. (2020) also pretrained translation models by predicting original source segments from generated CSW sentences and claimed better results compared to other pre-training methods (Conneau and Lample, 2019; Song et al., 2019b). Nevertheless, there barely exists work aimed at translating CSW sentences. Johnson et al. (2017) mentioned using a multilingual NMT system to translate CSW sentence to a third target language by showing only one example. To the best of our knowledge, only one parallel Arabic-English CSW corpus was specifically released for MT applications (Menacer et al., 2019). This CSW data was extracted from the UN data with Arabic as the matrix language: while translations into English were readily available, the purely Arabic side of the corpus was obtained using Google Translate to fill the missing Arabic bits.

6 Conclusion and outlook

In this study, we present a data augmentation method to generate artificial CSW data. We have shown that artificial data generated could be used to train NMT systems to translate both monolingual and CSW sentences (in one or even two different languages). With joint training of the two languages, we were able to build systems that were as good as a baseline bilingual system on monolingual texts, and much better for CSW texts. Our system does not need any explicit language identification and almost perfectly sorts out source tokens from target tokens in a CSW utterance. Another interesting feature of our system is that it always output monolingual translations. We finally report state-of-the-art results for the SemEval L2 Writing Assistant task for Es-En, while the related results for Fr-En are still somewhat lagging behind the best scores.

In the future, we would like to generate more realistic CSW data from monolingual sentences using a translation model. We also plan to explore ways to translate CSW texts simultaneously into both languages, so that the two decoding processes can mutually influence one another: in a first step in that direction, we have shown that training with a joint loss was actually beneficial for the translation into the two languages. Another line of research would be to continue experimenting with realistic language data, also containing other phenomena such as morphological binding. Finally, we also intend to study the somewhat more realistic condition where a mixture of languages A and B is translated into language C; we believe that the artificial CSW generation methods developed in our work would also be effective for this task.

7 Acknowledgements

This work was granted access to the HPC resources of IDRIS under the allocation 2021-[AD011011580R1] made by GENCI. The authors wish to thank Josep Crego for his comments of an earlier version of this work. We also would like to thank the anonymous reviewers for their valuable suggestions. The first author is partly funded by Systran and by a grant from Région Ile-de-France.

References

Gustavo Aguilar, Fahad AlGhamdi, Victor Soto, Mona Diab, Julia Hirschberg, and Thamar Solorio. 2018. Named entity recognition on code-switched data: Overview of the CALCS 2018 shared task. In *Proceedings of the Third Workshop on Computational Approaches to Linguistic Code-Switching*, pages 138–147, Melbourne, Australia. Association for Computational Linguistics.

Gustavo Aguilar, Sudipta Kar, and Thamar Solorio. 2020. LinCE: A Centralized Benchmark for Linguistic Code-switching Evaluation. In *Proceedings of The 12th Language Resources and Evaluation Conference*, pages 1803–1813, Marseille, France. European Language Resources Association.

Gustavo Aguilar and Thamar Solorio. 2020. From English to code-switching: Transfer learning with strong morphological clues. In *Proceedings of the 58th Annual Meeting of the Association for Computational Linguistics*, pages 8033–8044, Online. Association for Computational Linguistics.

Dzmitry Bahdanau, Kyunghyun Cho, and Yoshua Bengio. 2015. Neural machine translation by jointly learning to align and translate. In *3rd International Conference on Learning Representations, ICLR 2015, San Diego, CA, USA, May 7-9, 2015, Conference Track Proceedings*.

Kalika Bali, Jatin Sharma, Monojit Choudhury, and Yogarshi Vyas. 2014. "I am borrowing ya mixing ?" an analysis of English-Hindi code mixing in Facebook. In *Proceedings of the First Workshop on Computational Approaches to Code Switching*, pages 116–126, Doha, Qatar. Association for Computational Linguistics.

Kelsey Ball and Dan Garrette. 2018. Part-of-speech tagging for code-switched, transliterated texts without explicit language identification. In *Proceedings of the 2018 Conference on Empirical Methods in Natural Language Processing*, pages 3084–3089, Brussels, Belgium. Association for Computational Linguistics.

Hedi M Belazi, Edward J Rubin, and Almeida Jacqueline Toribio. 1994. Code switching and x-bar theory: The functional head constraint. *Linguistic inquiry*, pages 221–237.

Piotr Bojanowski, Edouard Grave, Armand Joulin, and Tomas Mikolov. 2017. Enriching word vectors with subword information. *Transactions of the Association for Computational Linguistics*, 5:135–146.

Bram Bulte and Arda Tezcan. 2019. Neural fuzzy repair: Integrating fuzzy matches into neural machine translation. In *Proceedings of the 57th Annual Meeting of the Association for Computational Linguistics*, pages 1800–1809, Florence, Italy. Association for Computational Linguistics.

Alexis Conneau and Guillaume Lample. 2019. Cross-lingual language model pretraining. In *Advances in Neural Information Processing Systems*, volume 32, pages 7059–7069. Curran Associates, Inc.

Josep M. Crego, José B. Mariño, and Adrià De Gispert. 2005. Reordered search, and tuple unfolding for Ngram-based SMT. In *In Proceedings of the MT Summit X*, pages 283–289.

Michael Denkowski and Alon Lavie. 2014. Meteor universal: Language specific translation evaluation for any target language. In *Proceedings of the Ninth Workshop on Statistical Machine Translation*, pages 376–380, Baltimore, Maryland, USA. Association for Computational Linguistics.

Georgiana Dinu, Prashant Mathur, Marcello Federico, and Yaser Al-Onaizan. 2019. Training neural machine translation to apply terminology constraints. In *Proceedings of the 57th Annual Meeting of the Association for Computational Linguistics*, pages 3063–3068, Florence, Italy. Association for Computational Linguistics.

Chris Dyer, Victor Chahuneau, and Noah A. Smith. 2013. A simple, fast, and effective reparameterization of IBM model 2. In *Proceedings of the 2013 Conference of the North American Chapter of the Association for Computational Linguistics: Human Language Technologies*, pages 644–648, Atlanta, Georgia. Association for Computational Linguistics.

Orhan Firat, Kyunghyun Cho, and Yoshua Bengio. 2016. Multi-way, multilingual neural machine translation with a shared attention mechanism. In *Proceedings of the 2016 Conference of the North American Chapter of the Association for Computational Linguistics: Human Language Technologies*, pages 866–875. Association for Computational Linguistics.

Saurabh Garg, Tanmay Parekh, and Preethi Jyothi. 2018. Code-switched language models using dual RNNs and same-source pretraining. In *Proceedings of the 2018 Conference on Empirical Methods in Natural Language Processing*, pages 3078–3083, Brussels, Belgium. Association for Computational Linguistics.

Hila Gonen and Yoav Goldberg. 2019. Language modeling for code-switching: Evaluation, integration of monolingual data, and discriminative training. In *Proceedings of the 2019 Conference on Empirical Methods in Natural Language Processing and the 9th International Joint Conference on Natural Language Processing (EMNLP-IJCNLP)*, pages 4175–4185, Hong Kong, China. Association for Computational Linguistics.

J. Edward Hu, Huda Khayrallah, Ryan Culkin, Patrick Xia, Tongfei Chen, Matt Post, and Benjamin Van Durme. 2019. Improved lexically constrained decoding for translation and monolingual rewriting. In *Proceedings of the 2019 Conference of the North American Chapter of the Association for Computational Linguistics: Human Language Technologies, Volume 1 (Long and Short Papers)*, pages 839–850, Minneapolis, Minnesota. Association for Computational Linguistics.

Fei Huang and Alexander Yates. 2014. Improving word alignment using linguistic code switching data. In *Proceedings of the 14th Conference of the European Chapter of the Association for Computational Linguistics*, pages 1–9, Gothenburg, Sweden. Association for Computational Linguistics.

Melvin Johnson, Mike Schuster, Quoc V. Le, Maxim Krikun, Yonghui Wu, Zhifeng Chen, Nikhil Thorat, Fernanda Viégas, Martin Wattenberg, Greg Corrado, Macduff Hughes, and Jeffrey Dean. 2017. Google's multilingual neural machine translation system: Enabling zero-shot translation. *Transactions of the Association for Computational Linguistics*, 5:339–351.

Simran Khanuja, Sandipan Dandapat, Anirudh Srinivasan, Sunayana Sitaram, and Monojit Choudhury. 2020. GLUECoS: An evaluation benchmark for code-switched NLP. In *Proceedings of the 58th Annual Meeting of the Association for Computational Linguistics*, pages 3575–3585, Online. Association for Computational Linguistics.

Philipp Koehn, Hieu Hoang, Alexandra Birch, Chris Callison-Burch, Marcello Federico, Nicola Bertoldi, Brooke Cowan, Wade Shen, Christine Moran, Richard Zens, Chris Dyer, Ondřej Bojar, Alexandra Constantin, and Evan Herbst. 2007. Moses: Open source toolkit for statistical machine translation. In *Proceedings of the 45th Annual Meeting of the Association for Computational Linguistics Companion Volume Proceedings of the Demo and Poster Sessions*, pages 177–180, Prague, Czech Republic. Association for Computational Linguistics.

Grandee Lee and Haizhou Li. 2020. Modeling code-switch languages using bilingual parallel corpus. In *Proceedings of the 58th Annual Meeting of the Association for Computational Linguistics*, pages 860–870, Online. Association for Computational Linguistics.

Esmé Manandise and Claudia Gdaniec. 2011. Morphology to the rescue redux: Resolving borrowings and code-mixing in machine translation. In

Systems and Frameworks for Computational Morphology, pages 86–97, Berlin, Heidelberg. Springer Berlin Heidelberg.

Mohamed Menacer, David Langlois, Denis Jouvet, Dominique Fohr, Odile Mella, and Kamel Smaïli. 2019. Machine Translation on a parallel Code-Switched Corpus. In *Canadian AI 2019 - 32nd Conference on Canadian Artificial Intelligence*, Lecture Notes in Artificial Intelligence, Ontario, Canada.

Giovanni Molina, Fahad AlGhamdi, Mahmoud Ghoneim, Abdelati Hawwari, Nicolas Rey-Villamizar, Mona Diab, and Thamar Solorio. 2016. Overview for the second shared task on language identification in code-switched data. In *Proceedings of the Second Workshop on Computational Approaches to Code Switching*, pages 40–49, Austin, Texas. Association for Computational Linguistics.

Carol Myers-Scotton. 1997. *Duelling languages: Grammatical structure in codeswitching*. Oxford University Press.

Myle Ott, Sergey Edunov, Alexei Baevski, Angela Fan, Sam Gross, Nathan Ng, David Grangier, and Michael Auli. 2019. fairseq: A fast, extensible toolkit for sequence modeling. In *Proceedings of the 2019 Conference of the North American Chapter of the Association for Computational Linguistics (Demonstrations)*, pages 48–53, Minneapolis, Minnesota. Association for Computational Linguistics.

Parth Patwa, Gustavo Aguilar, Sudipta Kar, Suraj Pandey, Srinivas PYKL, Björn Gambäck, Tanmoy Chakraborty, Thamar Solorio, and Amitava Das. 2020. SemEval-2020 task 9: Overview of sentiment analysis of code-mixed tweets. In *Proceedings of the Fourteenth Workshop on Semantic Evaluation*, pages 774–790, Barcelona (online). International Committee for Computational Linguistics.

Carol W Pfaff. 1979. Constraints on language mixing: Intrasentential code-switching and borrowing in Spanish/English. *Language*, pages 291–318.

Minh Quang Pham, Jitao Xu, Josep Crego, François Yvon, and Jean Senellart. 2020. Priming neural machine translation. In *Proceedings of the Fifth Conference on Machine Translation*, pages 462–473, Online. Association for Computational Linguistics.

Shana Poplack. 1978. *Syntactic structure and social function of code-switching*, volume 2. Centro de Estudios Puertorriqueños, City University of New York].

Shana Poplack. 1980. Sometimes i'll start a sentence in spanish y termino en espaÑol: toward a typology of code-switching 1. *Linguistics*, 18:581–618.

Matt Post. 2018. A call for clarity in reporting BLEU scores. In *Proceedings of the Third Conference on Machine Translation: Research Papers*, pages 186–191, Brussels, Belgium. Association for Computational Linguistics.

Matt Post and David Vilar. 2018. Fast lexically constrained decoding with dynamic beam allocation for neural machine translation. In *Proceedings of the 2018 Conference of the North American Chapter of the Association for Computational Linguistics: Human Language Technologies, Volume 1 (Long Papers)*, pages 1314–1324, New Orleans, Louisiana. Association for Computational Linguistics.

Adithya Pratapa, Gayatri Bhat, Monojit Choudhury, Sunayana Sitaram, Sandipan Dandapat, and Kalika Bali. 2018. Language modeling for code-mixing: The role of linguistic theory based synthetic data. In *Proceedings of the 56th Annual Meeting of the Association for Computational Linguistics (Volume 1: Long Papers)*, pages 1543–1553, Melbourne, Australia. Association for Computational Linguistics.

Adithya Renduchintala, Philipp Koehn, and Jason Eisner. 2019a. Simple construction of mixed-language texts for vocabulary learning. In *Proceedings of the Fourteenth Workshop on Innovative Use of NLP for Building Educational Applications*, pages 369–379, Florence, Italy. Association for Computational Linguistics.

Adithya Renduchintala, Philipp Koehn, and Jason Eisner. 2019b. Spelling-aware construction of macaronic texts for teaching foreign-language vocabulary. In *Proceedings of the 2019 Conference on Empirical Methods in Natural Language Processing and the 9th International Joint Conference on Natural Language Processing (EMNLP-IJCNLP)*, pages 6438–6443, Hong Kong, China. Association for Computational Linguistics.

Shruti Rijhwani, Royal Sequiera, Monojit Choudhury, Kalika Bali, and Chandra Shekhar Maddila. 2017. Estimating code-switching on Twitter with a novel generalized word-level language detection technique. In *Proceedings of the 55th Annual Meeting of the Association for Computational Linguistics (Volume 1: Long Papers)*, pages 1971–1982, Vancouver, Canada. Association for Computational Linguistics.

Younes Samih, Suraj Maharjan, Mohammed Attia, Laura Kallmeyer, and Thamar Solorio. 2016. Multilingual code-switching identification via LSTM recurrent neural networks. In *Proceedings of the Second Workshop on Computational Approaches to Code Switching*, pages 50–59, Austin, Texas. Association for Computational Linguistics.

Rico Sennrich, Barry Haddow, and Alexandra Birch. 2016. Neural machine translation of rare words with subword units. In *Proceedings of the 54th Annual Meeting of the Association for Computational Linguistics (Volume 1: Long Papers)*, pages 1715–1725, Berlin, Germany. Association for Computational Linguistics.

Sunayana Sitaram, Khyathi Raghavi Chandu, Sai Krishna Rallabandi, and Alan W. Black. 2019. A survey of code-switched speech and language processing. *CoRR*, abs/1904.00784.

Kai Song, Yue Zhang, Heng Yu, Weihua Luo, Kun Wang, and Min Zhang. 2019a. Code-switching for enhancing NMT with pre-specified translation. In *Proceedings of the 2019 Conference of the North American Chapter of the Association for Computational Linguistics: Human Language Technologies, Volume 1 (Long and Short Papers)*, pages 449–459, Minneapolis, Minnesota. Association for Computational Linguistics.

Kaitao Song, Xu Tan, Tao Qin, Jianfeng Lu, and Tie-Yan Liu. 2019b. Mass: Masked sequence to sequence pre-training for language generation. In *ICML*, volume 97 of *Proceedings of Machine Learning Research*, pages 5926–5936. PMLR.

Maarten van Gompel, Iris Hendrickx, Antal van den Bosch, Els Lefever, and Véronique Hoste. 2014. SemEval 2014 task 5 - L2 writing assistant. In *Proceedings of the 8th International Workshop on Semantic Evaluation (SemEval 2014)*, pages 36–44, Dublin, Ireland. Association for Computational Linguistics.

Ashish Vaswani, Noam Shazeer, Niki Parmar, Jakob Uszkoreit, Llion Jones, Aidan N Gomez, Ł ukasz Kaiser, and Illia Polosukhin. 2017. Attention is all you need. In I. Guyon, U. V. Luxburg, S. Bengio, H. Wallach, R. Fergus, S. Vishwanathan, and R. Garnett, editors, *Advances in Neural Information Processing Systems 30*, pages 5998–6008. Curran Associates, Inc.

Genta Indra Winata, Andrea Madotto, Chien-Sheng Wu, and Pascale Fung. 2019. Code-switched language models using neural based synthetic data from parallel sentences. In *Proceedings of the 23rd Conference on Computational Natural Language Learning (CoNLL)*, pages 271–280, Hong Kong, China. Association for Computational Linguistics.

Jitao Xu, Josep Crego, and Jean Senellart. 2020. Boosting neural machine translation with similar translations. In *Proceedings of the 58th Annual Meeting of the Association for Computational Linguistics*, pages 1580–1590, Online. Association for Computational Linguistics.

Zhen Yang, Bojie Hu, Ambyera Han, Shen Huang, and Qi Ju. 2020. CSP: Code-switching pre-training for neural machine translation. In *Proceedings of the 2020 Conference on Empirical Methods in Natural Language Processing (EMNLP)*, pages 2624–2636, Online. Association for Computational Linguistics.

Arkaitz Zubiaga, Iñaki San Vicente, Pablo Gamallo, José Ramom Pichel, Iñaki Alegria, Nora Aranberri, Aitzol Ezeiza, and Víctor Fresno. 2016. TweetLID: a benchmark for tweet language identification. *Language Resources and Evaluation*, 50(4):729–766.

On the logistical difficulties and findings of Jopara Sentiment Analysis

Marvin M. Agüero-Torales
DECSAI, University of Granada
Granada, Spain
maguero@correo.ugr.es

David Vilares
Universidade da Coruña, CITIC
A Coruña, Spain
david.vilares@udc.es

Antonio G. López-Herrera
DECSAI, University of Granada
Granada, Spain
lopez-herrera@decsai.ugr.es

Abstract

This paper addresses the problem of sentiment analysis for Jopara, a code-switching language between Guarani and Spanish. We first collect a corpus of Guarani-dominant tweets and discuss on the difficulties of finding quality data for even relatively easy-to-annotate tasks, such as sentiment analysis. Then, we train a set of neural models, including pre-trained language models, and explore whether they perform better than traditional machine learning ones in this low-resource setup. Transformer architectures obtain the best results, despite not considering Guarani during pre-training, but traditional machine learning models perform close due to the low-resource nature of the problem.

1 Introduction

Indigenous languages have been often marginalized, an issue that is reflected when it comes to design natural language processing (NLP) applications, where they have been barely studied (Mager et al., 2018). One of the places where this is greatly noticed is Latin America, where the dominant languages (Spanish and Portuguese) coexist together with hundreds of indigenous languages such as Guarani, Quechua, Nahuatl or Aymara.

In this context, the Guarani language plays a particular role. It is an official language in Paraguay and Bolivia. Besides, it is spoken in other regions, e.g. Corrientes (Argentina) or Mato Grosso do Sul (Brazil), alongside with their official languages. Overall, it has about 8M speakers. Its coexistence with other languages, mostly Spanish, has contributed to its use in code-switching setups (Muysken, 1995; Gafaranga and Torras, 2002; Matras, 2020) and led to Jopara, a code-switching between Guarani and Spanish, with flavours of Portuguese and English (Estigarribia, 2015).

Despite its official status, there is still few NLP resources developed for Guarani and Jopara. Abdelali et al. (2006) developed a parallel Spanish-English-Guarani corpus for machine translation. Similarly, Chiruzzo et al. (2020) developed a Guarani-Spanish parallel corpus aligned at sentence-level. There are also a few online dictionaries and translators from Guarani to Spanish and other languages.[1] Beyond machine translation, Maldonado et al. (2016) released a corpus for Guarani speech recognition that was collected from the web; and Rudnick (2018) presented a system for cross-lingual word sense disambiguation from Spanish to Guarani and Quechua languages. There also are a few resources for PoS-tagging and morphological analysis of Guarani, such as the work by Hämäläinen (2019) and Apertium;[2] and also for parsing, more specifically for the Mbyá Guarani variety (Dooley, 2006; Thomas, 2019), under the Universal Dependencies framework.

In the context of sentiment analysis (SA; Pang et al., 2002; Liu, 2012), and more particularly classifying the polarity of a text as positive, negative or neutral, we are not aware of any previous work; with the exception of (Ríos et al., 2014). They presented a sentiment corpus for the Paraguayan Spanish dialect, which also includes words in English and Portuguese. However, there were few, albeit relevant, words of Guarani (70) and Jopara[3] (10), in comparison to the amount of the ones in Spanish ($3,802$) (Ríos et al., 2014, p. 40, Table II). Overall, SA has focused on rich-resource languages for which data is easy to find, even when it comes to code-switching setups (Vilares

[1] https://gn.wiktionary.org/, https://es.duolingo.com/dictionary/Guarani/, https://www.paraguay.gov.py/traductor-guarani, https://www.iguarani.com/, https://glosbe.com/gn, and Mainumby (Gasser, 2018).

[2] https://github.com/apertium/apertium-grn

[3] Tokens that mix n-grams of characters from Guarani and Spanish, e.g.: *'I understand'* would be *'entiendo'* (es), *'ahechakuaa'* (gn) and *'aentende'* (jopara).

Proceedings of the Fifth Workshop on Computational Approaches to Linguistic Code-Switching, pages 95–102
June 11, 2021. ©2021 Association for Computational Linguistics
https://doi.org/10.26615/978-954-452-056-4_012

et al., 2016), maybe with a few exceptions such as English code-switched with languages found in India (Sitaram et al., 2015; Patra et al., 2018; Chakravarthi et al., 2020). In this context, although some previous work has developed multilingual lexicons and methods (Chen and Skiena, 2014; Vilares et al., 2017); for languages such as Guarani and other low-resource cases (where web text is scarce), it is hard to develop NLP corpora and systems.

Contribution Our contribution is twofold. First, we collect a corpus for polarity classification of Jopara tweets, which mixes Guarani and Spanish languages, being the former the dominating language in the corpus. We also discuss on the difficulties that we had to face when creating such resource, such as finding enough Twitter data that shows sentiment and contains a significant amount of Guarani terms. Second, we train a set of neural encoders and also traditional machine learning models, in order to have a better understand of how old versus new models perform in this low-resource setup, where the amount of data matters.

2 JOSA: The Jopara Sentiment Analysis dataset

In what follows, we describe our attempts to collect Jopara tweets. Note that ideally we are interested in tweets that are as Guarani as possible. However, Guarani is intertwined with Spanish, and thus we have focused on Jopara, aiming for Guarani-dominant tweets, in contrast to Ríos et al. (2014). We found interesting to report failed attempts to collect such data, since the proposed methods would most likely work to collect data in rich resource languages. We hope this can be helpful for other researchers interested in developing datasets for low-resource languages in web environments.

In this line, Twitter does not allow to automatically crawl Guarani tweets, since it is not included in its language identification tool. To overcome this, we considered two alternatives: (i) using a set of Guarani keywords (§2.1), and (ii) scrapping Twitter accounts that mostly tweet in Guarani (§2.2).

2.1 Downloading tweets using Guarani keywords - An unsuccessful attempt.

As the Twitter real-time streamer can deal with a limited number of keywords, we consider 50 different keywords which are renewed every 3 hours, and used them to sample tweets. To select such keywords, we considered two options:

1. *Dictionary-based keywords*: We used 5.1K Guarani terms from a Spanish-Guarani word-level translator.[4] We then downloaded 2.1M tweets and performed language identification with three tools: (i) `polyglot`,[5] (ii) `fastText`(Joulin et al., 2016) and (iii) `textcat`.[6] We assume that the text was Guarani if at least one of them classified the text as Guarani. After this, we got 5.3K tweets. Next, a human annotator was in charge of classifying such subset, obtaining that only 150 tweets, over the initial set of 2.1M samples, were prone to be Guarani-dominant.

2. *Corpus-based keywords*: We first merged two Guarani datasets[7] (Scannell, 2007), that were generated from web sources and included biblical passages, wiki entries, blog posts or tweets, among other sources. From there, we selected 550 terms, including word uni-grams and bi-grams with 100 occurrences or more. Again, we downloaded tweets using the keywords and collected 7M of tweets, but after repeating the language identification phase of step 1, we obtained a marginal amount of tweets that were Guarani-dominant.

Limitations This approach suffered from a low recall when it came to collect Guarani-dominant tweets, while similar approaches have worked when collecting data for rich-resource languages, where a few keywords were enough to succesfully download tweets in the target language (Zampieri et al., 2020). In this context, even if tweets contained a few Guarani terms, there were other issues: (i) words that have the same form in Spanish and Guarani such as *'mano'* (*'hand'* and *'to die'*), (ii) loanwords,[8] such as *'pororo'* (*'popcorn'*) or *'chipa'* (traditional Paraguayan food, non-translatable); (iii) or simply tweets where the majority of the content was written in Spanish. Overall, this has been a problem experienced in other low-resource setups (Hong et al., 2011; Kreutz and Daelemans,

[4] `https://github.com/SENATICS/traductor-espanhol-guarani`

[5] `https://polyglot.readthedocs.io/en/latest/Detection.html`

[6] `https://www.nltk.org/_modules/nltk/classify/textcat.html`

[7] BCP-47 *gn* and *gug* codes.

[8] Frequent in Paraguay and border countries (Pinta, 2013).

2020), so we decided instead to look for alternatives to find Guarani-dominant tweets.

2.2 Downloading tweets from Guarani accounts - A successful attempt.

In this case, we crawled Twitter accounts that usually tweet in Guarani.[9] We scrapped them, and obtained more than 23K Guarani and Jopara tweets from a few popular users (see Appendix A.1). Using the same Guarani language identification approach as in 1, we obtained 8,716 tweets. To eliminate very similar tweets that could contaminate the dataset, we removed tweets with a similarity greater than 60%, according to the Levenshtein distance. After applying this second cleaning step, we obtained a total of 3,948 tweets.

The dataset was then annotated by two native speakers of Guarani and Spanish. They were asked to: (i) determine whether the tweet was strictly written in Guarani, Jopara or other language (i.e., if the tweet did not have any words in Guarani); and determine whether the tweet was positive, neutral or negative. For sentiment annotations consolidation, we proceeded similarly to the SemEval-2017 Task 4 guidelines (Rosenthal et al., 2017, § 3.3).[10] We then filtered the corpus by language, including only those labeled as Guarani or Jopara, to ensure the samples are Guarani-dominant. This resulted into 3,491 tweets.

Limitations Although this second approach is successful when it comes to collect a reasonable amount of Guarani-dominant tweets, it also suffers from a few limitations. For instance, the first part of Table 1 shows that due to the nature of the crawled Twitter accounts (who tweet about events, news, announcements, greetings, ephemeris, tweets to encourage the use of Guarani, etc.), there is a tendency to neutral tweets. Also, as the number of selected accounts was small, the number of discussed topics might be limited too. We comment on this a bit further in the Appendix A.1.

Balanced and unbalanced versions As we are interested in identifying sentiment in Jopara tweets, we also created a balanced version of JOSA. Note that unbalanced settings are also interesting and might reflect real-world setups. Thus, we will report results both on the unbalanced and balanced setups. More particularly, we split each corpus into training (50%), development (10%), and test (40%). We show the statistics in Table 1.

For completeness, in Table 2 we show for the balanced corpus the top five most frequent terms (we only consider content tokens) for Guarani, Spanish and some language-independent tokens, such emoticons. This was done based on a manual annotation of a Guarani-Spanish native speaker.

<table>
<tr><th>Version</th><th>Total</th><th>Positive</th><th>Neutral</th><th>Negative</th></tr>
<tr><td>Unbalanced</td><td>3,491</td><td rowspan="2">349</td><td>2,728</td><td rowspan="2">414</td></tr>
<tr><td>Balanced</td><td>1,526</td><td>763</td></tr>
</table>

Version	Total	Train	Development	Test
Unbalanced	3,491	1,745	349	1,397
Balanced	1,526	763	152	611

Table 1: JOSA statistics and splits for the unbalanced/balanced versions.

Category	#Terms	Most frequent
Guarani	4,336	guaranime, ñe'ẽ, mba'e, guarani, avei
Spanish	1,738	paraguay, guaraní, no, es, día
Other*	1,440	alcaraz, su, rt, juan, francisco
Mixing	368	guaraníme, departamento-pe, castellano-pe, castellanope, twitter-pe
Emojis	112	[illegible] [illegible] [illegible] xD :)

*We include reserved words, proper nouns, acronyms, etc.

Table 2: Frequent terms for the balanced JOSA.

3 Models

Due to the low-resource setup, we run neural models and pre-trained language models, but also other machine learning models, such as complement naïve Bayes (CNB) and Support Vector Machines (SVMs) (Hearst et al., 1998), since they are less data hungry, and could help shed some light about the real effectiveness of neural models on Jopara texts. In all cases, the selection of the hyperparameters was done over a small grid search based on the dev set. We report the details in the Appendix A.2.

Naïve Bayes and SVMs We tokenized the tweets[11] and represented them as a 1-hot vector of unigrams with a TF-IDF weighting scheme. We used Pedregosa et al. (2011) for training.

Neural networks for text classification We took into account neural networks that process in-

[9]We followed http://indigenoustweets.com/gn/. We did not use an external human annotator as in 1, since the crawled accounts tend to tweet in Guarani.

[10]We obtained a slight agreement following Cohen's kappa metric (Artstein and Poesio, 2008).

[11]We used the TweetTokenizer from the NLTK library.

put tweets as a sequence of token vector representations. More particularly, we consider both long short-term memory networks (LSTM) (Hochreiter and Schmidhuber, 1997) and convolutional neural networks (CNN) (LeCun et al., 1995), as implemented in NCRF++ (Yang and Zhang, 2018). Although the former are usually more common in many NLP tasks, the latter have also showed traditionally a good performance on sentiment analysis (Kalchbrenner et al., 2014).

For the input word embeddings, we tested: (i) randomly initialized word vectors, following an uniform distribution, (ii) and pre-trained non-contextualized representations and more particularly, FastText's word vectors (Bojanowski et al., 2017) and BPEmb's subword vectors (including the multilingual version, which supports Guarani) (Heinzerling and Strube, 2018). In both cases, we also concatenate a second word embedding, computed through a char-LSTM (or CNN).

Pre-trained language models We also fine-tuned recent contextualized language models on the JOSA training set. We tested BERT (Devlin et al., 2019) including: (i) beto-base-uncased (a Spanish BERT) (Cañete et al., 2020), and (ii) multilingual bert-base-uncased (mBERT-base-uncased, pre-trained on 102 languages). We also tried more recent variants of multilingual BERT, in particular XLM (Lample and Conneau, 2019). Note that BERT models use a wordpiece tokenizer (Wu et al., 2016) to generate a vocabulary of the most common subword pieces, rather than the full tokens, and that in the case of the multilingual models, none of the language models used considered Guarani during pre-training.

4 Experiments

Reproducibility The baselines and tweet IDs[12] are available at `https://github.com/mmaguero/josa-corpus`.

We run experiments for the unbalanced and balanced versions of JOSA, evaluating the macro-accuracy (to mitigate the impact of the neutral class in the unbalanced setup). Table 3 shows the comparison. Note that all models, even the non-deep-learning models, only use raw word inputs and do not consider any additional information or hand-crafted features,[13] yet they obtained results that are in line with those of more recent approaches.

Model	Corpus Unbalanced	Corpus Balanced
CNB	0.50	0.55
SVM	0.55	0.54
^{C}CNN-^{W}BiLSTM	0.45	0.57
^{C}BiLSTM-^{W}CNN	0.49	0.53
$_{BPEmb,gn}$ ^{C}CNN-^{W}BiLSTM	0.46	0.53
$_{BPEmb,gn}$ ^{C}BiLSTM-^{W}CNN	0.42	0.50
$_{BPEmb,es}$ ^{C}CNN-^{W}BiLSTM	0.45	0.52
$_{BPEmb,es}$ ^{C}BiLSTM-^{W}CNN	0.45	0.50
$_{BPEmb,m}$ ^{C}CNN-^{W}BiLSTM	0.47	0.52
$_{BPEmb,m}$ ^{C}BiLSTM-^{W}CNN	0.43	0.48
$_{FastText,gn}$ ^{C}CNN-^{W}BiLSTM	0.46	0.53
$_{FastText,gn}$ ^{C}BiLSTM-^{W}CNN	0.42	0.51
$_{FastText,es}$ ^{C}CNN-^{W}BiLSTM	0.46	0.52
$_{FastText,es}$ ^{C}BiLSTM-^{W}CNN	0.46	0.46
BETO$_{base,uncased}$	**0.64**	**0.64**
mBERT$_{base,uncased}$	0.55	0.58
XLM-MLM-TLM-XNLI-15	0.46	0.49

^{C}Encodes character sequence. ^{W}Encodes word sequence.

Pre-trained embeddings are represented with a prefix together with their language ISO 639-1 code (except for m: multilingual).

Table 3: Experimental results on JOSA, both on the balanced and unbalanced setups.

With respect to the experiments with CNNs and BiLSTMs encoders, we tested different combinations using character representations, which output is first concatenated to a second external word vector (as explained in §3), and then fed to the encoder. Among those, the model that used a character-level CNN and a word-level BiLSTM encoder obtained the best results. Still, the difference with respect to traditional machine learning models is small. We hypothesize this might be due to the low-resource nature of the task. Finally, the pre-trained language models that use transformers architectures, in particular BETO, obtain overall the best results, despite not being pre-trained on Guarani. We believe this is partly due to the presence of Spanish words in the corpora and also to the cross-lingual abilities that BERT model might explode, independently of the amount of word overlap (Wang et al., 2019).

Error analysis on the balanced version of JOSA Figure 1 shows the confusion matrices for a representative model of each machine learning family (based on the accuracy): (i) CNB, (ii) the best BiLSTM-based model (CNN-BiLSTM), and (iii) Spanish BERT (BETO). There seems to be different tendencies in the miss-classifications that different models make. For instance, CNB tends to over-classify tweets as negative, while both deep

[12] Contact the authors for more details.

[13] In order to keep an homogeneous evaluation setup.

learning models show a more controlled behaviour when predicting this class. Although for the three models neutral tweets seem to be the easiest to identify, both deep learning models are clearly better at it. Finally, when it comes to identify positive tweets, BETO seems to show the overall best performance. These different tendencies indicate that an ensemble method could be beneficial for low-resource setups such as the ones that JOSA represent, since the models seem to be complementary to certain extent. In this context, we would like to explore this line of work in the future, following previous studies such as Jhanwar and Das (2018), which showed the benefits of combining different machine learning models for Hindi-English code-switching SA.

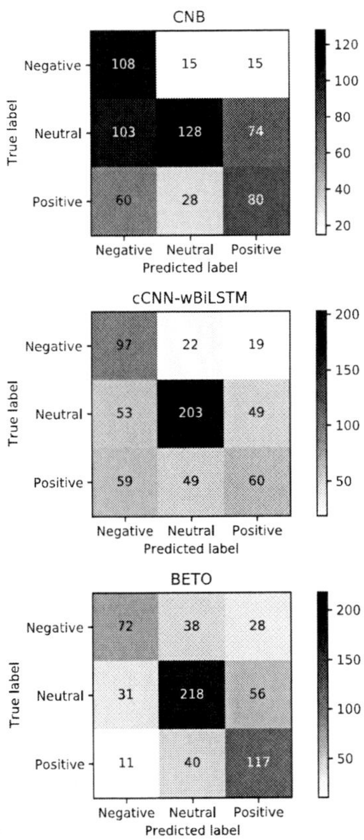

Figure 1: Confusion matrix for the balanced version of JOSA and the predictions of a representative member of each machine learning family: CNB, a BiLSTM-based model and Spanish BERT (BETO).

5 Conclusion

This paper explored sentiment analysis on Jopara, a code-switching language that mixes Guarani and Spanish. We collected the first Guarani-dominant dataset for sentiment analysis, and described some of the challenges that we had to face to create a collection where there is a significant number of Guarani terms. We then built several machine learning (naïve Bayes, SVMs) and deep learning models (BiLSTMs, CNNs and BERT-based models) to shed light about how they perform on this particular low-resource setup. Overall, transformers models obtain the best results, even if they did not consider Guarani during pre-training. This poses interesting questions for future work such as how cross-lingual BERT abilities (Wang et al., 2019) can be exploited for this kind of setups, but also how to improve language-specific techniques that can help process low-resource languages efficiently.

Acknowledgements

We thank the annotators that labelled JOSA. We also thank ExplosionAI for giving us access to the Prodigy annotation tool[14] with the Research License. DV is supported by a 2020 Leonardo Grant for Researchers and Cultural Creators from the FB-BVA.[15] DV also receives funding from MINECO (ANSWER-ASAP, TIN2017-85160-C2-1-R), from Xunta de Galicia (ED431C 2020/11), from Centro de Investigación de Galicia 'CITIC', funded by Xunta de Galicia and the European Union (European Regional Development Fund- Galicia 2014-2020 Program) by grant ED431G 2019/01.

References

Ahmed Abdelali, James Cowie, Steve Helmreich, Wanying Jin, Maria Pilar Milagros, Bill Ogden, Hamid Mansouri Rad, and Ron Zacharski. 2006. Guarani: a case study in resource development for quick ramp-up mt. In *Proceedings of the 7th Conference of the Association for Machine Translation in the Americas, "Visions for the Future of Machine Translation*, pages 1–9.

Ron Artstein and Massimo Poesio. 2008. Inter-coder agreement for computational linguistics. *Computational Linguistics*, 34(4):555–596.

[14] https://prodi.gy/

[15] The BBVA Foundation accepts no responsibility for the opinions, statements and contents included in the project and/or the results thereof, which are entirely the responsibility of the authors.

Piotr Bojanowski, Edouard Grave, Armand Joulin, and Tomas Mikolov. 2017. Enriching word vectors with subword information. *Transactions of the Association for Computational Linguistics*, 5:135–146.

José Cañete, Gabriel Chaperon, Rodrigo Fuentes, Jou-Hui Ho, Hojin Kang, and Jorge Pérez. 2020. Spanish pre-trained bert model and evaluation data. In *PML4DC at ICLR 2020*.

Bharathi Raja Chakravarthi, Vigneshwaran Muralidaran, Ruba Priyadharshini, and John P McCrae. 2020. Corpus creation for sentiment analysis in code-mixed tamil-english text. *arXiv preprint arXiv:2006.00206*.

Yanqing Chen and Steven Skiena. 2014. Building sentiment lexicons for all major languages. In *Proceedings of the 52nd Annual Meeting of the Association for Computational Linguistics (Volume 2: Short Papers)*, pages 383–389, Baltimore, Maryland. Association for Computational Linguistics.

Luis Chiruzzo, Pedro Amarilla, Adolfo Ríos, and Gustavo Giménez Lugo. 2020. Development of a Guarani - Spanish parallel corpus. In *Proceedings of the 12th Language Resources and Evaluation Conference*, pages 2629–2633, Marseille, France. European Language Resources Association.

Jacob Devlin, Ming-Wei Chang, Kenton Lee, and Kristina Toutanova. 2019. BERT: Pre-training of deep bidirectional transformers for language understanding. In *Proceedings of the 2019 Conference of the North American Chapter of the Association for Computational Linguistics: Human Language Technologies, Volume 1 (Long and Short Papers)*, pages 4171–4186, Minneapolis, Minnesota. Association for Computational Linguistics.

Robert A Dooley. 2006. Léxico guarani, dialeto mbyá, com informações úteis para o ensino médio, a aprendizagem e a pesquisa lingüística. e referências. *Cuiabá: Summer Institute of Linguistics*.

Bruno Estigarribia. 2015. Guarani-spanish jopara mixing in a paraguayan novel: Does it reflect a third language, a language variety, or true codeswitching? *Journal of Language Contact*, 8(2):183–222.

Joseph Gafaranga and Maria-Carme Torras. 2002. Interactional otherness: Towards a redefinition of codeswitching. *International Journal of Bilingualism*, 6(1):1–22.

Michael Gasser. 2018. Mainumby: un ayudante para la traducción castellano-guaraní. *arXiv preprint arXiv:1810.08603*.

Marti A. Hearst, Susan T Dumais, Edgar Osuna, John Platt, and Bernhard Scholkopf. 1998. Support vector machines. *IEEE Intelligent Systems and their applications*, 13(4):18–28.

Benjamin Heinzerling and Michael Strube. 2018. BPEmb: Tokenization-free Pre-trained Subword Embeddings in 275 Languages. In *Proceedings of the Eleventh International Conference on Language Resources and Evaluation (LREC 2018)*, Miyazaki, Japan. European Language Resources Association (ELRA).

Sepp Hochreiter and Jürgen Schmidhuber. 1997. Long short-term memory. *Neural computation*, 9(8):1735–1780.

Lichan Hong, Gregorio Convertino, and Ed Chi. 2011. Language matters in twitter: A large scale study. In *Proceedings of the International AAAI Conference on Web and Social Media*, volume 5.

Mika Hämäläinen. 2019. UralicNLP: An NLP library for Uralic languages. *Journal of Open Source Software*, 4(37):1345.

Madan Gopal Jhanwar and Arpita Das. 2018. An ensemble model for sentiment analysis of hindi-english code-mixed data. *CoRR*, abs/1806.04450.

Armand Joulin, Edouard Grave, Piotr Bojanowski, and Tomas Mikolov. 2016. Bag of tricks for efficient text classification. *arXiv preprint arXiv:1607.01759*.

Nal Kalchbrenner, Edward Grefenstette, and Phil Blunsom. 2014. A convolutional neural network for modelling sentences. In *Proceedings of the 52nd Annual Meeting of the Association for Computational Linguistics (Volume 1: Long Papers)*, pages 655–665.

Tim Kreutz and Walter Daelemans. 2020. Streaming language-specific Twitter data with optimal keywords. In *Proceedings of the 12th Web as Corpus Workshop*, pages 57–64, Marseille, France. European Language Resources Association.

Guillaume Lample and Alexis Conneau. 2019. Cross-lingual language model pretraining. *arXiv preprint arXiv:1901.07291*.

Yann LeCun, Yoshua Bengio, et al. 1995. Convolutional networks for images, speech, and time series. *The handbook of brain theory and neural networks*, 3361(10):1995.

Bing Liu. 2012. Sentiment analysis and opinion mining. *Synthesis lectures on human language technologies*, 5(1):1–167.

Manuel Mager, Ximena Gutierrez-Vasques, Gerardo Sierra, and Ivan Meza-Ruiz. 2018. Challenges of language technologies for the indigenous languages of the americas. In *Proceedings of the 27th International Conference on Computational Linguistics*, pages 55–69.

Diego Manuel Maldonado, Rodrigo Villalba Barrientos, and Diego P Pinto-Roa. 2016. Eñe'ẽ: Sistema de reconocimiento automático del habla en guaraní. In *Simposio Argentino de Inteligencia Artificial (ASAI 2016)-JAIIO 45 (Tres de Febrero, 2016)*.

Yaron Matras. 2020. *Language contact*. Cambridge University Press.

Pieter Muysken. 1995. Code-switching and grammatical theory. *The bilingualism reader*, pages 280–297.

Bo Pang, Lillian Lee, and Shivakumar Vaithyanathan. 2002. Thumbs up? sentiment classification using machine learning techniques. In *Proceedings of the 2002 Conference on Empirical Methods in Natural Language Processing (EMNLP 2002)*, pages 79–86. Association for Computational Linguistics.

Braja Gopal Patra, Dipankar Das, and Amitava Das. 2018. Sentiment analysis of code-mixed indian languages: an overview of sail_code-mixed shared task@ icon-2017. *arXiv preprint arXiv:1803.06745*.

F. Pedregosa, G. Varoquaux, A. Gramfort, V. Michel, B. Thirion, O. Grisel, M. Blondel, P. Prettenhofer, R. Weiss, V. Dubourg, J. Vanderplas, A. Passos, D. Cournapeau, M. Brucher, M. Perrot, and E. Duchesnay. 2011. Scikit-learn: Machine learning in Python. *Journal of Machine Learning Research*, 12:2825–2830.

Justin Pinta. 2013. Lexical strata in loanword phonology: Spanish loans in guaraní. Master's thesis, The University of North Carolina at Chapel Hill.

Jason D Rennie, Lawrence Shih, Jaime Teevan, and David R Karger. 2003. Tackling the poor assumptions of naive bayes text classifiers. In *Proceedings of the 20th international conference on machine learning (ICML-03)*, pages 616–623.

Adolfo A Ríos, Pedro J Amarilla, and Gustavo A Giménez Lugo. 2014. Sentiment categorization on a creole language with lexicon-based and machine learning techniques. In *2014 Brazilian Conference on Intelligent Systems*, pages 37–43. IEEE.

Sara Rosenthal, Noura Farra, and Preslav Nakov. 2017. Semeval-2017 task 4: Sentiment analysis in twitter. In *Proceedings of the 11th international workshop on semantic evaluation (SemEval-2017)*, pages 502–518.

Alexander James Rudnick. 2018. *Cross-Lingual Word Sense Disambiguation for Low-Resource Hybrid Machine Translation*. Ph.D. thesis, Indiana University.

Kevin P Scannell. 2007. The crúbadán project: Corpus building for under-resourced languages. In *Building and Exploring Web Corpora: Proceedings of the 3rd Web as Corpus Workshop*, volume 4, pages 5–15.

Dinkar Sitaram, Savitha Murthy, Debraj Ray, Devansh Sharma, and Kashyap Dhar. 2015. Sentiment analysis of mixed language employing hindi-english code switching. In *2015 International Conference on Machine Learning and Cybernetics (ICMLC)*, volume 1, pages 271–276. IEEE.

Guillaume Thomas. 2019. Universal Dependencies for Mbyá Guaraní. In *Proceedings of the Third Workshop on Universal Dependencies (UDW, SyntaxFest 2019)*, pages 70–77, Paris, France. Association for Computational Linguistics.

David Vilares, Miguel A Alonso, and Carlos Gómez-Rodríguez. 2016. En-es-cs: An english-spanish code-switching twitter corpus for multilingual sentiment analysis. In *Proceedings of the Tenth International Conference on Language Resources and Evaluation (LREC'16)*, pages 4149–4153.

David Vilares, Carlos Gómez-Rodríguez, and Miguel A Alonso. 2017. Universal, unsupervised (rule-based), uncovered sentiment analysis. *Knowledge-Based Systems*, 118:45–55.

Zihan Wang, Stephen Mayhew, Dan Roth, et al. 2019. Cross-lingual ability of multilingual bert: An empirical study. *arXiv preprint arXiv:1912.07840*.

Thomas Wolf, Lysandre Debut, Victor Sanh, Julien Chaumond, Clement Delangue, Anthony Moi, Pierric Cistac, Tim Rault, Remi Louf, Morgan Funtowicz, Joe Davison, Sam Shleifer, Patrick von Platen, Clara Ma, Yacine Jernite, Julien Plu, Canwen Xu, Teven Le Scao, Sylvain Gugger, Mariama Drame, Quentin Lhoest, and Alexander Rush. 2020. Transformers: State-of-the-art natural language processing. In *Proceedings of the 2020 Conference on Empirical Methods in Natural Language Processing: System Demonstrations*, pages 38–45, Online. Association for Computational Linguistics.

Yonghui Wu, Mike Schuster, Zhifeng Chen, Quoc V Le, Mohammad Norouzi, Wolfgang Macherey, Maxim Krikun, Yuan Cao, Qin Gao, Klaus Macherey, et al. 2016. Google's neural machine translation system: Bridging the gap between human and machine translation. *arXiv preprint arXiv:1609.08144*.

Jie Yang and Yue Zhang. 2018. Ncrf++: An open-source neural sequence labeling toolkit. *arXiv preprint arXiv:1806.05626*.

Marcos Zampieri, Preslav Nakov, Sara Rosenthal, Pepa Atanasova, Georgi Karadzhov, Hamdy Mubarak, Leon Derczynski, Zeses Pitenis, and Çağrı Çöltekin. 2020. SemEval-2020 task 12: Multilingual offensive language identification in social media (OffensEval 2020). In *Proceedings of the Fourteenth Workshop on Semantic Evaluation*, pages 1425–1447, Barcelona (online). International Committee for Computational Linguistics.

A Appendix

A.1 Twitter user accounts

We scraped the following Twitter user accounts and mentions: @ndishpy, @chereraugo, @Pontifex_grn, @lenguaguarani, @enga_paraguayo, @SPL_Paraguay, @rubencarlosoje1, as well as some keywords: *'guaranime'*, *'avañe'ẽme'*, *'remiandu'*, *'#marandu'*, *'reikuaavéta'*, *'hesegua'*, *'reheguápe'*, *'rejuhúta'*.

Note that accounts such as @Pontifex_grn, @SPL_Paraguay and @lenguaguarani belong to influential people and organizations. For instance, the first belongs to Pope Franscico, the second to the Secretariat of Linguistic Policy of Paraguay, and the third is the account of the General Director of the 'Athenaeum of the Guarani Language and Culture'. On the other hand, the terms *'marandu'* (news) and *'remiandu'* (feeling, sense) are related to news, where the first term means 'news' or 'to report' and the second is the name of a Paraguayan newspaper section[16] that publishes in Guarani.

A.2 Hyperparameters search and implementation details

To set the machine learning baselines, two standard classifiers were chosen: a variant of Naïve Bayes, Complement Naïve Bayes (CNB) (Rennie et al., 2003) to correct the 'severe assumptions' made by the standard Multinomial NB classifier; and Support Vector Machine (SVM) using weighted classes, to mitigate the effect of unbalanced classes. For the CNB, we set $\alpha = 0.1$ and considered only unigrams, except for the balanced version, where the combined use of unigrams and bigrams showed more robust results. To train the SVMs, we tested different values for the kernels: the `sigmoid` kernel obtained the best results for the unbalanced version of JOSA, and the `poly` kernel obtained the best results for the balanced version.

We used the NCRF++ Neural Sequence Labeling Toolkit (Yang and Zhang, 2018) to train our deep learning models and the Hugging face package (Wolf et al., 2020) for the transformer-based models. Table 4 shows the hyper-parameters used to train these models, both for the unbalanced and balanced corpus. The pre-trained embeddings used for Spanish, Guarani (and also the multilingual ones) have 300 dimensions. Finally, we trained the CNN and BiLSTM models for 20 epochs with a batch size of 10, and the transformer-based models were trained for up to 40 epochs relying on early stopping (set to 3). To train the models we used a NVIDIA Tesla T4 GPU with 16GB.

Parameter	Options
Sklearn	
TF-IDF-Lowercase	[True, False]
TF-IDF-n-grams	[(1,1) - (3,3)]
SVM-Kernel	[poly, sigmoid, linear, rbf]
CNB-alpha	[1.0, 0.1]
NCRF++	
Optimizer	[Adam, AdaGrad, SGD]
Avg. batch loss	[True, False]
Learning rate	[5e-5 - 0.2]
Char hidden dim.	[100, 200, 400, 800]
Word hidden dim.	[50, 100, 200]
Momentum	[0.0, 0.9, 0.95, 0.99]
LSTM Layers	[1, 2]
Hugging Face	
Eval. steps	[200]
Eval. strategy	[steps]
Disable tqdm	[False]
Eval. batch size	[16, 32]
Train batch size	[16, 32]
Learning rate	[2e-5 - 3e-5*]
Dropout	[0.1 - 0.6]
Epoch	[30 - 40]
Weight decay	[0.0 - 0.3]

*Except for the multilingual models, where 5e-5 was necessary to converge.

Table 4: Hyperparameters for the training of the models, both for the unbalanced and balanced corpus.

[16] `https://www.abc.com.py/especiales/remiandu/`

Unsupervised Self-Training for Sentiment Analysis of Code-Switched Data

Akshat Gupta[1], **Sargam Menghani**[1], **Sai Krishna Rallabandi**[2], **Alan W Black**[2]
[1]Department of Electrical and Computer Engineering, Carnegie Mellon University
[2]Language Technologies, Institute, Carnegie Mellon University
{akshatgu, smenghan}@andrew.cmu.edu, {srallaba, awb}@cs.cmu.edu

Abstract

Sentiment analysis is an important task in understanding social media content like customer reviews, Twitter and Facebook feeds etc. In multilingual communities around the world, a large amount of social media text is characterized by the presence of code-switching. Thus, it has become important to build models that can handle code-switched data. However, annotated code-switched data is scarce and there is a need for unsupervised models and algorithms. We propose a general framework called Unsupervised Self-Training and show its applications for the specific use case of sentiment analysis of code-switched data. We use the power of pre-trained BERT models for initialization and fine-tune them in an unsupervised manner, only using pseudo labels produced by zero-shot transfer. We test our algorithm on multiple code-switched languages and provide a detailed analysis of the learning dynamics of the algorithm with the aim of answering the question - 'Does our unsupervised model understand the Code-Switched languages or does it just learn its representations?'. Our unsupervised models compete well with their supervised counterparts, with their performance reaching within 1-7% (weighted F1 scores) when compared to supervised models trained for a two class problem.

1 Introduction

Sentiment analysis, sometimes also known as opinion mining, aims to understand and classify the opinion, attitude and emotions of a user based on a text query. Sentiment analysis has many applications including understanding product reviews, social media monitoring, brand monitoring, reputation management etc. Code switching is referred to as the phenomenon of alternation between multiple languages, usually two, within a single utterance. Code switching is very common in many bilingual and multilingual societies around the world including India (Hinglish, Tanglish etc.), Singapore (Chinglish) and various Spanish speaking areas of North America (Spanglish). A large amount of social media text in these regions is code-mixed, which is why it is essential to build systems that are able to handle code switching.

Various datasets have been released to aid advancements in Sentiment Analysis of code-mixed data. These datasets are usually much smaller and more noisy when compared to their high-resource-language-counterparts and are available for very few languages. Thus, there is a need to come up with both unsupervised and semi-supervised algorithms to deal with code-mixed data. In our work, we present a general framework called Unsupervised Self-Training Algorithm for doing sentiment analysis of code-mixed data in an unsupervised manner. We present results for four code-mixed languages - Hinglish (Hindi-English), Spanglish (Spanish-English), Tanglish (Tamil-English) and Malayalam-English.

In this paper, we propose the Unsupervised Self-Training framework and apply it to the problem of sentiment classification. Our proposed framework performs two tasks simultaneously - firstly, it gives sentiment labels to sentences of a code-mixed dataset in an unsupervised manner, and secondly, it trains a sentiment classification model in a purely unsupervised manner. The framework can be extended to incorporate active learning almost seamlessly. We present a rigorous analysis of the learning dynamics of our unsupervised model and try to answer the question - *'Does the unsupervised model understand the code-switched languages or does it just recognize its representations?'*. We also show methods for optimizing performance of the Unsupervised Self-Training algorithm.

2 Related Work

In this paper, we propose a framework called Unsupervised Self-Training, which is an extension to the semi-supervised machine learning algorithm called

Proceedings of the Fifth Workshop on Computational Approaches to Linguistic Code-Switching, pages 103–112
June 11, 2021. ©2021 Association for Computational Linguistics
https://doi.org/10.26615/978-954-452-056-4_013

Self-Training (Zhu, 2005). Self-training has previously been used in natural language processing for pre-training (Du et al., 2020a) and for tasks like word sense disambiguation (Yarowsky, 1995). It has been shown to be very effective for natural language processing tasks (Du et al., 2020b) and better than pre training in low resource scenarios both theoretically (Wei et al., 2020) and emperically(Zoph et al., 2020a). Zoph et al. 2020b show that self-training can be a more useful than pre-training in high resourced scenarios for the task of object detection, and a combination of pre-training and self-training can improve performance when only 20% of the available dataset was used. However, our proposed framework differs from self-training such that we only use the zero-shot predictions made by our initialization model to train our models and never use actual labels.

Sentiment analysis is a popular task in industry as well as within the research community, used in analysing the markets (Nanli et al., 2012), election campaigns (Haselmayer and Jenny, 2017) etc. A large amount of social media text in most bilingual communities is code-mixed and many labelled datasets have been released to perform sentiment analysis. We will be working with four code-mixed datasets for sentiment analysis, Malayalam-English and Tamil-English (Chakravarthi et al., 2020a,b,c) and Spanglish and Hinglish (Patwa et al., 2020).

Previous work has shown BERT based models to achieve state of the art performance for code-switched languages in tasks like offensive language identification (Jayanthi and Gupta, 2021) and sentiment analysis (Gupta et al., 2021). We will build unsupervised models on top of BERT. BERT (Devlin et al., 2018) based models have achieved state of the art performance in many downstream tasks due to their superior contextualized representations of language, providing true bidirectional context to word embeddings. We will use the sentiment analysis model from (Barbieri et al., 2020), trained on a large corpus of English Tweets (60 million Tweets) for initializing our algorithm. We will refer to the sentiment analysis model from (Barbieri et al., 2020) as the *TweetEval* model in the remainder of the paper. The TweetEval model is built on top of an English RoBERTa (Liu et al., 2019) model.

3 Proposed Approach: Unsupervised Self-Training

Our proposed algorithm is centred around the idea of creating an unsupervised learning algorithm that is able to harness the power of cross-lingual transfer in the most efficient way possible, with the aim of producing unsupervised sentiment labels. In its most fundamental form, our proposed Unsupervised Self-Training algorithm[1] is shown in Figure 1 is shown in Figure 1.

We begin by producing zero-shot results for sentiment classification using a selected pre-trained model trained for the same task. From the predictions made, we select the top-N most confident predictions made by the model. The confidence level is judged by the softmax scores. Making the zero-shot predictions and selecting sentences make up the *Initialization block* as shown in Figure 1. We then use the pseduo-labels predicted by the zero-shot model to fine tune our model. After that, predictions are made on the remaining dataset with the fine-tuned model. We again select sentences based on their softmax scores for fine-tuning the model in the next iteration. These steps are repeated until we've gone through the entire dataset or until a stopping condition. At all fine-tuning steps, we only use the predicted pseduo-labels as ground truth to train the model, which makes the algorithm completely unsupervised.

As the first set of predicted pseudo-labels are produced by a zero-shot model, our framework is very sensitive to initialization. Care must be taken to initialize the algorithm with a *compatible model*. For example, for the task of sentiment classification of Hinglish Twitter data, an example of a compatible initial model would be a sentiment classification model trained on either English or Hindi sentiment data. It would be even more compatible if the model was trained on Twitter sentiment data, the data thus being from the same domain.

3.1 Optimizing Performance

The most important blocks in the Unsupervised Self-Training framework with respect to maximizing performance are the *Initialization Block* and the *Selection Block* (Figure 1). To improve initialization, we must choose the most compatible model for the chosen task. Additionally, to improve performance, we can use several training strategies

[1]The code for the framework can be found here: https://github.com/akshat57/Unsupervised-Self-Training

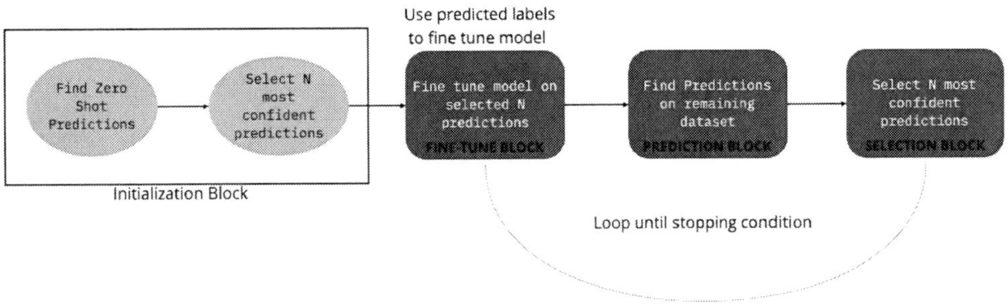

Figure 1: A visual representation of our proposed Unsupervised Self-Training framework.

in the Selection Block. In this section we discuss several variants of the Selection Block.

As an example, instead of selecting a fixed number of samples N from the dataset in the selection block, we could be selecting a different but fixed number N_i from each class i in the dataset. This would need an understanding of the class distribution of the dataset. We discuss this in later sections. Another variable number of sentences in each iteration, rather than a fixed number. This would give us a *selection schedule* for the algorithm. We explore some of these techniques in later sections.

Other factors can be incorporated in the Selection Block. Selection need not be based on *just* the most confident predictions. We can have additional selection criteria, for example, incorporating the Token Ratio (defined in section 8) of a particular language in the predicted sentences. Taking the example of a Hinglish dataset, one way to do this would be to select sentences that have a larger amount of Hindi and are within selection threshold. In our experiments, we find that knowing an optimal selection strategy is vital to achieving the maximum performance.

4 Datasets

We test our proposed framework on four different languages - Hinglish (Patwa et al., 2020), Spanglish (Patwa et al., 2020), Tanglish (Chakravarthi et al., 2020b) and Malayalam-English (Chakravarthi et al., 2020a). The statistics of the training sets are given in Table 1. We also use the test sets of the above datasets, which have similar distribution as their respective training sets. The statistics of the test sets are not shown for brevity. We ask the reader to refer to the respective papers for more details.

The choice of datasets, apart from covering three language families, incorporate several other important features. We can see from Table 1 that the four datasets have different sizes, the Malayalam-English dataset being the smallest. Apart from the Hinglish dataset, the other three datasets are highly imbalanced. This is an important distinction as we cannot expect an unknown set of sentences to have a balanced class distributions. We will later see that having a biased underlying distribution affects the performance of our algorithm and how better training strategies can alleviate this problem.

The chosen datasets are also from two different domains - the Hinglish and Spanglish datasets are a collection of Tweets whereas Tanglish and Malaylam-English are a collection of Youtube Comments. The TweetEval model, which is used for initialization is trained on a corpus of English Tweets. Thus the Hinglish and Spangish datasets are in-domain datasets for our initialization model (Barbieri et al., 2020), whereas the Dravidian language (Tamil and Malayalam) datasets are out of domain.

The datasets also differ in the amount of class-wise code-mixing. Figure 3 shows that for the Hinglish dataset, a negative Tweet is more likely to contain large amounts of Hindi. This is not the same for the other datasets. For Spanglish, both positive and negative sentiment Tweets have a tendency to use a larger amount of Spanish than English.

An important thing to note here is that each of the four code-mixed datasets selected are written in the latin script. Thus our choice of datasets does not take into account mixing of different scripts.

5 Models

Models built on top of BERT (Devlin et al., 2018) and its multilingual version like mBERT, XLM-

Language	Domain	Total	Positive	Negative	Neutral
Hinglish	Tweets	14000	4634	4102	5264
Spanglish	Tweets	12002	6005	2023	3974
Tanglish	Youtube Comments	9684	7627	1448	609
Malayalam-English	Youtube Comments	3915	2022	549	1344

Table 1: Training dataset statistics for chosen datasets.

RoBERTa (Conneau et al., 2019) have recently produced state-of-the-art results in many natural language processing tasks. Various shared tasks (Patwa et al., 2020) (Chakravarthi et al., 2020c) in the domain of code-switched sentiment analysis have also seen their best performing systems build on top of these BERT models.

English is a common language among all the four code-mixed datasets being considered. This is why we use a RoBERTa based sentiment classification model trained on a large corpus of 60 million English Tweets (Barbieri et al., 2020) for initialization. We refer to this sentiment classification model as the TweetEval model for the rest of this paper. We use the Hugging Face implementation of the TweetEval sentiment classification model [2]. The models are fine-tuned with a batch size of 16 and a learning rate of 2e-5. The TweetEval model preprocesses sentiment data to not include any URL's. We have done the same for for all the four datasets.

We compare our unsupervised model with a set of supervised models trained on each of the four datasets. We train supervised models by fine tuning the TweetEval model on each of the four datasets. Our experiments have shown that the TweetEval model performs the better in comparison to mBERT and XLM-RoBERTa based models for code-switched data.

6 Evaluation

We evaluate our results based on weighted average F1 and accuracy scores. When calculating the weighted average, the F1 scores are calculated for each class and a weighted average is taken based on the number of samples in each class. This metric is chosen because three out of four datasets we work with are highly imbalanced. We use the sklearn implementation for calculating weighted average F1 scores[3].

Language	F1	Accuracy
Hinglish	0.32	0.36
Spanglish	0.31	0.32
Tanglish	0.15	0.16
Malayalam-English	0.17	0.14

Table 2: Zero-shot prediction performance for the TweetEval model for each of the four datasets, for a two-class classification problem (positive and negative classes). The F1 scores represent the weighted average F1. These zero-shot predictions are for the training datasets in each of the four languages.

There are two ways to evaluate the performance of our proposed method, corresponding to two different perspectives with which we look at the outcome. One of the ways to evaluate the proposed method is to answer the question - 'How good is the model when trained in the proposed, unsupervised manner?'. We call this perspective of evaluation, having a *model perspective*. Here we're evaluating the strength of the unsupervised model. To evaluate the method from a model perspective, we compare the performance of best unsupervised model with the performance of the supervised model on the test set.

The second way to evaluate the proposed method is by looking at it from what we call an *algorithmic perspective*. The aim of proposing an unsupervised algorithm is to be able to select sentences belonging to a particular sentiment class from an unkown dataset. Hence, to evaluate from an algorithmic perspective, we must look at the training set and check how accurate the algorithm is in its annotations for each class. To do this, we show performance (F1-scores) as a function of the number of selected sentences from the training set.

7 Experiments

For our experiments, we restrict the dataset to consist of two sentiment classes - positive and negative sentiments. In this section, we evaluate our proposed unsupervised self-training framework

[2] https://huggingface.co/cardiffnlp/twitter-roberta-base-sentiment

[3] https://scikit-learn.org/stable/modules/generated/sklearn.metrics.classification_report.html

Train Language	Vanilla		Ratio		Supervised	
	F1	Accuracy	F1	Accuracy	F1	Accuracy
Hinglish	0.84	0.84	0.84	0.84	0.91	0.91
Spanglish	0.77	0.76	0.77	0.77	0.78	0.79
Tamil	0.68	0.63	0.79	0.80	0.83	0.85
Malayalam	0.73	0.71	0.83	0.85	0.90	0.90

Table 3: Performance of best Unsupervised Self-Training models for Vanilla and Ratio selection strategies when compared to performance of supervised models. The F1 scores represent the weighted average F1.

for four different code-swithced languages spanning across three language families, with different dataset sizes and different extents of imbalance and code-mixing, and across two different domains. We also present a comparison between supervised and unsupervised models.

We present two training strategies for our proposed Unsupervised Self-Training Algorithm. The first is a vanilla strategy where the same number of sentences are selected in the selection block for each class. The second strategy uses a selection ratio - where we select sentences for fine tuning in a particular ratio from each class. We evaluate the algorithm based on the two evaluation criterion described in section 6.

In the Fine-Tune Block in Figure 1, we fine-tune the TweetEval model on the selected sentences for only 1 epoch. We do this because we do not want our model to overfit on the small amount of selected sentences. This means that when we go through the entire training dataset, the model has seen every sentence in the train set *exactly* once. We see that if we fine-tune the model for multiple epochs, the model overfits and its performance and capacity to learn reduces with every iteration.

7.1 Zero-Shot Results

Table 2 shows the zero-shot results for the TweetEval model. We see that the zero-shot F1 scores are much higher for the Hinglish and Spanglish datasets when compared to the results for the Dravidian languages. Part of the disparity in zero-shot performance can be attributed to the differences in domains. This means that the TweetEval model is not as compatible to the Tanglish and Malayalam-English dataset than it is to the Spanglish and Hinglish datasets. Improved training strategies help increase performance.

The zero-shot results in Table 2 use the TweetEval model, which is a 3-class classification model. Due to this, we get a prediction accuracy of less than 50% for a binary classification problem.

7.2 Vanilla Selection

In the Vanilla Selection strategy, we select the same number of sentences for each class. We saw no improvement when selecting less than 5% sentences of the total dataset size in every iteration, equally split into the two classes. Table 3 shows the performance of the best unsupervised model trained in comparison with a supervised model. For each of these results, N = 0.05 * (dataset size), where N/2 is the number of sentences selected from each class at every iteration step. The best unsupervised model is achieved almost halfway through the dataset for all languages.

The unsupervised model performs surprisingly well for Spanglish when compared to the supervised counterpart. The performance for the Hinglish model is also comparable to the supervised model. This can be attributed to the fact that both datasets are in-domain for the TweetEval model and their zero-shot performances are better than for the Dravidian languages, as shown in Table 2. Also, the fact that the Hinglish dataset is balanced helps improve performance. We expect the performance of the unsupervised models to increase with better training strategies.

For a balanced dataset like Hinglish, selecting N > 5% at every iteration provided similar performance whereas the performance deteriorates for the three imbalanced datasets if a larger number of sentences were selected. This behaviour was somewhat expected as when the dataset is imbalanced, the model is likely to make more errors in generating pseduo-labels for one class more than the other. Thus it helps to reduce the number of selections as that also reduces the number of errors.

7.3 Selection Ratio

In this selection strategy, we select unequal number of samples from each class, deciding on a ratio of positive samples to negative samples. The aim of selecting sentences with a particular ratio is to incorporate the underlying class distribution of the dataset for selection. When the underlying distribution is biased, selecting equal number of sentences would leave the algorithm to have lower accuracy in the produced pseudo-labels for the smaller class, and this error is propagated with every iteration step.

The only way to truly estimate the correct selection ratio is to sample from the given dataset. In an unsupervised scenario, we would need to annotate a selected sample of sentences to determine the selection ratio empirically. We found that on sampling around 50 sentences from the dataset, we were accurately able to predict the distribution of the class labels with a standard deviation of approximately 4-6%, depending on the dataset. The performance is not sensitive to estimation inaccuracies of that amount.

Finding the selection ratio serves a second purpose - it also gives us an estimated stopping condition. By knowing an approximate ratio of the class labels and the size of the dataset, we now have an approximation for the total number of samples in each class. As soon as the total selections for a class across all iteration reaches the predicted number of samples of that class, according to the sampled selection ratio, we should stop the algorithm.

The results for using the selection ratio are shown in Table 3. We see significant improvements in performance for the Dravidian languages, with the performance reaching very close to the supervised performance. The improvement in performance for the Hinglish and Spanglish datasets are minimal. This hints that a selection ratio strategy was able to overcome the difference in domains and the affects of poor initialization as pointed out in Table 2.

The selection ratio strategy was also able to overcome the problem of data imbalance. This can be seen in Figure 2 when we evaluate the framework from an algorithmic perspective. Figure 2 plots the classification F1 scores of the unsupervised algorithm as a function of the selected sentences. We find that using the selection ratio strategy improves the performance on the training set significantly. We see improvements for the Dravidian languages, which were also reflected in Table 3.

This improvement is also seen for the Spanglish dataset, which is not reflected in Table 3. This means that for Spanglish, the improvement in the unsupervised model when trained with selection ratio strategy does not generalize to a test set, but the improvement is enough to select sentences in the next iterations more accurately. This means that we're able to give better labels to our training set in an unsupervised manner, which was one of the aims of developing an unsupervised algorithm. (Note : The evaluation from a model perspective is done on the test set, whereas from an algorithmic perspective is done on the training set.)

This evaluation perspective also shows that if the aim of the unsupervised endevour is to create labels for an unlabelled set of sentences, one does not have to process the entire dataset. For example, if we are content with pseudo-labels or noisy labels for 4000 Hinglish Tweets, the accuracy of the produced labels would be close to 90%.

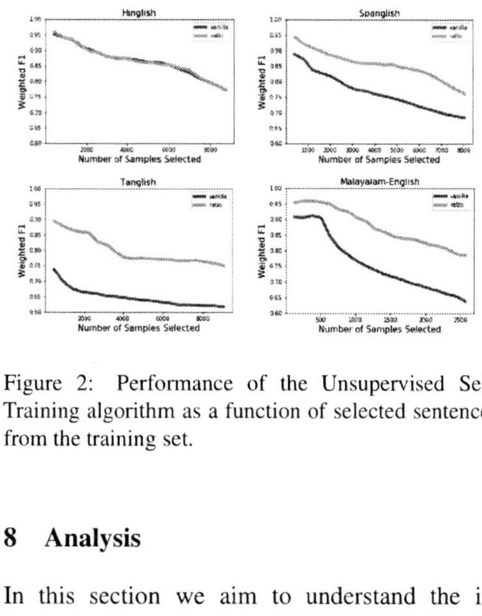

Figure 2: Performance of the Unsupervised Self-Training algorithm as a function of selected sentences from the training set.

8 Analysis

In this section we aim to understand the information learnt by a model trained under the Unsupervised Self-Training. We take the example of the Hinglish dataset. To do so, we define a quantity called *Token Ratio* to quantify the amount of code-mixing in a sentence. Since our initialization model is trained on an English dataset, the language of interest is Hindi and we would like to understand how well our model handles sentences with a large amount of Hindi. Hence, for the Hinglish dataset, we define the Hindi Token Ratio as:

$$\textit{Hindi Token Ratio} = \frac{\textit{Number of Hindi Tokens}}{\textit{Total Number of Words}}$$

(Patwa et al., 2020) provide three language labels for each token in the dataset - HIN, ENG, 0, where 0 usually corresponds to a symbol or other special characters in a Tweet. To quantify amount of code-mixing, we only use the tokens that have ENG or HIN as labels. Words are defined as tokens that have either the label HIN or ENG. We define the *Token Ratio* quantity with respect to Hindi, but our analysis can be generalized to any code-mixed language. The distribution of the Hindi Token Ratio (HTR) in the Hinglish dataset is shown in Figure 3. The figure clearly shows that the dataset is dominated by tweets that have a larger amount Hindi words than English words. This is also true for the other three datasets.

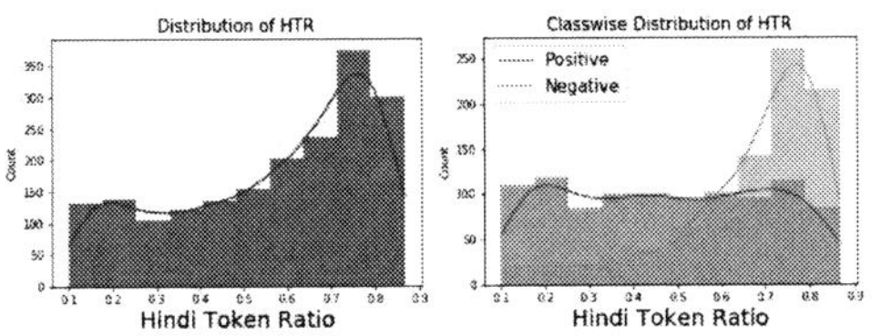

Figure 3: Distributions of Hindi Token Ratio for the Hinglish Dataset.

8.1 Learning Dynamics of the Unsupervised Model

To study if the unsupervised model understands Hinglish, we look at the performance of the model as a function of the Hindi Token Ratio. In Figure 4 , the sentences in the Hinglish dataset are grouped into buckets of Hindi Token Ratio. A *bucket* is of size 0.1 and contains all the sentences that fall in its range. For example, when the x-axis says 0.1, this means the bucket contains all sentences that have a Hindi Token ratio between 0.1 and 0.2.

Figure 4 shows that the zero shot model performs the best for sentences that have very low amount of Hindi code-mixed with English. As the amount of Hindi in a sentence increases, the performance of the zero-shot predictions decreases drastically. On training the model with our proposed Unsupervised Self-Training framework, we see a significant rise in the performance for sentences with higher HTR (or sentences with a larger amount of Hindi than English) as well as the overall performance of the model. This rise is gradual and the model improves at classifying sentences with higher HTR with every iteration.

Next, we refer back to Figure 3. Figure 3 shows

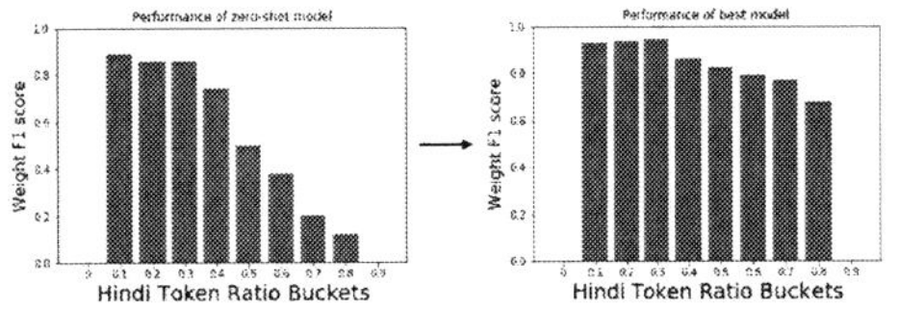

Figure 4: Model Performance for different Hindi Token Ratio buckets. For example, a bucket labelled as 0.3 contains all sentences that have a Hindi Token ration between 0.3 and o.4.

the distribution of the Hindi Token Ratio for each of the two sentiment classes. For the Hinglish dataset, we see that tweets with negative sentiments are more likely to contain more Hindi words than English. The distribution for the Hindi Token Ratio for positive sentiment is almost uniform, thus showing no preference for English or Hindi words when expressing a positive sentiment. If we look at the distribution of the predictions made by the zero-shot unsupervised model, shown in Figure 5, we see that majority of the sentences are predicted as belonging to the positive sentiment class. There seems to be no resemblance with the original distribution (Figure 3). As the model trains under our Unsupervised Self-Training framework, we see that the predicted distribution becomes very similar to the original distribution.

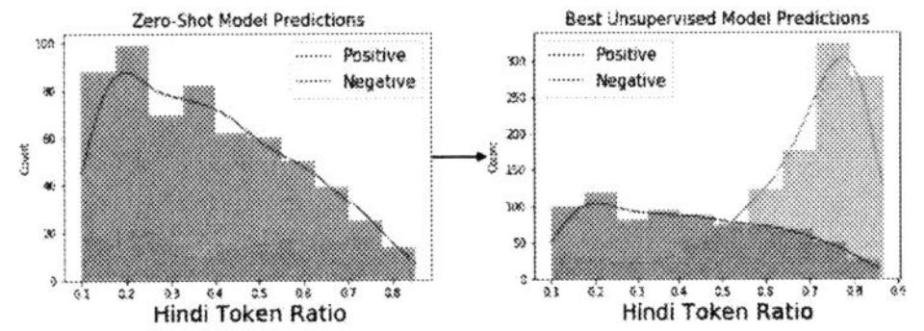

Figure 5: Comparison made between predictions made by the zero-shot and the best unsupervised model.

8.2 Error Analysis

In this section, we look at the errors made by the unsupervised model. Table 4 shows the comparison between the class-wise performance of the supervised and the best unsupervised model. The unsupervised model is better at making correct predictions for the negative sentiment class when compared to the supervised model. Figure 6 shows the classwise performance for the zero-shot and best unsupervised model for the different HTR buckets. We see that the zero-shot models performs poorly for both the positive and negative classes. As the unsupervised model improves with itera-

Model Type	Positive Accuracy	Negative Accuracy
Unsupervised	0.73	0.94
Supervised	0.93	0.83

Table 4: Comparison between class-wise performance for supervised and unsupervised models.

tions through the dataset, we see the performance for each class increase.

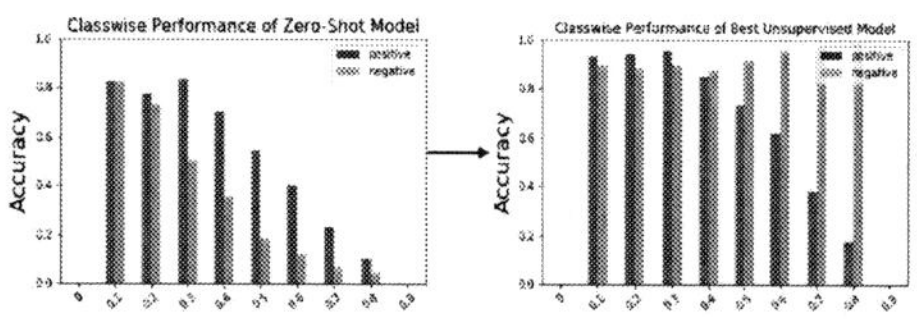

Figure 6: Class-wise performance of the zero-shot and the best unsupervised models for different Hindi Token Ratio buckets.

8.3 Does the Unsupervised Model 'Understand' Hinglish?

The learning dynamics in section 8.1 show that as the TweetEval model is fine-tuned under our proposed Unsupervised Training Framework, the performance of the model increases for sentences that have higher amounts of Hindi. In fact, the performance increase is seen across the board for all Hindi Token Ratio buckets. We saw the distribution of the predictions made by the zero-shot model, which preferred to classify almost all sentences as positive. But as the model was fine-tuned, the predicted distribution was able to replicate the original data distribution. These experiments show that the model originally trained on an English dataset is beginning to atleast recognize Hindi when trained with our proposed framework, if not understand it.

We also see a bias in the Hinglish dataset where the negative sentiments are more likely to contain a larger number Hindi Tokens, which are unknown tokens from the perspective of the initial TweetEval model. Thus the classification task would be aided by learning the difference in the underlying distributions of the two classes. Note that we do expect a supervised model to use this divide in the distributions as well. Figure 6 shows a larger increase in performance for the negative sentiment class than the positive sentiment class, although the performance is increased across the board for all Hindi Token Ratio buckets. (This difference in performance can be remedied by selecting sentences with high Hindi Token Ratio in the selection block.) Thus, it does seem like that the model is able to understand Hindi and this understanding is aided by the differences in the class-wise distribution of the two sentiments.

9 Conclusion

We propose the Unsupervised Self-Training framework and show results for unsupervised sentiment classification of code-switched data. The algorithm is comprehensively tested for four very different code-mixed languages - Hinglish, Spanglish, Tanglish and Malayalam-English, covering many variations including differences in language families, domains, dataset sizes and dataset imbalances. The unsupervised models performed competitively when compared to supervised models. We also present training strategies to optimize the performance of our proposed framework.

An extensive analysis is provided describing the learning dynamics of the algorithm. The algorithm is initialized with a model trained on an English dataset and has poor zero-shot performance on sentence with large amounts of code-mixing. We show that with every iteration, the performance on fine-tuned model increases for sentences with a larger amounts of code-mixing. Eventually, the model begins to understand the code-mixed data.

10 Future Work

The proposed Unsupervised Self-Training algorithm was tested with only two sentiment classes - positive and negative. An unsupervised sentiment classification algorithm is to be able to generate annotations for an unlabelled code-mixed dataset without going through the expensive annotation process. This can be done by including the neutral class in the dataset, which is going to be a part of our future work.

In our work, we only used one initialization model trained on English Tweets for all four code-mixed datasets, as all of them were code-mixed with English. Future work can include testing the framework with different and more compatible models for initialization. Further work can be done on optimization strategies, including incorporating the Token Ratio while selecting pseudo-labels, and active learning.

References

Francesco Barbieri, Jose Camacho-Collados, Leonardo Neves, and Luis Espinosa-Anke. 2020. Tweeteval: Unified benchmark and comparative evaluation for tweet classification. *arXiv preprint arXiv:2010.12421*.

Bharathi Raja Chakravarthi, Navya Jose, Shardul Suryawanshi, Elizabeth Sherly, and John P McCrae. 2020a. A sentiment analysis dataset for code-mixed malayalam-english. *arXiv preprint arXiv:2006.00210*.

Bharathi Raja Chakravarthi, Vigneshwaran Muralidaran, Ruba Priyadharshini, and John P McCrae. 2020b. Corpus creation for sentiment analysis in code-mixed tamil-english text. *arXiv preprint arXiv:2006.00206*.

BR Chakravarthi, R Priyadharshini, V Muralidaran, S Suryawanshi, N Jose, E Sherly, and JP McCrae. 2020c. Overview of the track on sentiment analysis for dravidian languages in code-mixed text. In *Working Notes of the Forum for Information Retrieval Evaluation (FIRE 2020). CEUR Workshop Proceedings. In: CEUR-WS. org, Hyderabad, India*.

Alexis Conneau, Kartikay Khandelwal, Naman Goyal, Vishrav Chaudhary, Guillaume Wenzek, Francisco Guzmán, Edouard Grave, Myle Ott, Luke Zettlemoyer, and Veselin Stoyanov. 2019. Unsupervised cross-lingual representation learning at scale. *arXiv preprint arXiv:1911.02116*.

Jacob Devlin, Ming-Wei Chang, Kenton Lee, and Kristina Toutanova. 2018. Bert: Pre-training of deep bidirectional transformers for language understanding. *arXiv preprint arXiv:1810.04805*.

Jingfei Du, Edouard Grave, Beliz Gunel, Vishrav Chaudhary, Onur Celebi, Michael Auli, Ves Stoyanov, and Alexis Conneau. 2020a. Self-training improves pre-training for natural language understanding. *arXiv preprint arXiv:2010.02194*.

Jingfei Du, Edouard Grave, Beliz Gunel, Vishrav Chaudhary, Onur Celebi, Michael Auli, Ves Stoyanov, and Alexis Conneau. 2020b. Self-training improves pre-training for natural language understanding. *arXiv preprint arXiv:2010.02194*.

Akshat Gupta, Sai Krishna Rallabandi, and Alan Black. 2021. Task-specific pre-training and cross lingual transfer for code-switched data. *arXiv preprint arXiv:2102.12407*.

Martin Haselmayer and Marcelo Jenny. 2017. Sentiment analysis of political communication: combining a dictionary approach with crowdcoding. *Quality & quantity*, 51(6):2623–2646.

Sai Muralidhar Jayanthi and Akshat Gupta. 2021. Sj_aj@ dravidianlangtech-eacl2021: Task-adaptive pre-training of multilingual bert models for offensive language identification. *arXiv preprint arXiv:2102.01051*.

Yinhan Liu, Myle Ott, Naman Goyal, Jingfei Du, Mandar Joshi, Danqi Chen, Omer Levy, Mike Lewis, Luke Zettlemoyer, and Veselin Stoyanov. 2019. Roberta: A robustly optimized bert pretraining approach. *arXiv preprint arXiv:1907.11692*.

Zhu Nanli, Zou Ping, Li Weiguo, and Cheng Meng. 2012. Sentiment analysis: A literature review. In *2012 International Symposium on Management of Technology (ISMOT)*, pages 572–576. IEEE.

Parth Patwa, Gustavo Aguilar, Sudipta Kar, Suraj Pandey, Srinivas PYKL, Björn Gambäck, Tanmoy Chakraborty, Thamar Solorio, and Amitava Das. 2020. Semeval-2020 task 9: Overview of sentiment analysis of code-mixed tweets. *arXiv e-prints*, pages arXiv–2008.

Colin Wei, Kendrick Shen, Yining Chen, and Tengyu Ma. 2020. Theoretical analysis of self-training with deep networks on unlabeled data. *arXiv preprint arXiv:2010.03622*.

David Yarowsky. 1995. Unsupervised word sense disambiguation rivaling supervised methods. In *33rd annual meeting of the association for computational linguistics*, pages 189–196.

Xiaojin Jerry Zhu. 2005. Semi-supervised learning literature survey.

Barret Zoph, Golnaz Ghiasi, Tsung-Yi Lin, Yin Cui, Hanxiao Liu, Ekin D Cubuk, and Quoc V Le. 2020a. Rethinking pre-training and self-training. *arXiv preprint arXiv:2006.06882*.

Barret Zoph, Golnaz Ghiasi, Tsung-Yi Lin, Yin Cui, Hanxiao Liu, Ekin D Cubuk, and Quoc V Le. 2020b. Rethinking pre-training and self-training. *arXiv preprint arXiv:2006.06882*.

A Implementation Details

We use the RoBERTa-base based model pre-trained on a large English Twitter corpus for initialization, which has about 125M paramters. The model was fine-tuned using the NVIDIA GeForce GTX 1070 GPU using python3.6. The Tanglish dataset was the biggest dataset which required approximately 3 minutes per iteration. One pass through the entire dataset required 20 iterations for the Vanilla selection strategy and about 30 iterations for the Ratio selection strategy. The time required per iteration was lower for the the other three datasets, with about 100 seconds per iteration for the Malaylam-English datasets.

CodemixedNLP: An Extensible and Open NLP Toolkit for Code-Mixing

Sai Muralidhar Jayanthi, Kavya Nerella, Khyathi Raghavi Chandu, Alan W Black
Language Technologies Institute
Carnegie Mellon University
{sjayanth, knerella, kchandu, awb}@cs.cmu.edu

Abstract

The NLP community has witnessed steep progress in a variety of tasks across the realms of monolingual and multilingual language processing recently. These successes, in conjunction with the proliferating mixed language interactions on social media have boosted interest in modeling code-mixed texts. In this work, we present CODEMIXEDNLP, an open-source library with the goals of bringing together the advances in code-mixed NLP and opening it up to a wider machine learning community. The library consists of tools to develop and benchmark versatile model architectures that are tailored for mixed texts, methods to expand training sets, techniques to quantify mixing styles, and fine-tuned state-of-the-art models for 7 tasks in Hinglish[1]. We believe this work has a potential to foster a distributed yet collaborative and sustainable ecosystem in an otherwise dispersed space of code-mixing research. The toolkit is designed to be simple, easily extensible, and resourceful to both researchers as well as practitioners[2].

1 Introduction

Code-mixing refers to fluid alteration between two or more languages in a given utterance. This phenomenon is ubiquitous and more natural in multilingual communities, and is highly prevalent in social media platforms. Developing tools that can comprehend mixed texts can have a multitude of advantages, ranging from socially responsible NLP applications such as moderating abusive content in social media to improve naturalness of ubiquitous technologies such as conversational AI assistants and further to develop socio-cultural studies around human cognition, such as why and when people code-mix.

NLP tools for monolingual and multilingual language processing have rapidly progressed in the past few years; thanks to the transformer-based models such as Multilingual BERT (Devlin et al., 2019) & XLM-RoBERTa (Conneau et al., 2020), and their *pretraining* techniques. On various mixed datasets, recent studies have shown that adopting multilingual pretrained models can perform better than their previous deep learning counterparts (Pires et al., 2019; Khanuja et al., 2020; Aguilar et al., 2020; Chakravarthy et al., 2020; Jayanthi and Gupta, 2021). While this looks promising for multilingual, the same is not translated to code-mixing. Hence, a critical investigation is required to understand generalizable modeling strategies to enhance performance on mixed texts (Winata et al., 2021; Aguilar and Solorio, 2020; Sitaram et al., 2020).

At the same time, practitioners who require an off-the-shelf tool into their downstream mixed text application (eg. sentiment or language identification), currently have to resort to monolingual toolkits such as NLTK, Flair, IndicNLP and iNLTK. On the other hand, while there have been several episodic works on mixed text processing, such as proposing novel datasets or shared-tasks or training strategies, there haven't been many initiatives to collate these resources into a common setting; doing so can benefit both researchers and practitioners, thereby accelerating NLP for mixed texts.

In this work, we address some of these shortcomings by creating an extensible and open-source toolkit for a variety of semantic and syntactic NLP applications in mixed languages. Our toolkit offers-

- simple **plug-and-play command line interfaces** with fine grained control over inputs, models and tasks for developing, quantifying, benchmarking, and re-using versatile model architectures tailored for mixed texts (§ 2.1, § 2.2, § 2.3)
- easy to use single stop interfacing for a variety

[1] Demo is available at: https://bit.ly/3rzOcWb

[2] The library and pretrained models are available at github.com/murali1996/CodemixedNLP.

Proceedings of the Fifth Workshop on Computational Approaches to Linguistic Code-Switching, pages 113–118
June 11, 2021. ©2021 Association for Computational Linguistics
https://doi.org/10.26615/978-954-452-056-4_014

of **data augmentation** techniques including transliteration, spelling variations, expansion with monolingual corpora etc., by leveraging a collation of publicly available tools

- a toolkit library to **import fine-tuned and ready-to-use models** for 7 different tasks in Hinglish, along with an easy-to-setup **web interface** wrapper based on flask server (§ 4)

We believe the fine grained plug and play interfacing of the toolkit can serve a multitude of purposes in both academia and industry. Such fine control over the individual components of the model can enable accelerated experimentation in training different model architectures, such as multi-tasking, representation-fusion, and language-informed modeling. This in-turn helps our understanding of utilizing pretrained transformer-models for mixed datasets. In addition, our toolkit also offers computation of metrics to quantify code-mixing such as Code-Mixing Index, Language Entropy, etc., which can be utilized to find peculiarities of low-performing subsets.

Like a curse in disguise, though code-mixing is widely prevalent and available on social media, it is accompanied with non-standard spellings, mixed scripts and ill-formed sentences are common in code-mixing. To combat this, our toolkit offers techniques to augment the training sets with multiple views of each input corresponding to the above problems.

Among many potential applications, we first demonstrate our toolkit's utility in *benchmarking* (§ 3). In addition, we publish state-of-the-art models for different NLP tasks in Hinglish and wrap them into a command line / deployable web interface (§ 4). Our toolkit is easily extensible–practitioners can incorporate new pretrained as well as fine-tuned models, include text processors such as tokenizers, transliterators and translators, and add wrappers on existing methods for downstream NLP applications.

2 Toolkit

Our toolkit is organized into components as depicted in Figure 1. In a nutshell, an end-to-end model architecture consists of one or more `encoder` components, a component for `combining encodings`, and one or more `adaptor` plus `task` components.

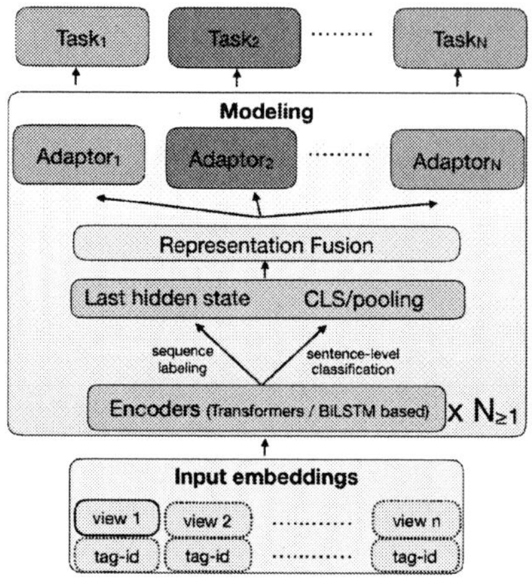

Figure 1: Customizable components in our toolkit. Marked in dashed box is an optional component.

2.1 Input Embeddings

Multi-view Integration: Tokens in mixed texts are often manifested in cross-script and mixed forms, that we refer to as *views*. This infusion motivates integration of text representations in varied forms, such as transliterated, translated, script-normalized, and tokens belonging to one of the participating languages. Especially in the context of pretrained multilingual models, this technique means extracting a holistic representation of a mixed text. To this end, the toolkit facilitates combining representations from different *views* of an input.

Text Tokenization: Motivated by some recent related works on using different word-level and sub-word-level embeddings (Winata et al., 2019; Aguilar and Solorio, 2020), our toolkit offers different tokenization methods for encoding text. Among the encoders available in our toolkit (§ 2.2), pretrained transformer-based encoders can either be tokenized using their default tokenization technique (i.e. subwords) or by using a character-CNN architecture (Boukkouri et al., 2020). LSTM-based models can take inputs in the form of tensor representations–eg. word-level FastText (Bojanowski et al., 2017) or semi-character (Sakaguchi et al., 2017) representations, or character-level representations–eg. char-BiLSTM[3].

Tag-Informed Modeling: Studies in the past have shown the usefulness of language tag-aware modeling for mixed and cross-lingual

[3]Sequence Tagging with Tensorflow

Benchmarking transformer based models (F1 / Accuracy)

Model	Text Classification Tasks							Sequence Tagging Tasks		
	Sentiment Classification			Aggression Identification	Hate Speech Identification	Offensiveness Identification	Youtube Comments Classification	Language Identification	NER	POS
	HIN-ENG$_1$	HIN-ENG$_2$	SPA-ENG†	HIN-ENG	HIN-ENG	TAM-ENG†	HIN-ENG	HIN-ENG†	HIN-ENG†	HIN-ENG
`mBert`	65.9 / 65.7	58.8 / 60.7	50.1 / 51.3	48.1 48.7	47.1 / 61.7	76.8 / 79.0	83.3 / 83.4	96.9 / 96.9	95.1 / 95.6	75.0 / 75.8
w/ Task adaptive	67.4 / 67.2	61.4 / 61.5	53.2 / 55.0	50.3 / 51.2	67.9 70.3	76.9 / **78.9**	83.6 / 83.7	97.1 / 97.1	97.1 / 97.1	**77.1 / 77.6**
w/ Domain adaptive	71.4 / 71.3	62.5 / 63.0	–	50.7 / 51.4	**65.5 / 70.3**	–	85.2 / 85.3	97.3 / 97.3	**97.2 / 97.3**	75.8 / 76.3
`XLM-RoBERTa`	68.9 / 69.1	61.5 / 61.5	54.4 / 54.6	49.0 / 49.6	64.4 / 69.6	76.7 / 77.4	85.7 / 85.8	97.1 / 97.1	96.1 / 96.3	73.7 / 74.8
w/ Task adaptive	70.4 / 70.4	63.0 / 63.0	**54.4 / 54.8**	55.3 / 55.4	64.6 / 69.8	**77.1** / 78.8	85.8 / 85.9	**97.6 / 97.6**	97.1 / 97.2	76.5 / 76.9
w/ Domain adaptive	**72.1 / 72.2**	**65.6 / 65.7**	–	**56.7 / 57.1**	65.2 / 70.4	–	**87.3 / 87.4**	97.5 / 97.5	96.9 / 97.0	74.9 / 75.7

Table 1: Results are reported for eight different tasks, namely, Sentiment Classification (HIN-ENG$_1$ (Patwa et al., 2020), HIN-ENG$_2$ (Patra et al., 2018), SPA-ENG(Aguilar et al., 2020)), Aggression Identification (Kumar et al., 2018), Hate Speech Identification (Bohra et al., 2018), Offensiveness Identification (Chakravarthi et al., 2020), Youtube Comments Classification (Kaur et al., 2019), Language Identification (Aguilar et al., 2020), Named Entity Recognition and Parts of Speech Tagging (Khanuja et al., 2020). † Implies results on *dev* split, otherwise on *test* splits.

Model	Sentiment Classification	
	HIN-ENG$_1$	HIN-ENG$_2$
`XLM-RoBERTa`	68.9 / 69.1	61.5 / 61.5
w/ multi-view integration	**71.1 / 71.3**	62.0 / 62.8
w/ language-tag informed	68.9 / 69.3	62.8 / 63.1
w/ fasttext-BiLSTM fusion	69.9 / 70.0	61.2 / 62.1
w/ char-BiLSTM fusion	69.3 / 69.1	62.0 / 62.3
w/ semi-char-BiLSTM fusion	69.4 / 68.9	60.0 / 60.8
w/ data noising	70.5 / 70.5	61.9 / 62.2
w/ monolingual corpora	68.9 / 69.3	**68.2 / 68.3**

Table 2: Results of various modelling techniques (F1 / Accuracy) when used with a pretrained transformers-based encoder. HIN-ENG$_1$ refers (Patwa et al., 2020) and HIN-ENG$_2$ refers to (Patra et al., 2018)

texts (Chandu et al., 2018; Lample and Conneau, 2019). However, their usefulness in the context of pretrained models and code-mixing is not thoroughly investigated. To this end, we offer a more generalized method in our toolkit to conduct *any* tag-aware fine-tuning, wherein representations for different kinds of tags can be added to the text representations. Examples of such tags include POS tags, Language IDs, etc.

2.2 Models

Encoders: An Encoder in our toolkit can consist of a transformer-based or BiLSTM-based architecture. Specifically, for the former, we utilize pretrained models from the HuggingFace library (Wolf et al., 2020) and the latter is implemented in Pytorch (Paszke et al., 2019).

Representation Fusion: Encodings from different encoders can be combined, and if required be augmented with (non-trainable) representations before passing through an adaptor. To combine encodings, one can either simply concat them or obtain a (trainable) weighted average, a more parameter-efficient choice than the former. Both choices are available in our toolkit.

Adaptors: An adaptor is a task-specific neural layer and currently, BiLSTM and Multi-Layer Perceptron (MLP) choices are available as part our toolkit. The inputs to adaptors are fused representations if multiple encoders are specified, else output from a single encoder. These adaptors serve as task-specific learnable parameters.

Multitasking: Multi-task learning can help models to pick relevant cues from one task to be applied to another. Such a setting was also previously investigated in the context of mixed texts, which showed promising improvements (Chandu et al., 2018). Furthermore, it is also shown in monolingual NLP that incorporating explicit semantics as an auxiliary task can enhance BERT's performance (Zhang et al., 2020). Motivated by these, our toolkit offers support to conduct training of one or more tasks. Once a final representation is produced by adaptors of each task, we use a training criterion to compute loss and perform gradient backpropagation.

2.3 Tasks

Tasks: Our toolkit currently supports two kinds of tasks– sentence-level text classification and word-level sequence tagging, the flow for each is demonstrated in Figure 1. The *decoupled* design of our toolkit helps in seamlessly creating multi-task training setups. The kinds of tasks for which we offer support currently are listed in Table 1.

Adaptive Pretraining: Following the successes of task-adaptive and domain-adaptive pretraining in monolingual and multilingual NLP tasks (Gururangan et al., 2020), users of our toolkit can also perform such adaptive pretrainings using mixed texts on top of pretrained transformer-based models.

2.4 Codemixed Quantification

Our toolkit offers 5 standardized metrics for quantifying mixing in text, namely Code-Mixing Index (Gambäck and Das, 2014), Average switch-points (Khanuja et al., 2020), Multilingual Index, Probability of Switching and Language Entropy (Guzmán et al., 2017). We offer simple command line methods to compute these metrics and also offer metric-based data sampling.

2.5 Data Augmentation

Our toolkit also offers techniques to do data augmentation. While data augmentation is useful in cases where there is training data scarcity, for mixed datasets, it is also essential to produce a more generalized model. As part of this feature, this toolkit currently offers augmentation through transliteration, spelling variations and monolingual corpora. We currently support transliteration of Indic languages through an off-the-shelf tool- `indic-trans` (Bhat et al., 2015). Spelling variations include noising spelling, such as randomly removing/replacing vowel characters. Monolingual corpora augmentation is task specific. For a given task, such as sentiment classification, we augment publicly available monolingual corpora based on the task type from one or all of the mixing languages and use it while fine-tuning models.

2.6 Data Format

Due to diverse data formats of existing mixed datasets, benchmarking and comparing results across tasks is not readily feasible. To this end, we propose a standardized data format for syntactic, semantic level understanding and generation tasks, and our toolkit offers command line methods to adopt a user's dataset to this standard format.

3 Experiments

Among many potential research applications of our toolkit, in this section, we demonstrate one – *benchmarking*. Table 1 presents performances of selected model architectures obtained using our toolkit on some popular mixed datasets. In Table 2, we also demonstrate the performances of different architectural choices implemented through our toolkit on two Hinglish datasets. For domain-adaptive pretraining of Hinglish datasets, we collate around 160K mixed sentences from several of the publicly available Hinglish datasets.

```
""" load toolkit """
from CodemixedNLP.cli import ModelCreator as HinglishToolkit
myToolkit = HinglishToolkit()

""" see what's available """
myToolkit.show_available_tasks()
#   >>> ['sentiment', 'aggression', 'hatespeech', 'lid', 'pos', 'ner', 'mt']

""" download models """
myToolkit.download_finetuned("all")

""" load model for your application and use """
# Sentiment Classification
sentiment_classifier = myToolkit.from_pretrained("sentiment")
results = sentiment_classifier.get_predictions("wo team kaafi acha hei, not all days are yours")
#   >>> results: positive

# Language Identification
lid_classifier = myToolkit.from_pretrained("lid")
results = lid_classifier.get_predictions("Aur mere projects bhi bohot hain", pretify=True)
#   >>> results: Aur/hi mere/hi projects/en bhi/hi bohot/hi hain/hi

# Machine Translation model
translator = myToolkit.from_pretrained("mt")
results = translator.get_predictions("anyways, wo team kaafi acha hei, glad to be a part of it")
#   >>> results: anyways, that team is very good, glad to be a part of it
```

Figure 2: Command line interface for utilizing fine-tuned models. We provide several functionality compatible with the popular Huggingface and Fairseq libraries. Marked in boxes are customizable input arguments.

For task-adaptive pretraining, we just use the training and testing data available in the dataset of interest. For training, we use standard optimizers and model configurations. [4]

4 Demo

We fine-tune and publish transformer-based models for 7 tasks in Hinglish. We include 3 task types– (1) **Semantic** (Sentiment Classification, Hate Speech and Aggression Identification), (2) **Syntactic** (NER, POS and Language Identification), and (3) **Generation** (Hinglish→English Machine Translation). We present some examples of utilizing these models in Figure 2.

5 Conclusion

In this work, we presented a unified toolkit for modeling code-mixed texts. Additionally, the toolkit contains various functionalities such as data augmentation, code-mixing quantification, and ready-to-use fine-tuned models for 7 different NLP tasks in Hinglish. Our toolkit is simple enough for practitioners to integrate new features as well as develop wrappers around its existing functionalities. We believe this contribution facilitates a sustainable and extensible ecosystem of models by adding novel pretraining techniques tailored for mixed texts, text normalization techniques to counter spelling variations, error analysis tools to identify peculiarities in incorrect predictions and so on.

[4]Due to the space limitations, we direct the reader to check github.com/murali1996/CodemixedNLP for toolkit usage patterns and for the list of modeling choices.

References

Gustavo Aguilar, Sudipta Kar, and Thamar Solorio. 2020. LinCE: A centralized benchmark for linguistic code-switching evaluation. In *Proceedings of the 12th Language Resources and Evaluation Conference*, pages 1803–1813, Marseille, France. European Language Resources Association.

Gustavo Aguilar and Thamar Solorio. 2020. From English to code-switching: Transfer learning with strong morphological clues. In *Proceedings of the 58th Annual Meeting of the Association for Computational Linguistics*, pages 8033–8044, Online. Association for Computational Linguistics.

Irshad Ahmad Bhat, Vandan Mujadia, Aniruddha Tammewar, Riyaz Ahmad Bhat, and Manish Shrivastava. 2015. Iiit-h system submission for fire2014 shared task on transliterated search. In *Proceedings of the Forum for Information Retrieval Evaluation*, FIRE '14, pages 48–53, New York, NY, USA. ACM.

Aditya Bohra, Deepanshu Vijay, Vinay Singh, Syed Sarfaraz Akhtar, and Manish Shrivastava. 2018. A dataset of hindi-english code-mixed social media text for hate speech detection. In *Proceedings of the second workshop on computational modeling of people's opinions, personality, and emotions in social media*, pages 36–41.

Piotr Bojanowski, Edouard Grave, Armand Joulin, and Tomas Mikolov. 2017. Enriching word vectors with subword information.

Hicham El Boukkouri, Olivier Ferret, Thomas Lavergne, Hiroshi Noji, Pierre Zweigenbaum, and Junichi Tsujii. 2020. Characterbert: Reconciling elmo and bert for word-level open-vocabulary representations from characters.

Bharathi Raja Chakravarthi, Vigneshwaran Muralidaran, Ruba Priyadharshini, and John Philip McCrae. 2020. Corpus creation for sentiment analysis in code-mixed Tamil-English text. In *Proceedings of the 1st Joint Workshop on Spoken Language Technologies for Under-resourced languages (SLTU) and Collaboration and Computing for Under-Resourced Languages (CCURL)*, pages 202–210, Marseille, France. European Language Resources association.

Sharanya Chakravarthy, Anjana Umapathy, and Alan W Black. 2020. Detecting entailment in code-mixed Hindi-English conversations. In *Proceedings of the Sixth Workshop on Noisy User-generated Text (W-NUT 2020)*, pages 165–170, Online. Association for Computational Linguistics.

Khyathi Chandu, Thomas Manzini, Sumeet Singh, and Alan W. Black. 2018. Language informed modeling of code-switched text. In *Proceedings of the Third Workshop on Computational Approaches to Linguistic Code-Switching*, pages 92–97, Melbourne, Australia. Association for Computational Linguistics.

Alexis Conneau, Kartikay Khandelwal, Naman Goyal, Vishrav Chaudhary, Guillaume Wenzek, Francisco Guzmán, Edouard Grave, Myle Ott, Luke Zettlemoyer, and Veselin Stoyanov. 2020. Unsupervised cross-lingual representation learning at scale. In *Proceedings of the 58th Annual Meeting of the Association for Computational Linguistics*, pages 8440–8451, Online. Association for Computational Linguistics.

Jacob Devlin, Ming-Wei Chang, Kenton Lee, and Kristina Toutanova. 2019. BERT: Pre-training of deep bidirectional transformers for language understanding. In *Proceedings of the 2019 Conference of the North American Chapter of the Association for Computational Linguistics: Human Language Technologies, Volume 1 (Long and Short Papers)*, pages 4171–4186, Minneapolis, Minnesota. Association for Computational Linguistics.

Flair. Flair toolkit. `https://github.com/flairNLP/flair`. Accessed: 2021-03-09.

Björn Gambäck and Amitava Das. 2014. On measuring the complexity of code-mixing. In *Proceedings of the 11th International Conference on Natural Language Processing, Goa, India*, pages 1–7.

Suchin Gururangan, Ana Marasović, Swabha Swayamdipta, Kyle Lo, Iz Beltagy, Doug Downey, and Noah A. Smith. 2020. Don't stop pretraining: Adapt language models to domains and tasks. In *Proceedings of ACL*.

Gualberto A Guzmán, Joseph Ricard, Jacqueline Serigos, Barbara E Bullock, and Almeida Jacqueline Toribio. 2017. Metrics for modeling code-switching across corpora. In *INTERSPEECH*, pages 67–71.

IndicNLP. Indic nlp library. `https://anoopkunchukuttan.github.io/indic_nlp_library/`. Accessed: 2021-03-09.

iNLTK. Natural language toolkit for indic languages (inltk). `https://github.com/goru001/inltk`. Accessed: 2021-03-09.

Sai Muralidhar Jayanthi and Akshat Gupta. 2021. SJ_AJ@DravidianLangTech-EACL2021: Task-adaptive Pre-Training of Multilingual BERT models for Offensive Language Identification.

Gagandeep Kaur, Abhishek Kaushik, and Shubham Sharma. 2019. Cooking is creating emotion: a study on hinglish sentiments of youtube cookery channels using semi-supervised approach. *Big Data and Cognitive Computing*, 3(3):37.

Simran Khanuja, Sandipan Dandapat, Anirudh Srinivasan, Sunayana Sitaram, and Monojit Choudhury. 2020. GLUECoS: An evaluation benchmark for code-switched NLP. In *Proceedings of the 58th Annual Meeting of the Association for Computational Linguistics*, pages 3575–3585, Online. Association for Computational Linguistics.

Ritesh Kumar, Atul Kr. Ojha, Shervin Malmasi, and Marcos Zampieri. 2018. Benchmarking aggression identification in social media. In *Proceedings of the First Workshop on Trolling, Aggression and Cyberbullying (TRAC-2018)*, pages 1–11, Santa Fe, New Mexico, USA. Association for Computational Linguistics.

Guillaume Lample and Alexis Conneau. 2019. Cross-lingual language model pretraining.

NLTK. Nltk sentiment analysis toolkit. `http://www.nltk.org/howto/sentiment.html`. Accessed: 2021-03-09.

Adam Paszke, Sam Gross, Francisco Massa, Adam Lerer, James Bradbury, Gregory Chanan, Trevor Killeen, Zeming Lin, Natalia Gimelshein, Luca Antiga, et al. 2019. Pytorch: An imperative style, high-performance deep learning library. *arXiv preprint arXiv:1912.01703*.

Braja Gopal Patra, Dipankar Das, and Amitava Das. 2018. Sentiment analysis of code-mixed indian languages: An overview of sail_code-mixed shared task@ icon-2017. *arXiv preprint arXiv:1803.06745*.

Parth Patwa, Gustavo Aguilar, Sudipta Kar, Suraj Pandey, Srinivas PYKL, Björn Gambäck, Tanmoy Chakraborty, Thamar Solorio, and Amitava Das. 2020. Semeval-2020 task 9: Overview of sentiment analysis of code-mixed tweets. In *Proceedings of the 14th International Workshop on Semantic Evaluation (SemEval-2020)*, Barcelona, Spain. Association for Computational Linguistics.

Telmo Pires, Eva Schlinger, and Dan Garrette. 2019. How multilingual is multilingual BERT? In *Proceedings of the 57th Annual Meeting of the Association for Computational Linguistics*, pages 4996–5001, Florence, Italy. Association for Computational Linguistics.

Keisuke Sakaguchi, Kevin Duh, Matt Post, and Benjamin Van Durme. 2017. Robsut wrod reocginiton via semi-character recurrent neural network. In *Proceedings of the Thirty-First AAAI Conference on Artificial Intelligence, February 4-9, 2017, San Francisco, California, USA.*, pages 3281–3287. AAAI Press.

Sunayana Sitaram, Khyathi Raghavi Chandu, Sai Krishna Rallabandi, and Alan W Black. 2020. A survey of code-switched speech and language processing.

Genta Indra Winata, Samuel Cahyawijaya, Zihan Liu, Zhaojiang Lin, Andrea Madotto, and Pascale Fung. 2021. Are multilingual models effective in code-switching?

Genta Indra Winata, Zhaojiang Lin, Jamin Shin, Zihan Liu, and Pascale Fung. 2019. Hierarchical meta-embeddings for code-switching named entity recognition. *arXiv preprint arXiv:1909.08504*.

Thomas Wolf, Lysandre Debut, Victor Sanh, Julien Chaumond, Clement Delangue, Anthony Moi, Pierric Cistac, Tim Rault, Remi Louf, Morgan Funtowicz, Joe Davison, Sam Shleifer, Patrick von Platen, Clara Ma, Yacine Jernite, Julien Plu, Canwen Xu, Teven Le Scao, Sylvain Gugger, Mariama Drame, Quentin Lhoest, and Alexander Rush. 2020. Transformers: State-of-the-art natural language processing. In *Proceedings of the 2020 Conference on Empirical Methods in Natural Language Processing: System Demonstrations*, pages 38–45, Online. Association for Computational Linguistics.

Zhuosheng Zhang, Yuwei Wu, Hai Zhao, Zuchao Li, Shuailiang Zhang, Xi Zhou, and Xiang Zhou. 2020. Semantics-aware bert for language understanding.

Normalization and Back-Transliteration for Code-Switched Data

Dwija Parikh and **Thamar Solorio**
Department of Computer Science
University of Houston
Houston, TX 77204-3010
{dkparikh, tsolorio}@uh.edu

Abstract

Code-switching is an omnipresent phenomenon in multilingual communities all around the world but remains a challenge for NLP systems due to the lack of proper data and processing techniques. Hindi-English code-switched text on social media is often transliterated to the Roman script which prevents from utilizing monolingual resources available in the native Devanagari script. In this paper, we propose a method to normalize and back-transliterate code-switched Hindi-English text. In addition, we present a grapheme-to-phoneme (G2P) conversion technique for romanized Hindi data. We also release a dataset of script-corrected Hindi-English code-switched sentences labeled for the named entity recognition and part-of-speech tagging tasks to facilitate further research in this area.

Original: bhai...*why r u crying, film* me to boht maza a aajyega...!!☺☺☺

Translation: brother why are you crying, the film will be fun!

Figure 1: An example of a code-switched Hindi-English tweet. English text appears in italics and Hindi text is underlined.

1 Introduction

Linguistic code-switching (CS) is the phenomenon of mixing two or more languages in the context of a single utterance. Multilingual speakers around the world engage in code-switching on a regular basis. Code-switched data differs from monolingual data to a great extent which discourages use of existing NLP technologies on code-switched text. Code-switching also combines the syntax and lexicon of the languages used, making it difficult for monolingual models to adapt to code-switched data (Çetinoğlu and Çöltekin, 2019).

In textual code-switching, text is frequently romanized[1] due to various technical constraints. This is especially true in the case of Hindi-English since the Devanagari script for Hindi is not widely available or efficient on modern technology. Figure 1 shows an example of a code-switched Hindi-English tweet. As we can see in the example, keyboard layouts force users to choose a single script during time of purchase or adapt to using the standard QWERTY layout for transliterating multiple scripts. Since most users need to use English in their daily life, it is impractical to choose a different keyboard layout. The ease of convenience due to Latin script keyboard layouts and the lack of a standardized transliteration process leads users to employ ad-hoc phonetic transcription rules when transcribing Hindi in the Roman script (Aguilar and Solorio, 2020). Variations in transliteration and the informality of social media adds noise which makes Hindi-English code-switched data increasingly different from standard script text and harder to process. Further, transliteration also prevents from leveraging the resources available for standard Devanagari text like Wikipedia entries and monolingual models for Hindi.

Recent trends in NLP research on code-switching have explored the performance of large pre-trained models on code-switching tasks. State-of-the-art multilingual models are typically trained on standard script text like Wikipedia and struggle at adapting to transliterated noisy code-switched input. Transfer learning has emerged as a promising method to adapt monolingual models trained on high resource languages like English to code-switched data. Large pre-trained models like multilingual BERT (henceforth, mBERT) (Devlin et al., 2019) have shown robust cross-lingual zero-shot performance with code-switching data. Aguilar and Solorio (2020) demonstrated the cross-lingual transfer ability of ELMo (Peters et al., 2018) ,

[1] Throughout this paper, we use *romanized* to mean transliterated to the Roman script

Proceedings of the Fifth Workshop on Computational Approaches to Linguistic Code-Switching, pages 119–124
June 11, 2021. ©2021 Association for Computational Linguistics
https://doi.org/10.26615/978-954-452-056-4_015

which was trained on English, to Spanish-English, Hindi-English, and Nepali-English code-switched data. They observe that mBERT is outperformed by their model (CS-ELMo) for Hindi-English, possibly due to the fact that mBERT is trained on Hindi in Devanagari and their code-switched input is Romanized. In another study, Pires et al. (2019) tested mBERT's zero-shot performance on code-switched data in two formats: transliterated, where Hindi words are written in the Roman script, and corrected, where Hindi words have been converted back to the Devanagari script by human annotators. Their results show a substantial increase in zero-shot performance with script-corrected data. Other studies have also shown improvement in performance after normalization and back-transliteration on various tasks like named entity recognition and part-of-speech tagging (Ball and Garrette, 2018; Bhat et al., 2018). Thus, there is often a need for computationally inexpensive systems to prepocess data by normalization and/or back-transliteration.

We begin by providing background for the normalization and back-transliteration tasks. Then, we describe our system for normalization, grapheme-to-phoneme, and back-transliteration. Finally, we provide results and statistics of our system against human annotated data. Our contributions include: (1) a model to normalize phonetic typing variations, (2) a simplified back-transliteration technique, (3) a grapheme-to-phoneme conversion technique for romanized Hindi, and (4) publicly available data sets of script corrected Hindi-English text.

2 Related Work

Normalization. Research in phonetic typing variations when transliterating Hindi has gained increasing attention recently due to the presence of code-switched data on social media. Singh et al. (2018c) proposed a normalization model using skip-gram and clustering techniques for Hindi-English data. Mandal and Nanmaran (2018) presented the first sequence-to-sequence model for normalizing Bengali-English code-switched data.

Transliteration. Previous work in Hindi transliteration has fallen in two classes: rule based systems and machine translation based approaches. Multiple libraries like indic-transliteration[2] exist for simple transliteration tasks using rule based systems; however, they require input to be normalized and fail at adapting to non-standard data that is typical on social media. Before the advent of neural machine translation, statistical machine translation tools such as Moses (Koehn et al., 2007) were deployed for transliteration. Neural machine translation based approaches have continued to treat transliteration as a translation problem and applied methods such as sequence-to-sequence learning successfully. For instance, Bhat et al. (2018) proposed a three step encoder-decoder model for normalization and transliteration of Hindi-English code-switched text.

Grapheme-to-Phoneme. Grapheme-to-phomene (G2P) is an important task for speech recognition. Mortensen et al. (2018) presented a multilingual G2P system for transcribing a multitude of languages using simple mappings. G2P for standard Hindi is a straightforward task using simple phonetic mappings. However, for non-standard transliterated Hindi, it can be tricky to generate accurate phonemic representations.

3 Background

User generated code-switched data is noisy and riddled with word variations, spelling mistakes, and grammatical errors. Since the Latin script does not possess all the consonants and vowels required to transliterate Hindi, users come up with the most convenient ways to transcribe Hindi. Common variations in transliterated Hindi are:

- Ambiguous consonant transliteration: For consonants not covered by the Roman script, users rely on the most appropriate transliteration available which leads to multiple sounds being transliterated to the same grapheme in the roman script. For example, both दिल *<heart>* and डब्बा *<box>* are transliterated as *dil* and *dabba* respectively but the character <d> corresponds to different consonants in Hindi.

- Vowel dropping: Since native speakers of Hindi do not require explicit notation for vowels that can be easily inferred, they tend to skip their transcription in text. For instance, the Hindi word यार is generally transliterated as *yaar*. However, vowel dropping changes it to *yr*.

- Long vowel transliteration: Users transliterate long vowels in various ways. For ex-

[2]https://pypi.org/project/indic-transliteration/

ample, the most standard way to transliterate the word काम would be *kaam* but it is often transliterated as *kam*. During back-transliteration, this can be confused as कम instead of काम.

- Double consonant transliteration: Singh et al. (2018c) describe informal variations in double consonant transliteration, similar to long vowel transliteration, where users use variants with or without repeating the respective consonant. For example, इज्ज़त can be transliterated as *izzat* or *izat*.

- Slang and abbreviations: We define some commonly used slang and abbreviations for both Hindi and English. Some examples include:

  btw -> by the way

  wassup -> what's up?

Besides the above, there are other non standard variations observed in transliterated Hindi as well. These variations make it difficult to properly transliterate text using simple phonetic mappings due to the lack of a standard transliteration scheme. Numerous schemes like WX notation (Chaitanya et al., 1996), BrahmiNet-ITRANS (Kunchukuttan et al., 2015), and others have been introduced. However, none of these have been widely employed by the general public.

4 Methodology

We follow a two step system to transliterate Romanized Hindi to the Devanagari orthography. First, we normalize the input using a sequence-to-sequence model. Then, for the back-transliteration task, we syllabify the token and transcribe to Devanagari. For the grapheme-to-phoneme task, we directly map the normalized tokens into the international phonetic alphabet (IPA).

5 Data

We use the hinglishNorm dataset by Makhija et al. (2020) to train the normalization model. The dataset comprises of romanized code-switched sentences and their normalized forms annotated by humans. The data contains both Hindi and English tokens along with their normalized forms. We create pairs of tokens and their normalized forms to train our model. We further augment the dataset with some frequently encountered Hindi words on social media and their variations.

6 Experiments

6.1 Normalization

Rule based systems are not the most efficient solution to normalization since they are not capable of capturing all possible variations. Instead, we treat normalization as a general machine translation problem. We train a character level sequence-to-sequence model for normalization following the architecture of Sutskever et al. (2014). The model is comprised of a Long Short-Term Memory(LSTM) encoder and LSTM decoder. We use the Keras library (Chollet, 2015) for training the model. Table 1 compares our model's performance with the baselines provided by Makhija et al. (2020). We evaluate our system using Word Error Rate (Nießen et al., 2000), BLEU score (Papineni et al., 2002), and METEOR score (Banerjee and Lavie, 2005).

Model	WER	BLEU	METEOR
(Makhija et al., 2020)	15.55	71.21	0.50
Ours	18.5	80.48	0.56

Table 1: Results showing the effectiveness of the normalization model using the WER, BLEU, and METEOR metrics.

It is likely that some of the errors are due to inconsistencies in the transcription scheme in the hinglishNorm dataset since it is annotated by humans. One such instance is the long vowel आ which is normalized to "aa" through most of the data. However, in some instances, the annotators normalize it to "a". For example, "bt control to krna pdega" from the training data is normalized to "but control to karana padega". A sample normalized output is shown in Table 2. Here we see that the Hindi token "bhai" has been normalized to "bhaai" while the English tokens "wher", "r", "u", and "frmm" have all been corrected to their correct spellings.

Original	**bhai**$_{\text{HIN}}$ wher r u frmm
Translation	*brother, where are you from?*
Normalized	**bhaai** where are you from

Table 2: An example of normalized output

6.2 Back-transliteration

Contemporary approaches treat transliteration using computationally intensive deep learning approaches. However, once data is normalized in effort to mitigate these variations, transliterating data does not require any sophisticated approaches.

Roman	IPA	Dev	Roman	IPA	Dev
k,q	kə	क	kh	kʰə	ख
g	gə	ग	gh	gʰə	घ
h	ɦə	ह	ch	t͡ʃə	च
chh	t͡ʃʰə	छ	j	d͡ʑə	ज
jh	d͡ʑʱə	झ	y	jə	य
sh	ʃə	श	t	tə	त
th	t̪ʰ	थ	d	d̪	द
dh	d̪ʱ	ध	r	ɹə	र
n	nə	न	l	lə	ल
s	sə	स	p	pə	प
f,ph	pʰ	फ़	b	bə	ब
bh	bʱə	भ	m	mə	म
v	ʋə	व	z	zə	ज़

Table 3: Mappings for consonants

Table 3 shows mappings between orthographic forms and phonemic forms for consonants. Table 4 describes the corresponding mappings for vowels.

Roman	IPA	Dev	Roman	IPA	Dev
a	ə	अ	aa	ɑ:	आ
i	i	इ	ee	i:	ई
u	u	उ	oo	u:	ऊ
ri, ru	r̩	ऋ	e	e:	ए
ai,ei	ɑ:i	ऐ	o	o:	ओ
ou	ɑ:u, ɔ:	औ	am	əm	अं
ah	əh	अः			

Table 4: Mappings for vowels

A sample process for transliteration is outlined in Table 5.

Original	let's go **bhaai**$_{\text{HIN}}$ **abhi**$_{\text{HIN}}$ **kitnaa**$_{\text{HIN}}$ wait **karoge**$_{\text{HIN}}$
Translation	*let's go brother how long will you wait*
Transliterated	let's go भाई अभी कितना wait करोगे

Table 5: An example of back-transliteration

We test our system against human annotated data from the Xlit-Crowd[3] corpus for Hindi-English transliteration (Khapra et al., 2014). The corpus provides crowd-sourced data for romanized Hindi back-transliterated by human annotators. Results show that our system is **78.6%** accurate. Most of the errors are due to inconsistencies in transcription schemes and the rest are due to mistakes in normalizing by our model. For comparison, the popular indic-trans[4] library achieves 63.56% on the same data set (Bhat et al., 2015).

6.3 Grapheme-to-Phoneme

For the grapheme-to-phoneme task, we describe many-to-one mappings from romanized Hindi to IPA and Devanagari as shown in Tables 4 and 3. We use the Epitran[5] library by Mortensen et al. (2018) for transcribing English tokens to IPA. We extend Epitran with customized mappings for the Hindi tokens. Since the Roman script doesn't cover all the consonants required for transcribing Hindi, there are multiple ways of transcribing the same phoneme. However, prepocessing by normalization reduces the variation to a large extent. An example of grapheme-to-phoneme is provided in Table 6.

Original	let's go **bhaai**$_{\text{HIN}}$ **abhi**$_{\text{HIN}}$ **kitnaa**$_{\text{HIN}}$ wait **karoge**$_{\text{HIN}}$
Translation	*let's go brother how long will you wait*
IPA	lets gəʊ baɪ kɪtnɑ weɪt kəro:ge:

Table 6: An example of Grapheme to Phoneme

7 Released Datasets

We use our system to back-transliterate the Hindi-English corpora from the LinCE[6] benchmark (Aguilar et al., 2020). The NER corpus is from Singh et al. (2018a) and has 2,079 tweets while the POS tagging corpus is from Singh et al. (2018b) and has 1,489 tweets. Some statistics about the datasets are presented in Table 7.

8 Conclusion and Future Work

Our method can easily be extended to other languages that employ variations of the Devanagari

[3]https://github.com/anoopkunchukuttan/crowd-indic-transliteration-data

[4]https://github.com/libindic/indic-trans

[5]https://github.com/dmort27/epitran

[6]https://ritual.uh.edu/lince/home

Task	Corpus	Hindi	English
NER	Singh et al. (2018a)	13,860	11,391
POS	Singh et al. (2018b)	12,589	9,882

Table 7: Statistics on the datasets

script, for instance Gujarati and Nepali. For other Romanized languages, simple phonetic mappings can be generated by domain experts. Using back-transliteration can help pre-process code-switched data to improve performance on a variety of tasks. We also plan to augment the normalization process with a dictionary of common word variations to make the normalization task more efficient. Our ongoing work includes testing performance of cross-lingual transfer on romanized and scrip-corrected text using multilingual models like mBERT.

9 Acknowledgements

This work was supported by the National Science Foundation (NSF) on the grant #1910192. We also thank Gustavo Aguilar for insightful discussions during preliminary investigations.

References

Gustavo Aguilar, Sudipta Kar, and Thamar Solorio. 2020. LinCE: A centralized benchmark for linguistic code-switching evaluation. In *Proceedings of the 12th Language Resources and Evaluation Conference*, pages 1803–1813, Marseille, France. European Language Resources Association.

Gustavo Aguilar and Thamar Solorio. 2020. From English to code-switching: Transfer learning with strong morphological clues. In *Proceedings of the 58th Annual Meeting of the Association for Computational Linguistics*, pages 8033–8044, Online. Association for Computational Linguistics.

Kelsey Ball and Dan Garrette. 2018. Part-of-speech tagging for code-switched, transliterated texts without explicit language identification. In *Proceedings of the 2018 Conference on Empirical Methods in Natural Language Processing*, pages 3084–3089, Brussels, Belgium. Association for Computational Linguistics.

Satanjeev Banerjee and Alon Lavie. 2005. METEOR: An automatic metric for MT evaluation with improved correlation with human judgments. In *Proceedings of the ACL Workshop on Intrinsic and Extrinsic Evaluation Measures for Machine Translation and/or Summarization*, pages 65–72, Ann Arbor, Michigan. Association for Computational Linguistics.

Irshad Bhat, Riyaz A. Bhat, Manish Shrivastava, and Dipti Sharma. 2018. Universal Dependency parsing for Hindi-English code-switching. In *Proceedings of the 2018 Conference of the North American Chapter of the Association for Computational Linguistics: Human Language Technologies, Volume 1 (Long Papers)*, pages 987–998, New Orleans, Louisiana. Association for Computational Linguistics.

Irshad Ahmad Bhat, Vandan Mujadia, Aniruddha Tammewar, Riyaz Ahmad Bhat, and Manish Shrivastava. 2015. Iiit-h system submission for fire2014 shared task on transliterated search. In *Proceedings of the Forum for Information Retrieval Evaluation*, FIRE '14, pages 48–53, New York, NY, USA. ACM.

Özlem Çetinoğlu and Çağrı Çöltekin. 2019. Challenges of annotating a code-switching treebank. In *Proceedings of the 18th International Workshop on Treebanks and Linguistic Theories (TLT, SyntaxFest 2019)*, pages 82–90, Paris, France. Association for Computational Linguistics.

Vineet Chaitanya, Rajeev Sangal, and Akshar Bharati (Group), editors. 1996. *Natural language processing: a Paninian perspective*, eastern economy ed edition. Prentice-Hall of India, New Delhi.

François Chollet. 2015. keras. `https://github.com/fchollet/keras`.

Jacob Devlin, Ming-Wei Chang, Kenton Lee, and Kristina Toutanova. 2019. BERT: Pre-training of deep bidirectional transformers for language understanding. In *Proceedings of the 2019 Conference of the North American Chapter of the Association for Computational Linguistics: Human Language Technologies, Volume 1 (Long and Short Papers)*, pages 4171–4186, Minneapolis, Minnesota. Association for Computational Linguistics.

Mitesh M. Khapra, Ananthakrishnan Ramanathan, Anoop Kunchukuttan, Karthik Visweswariah, and Pushpak Bhattacharyya. 2014. When transliteration met crowdsourcing : An empirical study of transliteration via crowdsourcing using efficient, non-redundant and fair quality control. In *Proceedings of the Ninth International Conference on Language Resources and Evaluation (LREC'14)*, Reykjavik, Iceland. European Language Resources Association (ELRA).

Philipp Koehn, Hieu Hoang, Alexandra Birch, Chris Callison-Burch, Marcello Federico, Nicola Bertoldi, Brooke Cowan, Wade Shen, Christine Moran, Richard Zens, Chris Dyer, Ondrej Bojar, Alexandra Constantin, and Evan Herbst. 2007. Moses: Open source toolkit for statistical machine translation. In *ACL*. The Association for Computational Linguistics.

Anoop Kunchukuttan, Ratish Puduppully, and Pushpak Bhattacharyya. 2015. Brahmi-Net: A transliteration and script conversion system for languages of the Indian subcontinent. In *NAACL: System Demonstrations*.

Piyush Makhija, Ankit Kumar, and Anuj Gupta. 2020. hinglishNorm - a corpus of Hindi-English code mixed sentences for text normalization. In *Proceedings of the 28th International Conference on Computational Linguistics: Industry Track*, pages 136–145, Online. International Committee on Computational Linguistics.

Soumil Mandal and Karthick Nanmaran. 2018. Normalization of transliterated words in code-mixed data using Seq2Seq model & Levenshtein distance. In *Proceedings of the 2018 EMNLP Workshop W-NUT: The 4th Workshop on Noisy User-generated Text*, pages 49–53, Brussels, Belgium. Association for Computational Linguistics.

David R. Mortensen, Siddharth Dalmia, and Patrick Littell. 2018. Epitran: Precision G2P for many languages. In *Proceedings of the Eleventh International Conference on Language Resources and Evaluation (LREC 2018)*, Miyazaki, Japan. European Language Resources Association (ELRA).

Sonja Nießen, Franz Josef Och, Gregor Leusch, and Hermann Ney. 2000. An evaluation tool for machine translation: Fast evaluation for MT research. In *Proceedings of the Second International Conference on Language Resources and Evaluation (LREC'00)*, Athens, Greece. European Language Resources Association (ELRA).

Kishore Papineni, Salim Roukos, Todd Ward, and Wei-Jing Zhu. 2002. Bleu: a method for automatic evaluation of machine translation. In *Proceedings of the 40th Annual Meeting of the Association for Computational Linguistics*, pages 311–318, Philadelphia, Pennsylvania, USA. Association for Computational Linguistics.

Matthew Peters, Mark Neumann, Mohit Iyyer, Matt Gardner, Christopher Clark, Kenton Lee, and Luke Zettlemoyer. 2018. Deep contextualized word representations. In *Proceedings of the 2018 Conference of the North American Chapter of the Association for Computational Linguistics: Human Language Technologies, Volume 1 (Long Papers)*, pages 2227–2237, New Orleans, Louisiana. Association for Computational Linguistics.

Telmo Pires, Eva Schlinger, and Dan Garrette. 2019. How multilingual is multilingual BERT? In *Proceedings of the 57th Annual Meeting of the Association for Computational Linguistics*, pages 4996–5001, Florence, Italy. Association for Computational Linguistics.

Kushagra Singh, Indira Sen, and Ponnurangam Kumaraguru. 2018a. Language identification and named entity recognition in Hinglish code mixed tweets. In *Proceedings of ACL 2018, Student Research Workshop*, pages 52–58, Melbourne, Australia. Association for Computational Linguistics.

Kushagra Singh, Indira Sen, and Ponnurangam Kumaraguru. 2018b. A Twitter corpus for Hindi-English code mixed POS tagging. In *Proceedings of the Sixth International Workshop on Natural Language Processing for Social Media*, pages 12–17, Melbourne, Australia. Association for Computational Linguistics.

Rajat Singh, Nurendra Choudhary, and Manish Shrivastava. 2018c. Automatic normalization of word variations in code-mixed social media text.

Ilya Sutskever, Oriol Vinyals, and Quoc V Le. 2014. Sequence to sequence learning with neural networks. In *Advances in Neural Information Processing Systems*, volume 27. Curran Associates, Inc.

Abusive content detection in transliterated Bengali-English social media corpus

Salim Sazzed
Old Dominion University
Norfolk, VA, USA
ssazz001@odu.edu

Abstract

Abusive text detection in low-resource languages such as Bengali is a challenging task due to the inadequacy of resources and tools. The ubiquity of transliterated Bengali comments in social media makes the task even more involved as monolingual approaches cannot capture them. Unfortunately, no transliterated Bengali corpus is publicly available yet for abusive content analysis. Therefore, in this paper, we introduce an annotated corpus of 3000 transliterated Bengali comments categorized into two classes, *abusive* and *non-abusive*, 1500 comments for each. For baseline evaluations, we employ several supervised machine learning (ML) and deep learning-based classifiers. We find support vector machine (SVM) classifier shows the highest efficacy for identifying abusive content. We make the annotated corpus publicly available for the researchers to aid abusive content detection in Bengali social media data.

1 Introduction

With the popularity of social media, nowadays, user-generated contents are available in many languages. In various social media platforms, such as review forums and social networking sites, users express their feelings, opinions, emotion, etc. Due to the open nature of social media, the presence of abusive, offensive, and hateful comments is common there (Schmidt and Wiegand, 2017; Wang et al., 2014).

Abusive language refers to the usage of demeaning, insulting, vulgar, or profane expression to attack individuals or groups (Nobata et al., 2016); However, there exist inconsistencies in the definitions of abusive language in various literature (Waseem et al., 2017). For example, Nobata et al. (2016) considered hate speech as a kind of abusive language, while Founta et al. (2018) distinguished it from abusive speech. As the presence of abusive and hatred content inflicts a negative impact on society and individuals (Nobata et al., 2016; Duggan, 2017; Park et al., 2018), it is important to identify them. While plenty of resources are available for abusive language detection in English (Poletto et al., 2020), limited research has been performed on abusive content analysis in low resource Bengali language.

Code-Mixing (CM) is a natural phenomenon of embedding linguistic units such as phrases, words, or morphemes of one language into an utterance of another (Myers-Scotton, 1993; Muysken et al., 2000). Transliteration can be considered as a special form of code-mixing where the phonetic transformations of the words from a source language to a target language is performed. The presence of code-mixing and transliterated Bengali (i.e., Bengali text using the Latin alphabet) is a common phenomenon in Bengali, as shown by the previous studies (Barman et al., 2014; Chanda et al., 2016).

The existing research on abusive content or hate speech detection in Bengali mainly investigated text written in Bengali (Kumar et al., 2021; Emon et al., 2019; Eshan and Hasan, 2017; Ishmam and Sharmin, 2019; Karim et al., 2020; Romim et al., 2020). Although a few works addressed the phenomenon of code-switching in word-level or sentence level (i.e., presence of both English and Bengali words written using the alphabet of the corresponding language), most of them did not consider transliterated Bengali. Only Jahan et al. (2019) utilized a small number of transliterated Bengali comments (around 200 abusive comments) in their study. English is the second language in Bangladesh, the country with the highest number of Bengali native speakers; therefore, transliterated Bengali is ubiquitous in Bengali social media content. Hence, to detect abusive content in Bengali social media, it is essential to consider the transliterated Bengali text. For example, "Dor besorom mor tui" is an abusive comment which is written in transliterated Bengali;

Proceedings of the Fifth Workshop on Computational Approaches to Linguistic Code-Switching, pages 125–130
June 11, 2021. ©2021 Association for Computational Linguistics
https://doi.org/10.26615/978-954-452-056-4_016

the corresponding English translation is, " You are shameless, you die". The monolingual approaches can not identify it as an abusive comment as the transliterated words neither exist in the Bengali or English dictionary nor available in the monolingual training data.

Supervised ML classifiers are more effective for abusive content detection than the word-list based approaches, as shown in previous studies (Nobata et al., 2016; Park and Fung, 2017). However, ML classifiers require annotated training data, which are missing for transliterated Bengali text. Therefore, in this work, we develop an annotated corpus for transliterated Bengali for abusive content detection and make them publicly available [1].

We manually annotate around 3000 transliterated Bengali comments collected from YouTube into abusive and non-abusive categories, 1500 for each category. To the best of our knowledge, this is the largest annotated transliterated Bengali corpus for abusive content analysis. We then employ popular ML classifiers, logistic regression (LR), support vector machine (SVM), random forest (RF), and deep learning-based bidirectional long short-term memory (BiLSTM) architecture for baseline evaluations.

1.1 Contributions

The major contributions of this work can be summarized as follows:

- We introduce a large transliterated Bengali corpus consisting of 3000 comments collected from YouTube.
- We manually annotate the transliterated comments into abusive and non-abusive categories.
- We provide the comparative performances of various supervised ML and deep learning-based classifiers for recognizing abusive content in the transliterated Bengali corpus.

2 Related Work

Researchers explored code-mixed and transliterated content for tasks like linguistic analysis, Part-of-Speech (POS) tagging, and sentiment analysis in various South Asian languages, such as Hindi and Bengali (Choudhury et al., 2010; Jamatia et al., 2015; Patwa et al., 2020). Mathur et al. (2018) introduced a Twitter dataset for the classification of offensive tweets written in the Hindi-English code-switched language. However, such a dataset for abusive content analysis in transliterated Bengali is not available yet.

2.1 Abusive Content Analysis in Bengali Text

Emon et al. (2019) applied linear support vector classifier (LinearSVC), logistic regression (LR), multinomial naïve bayes (MNB), random forest (RF), artificial neural network (ANN), and recurrent neural network (RNN) with a long short term memory (LSTM) to detect multi-type abusive Bengali text. They also introduced a stemming rule to improve the classifier performance. Eshan and Hasan (2017) investigated the performance of RF, MNB, SVM classifiers for abusive language detection using unigram, bigrams, and trigram based feature vectors. They found that the SVM classifier with linear kernel and tri-gram features showed the highest accuracy.

Ishmam and Sharmin (2019) employed traditional and deep learning-based ML algorithms for classifying different types of offensive comments collected from Facebook pages. They collected and annotated around 5000 Bengali comments and categorized them into six classes. They obtained the highest accuracy utilizing GRU based model, which is around 70.10%. Hussain et al. (2018) collected 300 comments from Facebook and an online newspaper for abusive content detection. They proposed a weighted-rule based method that utilized labeled data. Awal et al. (2018) employed Naïve Bayes (NB) classifier to detect the abusive content in Bengali; They collected text from YouTube and provided the performance of NB using 10-fold cross-validation. Chakraborty and Seddiqui (2019) employed MNB, SVM, Convolutional Neural Network (CNN) with LSTM classifiers. They leveraged both emoticons and Bengali characters as input. They found SVM with linear kernel performed best with 78% accuracy.

2.2 Abusive Content in Transliterated Bengali

In Jahan et al. (2019), the authors utilized Bengali-English code-mixed text and transliterated Bengali text in addition to the Bengali only text. They collected comments from several public Facebook pages. As input features, they used unigrams, bigrams, the number of likes, emojis along with their categories, sentiment

[1] https://github.com/sazzadcsedu/AbusiveCorpus.git

scores, offensive and threatening words used in the comments. They employed three Machine Learning classifiers, SVM, RF, and Adaboost for abusive speech detection.

As we mentioned earlier, most of the existing works considered only the Bengali text. Although few of them utilized code-switching text, transliterated Bengali is hardly explored. To the best of our knowledge, this is the first work that introduces a large annotated corpus of transliterated Bengali for abusive language detection and provides comparative performances of ML classifiers.

3 Corpus Creation

The developed corpus contains user-generated transliterated Bengali text regarding several Bengali dramas and celebrities (i.e., opinion data).

3.1 Data Collection

Using a web scraping tool, we first download the raw JSON data from YouTube that contains information such as user name, id, timestamp, comments, and like/dislike, etc. Utilizing a parsing script, we extract the viewer's comments from the JSON data.

3.2 Data Filtering

The comments are written in Bengali, English, transliterated Bengali, or using code-switching words. Since our goal is to create a corpus for transliterated Bengali (i.e., Bengali words in Latin alphabet), we exclude comments written using the Bengali alphabet (i.e., Bengali comments). We utilize a language detection tool[2] to distinguish comments written using the Latin alphabet and Bengali alphabet. However, the tool can not differentiate between English and transliterated Bengali words as both use the Latin alphabet. Since social media contains lots of non-dictionary and misspelled English words (especially when written by non-native speakers), checking the English dictionary is not a feasible option to distinguish English and Transliterated Bengali words. Therefore, we manually inspect all the comments to include them in the corpus. We discard comments which are written using only English words. Comments with both transliterated Bengali and English words are included in the corpus if they contain at least two transliterated Bengali words. Note that, unlike Bengali or English words, there is not fixed spelling for transliterated Bengali words; thus, the same transliterated word with different spellings can be present in the corpus.

[2]https://github.com/Mimino666/langdetect

3.3 Data Annotation

3.3.1 Annotation Guideline

For assigning the transliterated Bengali comments into abusive or non-abusive categories, we follow a similar guideline of Nobata et al. (2016). They labeled a piece of text as abusive if it contains either hate speech or derogatory language or profanity.

Based on that, we assign the class of the comments into two categories-

- *Abusive*: This class includes hate speech which attacks or demeans a group based on race, ethnic origin, religion, disability, gender, age, disability, etc. Besides, it consists of derogatory or demeaning remarks which attack an individual or a group and profanity towards individuals using sexually offensive and pornographic comments.

- *Non-abusive*: comments which do not fall into the abusive category. These comments could convey a positive, (non-abusive) negative or neutral opinion or could be objective in nature.

3.3.2 Inter-annotator Agreement

Two native Bengali speakers assign the class of the transliterated comments into two categories, *abusive* and *non-abusive*. Among the 3764 transliterated comments, both annotators assign 3000 comments into the same class; 323 comments are identified as abusive by the first annotator only, while 141 comments are rated abusive by the second annotator only. We observe a Cohen's kappa score of 0.733 between two annotators, which refers to substantial agreement.

3.4 Corpus Statistics

The final corpus includes the 3000 comments which are assigned to the same class by both annotators, 1500 from each category. To avoid ambiguity, we exclude the comments in which annotators disagree on class assignment (Awal et al., 2020; Waseem, 2016).

Each comment contains one or multiple sentences and 1-300 words. We purposely make the

Transliterated Bengali Comment	English Translation	Class
1. amar mathay dhorena somoy tv kivabe a khankire office aneche	I don't understand why shomoy TV brought this slut	Abusive
2. Really onk valolaglo vaia Apnr question gulo khubbi mojar silo	Really liked it a lot bro, your questions were very funny	Non-abusive
3. Magi tore to amio chudmo na	Whore not even I will fuck you	Abusive
4. Joy, tumar show r dekbona	Joy, I won't watch your show again	Non-abusive
5. Sobay to tor Moto khanki magi na tor family o khanki.	Not everyone is slut like you. Your family is slut too.	Abusive
6. Bro please tader k interview te ane highlights na kora tai valo	Bro Please don't highlight them in your interview	Non-abusive

Figure 1: Examples of annotated abusive and non-abusive reviews

corpus class-balanced to avoid introducing any bias in the classifier. Figure 1 shows some examples of original transliterated Bengali comments, corresponding English machine translations, and annotations.

3.4.1 Word Frequency Distribution

We manually investigate the presence of English and transliterated Bengali words in the comments by randomly selecting 100 abusive and 100 non-abusive comments. After tokenizing the 100 abusive comments, we find 1720 words. A manual inspection on them identifies 412 English words and 1308 Transliterated Bengali words, which indicates that 76% of the words are transliterated Bengali words. Among the 1088 words in the 100 non-abusive comments, we notice 858 transliterated Bengali and 230 English words, which reveals that nearly 80% of words are transliterated Bengali. As we discard the words written using the Bengali alphabet in the data filtering step, no Bengali words are present in the final corpus.

4 Baseline Classifiers

4.1 Traditional ML Classifiers

Three popular supervised ML classifiers, LR, RF, and SVM are employed to identify abusive comments. We extract unigrams and bigrams from the text and calculate the term frequency-inverse document frequency (TF-IDF) scores for them, which are used as an input for the ML classifiers. TF-IDF is a numerical statistic that aims to reflect the importance of a word to a document in a corpus. We utilize the LR, RF, and SVM implementation of scikit-learn (Pedregosa et al., 2011) library. The default parameter settings of ML classifiers are used.

4.2 Deep Learning Classifier

Furthermore, we apply the deep learning-based BiLSTM architecture for identifying abusive content. For BiLSTM, we use word embedding of 100-dimensional vectors trained on the transliterated corpus. A dropout rate of 0.25 is applied in the dropout layers; Rectified Linear Unit (ReLU) activation is used in the intermediate layers. In the final layer, softmax activation is employed. As an optimization function, Adam optimizer (Kingma and Ba, 2014), and as a loss function, binary-cross entropy is utilized. We set the batch size to 64, use a learning rate of 0.001, and train the model for 6 epochs. We use the Keras (Chollet et al., 2015) library for implementing BiLSTM model.

5 Results and Discussion

We report the precision (P_{abus}), recall (R_{abus}) and F1 scores ($F1_{abus}$) of various classifiers for identifying abusive comments. The TP, FP, and FN values of the abusive class are defined as follows-

TP = abusive review classified as abusive
FP = non-abusive review classified as abusive
FN = abusive review classified as non-abusive

$$R_{abus} = \frac{TP}{TP+FN}, P_{abus} = \frac{TP}{TP+FP}$$

$$F1_{abus} = \frac{2*P_{abus}*R_{abus}}{P_{abus}+R_{abus}}$$

We perform 10-fold cross-validation on the transliterated corpus. We run each classifier 10 times and provide the range of R_{abus}, P_{abus} and $F1_{abus}$ scores.

Table 1 shows the performance of various ML classifiers for abusive language detection in the translated Bengali corpus. We observe that among the three traditional ML classifiers, LR and SVM

Table 1: Performance of various classifiers for abusive language detection in the transliterated corpus

Classifier	R_{abus}	P_{abus}	$F1_{abus}$
SVM	0.790 ±0.008	0.865 ±0.015	0.827 ±0.010
LR	0.779 ±0.006	0.876 ±0.004	0.823 ±0.006
BiLSTM	0.781 ±0.031	0.800 ±0.036	0.790 ±0.031
RF	0.781 ±0.013	0.762 ±0.028	0.770 ±0.020

show similar R_{abus} and P_{abus} scores. RF classifier provides a similar R_{abus} score of LR and SVM; however, it attains a lower P_{abus} score. We find both LR and SVM yield lower R_{abus} scores than the P_{abus} scores. BiLSTM, the deep learning-based architecture, obtains a relatively lower $F1_{abus}$ score compared to LR and SVM, which could be attributed to the small size (i.e., 3000 comments) of the corpus.

6 Conclusion and Future Work

Identifying abusive content in social media is of paramount importance due to its detrimental impact. Not addressing this problem can lead to the increasing growth of harassment and cyberbullying in social media. While there have been few works for abusive speech detection in Bengali social media content, they mostly ignored the presence of transliterated Bengali. In this paper, we present the most comprehensive study of abusive content detection in transliterated Bengali text by providing an annotated corpus and baseline evaluations. Our future works will focus on expanding the size of the transliterated corpus, providing more rigorous analysis, and introducing a customized deep learning model to improve the performance of abusive content detection in transliterated Bengali text.

References

Md Abdul Awal, Md Shamimur Rahman, and Jakaria Rabbi. 2018. Detecting abusive comments in discussion threads using naïve bayes. In *2018 International Conference on Innovations in Science, Engineering and Technology (ICISET)*, pages 163–167. IEEE.

Md Rabiul Awal, Rui Cao, Roy Ka-Wei Lee, and Sandra Mitrović. 2020. On analyzing annotation consistency in online abusive behavior datasets. *arXiv preprint arXiv:2006.13507*.

Utsab Barman, Amitava Das, Joachim Wagner, and Jennifer Foster. 2014. Code mixing: A challenge for language identification in the language of social media. In *Proceedings of the first workshop on computational approaches to code switching*, pages 13–23.

Puja Chakraborty and Md Hanif Seddiqui. 2019. Threat and abusive language detection on social media in bengali language. In *2019 1st International Conference on Advances in Science, Engineering and Robotics Technology (ICASERT)*, pages 1–6. IEEE.

Arunavha Chanda, Dipankar Das, and Chandan Mazumdar. 2016. Unraveling the english-bengali code-mixing phenomenon. In *Proceedings of the Second Workshop on Computational Approaches to Code Switching*, pages 80–89.

François Chollet et al. 2015. Keras. `https://keras.io`.

Monojit Choudhury, Kalika Bali, Tirthankar Dasgupta, and Anupam Basu. 2010. Resource creation for training and testing of transliteration systems for indian languages. LREC.

Maeve Duggan. 2017. Online harassment 2017.

Estiak Ahmed Emon, Shihab Rahman, Joti Banarjee, Amit Kumar Das, and Tanni Mittra. 2019. A deep learning approach to detect abusive bengali text. In *2019 7th International Conference on Smart Computing & Communications (ICSCC)*, pages 1–5. IEEE.

Shahnoor C Eshan and Mohammad S Hasan. 2017. An application of machine learning to detect abusive bengali text. In *2017 20th International Conference of Computer and Information Technology (ICCIT)*, pages 1–6. IEEE.

Antigoni Founta, Constantinos Djouvas, Despoina Chatzakou, Ilias Leontiadis, Jeremy Blackburn, Gianluca Stringhini, Athena Vakali, Michael Sirivianos, and Nicolas Kourtellis. 2018. Large scale crowdsourcing and characterization of twitter abusive behavior. In *Proceedings of the International AAAI Conference on Web and Social Media*, volume 12.

Md Gulzar Hussain, Tamim Al Mahmud, and Waheda Akthar. 2018. An approach to detect abusive bangla text. In *2018 International Conference on Innovation in Engineering and Technology (ICIET)*, pages 1–5. IEEE.

Alvi Md Ishmam and Sadia Sharmin. 2019. Hateful speech detection in public facebook pages for the bengali language. In *2019 18th IEEE International Conference On Machine Learning And Applications (ICMLA)*, pages 555–560. IEEE.

Maliha Jahan, Istiak Ahamed, Md Rayanuzzaman Bishwas, and Swakkhar Shatabda. 2019. Abusive comments detection in bangla-english code-mixed and transliterated text. In *2019 2nd International Conference on Innovation in Engineering and Technology (ICIET)*, pages 1–6. IEEE.

Anupam Jamatia, Björn Gambäck, and Amitava Das. 2015. Part-of-speech tagging for code-mixed english-hindi twitter and facebook chat messages. Association for Computational Linguistics.

Md Rezaul Karim, Bharathi Raja Chakravarthi, John P McCrae, and Michael Cochez. 2020. Classification benchmarks for under-resourced bengali language based on multichannel convolutional-lstm network. In *2020 IEEE 7th International Conference on Data Science and Advanced Analytics (DSAA)*, pages 390–399. IEEE.

Diederik P Kingma and Jimmy Ba. 2014. Adam: A method for stochastic optimization. *arXiv preprint arXiv:1412.6980*.

Ritesh Kumar, Bornini Lahiri, and Atul Kr Ojha. 2021. Aggressive and offensive language identification in hindi, bangla, and english: A comparative study. *SN Computer Science*, 2(1):1–20.

Puneet Mathur, Rajiv Shah, Ramit Sawhney, and Debanjan Mahata. 2018. Detecting offensive tweets in hindi-english code-switched language. In *Proceedings of the Sixth International Workshop on Natural Language Processing for Social Media*, pages 18–26.

Pieter Muysken, Pieter Cornelis Muysken, et al. 2000. *Bilingual speech: A typology of code-mixing*. Cambridge University Press.

Carol Myers-Scotton. 1993. Common and uncommon ground: Social and structural factors in codeswitching. *Language in society*, pages 475–503.

Chikashi Nobata, Joel Tetreault, Achint Thomas, Yashar Mehdad, and Yi Chang. 2016. Abusive language detection in online user content. In *Proceedings of the 25th international conference on world wide web*, pages 145–153.

Ji Ho Park and Pascale Fung. 2017. One-step and two-step classification for abusive language detection on twitter. *arXiv preprint arXiv:1706.01206*.

Ji Ho Park, Jamin Shin, and Pascale Fung. 2018. Reducing gender bias in abusive language detection. *arXiv preprint arXiv:1808.07231*.

Parth Patwa, Gustavo Aguilar, Sudipta Kar, Suraj Pandey, Srinivas PYKL, Björn Gambäck, Tanmoy Chakraborty, Thamar Solorio, and Amitava Das. 2020. Semeval-2020 task 9: Overview of sentiment analysis of code-mixed tweets. *arXiv e-prints*, pages arXiv–2008.

F. Pedregosa, G. Varoquaux, A. Gramfort, V. Michel, B. Thirion, O. Grisel, M. Blondel, P. Prettenhofer, R. Weiss, V. Dubourg, J. Vanderplas, A. Passos, D. Cournapeau, M. Brucher, M. Perrot, and E. Duchesnay. 2011. Scikit-learn: Machine learning in Python. *Journal of Machine Learning Research*, 12:2825–2830.

Fabio Poletto, Valerio Basile, Manuela Sanguinetti, Cristina Bosco, and Viviana Patti. 2020. Resources and benchmark corpora for hate speech detection: a systematic review. *Language Resources and Evaluation*, pages 1–47.

Nauros Romim, Mosahed Ahmed, Hriteshwar Talukder, and Md Saiful Islam. 2020. Hate speech detection in the bengali language: A dataset and its baseline evaluation. *arXiv preprint arXiv:2012.09686*.

Anna Schmidt and Michael Wiegand. 2017. A survey on hate speech detection using natural language processing. In *Proceedings of the fifth international workshop on natural language processing for social media*, pages 1–10.

Wenbo Wang, Lu Chen, Krishnaprasad Thirunarayan, and Amit P Sheth. 2014. Cursing in english on twitter. In *Proceedings of the 17th ACM conference on Computer supported cooperative work & social computing*, pages 415–425.

Zeerak Waseem. 2016. Are you a racist or am i seeing things? annotator influence on hate speech detection on twitter. In *Proceedings of the first workshop on NLP and computational social science*, pages 138–142.

Zeerak Waseem, Thomas Davidson, Dana Warmsley, and Ingmar Weber. 2017. Understanding abuse: A typology of abusive language detection subtasks. *arXiv preprint arXiv:1705.09899*.

Developing ASR for Indonesian-English Bilingual Language Teaching

Zara Maxwell-Smith[1,3] **Ben Foley**[2,3]
1. The Australian National University, Canberra, ACT, Australia
2. The University of Queensland, Brisbane, QLD, Australia
3. ARC Centre of Excellence for the Dynamics of Language (CoEDL), Australia
Zara.Maxwell-Smith@anu.edu.au, B.Foley@uq.edu.au

Usage-based analyses of teacher corpora and *code-switching* (Boztepe, 2003) are an important next stage in understanding language acquisition. Multilingual corpora are difficult to compile and a classroom setting adds pedagogy to the mix of factors which make this data so rich and problematic to classify. Using quantitative methods to understand language learning and teaching is difficult work as the 'transcription bottleneck' constrains the size of datasets. We found that using an automatic speech recognition (ASR) toolkit with a small set of training data is likely to speed data collection in this context (Maxwelll-Smith et al., 2020).

For this study we used approximately 150 minutes of data from a project recording a single teacher's speech in a second-year, tertiary Indonesian language program. Our methodological considerations addressed the following: which ASR tool to use, how to prepare training data for this tool, and how to best manage the bias of the training data inherent in all transcription processes.

We chose the Elpis ASR system, which combines user-friendly data processing scripts with a Kaldi HMM/GMM (Hidden Markov Model/Gaussian Mixture Model) recipe. Elpis generates transcripts as time-aligned ELAN files, which was a good fit with the broader project investigating Indonesian language teaching.

A team of transcribers established guidelines which reflexively responded to a range of methodological considerations. Indonesian diglossic variants exist in a highly diverse linguistic ecosystem (Djenar and Ewing, 2015; Sneddon, 2003; Goebel, 2010). This was highlighted by transcriber subjectivity in the teaching context. For example, the task of analyzing and choosing orthography to transcribe teacher speech into over-simplified, binary L1 versus L2 categories (1st language: English, 2nd language: Indonesian) is influenced by transcriber expectations of language norms in 'high' vs. 'low' varieties of Indonesian. Further, the goal of modifying sociolinguistic norms which brings people to language classrooms precipitated a level of variance and unpredictability unusual in other speech contexts as teachers respond to student acquisition processes. We also provided examples of the development of a *Community of Practice* (Wenger, 1998) as another layer of complexity in the group classroom environment.

The dataset was transcribed using several "tiers" to create parallel structures for storing data. While predominately working from a code-switching paradigm, the data structure allowed us to train multiple models for comparative evaluation. We trained three models, two of which included all training data and multi-lingual pronunciation lexicons, resonating with work on *translanguaging* in educational settings (Garcia and Wei, 2014). The third model was trained with Indonesian data only. Our preliminary result of 64% word error rate (WER) is high in comparison to mono-lingual ASR systems (Maxwelll-Smith et al., 2020). However, WERs from code-switch bilingual data (Biswas et al., 2019) were more similar to our WER, especially given our small amount of training data.

By analysing the text spans in the machine transcription, we found a high incidence of resyllabification (word splitting), particularly with omission of initial or middle consonants. The analysis identified which model would include less disruptive errors than the others, and which would be more responsive to the addition of further training data.

The application of ASR tools is limited in this setting given the small set of training data, however using these tools has potential to expedite the transcription of teacher corpora. These tools could change workflow and decrease cognitive load for human transcribers by generating a draft transcript for revision. We highlight some of the benefits and risks of using these emerging technologies to analyze the complex work of language teachers, and in education more generally.

Proceedings of the Fifth Workshop on Computational Approaches to Linguistic Code-Switching, pages 131–132
June 11, 2021. ©2021 Association for Computational Linguistics
https://doi.org/10.26615/978-954-452-056-4_017

Acknowledgements

We acknowledge the contributions of Associate Professor Hanna Suominen (The Australian National University, Canberra, ACT, Australia, Data61/Commonwealth Scientific and Industrial Research Organisation, Canberra, ACT, Australia and University of Turku, Turku, Finland) and Simón González Ochoa (The Australian National University, Canberra, ACT, Australia).

References

Astik Biswas, Emre Yilmaz, Febe de Wet, Ewald van der Westhuizen, and Thomas Niesler. 2019. Semi-supervised acoustic model training for five-lingual code-switched asr. In *Interspeech 2019*.

Erman Boztepe. 2003. Issues in code-switching: Competing theories and models. *Issues in CS: Competing Theories and Models*, 3(2).

Dwi Noverini Djenar and Michael C. Ewing. 2015. Language varieties and youthful involvement in Indonesian fiction. *Language and Literature*, 24(2):108–128.

Ofelia Garcia and Li Wei. 2014. *Translanguaging: Language, Bilingualism and Education*. Palgrave Macmillan, New York.

Zane Goebel. 2010. Identity and social conduct in a transient multilingual setting. *Language in Society*, 39(02):203–240.

Max Planck Institute for Psycholinguistics - The Language Archive: Nijmegen. 2018. ELAN (Version 5.2) [Computer Software]. *Retrieved from https://archive.mpi.nl/tla/elan*.

Zara Maxwelll-Smith, Simón González Ochoa, Ben Foley, and Hanna Suominen. 2020. Applications of natural language processing in bilingual language teaching: An Indonesian-English case study. In *Proceedings of the Fifteenth Workshop on Innovative Use of NLP for Building Educational Applications*, pages 124–134, Seattle, WA, USA â†' Online. Association for Computational Linguistics.

James N. Sneddon. 2003. Diglossia in Indonesian. *Bijdragen tot de taal-, land- en volkenkunde / Journal of the Humanities and Social Sciences of Southeast Asia*, 159(4):519–549.

Etienne Wenger. 1998. *Communities of Practice: Learning, Meaning, and Identity*. Cambridge University Press, Cambridge.

Transliteration for Low-Resource Code-Switching Texts: Building an Automatic Cyrillic-to-Latin Converter for Tatar

Chihiro Taguchi*, **Yusuke Sakai***, and **Taro Watanabe**
{taguchi.chihiro.td0, sakai.yusuke.sr9, taro}@is.naist.jp
Nara Institute of Science and Technology

Abstract

We introduce a Cyrillic-to-Latin transliterator for the Tatar language based on subword-level language identification. The transliteration is a challenging task due to the following two reasons. First, because modern Tatar texts often contain intra-word code-switching to Russian, a different transliteration set of rules needs to be applied to each morpheme depending on the language, which necessitates morpheme-level language identification. Second, the fact that Tatar is a low-resource language, with most of the texts in Cyrillic, makes it difficult to prepare a sufficient dataset. Given this situation, we proposed a transliteration method based on subword-level language identification. We trained a language classifier with monolingual Tatar and Russian texts, and applied different transliteration rules in accord with the identified language. The results demonstrate that our proposed method outscores other Tatar transliteration tools, and imply that it correctly transcribes Russian loanwords to some extent.

1 Introduction

Modern Tatar has two orthographies: Cyrillic and Latin. The two alphabets are mostly mutually compatible when an input string consists of only Tatar-origin words. Effectively, however, modern Tatar has a massive amount of Russian loanwords, and, in colloquial texts, even a whole phrase may be switched to Russian. This linguistic phenomenon is known as code-switching or code-mixing.

A difficulty of transliteration from Cyrillic to Latin lies in the following two facts. First, a different set of transliteration rules has to be applied to Tatar and Russian words. This requires a language detection for each token, or worse, for each morpheme, which would additionally require morphological analysis. It is expected that a full implementation of such a system will produce heavy processes. Second, because modern Tatar frequently mixes Russian words, it is not easy to obtain a pure Tatar dataset for developing a language detector.

Existing methods are based on either Tatar monolingual rules or a huge bundle of ad-hoc rules aimed to cover Russian-origin words (Bradley, 2014; Korbanov, n.d.). The experimental results in Section 6 demonstrate that the former monolingual rule-based transliterators show low accuracy because Russian words are not supported. The latter extensively rule-based transliterator has better accuracy, but still misses a certain amount of words. This implies that a strictly rule-based method requires an ever-lasting process of adding rules ad hoc for exceptional words to further improve the accuracy. This is obviously unrealistic and inefficient.

In this study, in contrast, we pursue a simple yet high-accuracy automatic transliteration system from Cyrillic Tatar to Latin Tatar. We prepare two sets of simple rule-based monolingual transliteration rules for Tatar and Russian each. In addition, we train a classifier that automatically determines Tatar or Russian for each subword. Each token is then transliterated to Latin Tatar by applying the rules of the detected language to its subwords. The results demonstrate that our proposed method achieves higher accuracy than the previous tools. Also, our proposed method demonstrates higher accuracy than the transliterator with only Tatar-based rules, indicating that the method can correctly predict and transcribe Russian words to some extent.

2 Tatar: Linguistic Background

Tatar (ISO 639-1 Code: tt) is a Kipchak language of the Turkic language family mainly spoken in the Republic of Tatarstan, Russia. The number of the speakers is estimated to be around five million (Eberhard et al., 2021). The canonical word order is SOV, but allows for free word order with scrambling. Morphological inflections and declensions are derived by means of suffixation. The suffixation obeys the vowel harmony rule where backness

*Equal contribution

Proceedings of the Fifth Workshop on Computational Approaches to Linguistic Code-Switching, pages 133–140
June 11, 2021. ©2021 Association for Computational Linguistics
https://doi.org/10.26615/978-954-452-056-4_018

(or frontness) of vowels is kept consistent.

Through the long history of language contact with Russian, modern Tatar contains a large amount of Russian loanwords. Most of the speakers are bilingual along with Russian, and younger generations living in urbanized cities tend to have better competence in Russian than in Tatar. This bilingualism leads to frequent code-switching (CS) in text and speech, particularly of colloquial genre (Izmailova et al., 2018).

2.1 Tatar Orthographies

The mainstream orthography for modern Tatar is the Cyrillic alphabet, which comprises the Russian standard alphabet and six extended Cyrillic letters. Cyrillic Tatar is mostly used by Tatars living in Russian-speaking countries, while the Latin alphabet is used by Tatars living in other areas such as Turkey and Finland.

Until 1928, Tatar was exclusively written in the Arabic script. Along with the latinization project prevailing in the Soviet Union in 1920–30s, a Latin alphabet system *yañalif* was introduced to Tatar. In 1939, for political reasons, *yañalif* was superseded by the Cyrillic alphabet which has been officially used in Tatarstan as of now. After the demise of the Soviet Union, with the resurgence of the movement for restoring the Latin orthography, a new Latin-based orthography system was adopted by a republic law in 1999 (National Council of the Republic of Tatarstan, 1999). However, the law soon lost its validity in 2002 when a new paragraph stipulating that all the ethnic languages in Russia must be written in Cyrillic was added to the federal law (Yeltsin, 2020). The current Latin alphabet (2013Latin henceforth) based on the Common Turkic Alphabet was officially adopted by a republic law in 2013, and is commonly used in Tatar diaspora communities (National Council of the Republic of Tatarstan, 2013).

We define that the term "Latin alphabet" used in this paper refers to 2013Latin. A detailed rules for the conversion to 2013Latin is given in Timerkhanov and Safiullina (2019).

2.2 Code-switching in Tatar

An example of the former is displayed in (1) with transliteration in the Latin alphabet and the translation. Underlined класс (*klass* "class, grade") is a Russian word naturalized in Tatar, though it is pronounced with Russian phonology and therefore requires a different transliteration. In addition, a locative suffix -та (*-ta* "at, in") is attached in the example, as Russian loanwords may take Tatar suffixes, causing CS within a token (intra-word CS).

(1) Безнең класста кызлар сигезенчедән эчә башлаган иде.
translit.: Bezneñ klassta qızlar sigezençedän eçä başlağan ide.
"In our class, girls used to start drinking by the eighth grade."

3 Related Work

Code-Switching. Even though CS has attracted researchers in NLP, the lack of resource has been a major difficulty, because CS is an exclusively colloquial linguistic phenomenon and CS texts are seldom recorded. Jose et al. (2020) enumerates a list of available CS datasets at the time of the publication. In terms of both the availability of datasets and the popularity of research, CS language pairs in trend are Hindi–English (Srivastava et al., 2020, Singh and Lefever, 2020), Spanish–English (Alvarez-Mellado, 2020, Claeser et al., 2018), Arabic varieties and Modern Standard Arabic (Hamed et al., 2019).

As for the studies of intra-word CS in other languages, Mager et al. (2019) for German–Turkish and Spanish–Wixarika, Nguyen and Cornips (2016) for Dutch–Limburgish, and Yirmibeşoğlu and Eryiğit (2018) for Turkish–English have a similar approach to ours. The differences from ours are that Mager et al. (2019) employs segRNN (Lu et al., 2016) for segmentation and language identification, and that Nguyen and Cornips (2016) uses Morfessor (Creutz and Lagus, 2006) for morphological segmentation. However, our task that combines language detection of intra-word CS and transliteration has never been undertaken in any of these studies.

Tatar Transliteration. At the time of this writing, the following tools are available for Tatar Cyrillic-Latin conversion. The Tatar Transcription Tool (TTT henceforth) (Bradley, 2014) is a transliterator published online by Universität Wien as a part of the Mari Web Project. speak.tatar[1] is an anonymously developed transliteration service. FinTat[2] is a transliteration tool developed as a part of the Corpus of Written Tatar (Saykhunov et al., 2019). Aylandirow is a strictly rule-based transliteration tool

[1] https://speak.tatar/en/language/converter/tat/cyrillic/latin
[2] http://www.corpus.tatar/fintat

available online that extensively covers Russian-origin words as well as Tatar-origin (Korbanov, n.d.). The transliteration system employed in FinTat is based on the Latin alphabet used by Tatars in Finland, whose orthography is somewhat different from 2013Latin.

4 Method

We transliterate Cyrillic Tatar to Latin Tatar word by word, as each word does not affect other words in Tatar transliteration[3].

Taking into account the fact that Tatar has intra-word CS, we created a classifier that detects a language (Tatar or Russian) for each subword. To implement the language classifier, we prepared two monolingual corpora of Tatar and Russian. Given the lack of pure Tatar texts without CS in modern texts[4], we employed Tatar translation of Qur'an[5] (19,691 words with duplication) translated in 1912 that contains no Russian loanwords in order to avoid noise to train the classifier. Its Russian counterpart[6] (21,256 words with duplication) was translated by the Ministry of Awqaf, Egypt.

The training process is as follows. First, the words collected from the dataset were automatically divided into subwords by the Byte Pair Encoding algorithm (Sennrich et al., 2016). Banerjee and Bhattacharyya (2018) reports that, unlike Morfessor, BPE can flexibly solve the OOV problem because some subwords are character-level segments. In our case, due to the meagerness of the monolingual training data, we employed BPE to avoid the OOV problem. Then, assuming that longer subwords are less ambiguous with respect to labels to be assigned, we took the longest match to make it easier to distinguish between Russian and Tatar; for this reason, the subword merge operation was repeated until no further merge was possible. The obtained subwords are then represented in subword embeddings using fastText[7] (Bojanowski et al., 2017). The classification model is the supervised classifier provided by fastText, with the following hyperparameters that are known to perform high accuracy[8]: the number of dimensions is 16, the minimum and maximum character n-gram sizes are 2 and 4. Hierarchical softmax is used as the loss function. Together with this representation, the subword embeddings are annotated with a language label (Joulin et al., 2017).

It is worth noting that, unlike Mager et al. (2019), we do not employ deep learning approach. While the task in Mager et al. (2019) is multi-labeling, our language identification task is a binary classification with a low-resource training dataset; for this reason, deep learning is too superfluous and heavy for achieving our task.

To evaluate the performance of our model, we apply BPE also to the test data in the same manner, and predict a language label for each subword. Adjacent subwords are, when possible, combined to form a longer subword with a single language label for the sake of better accuracy; that is, for example, when two consecutive subwords are both labeled as `tt`, then they are combined into one subword labeled as `tt`. Finally, each subword is converted to the Latin alphabet with the transliteration rules of the predicted language, and combined into a word as an output.

5 Experimental Setup

For the evaluation of the performance, we prepared 700 sentences (shuffled; 8,466 words with duplication, 5,261 without duplication) from the Corpus of Written Tatar (Saykhunov et al., 2019) and their Latin counterpart as the gold data that was manually transcribed by us and verified by a native speaker. Also, we annotated the Cyrillic text data so that CS Russian morphemes are tagged. According to this, the text data contains 1,009 words (with duplication) with a Russian morpheme, and 598 words (with duplication) with intra-word CS.

For evaluation metrics, we calculated BLEU and longest common sequence (LCS) F-measure for each letter in a word as well as word accuracy (ACC) and character error rate (CER). The calculation of LCS F-measure and ACC is based on Chen et al. (2018).

To compare the performances of Tatar monolingual transliteration and of Tatar–Russian bilingual transliteration (i.e., our proposed method; "tt-ru hybrid" henceforth), we also evaluated the data with solely Tatar monolingual transliteration rules

[3]The code is available here: https://github.com/naist-nlp/tatar_transliteration. A demonstration page is published on the website: https://yusuke1997.com/tatar.

[4]In the evaluation dataset we prepared for this study, 1,009 words out of 8,466 contained at least one Russian morpheme.

[5]https://cdn.jsdelivr.net/gh/fawazahmed0/quran-api@1/editions/tat-yakubibnnugman.json

[6]https://cdn.jsdelivr.net/gh/fawazahmed0/quran-api@1/editions/rus-ministryofawqaf.json

[7]https://github.com/facebookresearch/fastText

[8]The training setting was inspired by the blog post by fastText: https://fasttext.cc/blog/2017/10/02/blog-post.html

	BLEU	LCS F-score	CER	ACC	# correct sentence	# error word
speak.tatar	0.869	0.953	0.049	0.952	67	1,747
TTT	0.879	0.956	0.054	0.946	121	1,505
Aylandirow	0.971	**0.994**	0.009	0.991	362	526
tt-based	0.968	0.989	0.011	0.989	365	552
tt-ru hybrid	**0.981**	**0.994**	**0.007**	**0.993**	**437**	**332**

Table 1: The experimental results with 700 sentences (5,261 words without duplication). CER and ACC are complementary in probability (i.e., $ACC = 1 - CER$). Note that the transliteration result is uniquely determined as the proposed method is rule-based.

("tt-based" henceforth). For the comparison with the existing transliteration tools, we computed the scores of speak.tatar, TTT, and Aylandirow[9].

6 Results

As shown in Table 1, the experimental results demonstrate that our tt-ru hybrid marked the best score in all the metrics. CER is the lowest, meaning that the total number of mistakes at a character level is the fewest. The difference is evident between monolingual transliterators (in particular, speak.tatar and TTT) that do not support Russian loanwords and bilingual transliterators (Aylandirow and tt-ru hybrid). Between the two groups, there is more or less a difference by 0.1 points in their BLEU scores. Furthermore, our monolingual tt-based marked higher scores than the other two monolingual transliterators. A possible explanation to this gap will be given in the next section.

Compared to Aylandirow, an extensive rule-based transliterator, CER (i.e., ACC also) in tt-ru hybrid was slightly better by 0.002 points. In LCS F-Score, in contrast, Aylandirow has the same score as our tt-ru hybrid. This fact means that Aylandirow returned transliterations somewhat closer to the gold data than our tt-ru hybrid.

Note that the perfection is not necessarily the ultimate goal of this transliteration. As described in detail in Section 7, there may be several ways of spelling in actual language use, particularly of the spelling of proper nouns. This variance in spelling foreign words is common among languages.

7 Analysis

The results illustrated that the bilingual transliterators generally have higher accuracy than the monolingual transliterators. However, it needs to be examined that tt-based also gained higher scores than the other monolingual ones, even though it does not support Russian loanwords. This is due to the fact that their transliteration rule sometimes does not follow the rules of 2013Latin. For example, тәнкыйть "criticism" is transliterated as *tänqit'* (with a *hamza* at the end) by the TTT, where it should be transliterated as *tänqit* according to 2013Latin. In fact, due to the de-facto absence of any institution that regulates the Latin orthography, different varieties in spelling styles can be observed on the Internet. For this reason, the seemingly high scores in tt-based are merely a product of the orthographical consistency.

Keeping this in mind, the improvement in the scores between tt-based and tt-ru hybrid indicates that the bilingual transliteration method designed to be adaptive to Russian loanwords successfully predicted the language and transcribed them.

Table 3 illustrates the number of error words categorized with respect to the transliteration rules (tt-based and tt-ru hybrid). We can see from the table that, among the error words observed in tt-based ($V(T)$), 336 words were correctly transliterated by tt-ru hybrid.

Examples of successful transliteration in our tt-ru hybrid are закон and совет shown in the upper example of Table 2. The tt-based transliteration converted them as *zaqon* and *sowet*, while tt-ru hybrid correctly returned *zakon* and *sovet*. This shows that tt-ru hybrid successfully identified the language, since they are Russian loanwords.

However, tt-ru hybrid wrongly transliterated 116 words that were correct in tt-based; for example, in the lower example of Table 2, the underlined transliteration *soklanıp* in tt-ru hybrid is a transliteration error, where the correct word form is *soqlanıp*. Because the language classifier identified

[9]Although we mentioned FinTat in Section 2, we excluded it from the evaluation because it is based on a spelling system slightly different from 2013Latin.

Source	РФ Закон чыгаручылар советы президиумы утырышында катнашты.
tt-based	RF Zaqon çığaruçılar sowetı prezidiumı utırışında qatnaştı.
tt-ru hybrid	RF Zakon çığaruçılar sovetı prezidiumı utırışında qatnaştı.
Source	һәр юлчы туктап, аның хозурлыгына сокланып китә.
tt-based	Här yulçı tuqtap, anıñ xozurlığına soqlanıp kitä.
tt-ru hybrid	Här yulçı tuqtap, anıñ xozurlığına soklanıp kitä.

Table 2: Examples of successful and unsuccessful transliterations in tt-ru hybrid based on subword tokenization. The underlined words are error words (Russian loanwords). The upper sentence is an example where tt-ru hybrid can correctly transliterate the underlined words while tt-based cannot. The lower example is, on the other hand, tt-ru hybrid mistakenly transliterates the underlined word that is correctly transliterated by tt-based.

set (total 5,261 words)	# words
$V(T)$	552
$V(H)$	332
$V(T) \cap V(H)$	216
$V(T) \setminus V(H)$	336
$V(H) \setminus V(T)$	116

Table 3: Comparison of the number of error words (without duplication) between the monolingual tt-based transliteration and our proposed tt-ru hybrid transliteration. $V(T)$ is the set of error words observed in tt-based, $V(H)$ in tt-ru hybrid, $V(T) \cap V(H)$ in both tt-based and tt-ru hybrid, $V(T) \setminus V(H)$ is the set of error words observed only in tt-based, and $V(H) \setminus V(T)$ only in tt-ru hybrid.

	ru words		CS words	
	#	accuracy	#	accuracy
speak.tatar	**805**	**0.798**	455	0.752
TTT	258	0.256	175	0.283
Aylandirow	738	0.731	461	0.762
tt-based	471	0.467	294	0.486
tt-ru hybrid	788	0.781	**464**	**0.767**

Table 4: A comparison of performance in Russian CS words. The left column (ru words) demonstrates the number of correctly transcribed words that contain Russian and its accuracy that is given by dividing by the total Russian words (1,009 with duplication). The right column (CS words) contains the number of correct transcriptions out of 605 words (with duplication) and its accuracy with respect to intra-word CS words.

the first subword as Russian, the Russian transliteration rule was applied, whereas in fact it is not a Russian loanword.

As for the high LCS F-score in Aylandirow (0.994), it implies that Aylandirow is good at correctly transcribing frequent words including Russian loanwords. Because Aylandirow is strictly rule-based without automatic language detection, it can easily suffer from the rule coverage problem; for example, the word такси (*taksi*, a Russian loanword) was mistakenly transliterated as *taqsi*.

As the comparison of performance with respect to Russian CS words in Table 4 shows, tt-ru hybrid demonstrated higher accuracy in transliterating words with Russian morphemes[10]. In particular, the tt-ru hybrid's performance adaptive to Russian morphemes is clearly visible in the accuracies of transcribing words containing Russian, where tt-ru hybrid scored 78.1% and tt-based 46.7%.

Considering that Russian CS in Tatar may arbitrarily occur, our proposed method with automatic language detection is expected to show a stable performance to any Russian words; in contrast, rule-based systems such as Aylandirow are less flexible to unknown Russian words, which, in effect, exist infinitely in natural languages as hapax legomena.

8 Conclusion

In this paper, we proposed a new transliteration system that converts Cyrillic Tatar to Latin Tatar. Taking into account the facts that different transliteration rules are applied to Russian loanwords and that intra-word CS is frequently observed, our proposed method involved language identification for each subword. Even though Tatar resources available at hand for training were limited, the results were significantly better than existing transliteration tools. The simple architecture of language detection employed in this approach is language-agnostic does not need detailed analyses such as syntactic parsing and POS tagging, our method is applicable to other low-resource languages that have intra-word CS.

[10] In this respect, speak.tatar scores the best for Russian words. This is merely because its transliteration rules are designed to work well for Russian words, and, in contrast, its performance to Tatar words is poor as shown in Table 1.

References

Elena Alvarez-Mellado. 2020. An annotated corpus of emerging anglicisms in Spanish newspaper headlines. In *Proceedings of the The 4th Workshop on Computational Approaches to Code Switching*, pages 1–8, Marseille, France. European Language Resources Association.

Tamali Banerjee and Pushpak Bhattacharyya. 2018. Meaningless yet meaningful: Morphology grounded subword-level NMT. In *Proceedings of the Second Workshop on Subword/Character LEvel Models*, pages 55–60, New Orleans. Association for Computational Linguistics.

Piotr Bojanowski, Edouard Grave, Armand Joulin, and Tomas Mikolov. 2017. Enriching word vectors with subword information. *Transactions of the Association for Computational Linguistics*, 5:135–146.

Jeremy Bradley. 2014. Tatar transcription tool. Available at: https://www.univie.ac.at/maridict/site-2014 [retrieved 28 March 2021].

Nancy Chen, Rafael E. Banchs, Min Zhang, Xiangyu Duan, and Haizhou Li. 2018. Report of NEWS 2018 named entity transliteration shared task. In *Proceedings of the Seventh Named Entities Workshop*, pages 55–73, Melbourne, Australia. Association for Computational Linguistics.

Daniel Claeser, Samantha Kent, and Dennis Felske. 2018. Multilingual named entity recognition on Spanish-English code-switched tweets using support vector machines. In *Proceedings of the Third Workshop on Computational Approaches to Linguistic Code-Switching*, pages 132–137, Melbourne, Australia. Association for Computational Linguistics.

Mathias Creutz and Krista Lagus. 2006. Morfessor in the morpho challenge. In *PASCAL Challenge Workshop on Unsupervised segmentation of words into morphemes*.

David M. Eberhard, Gary F. Simons, and Charles D. Fennig, editors. 2021. *Ethnologue*, 24th edition. SIL International, Dallas, Texas. Available at: http://www.ethnologue.com [retrieved 12 March 2021].

Injy Hamed, Moritz Zhu, Mohamed Elmahdy, Slim Abdennadher, and Ngoc Thang Vu. 2019. Code-switching language modeling with bilingual word embeddings: A case study for egyptian arabic-english.

Guzel A. Izmailova, Irina V. Korovina, and Elzara V. Gafiyatova. 2018. A study on tatar–russian code switching (based on instagram posts). *The Journal of Social Sciences Research*, Special Issue. 1:187–191.

N. Jose, B. R. Chakravarthi, S. Suryawanshi, E. Sherly, and J. P. McCrae. 2020. A survey of current datasets for code-switching research. In *2020 6th International Conference on Advanced Computing and Communication Systems (ICACCS)*, pages 136–141.

Armand Joulin, Edouard Grave, Piotr Bojanowski, and Tomas Mikolov. 2017. Bag of tricks for efficient text classification. In *Proceedings of the 15th Conference of the European Chapter of the Association for Computational Linguistics: Volume 2, Short Papers*, pages 427–431, Valencia, Spain. Association for Computational Linguistics.

Dinar Korbanov. n.d. Aylandirow. Available at: http://aylandirow.tmf.org.ru [retrieved 29 March 2021].

Liang Lu, Lingpeng Kong, Chris Dyer, Noah A. Smith, and Steve Renals. 2016. Segmental recurrent neural networks for end-to-end speech recognition. In *Proceedings of Interspeech 2016*, Interspeech, pages 385–389. International Speech Communication Association.

Manuel Mager, Özlem Çetinoglu, and Katharina Kann. 2019. Subword-level language identification for intra-word code-switching. *CoRR*, abs/1904.01989.

National Council of the Republic of Tatarstan. 1999. О восстановлении татарского алфавита на основе латинской графики [on the restoration of the tatar alphabet based on the latin script]. Available at: http://docs.cntd.ru/document/917005056 [retrieved 28 March 2021].

National Council of the Republic of Tatarstan. 2013. Об использовании татарского языка как государственного языка Республики Татарстан [on the use of the tatar language as the national language of the republic of tatarstan]. Available at: http://docs.cntd.ru/document/463300868 [retrieved April 26, 2021].

Dong Nguyen and Leonie Cornips. 2016. Automatic detection of intra-word code-switching. In *Proceedings of the 14th SIGMORPHON Workshop on Computational Research in Phonetics, Phonology, and Morphology*, pages 82–86, Berlin, Germany. Association for Computational Linguistics.

Mansur R. Saykhunov, R. R. Khusainov, T. I. Ibragimov, J. Luutonen, I. F. Salimzyanov, G. Y. Shaydullina, and A. M. Khusainova. 2019. Corpus of written tatar. Available at: http://www.corpus.tatar [retrieved 28 March 2021].

Rico Sennrich, Barry Haddow, and Alexandra Birch. 2016. Neural machine translation of rare words with subword units. In *Proceedings of the 54th Annual Meeting of the Association for Computational Linguistics (Volume 1: Long Papers)*, pages 1715–1725, Berlin, Germany. Association for Computational Linguistics.

Pranaydeep Singh and Els Lefever. 2020. Sentiment analysis for Hinglish code-mixed tweets by means of cross-lingual word embeddings. In *Proceedings of the The 4th Workshop on Computational Approaches to Code Switching*, pages 45–51, Marseille, France. European Language Resources Association.

Abhishek Srivastava, Kalika Bali, and Monojit Choudhury. 2020. Understanding script-mixing: A case study of Hindi-English bilingual Twitter users. In *Proceedings of the The 4th Workshop on Computational Approaches to Code Switching*, pages 36–44, Marseille, France. European Language Resources Association.

Aynur Akhatovich Timerkhanov and Gulshat Rafailevna Safiullina. 2019. *Tatarça-inglizçä, inglizçä-tatarça süzlek: Tatar-English, English-Tatar dictionary*. G. Ibragimov Institute of Language, Literature and Art, Kazan.

Boris Yeltsin. 2020. О языках народов Российской Федерации [on the languages of nations in the russian federation]. First published in 1991, last amended in 2020. Available at: http://pravo.gov.ru.

Zeynep Yirmibeşoğlu and Gülşen Eryiğit. 2018. Detecting code-switching between Turkish-English language pair. In *Proceedings of the 2018 EMNLP Workshop W-NUT: The 4th Workshop on Noisy User-generated Text*, pages 110–115, Brussels, Belgium. Association for Computational Linguistics.

A Appendix

Cyrillic	Latin (Tatar)	Latin (Russian)	Cyrillic	Latin (Tatar)	Latin (Russian)
а	a	a	у	u, uw, w	u
б	b	b	ф	f	f
в	w	v	х	x	x
г	g, ğ	g	ц	NA	ts
д	d	d	ч	ç	ç
е	e, ye, yı	e	ш	ş	ş
ё	NA	yo	щ	NA	şç
ж	j	j	ъ	—	—
з	z	z	ы	ı	ı
и	i	i	ь	—	—
й	y	y	э	e, '	e
к	k, q	k	ю	yu, yü, yuw, yüw	yu
л	l	l	я	ya, yä	ya
м	m	m	ә	ä	NA
н	n	n	ө	ö	NA
о	o	o	ү	ü, üw, w	NA
п	p	p	җ	c	NA
с	s	s	ң	ñ	NA
т	t	t	һ	h	NA

Table 5: Tatar's Cyrillic–Latin correspondence for Tatar- and Russian-origin words. NA (not applicable) means that the letter does not appear in the language. An em-dash means that the letter is ignored in Latin transcription.

original	РФ Президенты Владимир Путин Россия мөселманнарын изге Рамазан
gold (Latin)	RF Prezidentı Vladimir Putin Rossiyä möselmannarın izge Ramazan
speak.tatar	RF Prezidentı Vladimir Putin Rossiyä möselmannarın izge Ramazan
TTT	RF Prezidentı Wlädimir Pütin Rössiyä möselmannarın izge Ramazan
Aylandirow	RF Prezidentı Vladimir Putin Rossiä möselmännarın izge Ramazan
tt-based	RF Prezidentı Wladimir Putin Rossiyä möselmannarın izge Ramazan
tt-ru hybrid	RF Prezidentı Vladimir Putin Rossiyä möselmannarın izge Ramazan

Table 6: An example of comparison of transliterations. The sequence on the top is the original corpus sentence in Cyrillic, below which is the Latin counterpart manually transcribed. The three sentences in the middle row are transliterations by the previous tools. The first sentence in the bottom row is the monolingual tt-based transliteration, and the second is transcribed by our proposed method.

Code-Mixing on Sesame Street: Dawn of the Adversarial Polyglots

Samson Tan[§♮] **Shafiq Joty**[§‡]
[§]Salesforce Research Asia [♮]National University of Singapore [‡]Nanyang Technological University
{samson.tan,sjoty}@salesforce.com

Abstract

Multilingual models have demonstrated impressive cross-lingual transfer performance. However, test sets like XNLI are monolingual at the example level. In multilingual communities, it is common for polyglots to code-mix when conversing with each other. Inspired by this phenomenon, we present two strong black-box adversarial attacks (one word-level, one phrase-level) for multilingual models that push their ability to handle code-mixed sentences to the limit. The former (POLYGLOSS) uses bilingual dictionaries to propose perturbations and translations of the clean example for sense disambiguation. The latter (BUMBLEBEE) directly aligns the clean example with its translations before extracting phrases as perturbations. BUMBLEBEE has a success rate of 89.75% against XLM-R_{large}, bringing its average accuracy of 79.85 down to 8.18 on XNLI. Finally, we propose an efficient adversarial training scheme, Code-mixed Adversarial Training (CAT), that trains in the same number of steps as the original model. Even after controlling for the extra training data introduced, CAT improves model accuracy when the model is prevented from relying on lexical overlaps (+3.45), with a negligible drop (-0.15 points) in performance on the original XNLI test set. t-SNE visualizations reveal that CAT improves a model's language agnosticity.

Proceedings of the Fifth Workshop on Computational Approaches to Linguistic Code-Switching, page 141
June 11, 2021.
https://doi.org/10.26615/978-954-452-056-4_019

Are Multilingual Models Effective in Code-Switching?

Genta Indra Winata, Samuel Cahyawijaya, Zihan Liu, Zhaojiang Lin, Andrea Madotto, Pascale Fung
Center for Artificial Intelligence Research (CAiRE)
The Hong Kong University of Science and Technology
giwinata@connect.ust.hk

Abstract

Multilingual language models have shown decent performance in multilingual and cross-lingual natural language understanding tasks. However, the power of these multilingual models in code-switching tasks has not been fully explored. In this paper, we study the effectiveness of multilingual language models to understand their capability and adaptability to the mixed-language setting by considering the inference speed, performance, and number of parameters to measure their practicality. We conduct experiments in three language pairs on named entity recognition and part-of-speech tagging and compare them with existing methods, such as using bilingual embeddings and multilingual meta-embeddings. Our findings suggest that pre-trained multilingual models do not necessarily guarantee high-quality representations on code-switching, while using meta-embeddings achieves similar results with significantly fewer parameters.

1 Introduction

Learning representation for code-switching has become a crucial area of research to support a greater variety of language speakers in natural language processing (NLP) applications, such as dialogue system and natural language understanding (NLU). Code-switching is a phenomenon in which a person speaks more than one language in a conversation, and its usage is prevalent in multilingual communities. Yet, despite the enormous number of studies in multilingual NLP, only very few focus on code-switching. Recently, contextualized language models, such as mBERT (Devlin et al., 2019) and XLM-R (Conneau et al., 2020) have achieved state-of-the-art results on monolingual and cross-lingual tasks in NLU benchmarks (Wang et al., 2018a; Hu et al., 2020; Wilie et al., 2020; Liu et al., 2020; Lin et al., 2020). However, the effectiveness of these multilingual language models on code-switching tasks remains unknown.

Several approaches have been explored in code-switching representation learning in NLU. Character-level representations have been utilized to address the out-of-vocabulary issue in code-switched text (Winata et al., 2018c; Wang et al., 2018b), while external handcrafted resources such as gazetteers list are usually used to mitigate the low-resource issue in code-switching (Aguilar et al., 2017; Trivedi et al., 2018); however, this approach is very limited because it relies on the size of the dictionary and it is language-dependent. In another line of research, meta-embeddings have been used in code-switching by combining multiple word embeddings from different languages (Winata et al., 2019a,b). This method shows the effectiveness of mixing word representations in closely related languages to form language-agnostic representations, and is considered very effective in Spanish-English code-switched named entity recognition tasks, and significantly outperforming mBERT (Khanuja et al., 2020) with fewer parameters.

While more advanced multilingual language models (Conneau et al., 2020) than multilingual BERT (Devlin et al., 2019) have been proposed, their effectiveness is still unknown in code-switching tasks. Thus, we investigate their effectiveness in the code-switching domain and compare them with the existing works. Here, we would like to answer the following research question, *"Which models are effective in representing code-switching text, and why?."*

In this paper, we evaluate the representation quality of monolingual and bilingual word embeddings, multilingual meta-embeddings, and multilingual language models on five downstream tasks on named entity recognition (NER) and part-of-speech tagging (POS) in Hindi-English, Spanish-English, and Modern Standard Arabic-Egyptian. We study the effectiveness of each model by considering three criteria: performance, speed, and the

Proceedings of the Fifth Workshop on Computational Approaches to Linguistic Code-Switching, pages 142–153
June 11, 2021. ©2021 Association for Computational Linguistics
https://doi.org/10.26615/978-954-452-056-4_020

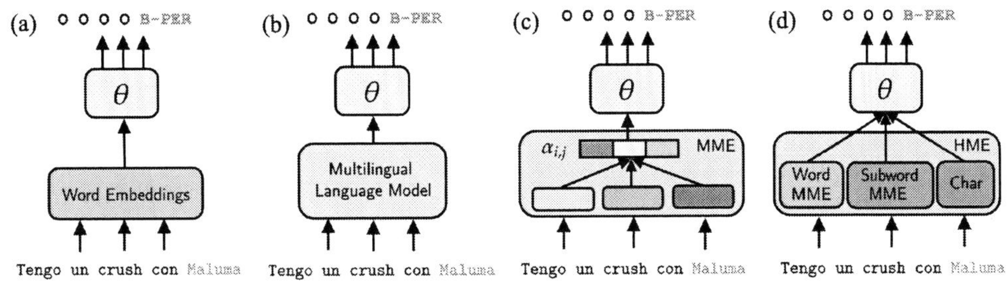

Figure 1: Model architectures for code-switching modeling: (a) model using word embeddings, (b) model using multilingual language model, (c) model using multilingual meta-embeddings (MME), and (d) model using hierarchical meta-embeddings (HME).

number of parameters that are essential for practical applications. Here, we set up the experimental setting to be as language-agnostic as possible; thus, it does not include any handcrafted features.

Our findings suggest that multilingual pre-trained language models, such as XLM-R_{BASE}, achieves similar or sometimes better results than the hierarchical meta-embeddings (HME) (Winata et al., 2019b) model on code-switching. On the other hand, the meta-embeddings use word and subword pre-trained embeddings that are trained using significantly less data than mBERT and XLM-R_{BASE} and can achieve on par performance to theirs. Thus, we conjecture that the masked language model is not be the best training objective for representing code-switching text. Interestingly, we found that XLM-R_{LARGE} can improve the performance by a great margin, but with a substantial cost in the training and inference time, with 13x more parameters than HME-Ensemble for only around a 2% improvement. The main contributions of our work are as follows:

- We evaluate the performance of word embeddings, multilingual language models, and multilingual meta-embeddings on code-switched NLU tasks in three language pairs, Hindi-English (HIN-ENG), Spanish-English (SPA-ENG), and Modern Standard Arabic-Egyptian (MSA-EA), to measure their ability in representing code-switching text.
- We present a comprehensive study on the effectiveness of multilingual models on a variety of code-switched NLU tasks to analyze the practicality of each model in terms of performance, speed, and number of parameters.
- We further analyze the memory footprint required by each model over different sequence lengths in a GPU. Thus, we are able to understand which model to choose in a practical scenario.

2 Representation Models

In this section, we describe multilingual models that we explore in the context of code-switching. Figure 1 shows the architectures for a word embeddings model, a multilingual language model, and the multilingual meta-embeddings (MME), and HME models.

2.1 Word Embeddings

2.1.1 FastText

In general, code-switching text contains a primary language the matrix language (ML)) as well as a secondary language (the embedded language (EL)). To represent code-switching text, a straightforward idea is to train the model with the word embeddings of the ML and EL from FastText (Grave et al., 2018). Code-switching text has many noisy tokens and sometimes mixed words in the ML and EL that produce a "new word", which leads to a high number of out-of-vocabulary (OOV) tokens. To solve this issue, we utilize subword-level embeddings from FastText (Grave et al., 2018) to generate the representations for these OOV tokens. We conduct experiments on two variants of applying the word embeddings to the code-switching tasks: FastText (ML) and FastText (EL), which utilize the word embeddings of ML and EL, respectively.

2.1.2 MUSE

To leverage the information from the embeddings of both the ML and EL, we utilize MUSE (Lample et al., 2018) to align the embeddings space of the ML and EL so that we can inject the information of the EL embeddings into the ML embeddings, and vice versa. We perform alignment in two directions: (1) We align the ML embeddings to the vector space of the EL embeddings (denoted as MUSE (ML $\rightarrow$ EL)); (2) We conduct the alignment in the opposite direction, which aligns the EL embeddings to the vector space of the ML embeddings (denoted as MUSE (EL $\rightarrow$ ML)). After the embeddings alignment, we train the model with the aligned embeddings for the code-switching tasks.

2.2 Multilingual Pre-trained Models

Pre-trained on large-scale corpora across numerous languages, multilingual language models (Devlin et al., 2019; Conneau et al., 2020) possess the ability to produce aligned multilingual representations for semantically similar words and sentences, which brings them advantages to cope with code-mixed multilingual text.

2.2.1 Multilingual BERT

Multilingual BERT (mBERT) (Devlin et al., 2019), a multilingual version of the BERT model, is pre-trained on Wikipedia text across 104 languages with a model size of 110M parameters. It has been shown to possess a surprising multilingual ability and to outperform existing strong models on multiple zero-shot cross-lingual tasks (Pires et al., 2019; Wu and Dredze, 2019). Given its strengths in handling multilingual text, we leverage it for code-switching tasks.

2.2.2 XLM-RoBERTa

XLM-RoBERTa (XLM-R) (Conneau et al., 2020) is a multilingual language model that is pre-trained on 100 languages using more than two terabytes of filtered CommonCrawl data. Thanks to the large-scale training corpora and enormous model size (XLM-R$_{\text{BASE}}$ and XLM-R$_{\text{LARGE}}$ have 270M and 550M parameters, respectively), XLM-R is shown to have a better multilingual ability than mBERT, and it can significantly outperform mBERT on a variety of cross-lingual benchmarks. Therefore, we also investigate the effectiveness of XLM-R for code-switching tasks.

2.2.3 Char2Subword

Char2Subword introduces a character-to-subword module to handle rare and unseen spellings by training an embedding lookup table (Aguilar et al., 2020b). This approach leverages transfer learning from an existing pre-trained language model, such as mBERT, and resumes the pre-training of the upper layers of the model. The method aims to increase the robustness of the model to various typography styles.

2.3 Multilingual Meta-Embeddings

The MME model (Winata et al., 2019a) is formed by combining multiple word embeddings from different languages. Let's define $\mathbf{w}$ to be a sequence of words with n elements, where $\mathbf{w} = [w_1, \ldots, w_n]$. First, a list of word-level embedding layers is used $E_i^{(w)}$ to map words $\mathbf{w}$ into embeddings $\mathbf{x}_i$. Then, the embeddings are combined using one out of the following three methods: concat, linear, and self-attention. We briefly discuss each method below.

Concat This method concatenates word embeddings by merging the dimensions of word representations into higher-dimensional embeddings. This is one of the simplest methods to join all embeddings without losing information, but it requires a larger activation memory than the linear method.

$$\mathbf{x}_i^{\text{CONCAT}} = [\mathbf{x}_{i,1}, ..., \mathbf{x}_{i,n}]. \tag{1}$$

Linear This method sums all word embeddings into single word embeddings with equal weight without considering each embedding's importance. The method may cause a loss of information and may generate noisy representations. Also, though it is very efficient, it requires an additional layer to project all embeddings into a single-dimensional space if one embedding is larger than another.

$$\mathbf{x'}_{i,j} = \mathbf{W}_j \cdot \mathbf{x}_{i,j},$$
$$\mathbf{x}_i^{\text{LINEAR}} = \sum_{j=0}^{n} \mathbf{x'}_{i,j}.$$

Self-Attention This method generates a meta-representation by taking the vector representation from multiple monolingual pre-trained embeddings in different subunits, such as word and subword. It applies a projection matrix $\mathbf{W}_j$ to transform the dimensions from the original space $\mathbf{x}_{i,j} \in \mathbb{R}^d$ to a new shared space $\mathbf{x'}_{i,j} \in \mathbb{R}^{d'}$. Then, it calculates attention weights $\alpha_{i,j} \in \mathbb{R}^{d'}$ with a non-linear scoring function ϕ (e.g., tanh) to take important information from each individual embedding $\mathbf{x'}_{i,j}$. Then, MME is calculated by taking the weighted sum of the projected embeddings $\mathbf{x'}_{i,j}$:

$$\mathbf{x'}_{i,j} = \mathbf{W}_j \cdot \mathbf{x}_{i,j}, \quad (2)$$

$$\alpha_{i,j} = \frac{\exp(\phi(\mathbf{x'}_{i,j}))}{\sum_{k=1}^{n} \exp(\phi(\mathbf{x'}_{i,k}))}, \quad (3)$$

$$\mathbf{u}_i = \sum_{j=1}^{n} \alpha_{i,j} \mathbf{x'}_{i,j}. \quad (4)$$

2.4 Hierarchical Meta-Embedings

The HME method combines word, subword, and character representations to create a mixture of embeddings (Winata et al., 2019b). It generates multilingual meta-embeddings of words and subwords, and then, concatenates them with character-level embeddings to generate final word representations. HME combines the word-level, subword-level, and character-level representations by concatenation, and randomly initializes the character embeddings. During the training, the character embeddings are trainable, while all subword and word embeddings remain fixed.

2.5 HME-Ensemble

The ensemble is a technique to improve the model's robustness from multiple predictions. In this case, we train the HME model multiple times and take the prediction of each model. Then, we compute the final prediction by majority voting to achieve a consensus. This method has shown to be very effective in improving the robustness of an unseen test set (Winata et al., 2019c). Interestingly, this method is very simple to implement and can be easily spawned in multiple machines, as in parallel processes.

3 Experiments

In this section, we describe the details of the datasets we use and how the models are trained.

3.1 Datasets

We evaluate our models on five downstream tasks in the LinCE Benchmark (Aguilar et al., 2020a). We choose three named entity recognition (NER) tasks, Hindi-English (HIN-ENG) (Singh et al., 2018a), Spanish-English (SPA-ENG) (Aguilar et al., 2018) and Modern Standard Arabic (MSA-EA) (Aguilar et al., 2018), and two part-of-speech (POS) tagging tasks, Hindi-English (HIN-ENG) (Singh et al., 2018b) and Spanish-English (SPA-ENG) (Soto and Hirschberg, 2017). We apply Roman-to-Devanagari transliteration on the Hindi-English datasets since the multilingual models are trained with data using that form. Table 1 shows the number of tokens of each language for each dataset. We classify the language with more tokens as the ML and the other as the EL. We replace user hashtags and mentions with <USR>, emoji with <EMOJI>, and URL with <URL> for models that use word-embeddings, similar to Winata et al. (2019a). We evaluate our model with the micro F1 score for NER and accuracy for POS tagging, following Aguilar et al. (2020a).

	#L1	**#L2**	**ML**	**EL**
NER				
HIN-ENG	13,860	11,391	HIN	ENG
SPA-ENG	163,824	402,923	ENG	SPA
MSA-EA†	-	-	MSA	EA
POS				
HIN-ENG	12,589	9,882	HIN	ENG
SPA-ENG	178,135	92,517	SPA	ENG

Table 1: Dataset statistics are taken from Aguilar et al. (2020a). We define L1 and L2 as the languages found in the dataset. For example, in HIN-ENG, L1 is HIN and L2 is ENG. †We define MSA as ML and EA as EL. #L1 represents the number of tokens in the first language and #L2 represents the number of tokens in the second language.

3.2 Experimental Setup

We describe our experimental details for each model.

3.2.1 Scratch

We train transformer-based models without any pre-training by following the mBERT model structure, and the parameters are randomly initialized, including the subword embeddings. We train transformer models with four and six layers with a hidden size of 768. This setting is important to measure the effectiveness of pre-trained multilingual models. We start the training with a learning rate of 1e-4 and an early stop of 10 epochs.

3.2.2 Word Embeddings

We use FastText embeddings (Grave et al., 2018; Mikolov et al., 2018) to train our transformer models. The model consists of a 4-layer transformer encoder with four heads and a hidden size of 200. We train a transformer followed by a Conditional Random Field (CRF) layer (Lafferty et al., 2001).

The model is trained by starting with a learning rate of 0.1 with a batch size of 32 and an early stop of 10 epochs. We also train our model with only ML and EL embeddings. We freeze all embeddings and only keep the classifier trainable.

We leverage MUSE (Lample et al., 2018) to align the embeddings space between the ML and EL. MUSE mainly consists of two stages: adversarial training and a refinement procedure. For all alignment settings, we conduct the adversarial training using the SGD optimizer with a starting learning rate of 0.1, and then we perform the refinement procedure for five iterations using the Procrustes solution and CSLS (Lample et al., 2018). After the alignment, we train our model with the aligned word embeddings (MUSE (ML $\rightarrow$ EL) or MUSE (EL $\rightarrow$ ML)) on the code-switching tasks.

3.2.3 Pre-trained Multilingual Models

We use pre-trained models from Huggingface. [1] On top of each model, we put a fully-connected layer classifier. We train the model with a learning rate between [1e-5, 5e-5] with a decay of 0.1 and a batch size of 8. For large models, such as XLM-R_{LARGE} and XLM-MLM_{LARGE}, we freeze the embeddings layer to fit in a single GPU.

3.2.4 Multilingual Meta-Embeddings (MME)

We use pre-trained word embeddings to train our MME. Table 2 shows the embeddings used for each dataset. We freeze all embeddings and train a transformer classifier with the CRF. The transformer classifier consists of a hidden size of 200, a head of 4, and 4 layers. All models are trained with a learning rate of 0.1, an early stop of 10 epochs, and a batch size of 32. We follow the implementation from the code repository. [2] Table 2 shows the list of word embeddings used in MME.

3.2.5 Hierarchical Meta-Embeddings (HME)

We train our HME model using the same embeddings as MME and pre-trained subword embeddings from Heinzerling and Strube (2018). The subword embeddings for each language pair are shown in Table 3. We freeze all word embeddings and subword embeddings, and keep the character embeddings trainable.

[1] https://github.com/huggingface/transformers

[2] https://github.com/gentaiscool/meta-emb

	Word Embeddings List
NER	
HIN-ENG	FastText: Hindi, English (Grave et al., 2018)
SPA-ENG	FastText: Spanish, English, Catalan, Portugese (Grave et al., 2018) GLoVe: English-Twitter (Pennington et al., 2014)
MSA-EA	FastText: Arabic, Egyptian (Grave et al., 2018)
POS	
HIN-ENG	FastText: Hindi, English (Grave et al., 2018)
SPA-ENG	FastText: Spanish, English, Catalan, Portugese (Grave et al., 2018) GLoVe: English-Twitter (Pennington et al., 2014)

Table 2: Embeddings list for MME.

	Subword Embeddings List
NER	
HIN-ENG	Hindi, English
SPA-ENG	Spanish, English, Catalan, Portugese
MSA-EA	Arabic, Egyptian
POS	
HIN-ENG	Hindi, English
SPA-ENG	Spanish, English, Catalan, Portugese

Table 3: Subword embeddings list for HME.

3.3 Other Baselines

We compare the results with Char2subword and mBERT (cased) from Aguilar et al. (2020b). We also include the results of English BERT provided by the organizer of the LinCE public benchmark leaderboard (accessed on March 12nd, 2021). [3]

4 Results and Discussions

4.1 LinCE Benchmark

We evaluate all the models on the LinCE benchmark, and the development set results are shown in Table 4. As expected, models without any pretraining (e.g., Scratch (4L)) perform significantly worse than other pre-trained models. Both FastText and MME use pre-trained word embeddings, but MME achieves a consistently higher F1 score than FastText in both NER and POS tasks, demonstrating the importance of the contextualized self-attentive encoder. HME further improves on the F1 score of the MME models, suggesting that encoding hierarchical information from sub-word level, word level, and sentence level representations can improve code-switching task performance. Comparing HME with contextualized pre-trained mul-

[3] https://ritual.uh.edu/lince

Method	Avg Perf.	NER HIN-ENG Params	NER HIN-ENG F1	NER SPA-ENG Params	NER SPA-ENG F1	NER MSA-EA Params	NER MSA-EA F1	POS HIN-ENG Params	POS HIN-ENG Acc	POS SPA-ENG Params	POS SPA-ENG Acc
Scratch (2L)	63.40	96M	46.51	96M	32.75	96M	60.14	96M	83.20	96M	94.39
Scratch (4L)	60.93	111M	47.01	111M	19.06	111M	60.24	111M	83.72	111M	94.64
Mono/Multilingual Word Embeddings											
FastText (ML)	76.43	4M	63.58	18M	57.10	16M	78.42	4M	84.63	6M	98.41
FastText (EL)	76.71	4M	69.79	18M	58.34	16M	72.68	4M	84.40	6M	98.36
MUSE (ML → EL)	76.54	4M	64.05	18M	58.00	16M	78.50	4M	83.82	6M	98.34
MUSE (EL → ML)	75.58	4M	64.86	18M	57.08	16M	73.95	4M	83.62	6M	98.38
Pre-Trained Multilingual Models											
mBERT (uncased)	79.46	167M	68.08	167M	63.73	167M	78.61	167M	90.42	167M	96.48
mBERT (cased)[‡]	79.97	177M	72.94	177M	62.66	177M	78.93	177M	87.86	177M	97.29
Char2Subword[‡]	81.07	136M	74.91	136M	63.32	136M	80.45	136M	89.64	136M	97.03
XLM-R$_{BASE}$	81.90	278M	76.85	278M	62.76	278M	81.24	278M	91.51	278M	97.12
XLM-R$_{LARGE}$	**84.39**	565M	**79.62**	565M	**67.18**	565M	**85.19**	565M	92.78	565M	97.20
XLM-MLM$_{LARGE}$	81.41	572M	73.91	572M	62.89	572M	82.72	572M	90.33	572M	97.19
Multilingual Meta-Embeddings											
Concat	79.70	10M	70.76	86M	61.65	31M	79.33	8M	88.14	23M	98.61
Linear	79.60	10M	69.68	86M	61.74	31M	79.42	8M	88.58	23M	98.58
Attention (MME)	79.86	10M	71.69	86M	61.23	31M	79.41	8M	88.34	23M	98.65
HME	81.60	12M	73.98	92M	62.09	35M	81.26	12M	92.01	30M	98.66
HME-Ensemble	**82.44**	20M	76.16	103M	62.80	43M	81.67	20M	**92.84**	40M	**98.74**

Table 4: Results on the development set of the LinCE benchmark. [‡] The results are taken from Aguilar et al. (2020b). The number of parameters of mBERT (cased) is calculated by approximation.

Method	Avg Params	Avg Perf.↑	NER HIN-ENG	NER SPA-ENG	NER MSA-EA	POS HIN-ENG	POS SPA-ENG
English BERT (cased)[†]	108M	75.80	74.46	61.15	59.44	87.02	96.92
mBERT (cased)[‡]	177M	77.08	72.57	64.05	65.39	86.30	97.07
HME	36M	77.64	73.78	63.06	66.14	88.55	96.66
Char2Subword[‡]	136M	77.85	73.38	64.65	66.13	88.23	96.88
XLM-MLM$_{LARGE}$	572M	78.40	74.49	64.16	67.22	89.10	97.04
XLM-R$_{BASE}$	278M	78.75	75.72	64.95	65.13	91.00	96.96
HME-Ensemble	<u>45M</u>	<u>79.17</u>	75.97	65.11	**68.71**	89.30	96.78
XLM-R$_{LARGE}$	565M	**80.96**	**80.70**	**69.55**	65.78	**91.59**	**97.18**

Table 5: Results on the test set of the LinCE benchmark.[‡] The results are taken from Aguilar et al. (2020b). [†] The result is taken from the LinCE leaderboard.

tilingual models such as mBERT and XLM-R, we find that HME models are able to obtain competitive F1 scores while maintaining a 10x smaller model sizes. This result indicates that pre-trained multilingual word embeddings can achieve a good balance between performance and model size in code-switching tasks. Table 5 shows the models' performance in the LinCE test set. The results are highly correlated to the results of the development set. XLM-R$_{LARGE}$ achieves the best-averaged performance, with a 13x larger model size compared to the HME-Ensemble model.

4.2 Model Effectiveness and Efficiency

Performance vs. Model Size As shown in Figure 2, the Scratch models yield the worst average score, at around 60.93 points. With the smallest pre-trained embedding model, FastText, the model performance can improve by around 10 points compared to the Scratch models and they only have 10M parameters on average. On the other hand, the MME models, which have 31.6M parameters on average, achieve similar results to the mBERT models, with around 170M parameters. Interestingly, adding subwords and character embeddings to MME, such as in the HME models, further im-

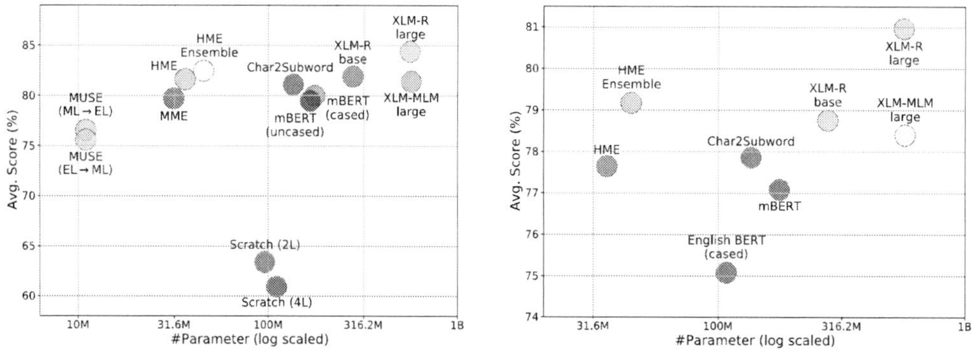

Figure 2: Validation set (left) and test set (right) evaluation performance (y-axis) and parameter (x-axis) of different models on LinCE benchmark.

proves the performance of the MME models and achieves a 81.60 average score, similar to that of the XLM-R_{BASE} and XLM-MLM_{LARGE} models, but with less than one-fifth the number of parameters, at around 42.25M. The Ensemble method adds further performance improvement of around 1% with an additional 2.5M parameters compared to the non-Ensemble counterparts.

Inference Time To compare the speed of different models, we use generated dummy data with various sequence lengths, [16, 32, 64, 128, 256, 512, 1024, 2048, 4096]. We measure each model's inference time and collect the statistics of each model at one particular sequence length by running the model 100 times. The experiment is performed on a single NVIDIA GTX1080Ti GPU. We do not include the pre-processing time in our analysis. Still, it is clear that the pre-processing time for meta-embeddings models is longer than for other models as pre-processing requires a tokenization step to be conducted for the input multiple times with different tokenizers. The sequence lengths are counted based on the input tokens of each model. We use words for the MME and HME models, and subwords for other models.

The results of the inference speed test are shown in Figure 3. Although all pre-trained contextualized language models yield a very high validation score, these models are also the slowest in terms of inference time. For shorter sequences, the HME model performs as fast as the mBERT and XLM-R_{BASE} models, but it can retain the speed as the sequence length increases because of the smaller model dimension in every layer. The FastText, MME, and Scratch models yield a high throughput in short-sequence settings by processing more than 150

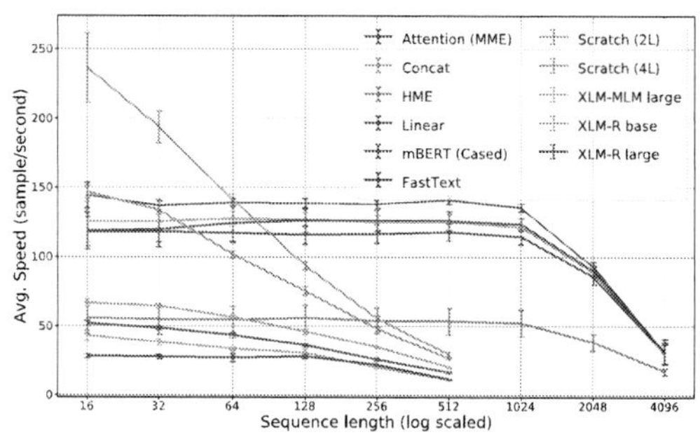

Figure 3: Speed-to-sequence length comparison of different models.

samples per second. For longer sequences, the same behavior occurs, with the throughput of the Scratch models reducing as the sequence length increases, even becoming lower than that of the HME model when the sequence length is greater than or equal to 256. Interestingly, for the FastText, MME, and HME models, the throughput remains steady when the sequence length is less than 1024, and it starts to decrease afterwards.

Memory Footprint We record the memory footprint over different sequence lengths, and use the same setting for the FastText, MME, and HME models as in the inference time analysis. We record the size of each model on the GPU and the size of the activation after performing one forward operation to a single sample with a certain sequence length. The result of the memory footprint analysis for a sequence length of 512 is shown in Table 6. Based on the results, we can see that meta-embedding models use a significantly smaller memory footprint to store the model and activation memory. For instance, the memory footprint of the HME model is less than that of the Scratch (4L) model, which has only four transformer encoder layers, a model dimension of 768 and a feed-forward dimension of 3,072. On the other hand, large pre-trained language models, such as XLM-MLM$_{\text{LARGE}}$ and XLM-R$_{\text{LARGE}}$, use a much larger memory for storing the activation memory compared to all other models. The complete results of the memory footprint analysis are shown in Appendix A.

Model	Activation (MB)
FastText	79.0
Concat	85.3
Linear	80.8
Attention (MME)	88.0
HME	154.8
Scratch (2L)	133.0
Scratch (4L)	264.0
mBERT	597.0
XLM-R$_{\text{BASE}}$	597.0
XLM-R$_{\text{LARGE}}$	1541.0
XLM-MLM$_{\text{LARGE}}$	1158.0

Table 6: GPU memory consumption of different models with input size of 512.

5 Related Work

Transfer Learning on Code-Switching Previous works on code-switching have mostly focused on combining pre-trained word embeddings with trainable character embeddings to represent noisy mixed-language text (Trivedi et al., 2018; Wang et al., 2018b; Winata et al., 2018c). Winata et al. (2018a) presented a multi-task training framework to leverage part-of-speech information in a language model. Later, they introduced the MME in the code-switching domain by combining multiple word embeddings from different languages (Winata et al., 2019a). MME has since also been applied to Indian languages (Priyadharshini et al., 2020; Dowlagar and Mamidi, 2021).

Meta-embeddings have been previously explored in various monolingual NLP tasks (Yin and Schütze, 2016; Muromägi et al., 2017; Bollegala et al., 2018; Coates and Bollegala, 2018; Kiela et al., 2018). Winata et al. (2019b) introduced hierarchical meta-embeddings by leveraging subwords and characters to improve the code-switching text representation. Pratapa et al. (2018b) propose to train skip-gram embeddings from synthetic code-switched data generated by Pratapa et al. (2018a). This improves syntactic and semantic code-switching tasks. Winata et al. (2018b); Lee et al. (2019); Winata et al. (2019d); Samanta et al. (2019), and Gupta et al. (2020) proposed a generative-based model for augmenting code-switching data from parallel data. Recently, Aguilar et al. (2020b) proposed the Char2Subword model, which builds representations from characters out of the subword vocabulary, and they used the module to replace subword embeddings that are robust to misspellings and inflection that are mainly found in a social media text. Khanuja et al. (2020) explored fine-tuning techniques to improve mBERT for code-switching tasks, while Winata et al. (2020) introduced a meta-learning-based model to leverage monolingual data effectively in code-switching speech and language models.

Bilingual Embeddings In another line of works, bilingual embeddings have been introduced to represent code-switching sentences, such as in bilingual correlation-based embeddings (BiCCA) (Faruqui and Dyer, 2014), the bilingual compositional model (BiCVM) (Hermann and Blunsom, 2014), BiSkip (Luong et al., 2015), RCSLS (Joulin et al., 2018), and MUSE (Lample et al., 2017, 2018), to align words in L1 to the corresponding words in L2, and vice versa.

6 Conclusion

In this paper, we study multilingual language models' effectiveness so as to understand their capability and adaptability to the mixed-language setting. We conduct experiments on named entity recognition and part-of-speech tagging on various language pairs. We find that a pre-trained multilingual model does not necessarily guarantee high-quality representations on code-switching, while the hierarchical meta-embeddings (HME) model achieve similar results to mBERT and XLM-R$_{\text{BASE}}$ but with significantly fewer parameters. Interestingly, we find that XLM-R$_{\text{LARGE}}$ has better performance by a great margin, but with a substantial cost in the training and inference time, using 13x more parameters than HME-Ensemble for only a 2% improvement.

Acknowledgments

This work has been partially funded by ITF/319/16FP and MRP/055/18 of the Innovation Technology Commission, the Hong Kong

SAR Government, and School of Engineering Ph.D. Fellowship Award, the Hong Kong University of Science and Technology, and RDC 1718050-0 of EMOS.AI.

References

Gustavo Aguilar, Fahad AlGhamdi, Victor Soto, Mona Diab, Julia Hirschberg, and Thamar Solorio. 2018. Named entity recognition on code-switched data: Overview of the calcs 2018 shared task. In *Proceedings of the Third Workshop on Computational Approaches to Linguistic Code-Switching*, pages 138–147.

Gustavo Aguilar, Sudipta Kar, and Thamar Solorio. 2020a. Lince: A centralized benchmark for linguistic code-switching evaluation. In *Proceedings of The 12th Language Resources and Evaluation Conference*, pages 1803–1813.

Gustavo Aguilar, Suraj Maharjan, Adrian Pastor López-Monroy, and Thamar Solorio. 2017. A multi-task approach for named entity recognition in social media data. In *Proceedings of the 3rd Workshop on Noisy User-generated Text*, pages 148–153.

Gustavo Aguilar, Bryan McCann, Tong Niu, Nazneen Rajani, Nitish Keskar, and Thamar Solorio. 2020b. Char2subword: Extending the subword embedding space from pre-trained models using robust character compositionality. *arXiv preprint arXiv:2010.12730*.

Danushka Bollegala, Kohei Hayashi, and Ken-Ichi Kawarabayashi. 2018. Think globally, embed locally: locally linear meta-embedding of words. In *Proceedings of the 27th International Joint Conference on Artificial Intelligence*, pages 3970–3976. AAAI Press.

Joshua Coates and Danushka Bollegala. 2018. Frustratingly easy meta-embedding–computing meta-embeddings by averaging source word embeddings. In *Proceedings of the 2018 Conference of the North American Chapter of the Association for Computational Linguistics: Human Language Technologies, Volume 2 (Short Papers)*, pages 194–198.

Alexis Conneau, Kartikay Khandelwal, Naman Goyal, Vishrav Chaudhary, Guillaume Wenzek, Francisco Guzmán, Édouard Grave, Myle Ott, Luke Zettlemoyer, and Veselin Stoyanov. 2020. Unsupervised cross-lingual representation learning at scale. In *Proceedings of the 58th Annual Meeting of the Association for Computational Linguistics*, pages 8440–8451.

Jacob Devlin, Ming-Wei Chang, Kenton Lee, and Kristina Toutanova. 2019. Bert: Pre-training of deep bidirectional transformers for language understanding. In *Proceedings of the 2019 Conference of the North American Chapter of the Association for Computational Linguistics: Human Language Technologies, Volume 1 (Long and Short Papers)*, pages 4171–4186.

Suman Dowlagar and Radhika Mamidi. 2021. Cmsaone@ dravidian-codemix-fire2020: A meta embedding and transformer model for code-mixed sentiment analysis on social media text. *arXiv preprint arXiv:2101.09004*.

Manaal Faruqui and Chris Dyer. 2014. Improving vector space word representations using multilingual correlation. In *Proceedings of the 14th Conference of the European Chapter of the Association for Computational Linguistics*, pages 462–471.

Edouard Grave, Piotr Bojanowski, Prakhar Gupta, Armand Joulin, and Tomas Mikolov. 2018. Learning word vectors for 157 languages. In *Proceedings of the International Conference on Language Resources and Evaluation (LREC 2018)*.

Deepak Gupta, Asif Ekbal, and Pushpak Bhattacharyya. 2020. A semi-supervised approach to generate the code-mixed text using pre-trained encoder and transfer learning. In *Proceedings of the 2020 Conference on Empirical Methods in Natural Language Processing: Findings*, pages 2267–2280.

Benjamin Heinzerling and Michael Strube. 2018. Bpemb: Tokenization-free pre-trained subword embeddings in 275 languages. In *Proceedings of the Eleventh International Conference on Language Resources and Evaluation (LREC-2018)*.

Karl Moritz Hermann and Phil Blunsom. 2014. Multilingual models for compositional distributed semantics. In *Proceedings of the 52nd Annual Meeting of the Association for Computational Linguistics (Volume 1: Long Papers)*, pages 58–68, Baltimore, Maryland. Association for Computational Linguistics.

Junjie Hu, Sebastian Ruder, Aditya Siddhant, Graham Neubig, Orhan Firat, and Melvin Johnson. 2020. Xtreme: A massively multilingual multi-task benchmark for evaluating cross-lingual generalisation. In *International Conference on Machine Learning*, pages 4411–4421. PMLR.

Armand Joulin, Piotr Bojanowski, Tomáš Mikolov, Hervé Jégou, and Édouard Grave. 2018. Loss in translation: Learning bilingual word mapping with a retrieval criterion. In *Proceedings of the 2018 Conference on Empirical Methods in Natural Language Processing*, pages 2979–2984.

Simran Khanuja, Sandipan Dandapat, Anirudh Srinivasan, Sunayana Sitaram, and Monojit Choudhury. 2020. Gluecos: An evaluation benchmark for code-switched nlp. In *Proceedings of the 58th Annual Meeting of the Association for Computational Linguistics*, pages 3575–3585.

Douwe Kiela, Changhan Wang, and Kyunghyun Cho. 2018. Dynamic meta-embeddings for improved sentence representations. In *Proceedings of the 2018 Conference on Empirical Methods in Natural Language Processing*, pages 1466–1477.

John D Lafferty, Andrew McCallum, and Fernando CN Pereira. 2001. Conditional random fields: Probabilistic models for segmenting and labeling sequence data. In *Proceedings of the Eighteenth International Conference on Machine Learning*, pages 282–289.

Guillaume Lample, Alexis Conneau, Ludovic Denoyer, and Marc'Aurelio Ranzato. 2017. Unsupervised machine translation using monolingual corpora only. *arXiv preprint arXiv:1711.00043*.

Guillaume Lample, Alexis Conneau, Marc'Aurelio Ranzato, Ludovic Denoyer, and Hervé Jégou. 2018. Word translation without parallel data. In *International Conference on Learning Representations*.

Grandee Lee, Xianghu Yue, and Haizhou Li. 2019. Linguistically motivated parallel data augmentation for code-switch language modeling. In *INTERSPEECH*, pages 3730–3734.

Zhaojiang Lin, Zihan Liu, Genta Indra Winata, Samuel Cahyawijaya, Andrea Madotto, Yejin Bang, Etsuko Ishii, and Pascale Fung. 2020. Xpersona: Evaluating multilingual personalized chatbot. *arXiv preprint arXiv:2003.07568*.

Zihan Liu, Genta Indra Winata, Zhaojiang Lin, Peng Xu, and Pascale Fung. 2020. Attention-informed mixed-language training for zero-shot cross-lingual task-oriented dialogue systems. In *Proceedings of the AAAI Conference on Artificial Intelligence*, volume 34, pages 8433–8440.

Thang Luong, Hieu Pham, and Christopher D. Manning. 2015. Bilingual word representations with monolingual quality in mind. In *Proceedings of the 1st Workshop on Vector Space Modeling for Natural Language Processing*, pages 151–159, Denver, Colorado. Association for Computational Linguistics.

Tomas Mikolov, Edouard Grave, Piotr Bojanowski, Christian Puhrsch, and Armand Joulin. 2018. Advances in pre-training distributed word representations. In *Proceedings of the International Conference on Language Resources and Evaluation (LREC 2018)*.

Avo Muromägi, Kairit Sirts, and Sven Laur. 2017. Linear ensembles of word embedding models. In *Proceedings of the 21st Nordic Conference on Computational Linguistics*, pages 96–104.

Jeffrey Pennington, Richard Socher, and Christopher Manning. 2014. Glove: Global vectors for word representation. In *Proceedings of the 2014 conference on empirical methods in natural language processing (EMNLP)*, pages 1532–1543.

Telmo Pires, Eva Schlinger, and Dan Garrette. 2019. How multilingual is multilingual bert? In *Proceedings of the 57th Annual Meeting of the Association for Computational Linguistics*, pages 4996–5001.

Adithya Pratapa, Gayatri Bhat, Monojit Choudhury, Sunayana Sitaram, Sandipan Dandapat, and Kalika Bali. 2018a. Language modeling for code-mixing: The role of linguistic theory based synthetic data. In *Proceedings of the 56th Annual Meeting of the Association for Computational Linguistics (Volume 1: Long Papers)*, volume 1, pages 1543–1553.

Adithya Pratapa, Monojit Choudhury, and Sunayana Sitaram. 2018b. Word embeddings for code-mixed language processing. In *Proceedings of the 2018 Conference on Empirical Methods in Natural Language Processing*, pages 3067–3072, Brussels, Belgium. Association for Computational Linguistics.

Ruba Priyadharshini, Bharathi Raja Chakravarthi, Mani Vegupatti, and John P McCrae. 2020. Named entity recognition for code-mixed indian corpus using meta embedding. In *2020 6th International Conference on Advanced Computing and Communication Systems (ICACCS)*, pages 68–72. IEEE.

Bidisha Samanta, Sharmila Reddy, Hussain Jagirdar, Niloy Ganguly, and Soumen Chakrabarti. 2019. A deep generative model for code-switched text. *arXiv preprint arXiv:1906.08972*.

Kushagra Singh, Indira Sen, and Ponnurangam Kumaraguru. 2018a. Language identification and named entity recognition in hinglish code mixed tweets. In *Proceedings of ACL 2018, Student Research Workshop*, pages 52–58.

Kushagra Singh, Indira Sen, and Ponnurangam Kumaraguru. 2018b. A twitter corpus for hindi-english code mixed pos tagging. In *Proceedings of the Sixth International Workshop on Natural Language Processing for Social Media*, pages 12–17.

Victor Soto and Julia Hirschberg. 2017. Crowdsourcing universal part-of-speech tags for code-switching. *Proc. Interspeech 2017*, pages 77–81.

Shashwat Trivedi, Harsh Rangwani, and Anil Kumar Singh. 2018. Iit (bhu) submission for the acl shared task on named entity recognition on code-switched data. In *Proceedings of the Third Workshop on Computational Approaches to Linguistic Code-Switching*, pages 148–153.

Alex Wang, Amanpreet Singh, Julian Michael, Felix Hill, Omer Levy, and Samuel Bowman. 2018a. Glue: A multi-task benchmark and analysis platform for natural language understanding. In *Proceedings of the 2018 EMNLP Workshop BlackboxNLP: Analyzing and Interpreting Neural Networks for NLP*, pages 353–355.

Changhan Wang, Kyunghyun Cho, and Douwe Kiela. 2018b. Code-switched named entity recognition with embedding attention. In *Proceedings of the*

Third Workshop on Computational Approaches to Linguistic Code-Switching, pages 154–158.

Bryan Wilie, Karissa Vincentio, Genta Indra Winata, Samuel Cahyawijaya, Xiaohong Li, Zhi Yuan Lim, Sidik Soleman, Rahmad Mahendra, Pascale Fung, Syafri Bahar, et al. 2020. Indonlu: Benchmark and resources for evaluating indonesian natural language understanding. In *Proceedings of the 1st Conference of the Asia-Pacific Chapter of the Association for Computational Linguistics and the 10th International Joint Conference on Natural Language Processing*, pages 843–857.

Genta Indra Winata, Samuel Cahyawijaya, Zhaojiang Lin, Zihan Liu, Peng Xu, and Pascale Fung. 2020. Meta-transfer learning for code-switched speech recognition. In *Proceedings of the 58th Annual Meeting of the Association for Computational Linguistics*, pages 3770–3776.

Genta Indra Winata, Zhaojiang Lin, and Pascale Fung. 2019a. Learning multilingual meta-embeddings for code-switching named entity recognition. In *Proceedings of the 4th Workshop on Representation Learning for NLP (RepL4NLP-2019)*, pages 181–186.

Genta Indra Winata, Zhaojiang Lin, Jamin Shin, Zihan Liu, and Pascale Fung. 2019b. Hierarchical meta-embeddings for code-switching named entity recognition. In *Proceedings of the 2019 Conference on Empirical Methods in Natural Language Processing and the 9th International Joint Conference on Natural Language Processing (EMNLP-IJCNLP)*, pages 3532–3538.

Genta Indra Winata, Andrea Madotto, Zhaojiang Lin, Jamin Shin, Yan Xu, Peng Xu, and Pascale Fung. 2019c. Caire_hkust at semeval-2019 task 3: Hierarchical attention for dialogue emotion classification. In *Proceedings of the 13th International Workshop on Semantic Evaluation*, pages 142–147.

Genta Indra Winata, Andrea Madotto, Chien-Sheng Wu, and Pascale Fung. 2018a. Code-switching language modeling using syntax-aware multi-task learning. In *Proceedings of the Third Workshop on Computational Approaches to Linguistic Code-Switching*, pages 62–67.

Genta Indra Winata, Andrea Madotto, Chien-Sheng Wu, and Pascale Fung. 2018b. Learn to code-switch: Data augmentation using copy mechanism on language modeling. *arXiv preprint arXiv:1810.10254*.

Genta Indra Winata, Andrea Madotto, Chien-Sheng Wu, and Pascale Fung. 2019d. Code-switched language models using neural based synthetic data from parallel sentences. In *Proceedings of the 23rd Conference on Computational Natural Language Learning (CoNLL)*, pages 271–280.

Genta Indra Winata, Chien-Sheng Wu, Andrea Madotto, and Pascale Fung. 2018c. Bilingual character representation for efficiently addressing out-of-vocabulary words in code-switching named entity recognition. In *Proceedings of the Third Workshop on Computational Approaches to Linguistic Code-Switching*, pages 110–114.

Shijie Wu and Mark Dredze. 2019. Beto, bentz, becas: The surprising cross-lingual effectiveness of bert. In *Proceedings of the 2019 Conference on Empirical Methods in Natural Language Processing and the 9th International Joint Conference on Natural Language Processing (EMNLP-IJCNLP)*, pages 833–844.

Wenpeng Yin and Hinrich Schütze. 2016. Learning word meta-embeddings. In *Proceedings of the 54th Annual Meeting of the Association for Computational Linguistics (Volume 1: Long Papers)*, volume 1, pages 1351–1360.

A Memory Footprint Analysis

We show the complete results of our memory footprint analysis in Table 7.

Model	Activation (MB)								
	16	**32**	**64**	**128**	**256**	**512**	**1024**	**2048**	**4096**
FastText	1.0	2.0	4.0	10.0	26.0	79.0	261.0	941.0	3547.0
Linear	1.0	2.0	4.0	10.0	27.4	80.8	265.6	950.0	3562.0
Concat	1.0	2.0	5.0	11.2	29.2	85.2	274.5	967.5	3596.5
Attention (MME)	1.0	2.0	5.4	12.4	31.0	89.0	283.2	985.6	3630.6
HME	3.2	6.6	13.4	28.6	64.2	154.8	416.4	1252.0	4155.0
Scratch (2L)	2.0	4.0	8.0	20.0	46.0	133.0	-	-	-
Scratch (4L)	3.0	7.0	15.0	38.0	90.0	264.0	-	-	-
mBERT (uncased)	10.0	20.0	41.0	100.0	218.0	597.0	-	-	-
XLM-R_{BASE}	10.0	20.0	41.0	100.0	218.0	597.0	-	-	-
XLM-R_{LARGE}	25.0	52.0	109.0	241.0	579.0	1541.0	-	-	-
XLM-MLM_{LARGE}	20.0	42.0	89.0	193.0	467.0	1158.0	-	-	-

Table 7: Memory footprint (MB) for storing the activations for a given sequence length.

Author Index

Association for Computational Linguistics
209 N. Eighth Street
Stroudsburg, Pennsylvania 18360

ISBN 978-1-7138-3018-4
9 781713 830184

CURRAN ASSOCIATES INC.
proceedings.com